Managerial
Psychology

Fifth Edition

Managerial Psychology

Managing Behavior in Organizations

Harold J. Leavitt
and
Homa Bahrami

The University of Chicago Press
Chicago and London

Harold J. Leavitt is Walter Kenneth Kilpatrick Professor of Organizational Behavior and Psychology in
the Graduate School of Business, Stanford University.
He is the author of *Corporate Pathfinders* and the co-
editor of *Readings in Managerial Psychology,* published by the University of Chicago Press. **Homa
Bahrami** is lecturer in organizational behavior in the
School of Business Administration, University of California, Berkeley, and research associate in the Graduate
School of Business, Stanford University.

The University of Chicago Press, Chicago 60637
The University of Chicago Press, Ltd., London
© 1958, 1964, 1972, 1978, 1988 by
The University of Chicago
All rights reserved. Published 1988
Fifth edition 1988
Printed in the United States of America
98 97 96 95 94 93 92 91 90 89   5 4 3 2

Library of Congress Cataloging-in-Publication Data

Leavitt, Harold J.
    Managerial psychology : managing behavior in orga-
nizations / Harold J. Leavitt and Homa Bahrami.—
5th ed.
        p.   cm.
    Bibliography: p.
    Includes index.
    1. Psychology, Industrial.   I. Bahrami, Homa.
II. Title.
HF5548.8.L35   1988
158.7—dc19   87-16820
ISBN 0-226-46973-5   CIP

Contents

Preface to the fifth edition

Things have changed—again. And they have also remained the same. The last edition of this book was written just as Americans had recovered from student revolt, Vietnam, and black-white and male-female confrontations. Now, almost 10 years later, we have cooled way down, probably too far down. Indeed, on the managerial front we're faced with some serious challenges. The Japanese have been on our tails for a decade, and the Koreans are coming along behind them. Trade wars are looming. Technology seems to move faster than we can handle it. Instead of concentrating on producing better goods and services, we have been overtaken by a mania for takeovers.

But American managers respond. They experiment. They adapt. So the next decade could become a decade of managerial experimentation and innovation. It *could,* if we are willing to pick up the challenge.

As to this fifth edition of *Managerial Psychology,* it too has changed. Something like 70 percent of the material is new. But the overall structure remains about the same, working from the small to the large, from the individual to the organization.

Part 1 is about the psychology of the individual. It tries to pull together a few key concepts and ideas about individual human beings in organizational settings. But psychological beliefs, theories, and findings have changed over this last decade, and perhaps even progressed. So Part 1 is redesigned. It tries to incorporate more from the burgeoning field of cognitive psychology. There's a lot more on human thinking, on current views about motivation, and on how attitudes and values change.

In part 2 we shift our focus from one person to relationships between people; to how our person can try to change the behavior of another. This part is considerably different, too, There's more material on alternative forms of influence, and their costs and benefits, and a revised chapter on incentives, new models and old.

Part 3, on small groups, has been modified less than the others because not much basic new research has been done on groups. The real-world application of ideas about groups, however, has made great strides. So a new chapter on the uses of groups in modern organizations replaces our old one.

Big changes show up again in part 4, in which we broaden our focus to look at the whole organization and at the complex process of managing. Our knowledge of macro-organizational processes has increased considerably in the last few years, so we have expanded and updated the material on organizations. Current concerns about organizational leadership, organizational culture, and organizational structure are all reflected in this revised section.

An entirely new section, part 5, has now been added to the book. Its purpose is to take one full step that was only partially taken in the fourth edition. Part 5 is about the relationship between contemporary organizations and their environments. We've added this section, of course, because contemporary managers live in a very small, very crowded, very intrusive world. Strong competitors are popping up in different parts of the world, and, although they may speak in different tongues, they nevertheless seem to operate rather effectively in "our" market places. Government regulations, lawsuits, international crises, and pressure groups all nip at the modern manager's heels. Managers no longer just manage the inside of their organizations. They have to try to manage the outside, too—or at least their interactions with the outside.

A couple of other issues. We have tried to avoid the awkwardness of using both masculine and feminine third-person pronouns. We have done it simply by using the masculine form throughout. We hope readers of both sexes will forgive what may appear to some to be a breach of principle in exchange for simplicity and convenience in communication.

Readers even faintly familiar with past editions will also note two other major changes that show up on the cover of this edition. Because we have extended our coverage to encompass much of what is now called "organizational behavior," we have also extended the book's title to reflect the change. More important, we now have an additional author, someone with more expertise than the original on matters of organizational design and strategy.

We are both most grateful to Mrs. Arleen Danielson for working and reworking our manuscript, and to the many friends, students, and colleagues who have contributed to our thinking along the way.

H. J. L.
H. B.

1   People one at a time: The individual in the organization

Introductory note

Part 1 of this book is the most psychological part. It tries to pull together some important ideas about individual human beings. But this book is not primarily about the psychology of the individual. It's about individuals in organizations and about managing small and large numbers of individuals in organizational settings. So we have tried to select from contemporary psychological research and theory those ideas, concepts, and findings that seem particularly relevant to the world of managerial work.

Why do we need this first part? Because organizations are still—despite all our modern technology—*human* institutions. They are created by people, populated by people, managed by people, developed by people, and operated by people. And people are flexible, intelligent, fallible, often unpredictable, emotional, creative, and more. So we'll try to get as useful a picture as we can of what does and what doesn't make them tick.

Part 1 is designed like this:

Chapter 1 is about ideas that apply to all people alike. Despite our individuality, human similarities are more impressive than human differences. In chapter 1 we outline three key ideas about people that will recur again and again throughout the remainder of the book.

Then, in chapter 2, we turn to the other side, to look at how each of us gets to be different from every other one of us. Both the similarities and the differences are critical in the managing process. Managers often have to manage large numbers of people at the same time, so understanding human commonalities is critical. But managers also manage small numbers of people, small teams, groups, and individuals. And to do that job well managers should also understand the unique attributes of individuals.

Chapter 3 is about emotions. Managers may dream of a cool and unemotional organizational world, but they will never find it. The real world is full of loving, hating, searching, inquiring, laughing, and crying people. And good managers don't treat that cauldron of human emotions as a load of noise and trouble. They realize that all that emotion is the stuff from which loyalty and commitment and effort are made. Good managers are aware that a large part of their job is to manage emotions.

But of course, people aren't just emotional. They also think and plan and reason. So chapter 4 is about the reasoning parts of people, about how we use our heads to plan, create, and solve problems.

The next chapter, chapter 5 then tries to put those two big pieces—emotion and reason—back together, which is the way the two exist in the real, human world.

We then return to the thinking process, in chapter 6. This time the focus is more applied. We look at different styles of thinking, at how each of us develops our own style; and we also consider the marginal costs and benefits of different cognitive styles.

Finally, as we will do at the end of four parts of this book, we end part 1 with an application chapter that tries to put some of our concepts and ideas to work on a few real managerial problems. In this case, in chapter 7, the spotlight is on managers' endless need to assess, evaluate, and judge the people they encounter as well as those they manage. We look at different approaches to evaluation and assessment, and at some of the costs—economic, psychological, and ethical—of different ways of going about it.

1

People are
all alike:
Three key ideas

Managers' decisions, like other people's, are usually based on some combination of fact and theory. They are choices made by interpreting things observed in the light of things believed. And in most of their decisions, managers are reasonably aware of the particular theories they use in interpreting what they observe. They take supply-and-demand ideas into account in making marketing decisions, for example. And they often use high-level technical theory in attacking engineering and production problems.

Managers also use theory in dealing with human problems. But in the human area, theorizing is usually a much more implicit or even unconscious process. Manager's theories of human behavior also seem to be much more diverse than their economic and engineering theories, perhaps because they are more the private property of individual executives. Here, for instance, are some pairs of assertions that have been made by business executives. Each reflects a number of basic theoretical assumptions about the nature of human beings:

- People are basically lazy. Or, people just want a chance to show what they can do.
- Always be careful of executives who lose their temper. Or, watch out for executives who never lose their temper.
- Good salespeople sell themselves before their products. Or, a good product sells itself.
- Men think more logically; women think more intuitively.
- If you give people a finger, they'll take the whole arm. Or, kindness begets kindness.
- You can never get a high-quality decision from a group. Or, if your group isn't involved in making a decision, that decision won't be implemented.
- People need to know exactly what their jobs are. Or, people will work best when they have room to define their own jobs.

Each of these statements (and the list is not exhaustive) is either an assumption about the nature of people or a derivation from such an assumption. Each is a flat, unequivocal generalization, much like the statement, "Air is lighter than water."

The fact that many of these generalizations contradict one another suggests that they cannot all be correct, so difficult questions of proof and consistency arise. This first section of our book does *not* aim to prove that some are true and others are false. What it does aim to do is to provide a set of internally consistent generalizations—generalizations that should be useful for those who want to manage human organizations.

Managers have a reputation for practicality and hardheadedness, a reputation fledgling managers may mistakenly equate with entirely concrete and nongeneral thinking. Yet statements like those above are extremely general, extremely theoretical. Some kind of psychological theory is just as necessary for managers dealing with human problems as is electrical and mechanical theory for engineers dealing with machine problems. Without theory, engineers have no way of diagnosing what might be wrong when an engine stops, no way of estimating the effects of a proposed change in design. Without some kind of psychological theory, managers cannot attach meaning to the red flags of human disturbance; nor can they predict the likely effects of changes in organizational structure or personnel policy.

The theoretical positions outlined in these early chapters will not be new to most readers. Most of us already accept them, though often we do not use them. If they are good theories they should lead to useful predictions. Incidentally, if they are good theories, they may not necessarily turn out to be true theories. No one knows whether some of the things said here are, in some absolute sense, true or false. You can decide for yourself whether or not they are reasonably useful.

Three ideas about human behavior

Consider three theoretical ideas that are pervasive in contemporary psychological theory and practice: *motivation, reinforcement,* and *cognition.*

Motivation is about people's drives, needs, wants; about tensions emanating from within the individual that drive behavior, that push people out into the world in search of straightforward things like food or shelter and not so straightforward things like love or achievement or personal fulfillment. Behind most ideas about motivation lie ideas about the dynamics of human personality and human potential. We'll talk more about those later.

The idea of *reinforcement* is about rewards and punishments, emanating mostly from the world outside the person. Behind the notion of reinforcement lie ideas about the ways people learn, ideas like "the law of effect." The law of effect says, in effect, "That which satisfies is learned." "That which satisfies" is a reinforcer. So reinforcement is important because it directs and shapes human behavior by causing selective learning. If doing X is reinforced, we tend to do it again. If it isn't we tend to forget it.

Cognition is, among other things, about thinking, anticipating reinforcements before they occur, and learning vicariously when we observe something happening to somebody else. Behind the broad concept of cognition lie ideas about the richness of the human mind, its capacity to imagine, to expect, to estimate, to generalize. We don't just do it again if it satisfies; we also think about it and look for ways to make it happen again.

Those three ideas apply to the behavior of everybody, everywhere, at all times. In relation to those three concepts, that is, people are all alike. We are all motivated. Selective reinforcement works for everybody. And all of us, everywhere, think and imagine and forecast things that may happen in the future.

It's useful to treat those three ideas as gateways to three levels of human complexity. The motivational idea, which evolved largely out of Freudian psychoanalytic thinking, is a kind of basic gateway. It tries to account for mankind's pervasive drives not only to eat and reproduce but to achieve, explore, and group into communities. Classical motivation theories seek understanding by looking mostly *inside* the person; they hypothesize inner tensions and hungers that drive the individual into action in search of relief or fulfillment.

Reinforcement theory (out of Pavlov, Watson, and Skinner) is a second gateway, which treats man as an almost mechanical beast, one who learns in small, simple increments. If I found candy there last time, I'll probably learn to go back to the same place. People can be "conditioned" like chickens and kittens, through manipulation of rewards and punishments, to repeat behaviors that are rewarded and to "extinguish" behaviors that are not. Thus, people can be trained to develop finely honed skills. And they can be socialized through suitable reinforcement procedures to behave in approved ways.

Notice that, although true believers in reinforcement and true believers in dynamic motivational theories often fight like the devil, they still need each other. The reinforcement gateway needs some kind of motivation to work. Reinforcement requires reward, payoff. But when is a reward a reward? Only when it is "wanted" or "needed." So some kind of built-in wants (or motives) are required if reinforcers are to have any way of reinforcing anything.

On the other hand, the motivationists need reinforcement to account for the learning and development of new motives. For everyone agrees that humans are learning animals, and what motivates them as adults are not all the same things that motivated them as infants. Motivationists need to explain why some adults develop strong power motivation whereas others disdain power and want only to achieve, affiliate, or become competent.

So now we have the inner person, motivated by internal tensions (like hunger or fear) who learns by experiencing positive and negative reinforcements, to shape and narrow behavior in order to get those positive reinforcements that will eliminate those motivational tensions. We've added man's ability to *learn* from experience to the recipe for understanding human behavior.

Finally, there is that third gateway that's relevant here. People also think. We notice what other people do and what happens when they do it. We wonder how the candy got there in the first place. We also ask, "Why?" We attribute causes to things that happen, sometimes correctly, sometimes quite incorrectly.

Cognition is about those thinking parts of people—expectations, anticipations, and attributions, as well as learning vicariously (what happened to that other guy could happen to me), hypothesizing (what would happen if . . . ?), and estimating costs and benefits (how hard would I have to work to get what I want, and what's the probability that I would get it even if I did work very hard?). The cognition idea is the gateway to the enormous variety and complexity of human thinking. And, we should add, although great strides have been made in the last decade, we still don't know very much about it.

Let's back up now and look at each of those three ideas in a little more detail.

Motivation 1
Deficiency models

Motivation means drive, interest in trying to get something. Unmotivated people just sit there. Motivated people get up and go searching, building, doing. No wonder managers worry about motivating people at work.

One classical model of how motivation works has been called the *deficiency* model. It looks at human behavior as a kind of closed circuit in which motivation (tension, resulting from a deficiency) causes people to behave. That behavior continues until it leads to something that eliminates the motivation (reduces the tension) and thereby stops the behavior. Thus, for instance, your stomach is empty. The emptiness stimulates impulses interpreted as "hunger." The feeling of hunger stimulates the behavior of searching for food. You find food. The food fills the stomach, causing the "feeling hungry" impulse to stop, which in turn stops the behavior in search of food.

This simple closed-circuit motives-as-tensions conception has many weaknesses. For instance, "psychological," as distinct from "physical," motives are not finite and specific. One can consume a specific quantity of food and thereby temporarily stop feeling hungry. It is doubtful, however, that one can consume a specific quantity of prestige, for instance, and feel sated. Prestige and other "psychological" wants seem to be boundless; enough may never be obtained to inactivate the tensions, and hence the behavior.

Moreover, this deficiency view is ideologically unattractive to most of us. It offers a lazy view of behavior. It treats human behavior as an attempt to get rid of tension, so we won't have to behave anymore. No tensions, no behavior.

Deficiency models, although weak and unattractive, have their uses. They put the emphasis on the *push* from inside the person, rather than on the *pull* from outside. Managers, for instance, often encounter problems with subordinates who "don't know what they want," people who feel restless and disturbed but can't seem to say what it is they are after. Most of us feel that way a good deal of the time, experiencing the push of tension from inside but not being able to identify the precise goal that might eliminate that tension. We search vaguely, trying one job or another, one boss or another, one idea or another, until—if we are lucky—we hit on something that does the trick. Only then may we be able to tie up that particular tension to some clear goal, so that next time we can head directly for where we want to go. Babies, after all, don't start out crying, "I want a bottle." They start out with something like, "I feel discomfort somewhere inside." They then go on to try all the variety of behaviors they can muster until they discover that the bottle eliminates that particular discomfort. Then they can narrow down their behavior in order to get to the goal next time without exhaustion.

Once again the reader will notice that this idea about motivation brings us very close to the reinforcement idea. Reinforcement types would tell the same story in different words: The bottle is a reinforcer, and the probability that the baby will go for it again will increase.

But no matter how one views this deficiency model, it suggests that the ultimate condition of mankind can be thought of as an equilibrium condition in which no behavior occurs. This ultimate condition, will, of course, be unattainable so long as one fly after another goes on landing on man's rump to stir up some tension and to force him to go on swishing his tail.

Of course, the same landscape can be drawn from a brighter perspective. The tendency not to behave except when driven can also account for the human capacity to learn. It can account for the baby's rapidly improving skill at finding food. The diffuse kicking, squalling, and rolling of the first few months give way over time to the simpler and more efficient behavior of finding and opening the cookie jar.

Motivation 2
Growth models

The big problem with deficiency models is that they don't account very well for the enormous growth and expansion of human behavior over time. Given a benevolent environment, the deficiency approaches would have all of us lazing around and snoozing. But people don't really seem to behave that way, even when they're well fed. Well-fed children don't just quit. They're curious; they explore; they invent games; they make friends; they try all kinds of things.

Some growth models handle that problem by positing an inside-the-person triggering mechanism that sets off a new set of motives whenever one reaches some reasonable degree of satiation of the present set. When our bellies finally feel full, that position holds, we will then be motivated by new motives, this time focusing on longer-term safety and security, rather than on satisfying our short-term hunger. When those, in turn, are reasonably under control, the social needs pick up, the needs for membership and belonging. And so on up a hypothesized hierarchy of motivational levels.

Growth models are open-ended in their view of human potential. They see human beings as forever developing, forever moving on from one level of motivation to a next higher one, and thereby continuously repositioning themselves to accomplish ever "higher" ends.

This more optimistic and rather Western view leads toward a more positive approach to the question of motivating people in organizations. The deficiency models viewed motivation as arising exclusively out of deficiencies. So how does one motivate people? Obviously by *creating deficiencies*. One of the fathers of modern organizational psychology, Douglas McGregor, dubbed that idea "Theory X." "Let's keep 'em barefoot and hungry, then they'll work." The growth motivators argue an almost opposite position, more in line with what McGregor called "Theory Y." Only when human beings have satisfied their more basic motives can the "higher" needs come into flower. It is precisely when people are freed from their basic deficiencies, when they are *not* barefoot and hungry, that they can really begin to work as complete human beings.

Notice, however, that both the deficiency and growth views still focus on the dynamics of the inner person much more than on the dynamics of the external situation. According to these views, human potential lies largely inside the individual, waiting to be let out. The situation is important only as a limiting factor. Dissatisfying situations prevent people from flowering, and satisfying situations permit people to flower. But the motivational potential is the key, and that resides inside the person. As we shall see, more recent views of motivation include reinforcement and cognitive components, treating motivation as part of a broader learning and thinking process.

Reinforcement theory

Classical reinforcement theory, in contrast to both deficiency and growth views of motivation, doesn't give much credit to what's inside the person—just as long as there's enough internal tension to allow for reinforcements to work, for rewards to be rewarding. Reinforcement theorists worry about what and how people learn.

The reinforcement idea adds a critical *outside* component to the picture—a situational component to those minimal internal drives (or tensions or needs or motives—pick your own word). Its emphasis is on how people *learn* from their experiences in the big world. Given the reinforcement notion, two babies with identical initial motives can (and probably will) turn into very different adults because they will encounter different experiences of success and failure. For example, baby A is always reinforced (or better still, is *often* reinforced) when he smiles. Baby B gets nothing from smiling, but frequent reinforcement when he kicks his left foot. A begins to smile more and more; and B just keeps kicking that left foot. Take it from there; the network of possibilities becomes enormous, allowing for almost infinite variations in human behavior. J. B. Watson, one of the great founding figures of this notion, once asserted back in the early part of this century that he could turn babies into heroes or criminals or almost anything else if he could get hold of them early enough, by selectively reinforcing their initial random behaviors.

So classical reinforcement theory focuses on the outside, on how those other people—parents, teachers, managers—do or don't reinforce particular behaviors and thereby shape the individual.

Human cognition

When we add in the concept of human cognition, new dimensions open up, dimensions that add both depth and breadth to our picture of human nature. People are driven, they learn to go where the goodies are, but they also think. They remember, forecast, observe, imagine. They process information. They compare what happened today with what happened yesterday and hypothesize explanations that cover both. They invent gods to explain things they can't otherwise understand. They balance (not always logically) benefits (like "How much will I win?") against costs ("What are the odds of my winning?").

These more cognitive views of behavior grant to human beings more control than simple reinforcement views and more proactive possibilities, too. (We use the term *proactive* to mean the opposite of reactive.) We are not *just* driven by our needs. We do not *just* tend mindlessly to repeat our last behavior if reinforcement accompanied it. We intentionally suppress some of our needs. We delay gratifications. We forecast the future. We make choices among alternatives. We avoid holes that we have seen others fall into. We try to explain why events happened. We use our heads.

That doesn't mean humans are necessarily entirely logical, orderly, or analytic creatures—only that mind is as much a part of the behavioral equation as heart. To understand and predict behavior, we will need to understand how humans think, how they process information, along with understanding their drives and the environmental forces that act on them. Even the simplest of people is rather complex.

In summary

Since managers manage people, this opening chapter takes a first look at the basic concepts that help explain human behavior. It puts forth three central and managerially useful ideas that have evolved out of Western psychology in this century:

1. *The idea of motivation.* People are internally driven initially by innate and later by learned "needs," "wants," or "tensions." That idea provides a basis for understanding what makes people even interested in working and learning.

2. *The idea of reinforcement.* Reinforcing a particular act increases the probability that people (and other organisms) will perform that act again—hence, another lever for human learning and development, this time generated from outside the person. The emphasis here is on the outside situation more than on what's going on inside the person. The reinforcement idea provides a basis for thinking about how outsiders—like parents and bosses—can shape behavior in the directions in which they want it to go—with all the ethical questions that such power carries with it.

3. *The overarching idea of human cognition.* This idea brings people's brains and minds into the picture. We may be driven by our needs, and we may salivate when the buzzer buzzes; but we do more than that. We are active participants in the learning and growing processes. We think, we observe, we hypothesize, we learn vicariously, we attribute causality (often wrongly), and we rationalize to make things orderly where there may have been no order to begin with.

These three ideas may look mutually contradictory, and in some ways they are. But they can be integrated. Together they give us a picture of the human being as a dynamic, proactive, thinking organism—complicated but understandable, and not easily managed by reliance on any simplistic set of rules. It follows that if managers expect to manage such complicated critters, they had better try to understand their nature.

2

People are different: The development of individuality

People are all alike, the preceding chapter asserted. We are driven (motivation is real), we learn to go where the cookies are (reinforcement works), and we even use our heads to think, observe, and generalize (cognitive processes operate in each of us).

But although we all operate by the same basic rules, each of us is also different. Somehow, despite our common human attributes, every one of us ends up clearly and recognizably different, not only physically but psychologically, from everyone else. Each of us has idiosyncratic styles, beliefs, attitudes, values, and skills.

It would be foolish to suggest that this chapter is going to tell you exactly how that individuality takes shape. The processes are complex and poorly understood, even by experts. But it is nevertheless important for managers to get a broad fix on the mechanisms that shape and sculpt each of us. Managers after all, are shapers and sculptors of other people, whether they intend to be or not. This chapter, then, tries to spotlight some of the forces that shape individuality and to highlight the manager's role as a director of some of those forces.

In one sense it isn't a very hard job to describe how people become unique individuals. People get to be different and unique because their drives and motives differ to begin with, because they encounter different and diverse experiences of positive and negative reinforcement, and because their thinking equipment is different and they encounter different things to think about.

But let's get a bit more specific. One of the mechanisms that generates individuality is *dependency*.

The key role of dependency

A theory, it has been said, is as good as its ratio of predictions to assumptions. To economize on assumptions, let's assume first that only people's basic physical motives (or needs or drives) are inherited—motives such as hunger and thirst—and then go on from there. But that certainly isn't all

13

that each of us starts out with. In addition to those innate motives, people have built-in learning systems: sense organs; memory—a mechanism for retaining information picked up by the sense organs; a decision-making and information-processing mechanism; plus a tendency to be stingy in the expenditure of energy. Add to all those a muscular system that allows people to move and act on their environment. If all those make up people's original, factory-installed equipment, we have almost enough to account for all the accessories that each of them will add later to make them unique and special by the age of ten, twenty, or forty. That equipment—motivation plus learning capacity plus a kind of metasystem for noticing what they are learning—provides an enormous potential for individual development.

But our little, individual person still needs one more characteristic, a characteristic that is not so much a part of the person as of the relationship between the person and the world. That additional characteristic is *dependency*—the dependency of human beings on one another for their very survival, especially in early childhood. Dependency is pervasive and important. The child is dependent on parents, the husband on wife, the wife on husband, employees on their employers, and employers on their employees.

If human infants came into the world with almost complete physical development, like some other animal young, they might be much less dependent on others, and we might then have to devise quite different theories to account for differences among adults. In fact, if infants could fend for themselves from the start, adults would surely be noticeably different characters from what they now are.

But it is in the nature of things that any infant who survives to adulthood has *necessarily* passed through an extended period of great dependency on other people, for food, care, affection, and lots more. And that dependency, coupled with the good but still incomplete physical plant of the young child, plus the capacity to learn, gives us the leverage to account for the development of a great many secondary and tertiary mental characteristics. The network that evolves for each individual is both massive and unique.

To see how that dependency lever might work, consider this entirely hypothetical illustration:

Suppose that you suffer from a magical ailment. The major symptom of the ailment is paralysis—complete paralysis. But though you are paralyzed, your head is perfectly clear and your senses perfectly keen. You can hear, you can see, you can feel, you can think—but you can't move.

You have a brother or a sister—pick either one—who possesses a magical gift. Let's use a brother for this example. Whenever his hand is on your shoulder, you are temporarily cured; your paralysis evaporates; you can move as well as anyone else. But when he takes his hand away, the paralysis returns immediately.

Assume that this sibling of yours is really a good person. He spends a good deal of his time with his hand on your shoulder, and he goes through considerable inconvenience to do so. You have not had this disease very long, but by now you have gotten over the shock that it entailed at first. You are trying, with his help, to settle down to the best life you can work out.

On this particular morning, you awake, but of course you cannot move. You lie in bed until your brother comes in to put his hand on your shoulder. At that time you rise, dress, and wash. You have breakfast, chat, and read the morning paper. You do everything that you would have done before you had the disease. Over breakfast your brother reminds you that he has a dentist's appointment this morning. He will have to leave the house at about ten o'clock. He probably will not be able to get back until noon. This is a matter of some concern to you, but it's not a big deal since it's just a two-hour absence.

With his hand on your shoulder you fix a comfortable place in which you can sit while your brother is gone. You arrange an easy chair by the window, put your feet on an ottoman, and tune in to a radio program you particularly like. You open the window to let the warm air and sun in and to see what's going on outside. You settle down for the two-hour absence. Your brother leaves.

For half an hour or so, as you expected, things are fine. You are perfectly comfortable; there's enough activity outdoors to keep you interested; and the radio program is good. But at 10:30 the program changes to what you hate most—country music—but that's of no major concern. A fly manages to get through a hole in the screen and begins to buzz around your nose. That too is just one of those minor inconveniences you have long since learned to bear.

By eleven o'clock there's a little itch developing from a rough place in the chair you're sitting in, but that's bearable, too. The fly is still buzzing around. The country music goes on. It seems to grow louder and louder. At 11:30 the sky clouds over. It begins to rain. At a quarter to twelve it's raining hard and the wind is picking up. You're getting wet and cold. If you could shiver you would. The itch is getting worse. And your bladder begins to feel a little too full for comfort. But you reassure yourself, after all, it's only fifteen minutes more. At noon you're waiting for your brother's step, but you don't hear it. He hasn't shown up at 12:15. The terrible mix of the cold, the wet, the itches, the bladder, the fly, and the radio become almost unbearable. By 12:45 you're on the verge of explosion. One o'clock and still no brother. But there is more rain, more discomfort.

At just about one-thirty you hear footsteps. Brother walks in, puts his hand on your shoulder, and says, "The dentist was way behind schedule and I got caught in a traffic jam on the way home. I'm sorry I'm late."

Now seriously ask yourself these questions: (1) Just how would you *feel* about your brother at this moment? (2) What do you think you would *do* to your brother at the moment he frees you by putting his hand on your shoulder?

Your answers probably fall into one of these major categories: (1) I would feel angry and resentful; (2) I would feel extremely relieved, extremely grateful that he had finally arrived; or (3) I would have mixed feelings of anger and resentment, on the one hand, and relief and gratefulness, on the other.

To the action question, answers range from: I would sock him on the nose, to I would throw my arms around him and kiss him.

A wide range of seemingly contradictory answers is appropriate and understandable. Together they represent the necessary conflict of feelings that derive from the complete dependency of one individual on another. If you say you would feel angry and hostile, you will probably be ready to admit that those would be predominant, but not exclusive, feelings. Although you feel angry, you may at the same time feel affectionate and grateful. If you say you will feel grateful and relieved, you will probably admit to being just a little angry and irritated. Some mixture of these almost polar feelings will probably be present in everyone. This is the peculiar phenomenon of *ambivalence,* the simultaneous existence of opposite feelings in the same place at the same time.

Ambivalence will show up at the action level, too. If you say, "I would sock my brother on the nose," you might reluctantly add, "But I'd feel awfully sorry afterward." And if you say, "I would throw my arms around him," you might add that your embrace could easily convert to a bear hug.

Suppose further that this sort of incident happened often, month after month. Might you not then start thinking about ways to escape, possible routes to independence from your brother? Might you not then also start thinking creatively about possible ways to control your brother, by "getting something on him" perhaps, so that you would not have to count just on his goodwill? And suppose he was a particularly bad brother who didn't care much for you? Wouldn't that intensify your search for independence from him and for power over him?

Dependency coupled with our three ideas of motivation, reinforcement, and cognition thus serves as a lever for initiating new kinds of attitudes, motives, and expectations. To a certain extent dependency yields ready satisfactions that one cannot supply for oneself independently; to that extent one's feelings are likely to grow positive, friendly, affectionate, protective, grateful toward the provider of all those goodies. But also dependency may not satisfy, it may rather frustrate; to that extent one is likely to develop feelings of anger and hostility and to wish for and search for independence and autonomy.

All human infants suffer from that kind of magical paralysis. They are entirely dependent on adults for the satisfaction of those basic survival requirements. But because no parent (whether they want to or not) can be entirely satisfying (or entirely frustrating), each child must necessarily develop some mixture of positive and negative feelings, first toward the parents, since the parents often are the world, and then toward the world. And not just feelings develop. Because humans think as well as feel, attitudes and expectations develop about what those adult people out there will or won't do. And from there the child moves on to a search for workable methods for dealing with those folks.

No parent can have either entirely satisfied or entirely frustrated a now adult infant for these reasons: Infants who encountered only frustration in their very early attempts to satisfy basic needs simply didn't survive. Children who didn't get fed, died. At the other end of the scale, too, no infant was ever perfectly satisfied. No parents could have had the prescience to foresee all the infant's wants before they arose or the patience and resources to satisfy every want they did foresee. So no real adult in the real world has grown up completely frustrated in infancy or completely satisfied.

The working range is the range between the extremes on a satisfaction-to-frustration scale. Parents can consciously or inadvertently work predominantly near one or the other end of the scale, reinforcing positively or ignoring or even punishing the child's efforts to satisfy needs. And the extent to which the predominance is at one end or the other, together with the physiological givens, probably accounts for the general pattern of early personality development in any particular child. Managers (as well as teachers and others) can also satisfy or frustrate whatever people are seeking anywhere along the same broad band later in life. They can contribute further to the unique and always pliable pattern that continuously evolves for each of us throughout our lives.

To be more accurate, one can put it this way: Some infants encounter a world that is frustrating from the start, a world that is unpredictable and uncontrollable; other infants encounter a world that is more satisfying, more predictable, and more controllable. Children faced with unpredictable and uncontrollable worlds are more likely to grow fearful and hostile early. They are more likely to wish strongly for and to seek independence. And they are more likely to be concerned with the instrumental mechanisms by which independence may seem to be gained—that is, with power, ingratiation, acquisition of goods that others value, and so on.

On the other hand, children whose early years are mostly satisfying are more likely to feel secure and to accept more dependence willingly. They are more likely to develop predominantly positive social attitudes and behaviors, with only secondary concern (unless they learn it later) for autonomy and independence.

These acquired sets of feelings can now be thought of as new classes of learned motives, beliefs, and wants. One set may be essentially social, feeling that it is OK to be somewhat dependent on others, to be affiliated with people, to like, to like to be liked, and so on. Another set may be essentially independent, concerned with ways of controlling and using other people, of freeing oneself from dependency on them. The important concerns become autonomy, power (over other people), status (one kind of power over other people), knowledge (another path toward independence), and the like.

The extent of parental control

The relative degree to which one or another of these sets of needs (or drives, wants, or concerns) develops in a young child is partially controllable by outsiders, most often by parents. Parents can encourage the social side by satisfying the child's physical needs, and they can encourage the independent side by limiting their satisfaction of those needs.

In practice the problem is not simple. There is another important factor in this picture. When children, or adults for that matter, are prevented from getting what they want, they are apt to become angry and to attack the things that block their way. Young children strike out blindly at Mama or Papa, adolescents use their fists, adults often attack with words. Suppose our hypothetical parent blocks the child, who responds to that frustration by attacking the parent with kicking, biting, and howling. Does the parent now decide to tolerate or punish this new behavior? Do Papa or Mama let themselves be attacked successfully, or do they instead block the new attack behavior by using superior force to retaliate? If they do the first, what becomes of their parental dignity? If they do the second, what do they teach the child? Probably that the child must suppress hostility. But the suppression of hostility is not the *absence* of hostility. The child who is not allowed to kick may still want to kick. Extend such behaviors over time, day after day, incident after incident, and the patterns that emerge will vary, but they will probably include internalized, unexpressed, "sat upon" hatred and anger, accompanied perhaps by a cover of equanimity and calm. Depending on the child's particular experiences, the pattern might also include a sense of helplessness and hopelessness.

All this is not to say that children are forever what they become in, say, their first year of life. On the contrary, each of us is always something more than our history. And present motives plus dependency plus the capacity to think and learn plus a volatile environment can account for the development of new motives and attitudes in adults as well as in children.

The first years have a good deal to do with determining whether or not children feel essentially secure or insecure about their place in the world and essentially optimistic or pessimistic about other people. And those first years also prompt us to think, plan, and search for ways to cope with what we now believe to be the nature of that big world.

Dependency and the manager

Managers aren't parents, and employees aren't children. However, like the parent-child relationship, the manager-employee relationship is a dependent one. Managers can reinforce and punish. They can act more like good brothers or more like bad brothers, and by so doing they can influence and modify the behavior of their employees.

If managers act like good brothers, the probability that employees will learn to feel trustful and affiliative is quite high—if they have already learned to be reasonably trusting of people with power. If people in the company are bad brothers, the predominant local feelings are more likely to become hostile and competitive.

It is important to point out here that this "positive reinforcement" view about early dependency may come into conflict with some widespread beliefs about training, both of children and of employees. For example, this position suggests that strong discipline for the infant will probably generate hostility and fear, and perhaps lead to active power and independence seeking. It suggests further that a history of denials probably makes later denials more emotionally difficult rather than easier. And who, by this point of view, is likely to hold up best under high pressure and stress? "Positive reinforcement" types would *not* put their money on the adult who had gone through a childhood school of psychological hard knocks. They would, instead, pick people whose parental relationships (and preferably later relationships, too) had been comfortable and relatively free from psychological want. (Incidentally, the evidence from studies of successful executives is consistent with this view. Successful executives tend to come from harmonious, higher-income homes and to have liked their families and teachers.) Therefore, for the first year or two, the best way to "spoil" children would seem to be to deny them what they want. The best way not to spoil them would be first to help them get what they want and then to encourage them to get what they want for themselves. And, if one considers the new employee instead of the new baby, the same conclusions might hold. But more of this in later chapters.

Managing the unique individual

It's time to raise questions about the relevance of this whole issue of individuality to the managing process. We've already suggested a couple of points of relevance. If we accept a deficiency model of motivation (and many managers used to) and couple it with reinforcement theory, it becomes easy to think about increasing employee productivity simply by increasing deficiencies. If we keep 'em hungry, they'll work to eat. That, of course, is not only an ethically questionable route, but a dangerously simplistic and shortsighted one. People don't just look for ways to eat; they also think, expect, and plan. Deficiencies may motivate more active behavior all right, but the behavior they generate will not necessarily be the productive kind the manager wants. If I am very hungry and I know that by working harder I will be able to get more pay to buy more food, I might work harder. But I might also decide to break the windows in the local bakery. Or I might attack what I believe to be the cause of my hunger—you! Or I might organize a union. Motivating by creating deficiencies may generate a wide spectrum of behaviors, including many that the manager may not be able to control.

We also spoke a little, in earlier pages, about the implications of the growth-motivation models for the managing process. One key point that growth protagonists make is that a reward is only a reward if it matches some unsatisfied motive. We will not get much behavior—good or bad—by offering food to someone whose belly is full. Thinking in terms of the growth model points managers toward searching for *relevant* reinforcements, rewards matched to currently operating motives. In developed America, most of us are probably operationally motivated more by social esteem or self-actualization needs than by hunger. So we need to rethink old deficiency-based reward systems designed for people motivated mostly by physical and safety needs. Only operational motives generate active behavior.

Managing and intrinsic versus extrinsic motivation

If, as managers, we lay on new reinforcements, will those simply be added on to the personal, *intrinsic* motivation to work that people may bring with them into the organization?

Intrinsic motivation means what it sounds like—motivation from inside the self, doing something because we want to do it. *Extrinsic* motivation is reinforcement generated from the outside. One does something to win a reward that others offer for that behavior.

Imagine, for example, that I am a crossword puzzle junkie. I am intrinsically motivated to do crossword puzzles. I do them just because I enjoy doing them. Now suppose it is in your interest to try to get me to do more of them. Suppose that completely solved crossword puzzles are a product you can sell at a profit. You want more of them because you run the local finished crossword shop. Having "discovered" me (the world's fastest crossword puzzle solver) you grab me and say, "I will pay you for those finished puzzles at the rate of X dollars per puzzle." You are adding a new extrinsic reward on top of my existing intrinsic motivation.

Will the two forms of motivation simply add up? Will I now be more motivated because I both enjoy the work and can now *also* earn money by doing it? The evidence suggests that the two do not usually add up. Instead, the added extrinsic motivation can, under certain circumstances, even cancel the old intrinsic motivation. Now that you are paying me to do puzzles, I may begin to find them much less interesting; they are work, not fun. I'm doing them for money, not for kicks. The outcome is a little like the scene from Tom Sawyer in reverse. He got his friends to help him whitewash the fence by getting them to see it as intrinsic fun and not as depressing hard labor.

Perhaps we had better be careful, in managing, of the implicit assumption we often make that different kinds of extrinsic rewards and reinforcements can just be piled on one another. Give 'em more money and gold medals and picnics, and those will either compensate for uninteresting work or add to already interesting work.

Individualism in organizations

The biggest question about individualism and management is a familiar one—the question of individual freedom versus organizational constraints. Although it's a very old question, it's still alive and well. If each person is unique and special, how can we *organize* great numbers of people in ways that permit, indeed enhance, that uniqueness. *Organization,* after all, means (in human terms) limiting, controlling, and sequencing the behavior of each person in the interest of the whole. Organizations thrive on uniform, lockstepped behavior. People in organizations have to get to work on time in order to perform certain standard routines in standard ways at standard intervals so that the whole shop will work smoothly. There isn't much room for uniqueness and individuality on the assembly line. And yet people, whether the organization wishes it or not, remain individuals.

In the old days we tried to solve that problem by designing highly structured organizations composed of many narrowly defined jobs, and then squeezing all sizes and shapes of people into those jobs. The essential effort was to squeeze individualism out of working hours. Be your unique self when you go home, buddy, but while you're here you're a "factor of production." While that idea is still alive, it's not very vigorous any more.

A more recent alternative is partially to reverse the process, to take a less rigid view, leaving room to modify the organization to fit its people and to try to give individual people a little room to be individual even inside the organizational structure. That choice has come to look better and better as the organizational world has grown more complex, technical, and diverse. But we will speak much more of the person-organization relationship in later chapters.

In summary

While people are all alike, they are also all different. From the beginning, each of us is different from everyone else. Then, as we make our way through our own unique network of reinforcements—observing, thinking, and generalizing as we go—our uniqueness is enhanced as we are socialized. So even in a world of nearly 5 billion human beings, no two people are identical.

One key lever that starts us off on our individual paths is the dependency of the child on the adult. The way that leverage is applied heads each child toward an overall perspective and a set of expectations about other people and about the likely benevolence or malevolence of that big world out there. Adults, by the way they handle that dependency lever, can make that dependency predominantly satisfying or predominantly frustrating. Satisfaction tends to build security and social needs; frustration tends to build insecurity, hostility, and egoistic needs.

The dependency conditions of infancy recur again and again in later life, in organizations, in education, and elsewhere: The same infantile learning formula may prevail at the adult level.

Motivational and reinforcement issues related to dependency become relevant to the managing process in many different ways. If we accept the old deficiency models of motivation, we had better make sure that we know how to create deficiencies that will lead to the behavior we want, and not to behavior we don't want. If we use growth models, we need to worry about the kinds of motives that operate in particular people in a particular society at a particular time; and we need to design reward systems consistent with those motivations. To complicate the issue even more, extrinsic rewards proffered by others may not simply add on to one's intrinsic motivation. Sometimes extrinsic rewards cancel intrinsic motives. So offering more goodies may not always generate more of what the manager wants.

An old overarching issue of individualism, however, still remains for the manager: How can unique, free individuals find happiness within the imprisoning cages of large, impersonal organizations? And how can organizations find happiness (and productivity) trying to manage large numbers of unique and individualistic human beings? That issue and ways of dealing with it will come up in the chapters that follow.

3

People are emotional: Human feelings and the manager

Human beings—on the job and off—reason; think, and plan. Those same people—on and off the job—also love, hate, laugh, fear, and envy. Emotions are as much a part of human character as reason. And managers can't just manage the reasoning parts of people; they have to manage the whole show, including the emotional bits.

This chapter—still using our three ideas of motivation, reinforcement, and cognition—looks at a few important aspects of human emotions and at their development, the functions they perform, and their relevance to the manager.

Frustration
The obstacle course

Consider the following example. It is written from a male perspective, but female readers will surely find it quite easy to recast this sad but familiar story (with appropriate changes in the sexes of the characters):

> Let's go back, if we can, to the days when you were seventeen or so. You have met a girl named Mary and taken her out once, and you like her. Now the junior prom is coming up and you decide to invite her. You extend your invitation, and Mary accepts.
>
> This prom is important. It's the big event of the year. It will cost some money, and you don't have much, so you start saving your pennies. You take on extra odd jobs, wash cars, and deliver groceries. You manage to borrow a car. You even work it so that a close friend and his date will come with you and share the cost of the gas. You manage to scrounge up enough money so that by prom night you've rented a tux, put gas in the car, and bought a corsage. Ready, combed, and polished, you drive over to pick up your friend and his date, and from there to Mary's house. You park at the gate and go up the walk with a corsage clutched in your little hot fist.
>
> You've never met Mary's parents. When you ring the doorbell and a man appears, you correctly assume it is Mary's father.

You: "Is Mary home?"

Mary's Dad, gruffly, newspaper in one hand, cigar in the other: "Why no, Mary's gone out for the evening."

End of scene.

Two questions for the reader: (1) At that moment (and the moments that follow) how would you *feel?* (2) How would you *act?*

The answers will by no means be the same for everyone. People's feelings in situations like this can be roughly broken into three broad classes:

First, there are those of us whose predominant reaction would be *anger*— mostly directed at Mary.

Second, there are those who do not feel much anger but do feel ashamed, embarrassed, and disappointed—*in themselves.*

Third—and very rarely—fairly cool, rational analysis rather than highly emotional feelings may occur; for example, "I wonder which one of us forgot the right date?"

The *actions* that may follow these feelings can, of course, follow directly from the feelings. The angry teenager may express his anger by attacking, slamming doors, cursing, or by seeking out Mary for verbal or even physical attack.

But there is another possibility. The angry teenager may suppress his feelings and *act* as though he feels calm. Similarly, the person who feels ashamed and inadequate may act accordingly—with weeping, wailing, and wringing of hands. On the other hand, he may act in many other ways. He may, for example, *act* angry as a face-saving device, even though he doesn't feel angry.

The rare third person (and he would be very rare among teenagers) may feel neither angry nor ashamed. He may simply view the situation as a not-very-important problem to be solved. He then has a large variety of actions open to him—to double-check, find another date, go alone, or spend his money elsewhere—all without major emotional upset.

Two kinds of aggression and who shows them

That third person is hard to find. Most people would feel like one of the other two. Those other two have one thing in common: intense emotional feelings of anger. But in one case the anger is outward-directed toward some outside object—toward Mary, her parents, or women in general. In the other case it is inward-directed, toward oneself, one's lack of ability in these realms, one's unattractiveness to women, one's stupidity for getting involved with someone like Mary.

Probably there is some admixture of these feelings in almost everyone, much as in the dependency relationship of infancy. But the sets of feelings that would predominate can be guessed fairly accurately if we know just a little more about the person—that is, if we know about other, past situations and how the positive and negative reinforcements in those situations have shaped expectations.

For example, suppose young man A is the Beau Brummel of the high school. He has a history of successes. Every young woman in town would love to go out with him. He is perfectly self-confident about his ability to deal with women. Now he gets stood up by Mary.

Contrast him with B, the low boy on the high school totem pole. He has acne. He has not been very successful in his social relationships. Girls tease him but pay little serious attention to him. He didn't want to go to the prom in the first place, but you (one of his friends), urged him to go. You almost had to force him ("for his own good") to call Mary.

What differences would one expect in the way these two, shaped by their quite different histories of success and failure, would handle this situation?

Secure, self-confident A, moving toward an important goal and encountering an entirely unexpected and apparently insurmountable obstacle, will probably want to attack the obstacle directly. He will be angry. He will want to fight.

B, pessimistic about his abilities but nevertheless wishing very much to be successful, might behave quite differently. When he encounters this sudden, insurmountable obstacle, his anger and hostility will probably be directed much more toward himself—at this further proof of his own inadequacy, at his stupidity in even venturing into this danger area. And he will be just that much harder to entice into a relationship in the future.

Frustration is a feeling

One situational platform for evoking emotional behavior occurs when people meet serious, unexpected obstacles between themselves and something they want. Initially, the "natural" emotion tends toward anger and the natural behavior toward aggression. Indeed, those natural reactions may have a functional basis in the evolution of the species. People who are optimistic about their competence, who expect to get what they want, aim their aggression outward; they attack the obstacle. If they have become pessimistic about their own competence they tend to turn the aggression inward, to attack themselves.

Clearly a *series* of frustrating situations may begin to turn the secure optimist into an insecure pessimist. The Beau Brummel may lose his confidence if, having been stood up once, he bounces back only to find himself stood up again—and again and again and again. He will reach a point at which he can no longer feel certain that it's the world that's gone wrong. He will begin unhappily to worry about himself. Similarly, a series of success experiences may turn our shy, self-doubting youngster toward feeling secure and self-confident in his relationships.

The rare third person is still worth thinking about. He is the one who *feels* little emotional upset—little anger either at Mary or at himself. He treats the incident the way most of us might treat running out of ink while writing a letter—troublesome, but not worth getting into a stew about.

An explanation of the third person requires us to consider the nature of human perception. Different people perceive the world in different ways. What kind of world can the third person be perceiving that permits him to toss off this obstacle so lightly? His world probably includes, for one thing, a wide range of alternative behaviors to fall back on when he meets road-blocks, so that no single roadblock seems insurmountable. His is a bigger world. It is probably also a world that has mostly been positively reinforcing. In such a world of self-confidence coupled with many perceived alternatives, being stood up on one occasion may not seem very important.

But what makes some things seem important and others unimportant? The word *important* here means something like "dear to one's self-esteem." Just what is it, for example, that is so frustrating for our frustrated young swain? Is he upset because he cannot get to the dance? Probably not nearly as much as he is upset because his personal feelings of self-esteem have been shaken by Mary's absence.

Most of us can empathize. Being stood up on an important date might have been a major cause of frustration when we were adolescents. But if the same event occurred later, as older adults whose social relationships have jelled, whose range of interests have expanded, wouldn't we feel a little more like that third person? Just the experience of a few years may make the same huge emotional problem feel emotionally trivial. Adult security and self-assurance usually hang on firmer threads, not so readily ruptured by a single social setback.

Incidentally, we usually save the word *frustration* for obstacles that generate emotional reactions. For the third person, and for most "minor" obstacles, we describe the situation as a "deprivation." Notice that it is not the facts of the situation but the person's perception of them that determines whether they are "frustrating" or only "depriving."

Should managers blow off?

Some odd implications evolve out of these generalizations about who reacts to frustration in one way and who reacts in another. The position taken here is, in effect, that confident, secure people will be less likely to encounter obstacles that are serious (for them), but that they will be more likely emotionally to attack the few they do perceive as serious blocks.

Yet organizations are likely to look askance at executives who are given to emotional outbursts, even rare ones. Emotional blow-offs are unbusinesslike and usually earn young executives poor marks on performance evaluation sheets. Given that squeeze, behavior may not correspond with feelings. We are likely to find many cases of emotional turmoil on the inside coupled with the appearance of orderly control on the outside.

Thus, it is possible for the secure optimist to *feel* like blowing up but then stifle corresponding actions so that what the boss sees is a controlled and rational facade. In fact, many executives probably do just that, perhaps contributing to those psychosomatic illnesses that executives are supposed to be prone to. Chronic failure to express intense emotion, and through that expression to utilize the physiological products of emotion, may well generate physiological disturbances. Moreover, that triple play—first encountering a serious obstacle, then wanting to attack it, and then finding the route of attack cut off by the disapproval of organizational superiors—sets up a secondary set of debilitating frustrations. Now I feel even madder because I'm not allowed to get mad.

Occasional blow-offs, therefore, ought to be treated much more tolerantly than they usually are—as appropriate reactions by imperfect but motivated, hard-working individuals when they encounter, as they must at times, difficult, unexpected, and important obstacles in their paths.

Executives might be even better executives if they were our third man—if, that is, they did not get frustrated to begin with. Obstacles that seemed insurmountable to other people would seem quite surmountable to them; ergo, no anger and no need to try to control it. Most of us would love to be that rare third man, wouldn't we, who, when encountering a crisis, simply shrugs his shoulders (both at himself and at the world) and starts thinking about alternative ways to handle it and where to go from there? One ideal for executives might be to develop a tolerance of frustrations that would be so great, a range of personal security that would be so broad, a breadth of perception that would be so wide that only very, very few incidents in their lifetimes would present seemingly insurmountable obstacles (because they would always have ways around them) or really important threats to their self-esteem (because their faith in their own competence would be rock solid). Their orientation instead would be toward the accomplishment of their goals.

The general problem is one of expectations. Expectations are largely determined by past experiences of success and failure, by one's history of reinforcements, both direct and indirect. If through life you have come to expect failure, to feel unsure of your ability to get what you want, you will generate second-order wants that will loom larger in your perceptions than they will for others. The martini that is not dry enough stops being just a deprivation—that is, just the wrong martini. It becomes instead a sign of disrespect by the bartender—a threat to one's already fragile self-esteem.

It follows that people whose self-esteem is easily threatened are less likely than others to act rationally as they encounter that jungle out there. It follows, too, that if one (as parent, teacher, friend, or manager) can help build up people's feelings of self-confidence and personal competence, they will deal with their worlds less impulsively, more objectively, and less stressfully.

Emotions and standards of success

Perhaps the most important key to whether or not we encounter frequent frustration is our own individual standard of success, and even that can be changed by changing patterns of reinforcement. You and your neighbor may both want to make money, but "to make money" for you may mean $30,000 a year, whereas for your neighbor "to make money" means $300,000. If the two of you are of about equal ability and have about equal opportunity, and if both of you actually achieve $50,000 a year, then you will consider yourself a success and your neighbor a failure.

This "level of aspiration" has many facets. It is a question of the relationship between our aspirations and our realistic ability to achieve our aspirations. If the two are close together, frustration is relatively unlikely. If our ability exceeds our level of aspiration—if we can achieve much more than we want to—then we are underachievers and society probably suffers because we do not contribute as much as we can.

If aspiration and ability are out of line in the other direction—if we want very much to attain what we are very unlikely to be able to obtain—then we have both a potential source of serious frustration and a possible route to withdrawal and depression. But that same gap has a positive side. It is a springboard for tremendous human effort, the kind of effort we often associate with stubborn, determined, dedicated innovators or entrepreneurs who fight the odds all the way. But more of that later.

How high is high?
And how do I reach up there from here?

Suppose someone puts a target on a wall and then leaves you alone with a set of darts and the target. Suppose you have never thrown darts before. Do you set yourself a score to shoot at before you throw the first dart? Probably not. But suppose you throw five darts and score 75 out of a possible 250? What do you do next? Before you throw the next dart do you set yourself a goal? Is the standard 250? Or is it just something better than 75? For most of us it would be the latter. In situations in which we are perfectly free to set our own standards, we are most likely to set our goals incrementally, just slightly ahead of our past performance.

Suppose, however, that instead of being alone in that room, someone else is present, who, let's say, has been a constant competitor of yours. The other person throws first and hits 100. Now what is your goal? And now how do you feel when you hit only 75? The point is that our personal standards are partially set by the people around us, by *social* processes; they are set by what we observe of the performance of others and by the expectations others (such as parents) set for *our* performance.

Once other people enter into the goal-setting process, the more or less "natural" tendency to set our goals a little ahead of past achievement begins to give way. Goals may then, in fact, be set without any regard to ability. Thus, one occasionally encounters a person who *must* become a great pianist because the parents have hammered in that notion since childhood. Failure in that endeavor now constitutes failure to satisfy other people the person wants most to satisfy and, hence, means frustration.

Consider the case of a young engineering student who was unhappy at school and who wasn't a very good student either. He had never wanted to be an engineer; he had always wanted to be a football coach. But his father had been an engineer. The father, on his deathbed, had extracted a promise from the student that he would become an engineer, and a good one. So the fellow was stuck with a goal that had been imposed on him, but with abilities and interests not likely to permit him to reach that goal. He had no good solution to the problem except to continue through life jumping for the ring he would probably never reach—unless he could somehow change his attitude toward his now unreachable father.

It is commonplace in organizational situations to feel that you must set high standards for employees in order to "motivate" them. But may not standards beyond your reach lead to one of two other behaviors? They may lead you into a hopeless struggle to reach a goal that your abilities will not allow you to reach; resulting in a series of frustrating failures and in panic and insecurity. Or else overly high standards may lead a better-adjusted individual simply to flee physically or psychologically from the situation, to refuse to accept the unrealistic standards that have been set. There's no free lunch. Higher standards *do* generate greater effort, but often at a high emotional cost.

If those high standards are set internally, they can lead to dedication and commitment. But if others are setting them, watch out. And others almost always play a major role in setting them. Perhaps one can argue that a person who is in a position to set standards for other people has a responsibility to set those standards neither so low as to provide inadequate opportunity for full expression nor so high as to guarantee feelings of failure. And maybe a joint goal-setting process can help to reach that happy medium.

Achieving styles

There is another important management issue here. It isn't just the *level* to which one aspires that is important; it is also the *methods* that one learns for trying to achieve that level. Some people discover that they can get what they want by one means, some by another. Joe and Mary both want to get all A's in their math course. Mary studies hard for the final exam; Joe writes problem answers on the cuffs of his shirt and sits beside Mary so he can look at her answers. They both get A's in the course. What *styles* of achieving behavior have been reinforced in each? And to complicate the picture further, suppose Mary learns that Joe got that A by cheating—indeed, by copying her hard-won answers?

Probably even more important for the manager than the *levels* of achievement motivation of the people in the organization is the set of achieving styles that is characteristic of the organization. People bring their own styles into the organization, but they are further reinforced or modified by managers' actions. What do people learn about how one "really" makes it in this organization? What's the "right" way of doing things? Is it, for example, to play *instrumental* games, parlaying relationships to get what one wants? Or do we learn *collaborative* styles to get things done? Or is it crucial to be *competitive,* to show yourself better than your peers? Should one act passive and dependent with the boss, or go after problems directly and aggressively? Organizations set achieving styles for their members, often quite unconsciously; but they are worth a conscious review.

By the time we are adults, our characteristic and preferred achieving styles are probably fairly set. Nevertheless, a strong organizational style can modify our own behavioral styles considerably. We can learn soon enough that in this organization we need to play power games to survive, or that competing with our peers earns more positive reinforcement than cooperating with them, or that we should get to know the right people even more than we should get to know the right answers.

So it is relevant for managers to diagnose for themselves their own characteristic styles for trying to reach their goals (because employees may use their managers as behavior models), and to consider what prevailing styles they want their organizations to reinforce. The organization's achieving style is an important attribute of its culture and a significant contributor to the organization's productivity.

Conflict
Emotional roadblocks on the inside

It's not just obstacles in the outside world that can generate frustration. We all encounter internal roadblocks as well. Some are moral or ethical roadblocks. We want to do it, but we know it's wrong. So we set up internal roadblocks against the more impulsive and amoral parts of ourselves. Another type of conflict has a rubber band quality. We want both A and B, but the more we move toward A the further we get from B, which causes the pull from B to grow stronger and tends to drag us back from A. No moral issues are necessary in that kind of conflict. The only issue is the multitude of our own wants and the fact that the world sets some of them up in mutually exclusive or mutually contradictory ways—or so it appears to us.

For example, I'm really hungry. That delicatessen window is full of edible goodies. But I've got no money, and breaking and entering is plain wrong. Or, we really need that big order, but that guy expects a private payoff before he'll sign the contract. And we don't play that game. Or think back to the dependency example in the preceding chapter. I want to sock my brother on the nose, but that makes it impossible to throw my arms around him at the same time. I want to eat that sundae, but it's got too many calories.

So conflicts are emotion-producing choice situations, characterized by a pull in two (or more) directions at the same time. The obstacles one meets here are not brick walls, but internal drags that pull one back even as one goes forward. Conflict situations are frying-pan-and-fire situations, ambivalent situations. They are emotional-choice situations, decision-making situations. And this large class of psychological situations underlies considerable emotional upset and considerable irrationality in everyday life and everyday management.

Emotion-producing conflicts can occur with different degrees of importance. Some are minor. Few of us are likely to be psychologically crippled by trying to decide between two attractive movies, though the presence of conflict often makes itself visible as a tendency to vacillate before the choice is made. And notice that even such an apparently trivial choice can generate emotion if our self-esteem as well as the movie is involved in the choice. Nor is the donkey nearly so likely to be paralyzed between the bales of hay as the old story makes out. On the contrary, most of us encounter numberless conflicts in the course of everyday life, conflicts we manage to resolve in short order and without permanent scars.

But as in the case of frustration, some conflict situations can be central to the person while appearing to involve inescapably opposing forces. Such conflicts can be a real threat to the personality. Perhaps the reader can catch the flavor of the dynamics of such important conflicts through this unlikely example:

Suppose I put you into a cage on a starvation diet with no way out. Suppose every effort you made to escape was a failure. Again and again over long periods of time you were utterly unable to do anything to control your world. You tried to cajole me into letting you out, and that failed. You begged for more food; no way. You kicked and screamed; that had zero effect.

How would you solve the problem?

Eventually, mightn't you "solve" it by quitting and retiring quietly into a dark corner, not responding any more to any thing that might happen to you? That retreat into a dark corner might be viewed from the outside as a kind of insanity. You might be huddling there in a dazed and stuporous state. If we opened the cage and took you out, you would probably stay dazed and stuporous for a long time. If we tried to feed you, you probably wouldn't eat. If we tried to wake you, you probably wouldn't wake up. You're gone—even though you're alive and there's no specific physical defect.

Now suppose that we were to step inside your mind during that early stuporous state. What will we be likely to find? You may be off in some fantasy world. You may be in Paris, eating your way through three-star restaurants, while in one fist you hold the only key to the cage. You would be dealing with the conflict by escaping upward into the realm of fantasy. You cannot escape physically; you cannot handle the stresses as they exist; so you escape psychologically.

Such behavior becomes, in a sense, reasonable behavior. It fits with the view that the organism defends itself from intolerable attack and seeks to keep itself together. Cutting off one's communication with the real world in favor of a world of fantasy is a desperation measure for meeting intolerable conflict. It is not necessarily a healthy way of meeting it, but to a person at a particular time it may be the best available way.

If we sent you down to Florida and put you out to bask in the sun, if we held your hand and talked with you and reassured you, we might be able to get back into contact with you. We might tease you into accepting food and into discovering that things have changed; the world is no longer what it had been during those terrible days in the cage. The cure might be almost complete, but most probably, no matter how many years passed, you would still get upset when you encountered cages.

That illustration is extreme, of course. And it can only work because a cage exists. If we had not enclosed you in the cage, then you would simply have walked away. In fact, one might say that the presence or absence of the cage makes the difference between conflicts that lead to extreme emotional reaction, especially withdrawal reaction, and conflicts that are handled more easily. But the cages one encounters in real life are usually built of social bars rather than steel ones.

Consider just one more illustration of emotion-producing conflict. Consider two women, A and B, each married to an impossible partner. Both have been married for a long time and have children. A has a political job, in the public eye, has no religious values of any significance, is not interested in children, and has no scruples about divorce. B loves her children, is intensely religious, and feels that divorce is sinful. Assume that the respective partners of A and B continue to make their lives miserable, and suppose further that the intensity of this misery increases continually. Suppose that A and B reach the same point at about the same time. Each decides that the situation is unbearable and runs away.

Which will be more likely to escape successfully? Which will be able to settle down to live and work in a new community? The answer clearly is that A may be quite successful and B quite unsuccessful.

The reason is that A's conflict is between career and desire to escape. Though much intensified in degree, that choice is not essentially different from the choice one must make in deciding between two TV programs broadcast at the same time. A's choice involves little guilt, little threat to her idealized picture of herself. The stimuli are largely external to her person. All she can lose is her career. But for B, leaving the field is no escape at all. Her conflict resides entirely within her. It involves conscience and self-esteem. No matter how far she may go from the physical location of the conflict, feelings of guilt and loss of self-respect will be with her, for she has no easy way of cutting off communication within her.

The most troublesome conflicts, then, are those that involve issues "central" or "internal" to the personality. Usually these turn out to be conflicts between different *levels* of the personality—between more or less basically impulsive needs and "conscience" needs. But also note that there are still a variety of possible ways of dealing (with varying success) even with such conflicts. B could see a therapist, join a community that supported her decision, reject her religion, or try to believe that her husband's villainy justified her departure.

Frustration and conflict in people in organizations

Managing often involves setting up frustrating or conflicting situations for other people. For example, the threat of discipline to prevent unwanted behavior is an attempt to introduce a conflict into another person's (C's) perceptual world. At time 1, let's say, C's objective was just to get something he desires; now, at time 2, C has a second and conflicting objective—to avoid the punishment that fulfilling that desire now entails.

Such control, through engendering conflict, cannot be classed glibly as either good or bad. For the most part, such measures do not introduce serious conflicts because they do not set up situations that involve feelings of guilt, nor do they threaten people's feelings of self-esteem. They are largely external to the personality. But insofar as some people may see rules as a challenge to their basic autonomy, the reaction may be intense.

Other uses of conflict as devices for controlling behavior can get more serious. Suppose, instead of the threat of discipline, we choose to try to develop "positive" feelings of loyalty and duty to the company. Suppose we try to build a "company conscience" into our employees, as many of us try to do with our children. If we succeed, this time we are setting up *internal* conflicts. Now it is not the boss that the employees must worry about, but their own feelings of guilt. People who begin in this way to feel honor-bound can get themselves into a tense emotional tizzy. And the likelihood of an irrational emotional blow-off is consequently greater. Paternalistic company cultures can generate that kind of problem. One simply showers employees with gifts or benefits and then makes it clear that they are expected to show their gratitude by playing by the company rules. For those with strong needs for independence, the resulting conflict is essentially internal, and it includes the possibility of violent reaction. And how about developing a "loyal" organization? Is that an unmitigated good?

The reader can identify many other spots in organizations where frustrations and emotional conflicts are commonplace. Some think of that old conflict between desire for independence, on the one hand, and for dependence and support, on the other. The whole pattern of industrial organization encourages that sort of conflict. Subordinates are, by contract, dependent on their managers. Subordinates are therefore bound to feel ambivalent to some degree—that is, to feel uncomfortably bound and yet pleasantly protected.

Some of the emotions derive from a gap between effort and outcome. One department store chain, for example, had developed a method of using the level-of-aspiration idea as a "motivator." Buyers received bonuses in proportion to the improvement in the year's departmental sales level over the previous year's. So even as individual buyers celebrated this year's big bonus, they had to stay up all night trying to figure out how to beat this year's performance next year. The carrot was always put a little out of reach, no matter how much one improved one's reach. From the store's point of view, the scheme worked well, at least in the short run. But for the buyer the emotional stress was enormous.

Here's a related issue. Sometimes one finds individual executives who have managed to strike a balance between their concerns for autonomy and for dependency. Perhaps they have found a particular job at a particular level that satisfied both, thus allowing them to exploit their most comfortable achieving style. Or take the example of a middle-level executive who feels both competent to do his job and also satisfied with the prestige and status that accompanies it. As often happens, however, senior management, blind to that subordinate's perception of the world, decides to "reward" him by promoting him. Promotion in such a case may result only in reinstating an old conflict with greater intensity than ever. Now, perhaps, our executive begins to feel panicky about his ability to do this bigger job. It frightens him. But he wants the status and the money it will bring, and he wants to conform to the social pressure toward accepting a promotion. ("You'd be crazy to refuse an offer like that!") Shortly following such a promotion, one often sees beginning signs of active conflict: anxiety, "unpredictable" lashing out against subordinates, "inexplicable" refusal to delegate authority, self-isolation from peers and subordinates and, if possible, from superiors. In fact, many cases end up in physical illness, alcoholic escapes, or some other unacceptable solution. Top management then usually decide they have misjudged the person—he wasn't as good as he looked.

This is not to suggest that fear of promotion should keep people from accepting promotion. Fears can be overcome by success in meeting them. But awareness of the existence of pressures that drag against the rewards of promotion can help a promoter to plan the promotional process more wisely.

Sometimes a job demands of people activities that do not mesh with their conception of what is right or their conception of what is dignified or proper. Salespeople seem to suffer from this conflict more than some other occupational groups. Sales managers beat the drums and wave the flags to get them to go out to sell Ajax iceboxes to Eskimos. But some Eskimos seem not to need iceboxes; or some other kinds of iceboxes look better than Ajax; or the salesperson feels uneasy and uncomfortable about putting a foot in people's doors.

Some sales managers try to resolve this job versus moral values conflict by "proving" the social importance of selling. They point up salespeople's responsibility to carry the good life to the ignorant consumer. They try to resolve the conflict by building up the pressure on one side to such an extent that it overrides the other. The difficulties here are two. First is the problem of the morning after. Their enthusiasm drummed up by "inspirational" sales meetings, the salepeople go out and sell—temporarily reducing one set of pressures to zero. They then find themselves feeling depressed and guilty because the still unsatisfied moral-social needs are now naked and exposed. The second difficulty is more pragmatic. The inspirational method requires continual recharging. The sales manager must maintain the initiative by injecting periodic shots of enthusiasm, lest the salespeople wake up one morning deciding their product and job are really no good.

Conscience

People do not grow up with clear, well-integrated goals and purposes, with goals that will always harmonize with their abilities and with one another. Both in the inside and outside worlds, roadblocks and conflicts are manufactured faster than razor blades. People get hungry and sleepy at the same time; they want to fight and to run at the same time; to love and to hate; to overpower and to submit. And when they want to eat, the clock (and the boss) tell them it won't be lunch time for another hour. But all people don't deal with the same pressures in the same way. The variety and complexity of responses is enormous. We need another concept to help explain these individual differences, and the concept of *conscience* can serve that purpose.

Conscience seems to develop in people through several stages. Often you can see some of those stages going on in children. First, children do what they want to do. Then, having been punished or rewarded, they begin to avoid some things they want to do because they have learned to fear reprisals from parents or because they want to please them by showing self-restraint. At first they may respond to punishment by trying to do what they want to do when Mama's not looking. But as the socialization process goes on, they begin to internalize and accept as their own the restrictions that originally came from outside. At this point they begin to play two roles: to act like themselves; and also to act like their parents. They may throw a glass of milk to satisfy the impulse, but then they will slap their own wrist as punishment for what was done. The final stage in this process is the refusal to throw the milk; the *child* now feels it is wrong.

That's conscience. It's an internal control stystem. It is the difference between being aware of the law but afraid only of getting caught and feeling that the law is right and proper and that to break it is morally wrong. So the pressures from conscience can be satisfied only by denying pressures from other sources.

Some of the conflicts that cause us emotional difficulty are those long-term conflicts between increasingly strong attractions that must be denied because of severe conscience. Thus, one troublesome conflict may center in the infantryman's sense of duty and responsibility (the conscience issues) and his more basic need to stay alive. Or in marriage, the conflict may be between the conscience notions of morality and propriety and the desire to escape physical and psychological harassment at the hands of the other. In organizations, the conflict may be between ambition or greed and the conscience-based pressure to behave ethically.

If we develop an oversized conscience—if a wide range of behaviors comes to be seen as improper or dangerous—then we may encounter many serious conflicts. If one learns early that aggression or sensuality or hostility are wrong and to be feared, and yet, in the course of living, one encounters situations that call for aggression or stir up sensual impulses or engender hostility, then one may be caught up in conflict much more than the person with a different pattern of conscience-based constraints. And if one's perceptual breadth is too limited to find ways around such problems, then the emotional consequences may be large.

On the other hand, if one develops an *under*sized conscience, if one can lie, or steal, or turn on the "showers" at Auschwitz without guilt, then one may suffer very little, although society may suffer a whole lot. At the extreme, people with minimal conscience are usually labeled "psychopaths." They get put in a special psychiatric filing category because, although they present a real problem for society, they are not internally *emotionally* sick. They make other people sick, but they themselves feel fine.

Unconsciousness

At this point we must add one more concept to the whole picture of human emotions: the concept of unconsciousness. One extreme way to handle conscience-impulse conflicts is to *deny* to oneself the existence of one or both of the competing forces. This process of essentially pushing out of memory something the conscience disapproves is labeled, in psychoanalytic terms, *repression*. It can be viewed as one kind of functional "defense mechanism," a way of holding a personality together in the face of otherwise insoluble internal dilemmas. If there is no acceptable solution to be found in the real world, then the solution must somehow be found by rejecting reality. Repression is denying reality by simply and literally forgetting about it. Thus the soldier suffering from what used to be called combat fatigue may appear to remember nothing of the traumatic occurrences that caused his condition. Of course, he does remember. It's all in there somewhere. Indeed, one might say he remembers too well, since his memories may be so threatening and so dangerous that he must deny them to himself.

So, unconsciousness is in part a burial ground for dangerous or guilt-provoking memories. Daydreaming and night dreaming are very probably cues to such unconscious activity. All of us use such mechanisms, albeit in less extreme ways. We may voluntarily escape into unconsciousness with alcohol or drugs, or with hobbies or movies and other less extreme devices. They are all temporary efforts to hold oneself together by erasing one's disturbing memories.

Handling conflict

Obviously, most unconscious or semiconscious methods of handling conflict are not particularly conducive to good mental health. They tend to be last-ditch holding actions that themselves require a great deal of mental energy. So much energy, in fact, may be devoted to repressing what is feared that not much may be left for the behavior required to satisfy the multitudes of other more mundane needs that most of us must satisfy in order to survive.

So we are left with this question: How can one *really* resolve emotional conflicts? No full answer is possible, but here's a useful hint. Most conflicts, like other psychological phenomena, are conflicts only because they are perceived as such. They are less part of the real than of the perceived world. Often, conflicts exist for people because to them certain pressures seem to demand behaviors that are mutually exclusive. Their conflicts would be resolved if (1) they could find some new, previously unknown means to deal with both sides fully, (2) they could change their mind about one of the pressures so that they were no longer concerned with it, or (3) they could reorganize, in one of a number of other ways, their view of the world to set the whole conflict in a new and less significant perspective.

For example, consider again that woman caught between an impossible spouse and social duty. Several alternative resolutions are *theoretically* available. First, she may come to feel differently about her notions of duty. If she decides, say, that it is socially, religiously, and morally appropriate to leave the partner, then perhaps it can be done without trouble. Or she may come to redefine her partner in a new light. Instead of a vicious, unforgiving demon, the spouse may be converted into a miserable soul much in need of help and support. Still again, one may be able to lower one's levels of aspiration, to reorient one's standards so that those sufferings one endures are not so much sufferings as "the things one must expect from life."

This is not to say that one can resolve conflicts simply by asserting, "I feel differently about this." The problem is *really* to feel differently. The counselor and the psychiatrist, as well as time and experience, can help one reorganize perceptions so that new solutions become possible.

One way to illustrate the idea of "reorganizing perceptions" is to ask you to compare yourself today with yourself as an adolescent. Consider what a skin rash might have meant in adolescence and what it would mean when you are thirty or forty-five and settled down. The problem is simply not the same problem. As our worlds have grown, as new knowledge and new experiences have been added, we have changed our perspectives and reorganized our perceptions.

Sometimes an adult conflict exists only because a person cuts off channels of information from the world. Combat-fatigue victims, for example, may withdraw completely into themselves, apparently seeking to avoid emotional repetition of their terribly arduous experiences. But unless they eventually open their channels, they will never get an opportunity to learn that the world has changed and that they are in a world of sunlight rather than darkness. Similarly, the energetic work of repressing old conflicts may so preoccupy many of us that we cannot observe our own changing roles in changing environments. We do not learn that our elaborate defenses are no longer necessary because we do not realize that we and the world have both changed. Thus, executives who feel they are not as technically up to date as their young colleagues may, after a series of perceived failures, go on avoiding new technologies, never realizing that now they are—if they can bring themselves to try it—perfectly capable of handling the new tools that are now available. This tendency to narrow one's incoming communication channels in order to avoid psychological dangers is one major organizational and social cost of conflict. People avoid much of the world because they fear much of themselves.

But though many reactions to emotional conflict are psychologically unhealthy and inefficient, they remain psychologically lawful reactions. They, like other behavior, can be thought of as attempts by the organism to bring itself into equilibrium with the world out there.

Conflicts, beliefs, and decisions
The great balancing act

These methods for trying to cope with emotional conflict—by reorganizing perceptions or restricting incoming communication—have their paral-
lels even as managers confront "rational" decision-making situations. In
the next chapter we will focus on the rational part of the human being,
what we usually consider the part that makes our important decisions. But
before going on, it is appropriate at the end of this chapter to build a bridge
between the gutsy, emotional side of people and that other brainy, decision-
making side. The methods we use to cope with conflict provide such a
bridge. Decisions, the essence of managerial life, are, after all, attempts at
resolving conflicts.

Some of those "resolutions" are fact-based and logical; but some, even
at top levels of organizations, are impulse-based and irrational. Why do
even hardheaded business decisions in retrospect often turn out to have
been foolish and irrational? Why do executives often fail to abandon a
course of action even after it seems obviously hopeless? Why do we often
fight for our programs even more after they are clearly in trouble than we
ever did before?

All of these and more can usefully be considered part of a great human
balancing act in which each of us is highly skilled. Humans search for consistency and balance in business decisions as well as in the choices of
everyday life. When we have invested a large amount of money, effort, or
emotion into a course of action, we find it hard to accept evidence showing
that those actions are not working out. To maintain an internal balance, to
reduce psychological dissonance, we often do "irrational" things—such as
blaming the sales force for a product's failure or investing *more* in promotion and advertising after failure than after success.

So emotions do not sit in an isolated backwater of human affairs. They
are there all the time, even when kings, presidents, and generals are making
decisions about the fate of the world.

That critical but rocky marriage between emotion and reason will come
up in more detail in later chapters.

Managing emotions
Five thoughts for the manager

People, this chapter has intoned, are emotional beings. They don't just
think; they feel. They get frustrated at the obstacles the world throws in
their paths (or those they perceive the world to be throwing in their paths).
They want to go in opposite directions at the same time, and they get upset
when they can't. They blow up; they go into depressions; they blame the
innocent; they rationalize away their own mistakes. Yet many of those "ir-

rational" behaviors carry a special kind of reason of their own. Emotions perform protective functions that help keep the whole person together, often in situations where staying together isn't easy. And they drive humans forward to great achievements against long odds. Emotions are as natural and as useful as rational thought. So, for the manager, an appreciation of the nature of human emotions becomes absolutely critical.

Many of us, including managers, have been trained and educated to worship at the church of reason—with its denominations of Logic, Consistency, and Fact. So we may treat emotionality, both in those around us and in ourselves, as a kind of inadequacy, a fault, as noise in the system. If God had done the job properly, He (or She) would have created only rational human beings. Emotions, with good luck, might disappear in a few more million years of evolution.

But, of course, God didn't make a mistake. Emotions were built into us, and they can serve us well. Love, passion, commitment, and even greed are emotional processes that can drive humans forward. Managing one's own emotions, and those of employees is as much a critical managerial function as managing markets or finances.

So let's turn from the nature of emotionality to the issue of managing emotionality. Here are five derivations from what we have said so far:

1. Managers are emotional creatures, too, and just as much given to disguising emotion in the cloak of reason as are the people who work with them. Manager, know thyself.

2. Managers had better not try to act *un*emotionally. The cool, distant, impersonal manager is not a good fit for today's managerial world. Leadership, after all, is a heavily emotional process. One managerial job is to stir up motives to challenge, stimulate, and lead. And those activities require managers who are themselves emotionally committed to their missions.

3. Emotions are close to morality. Conscience is where feelings about duty and responsibility come from. While conscience inhibits and controls behavior, it also *directs* behavior. Managers without a clear sense of conscience run ships without rudders. Managers are people who hold the fates of other people in their hands. They had better *feel* responsible.

4. Emotions are one critical driver of productivity. Turned-on people work hard; dedicated people make things happen. Apathetic people don't.

5. If managers want to manage other people's emotions sensibly, they must be prepared to step on their own brakes now and then. When people become emotionally upset, what will usually help them most is not orders to cool it or sage advice or argument, but acceptance, good listening, and support. Let's not treat irrationality as though it were rational just because we know how to deal with rationality.

This whole issue—the management of other people's emotionality receives more thorough coverage in part 2, when we look at problems of influencing and changing other people's behavior.

In summary

Emotions are a pervasive part of human nature. One class of strong emotions are feelings of frustration, feelings that arise when one encounters unexpected and threatening blocks in one's path. When people encounter such blocks, they usually react with aggression. When we are sure of our own ability, that aggression is mostly directed toward the obstacle; when we are pessimistic about our ability or when we have had a history of failure in this area of our lives, the aggression is mostly directed toward ourselves.

Many block situations deprive rather than frustrate because the obstacles do not seem insurmountable or the goals are not central to the self. Some people may therefore meet fewer frustrations than others because they can find more ways around more obstacles, or because they are self-confident enough that their self-esteem does not have to be proved again with every new problem they encounter.

Moreover, if your objectives are in line with your abilities, then you may avoid another major source of frustration. If your objectives extend far beyond your abilities, you may consider yourself a chronic failure simply because you cannot see that the carrot is tied to your own nose.

Similar feelings can be generated by psychological conflicts, pulls and pushes in different directions at the same time. Conflicts that require extreme solutions usually involve "conscience" needs, centering on morality and social propriety. Extreme solutions often require the person to push one of the needs into unconsciousness and thereby—by forgetting—deny the conflict.

But such repressive defenses cost energy. Less enervating solutions call for reorganization of perceptions, finding new ways out of apparently dead-end situations.

Serious chronic conflicts may develop in organizations. Conflicts between needs for dependence and for independence are especially prevalent because the large organizational environment emphasizes dependency, but professes to value independence.

Less deep but equally important conflicts occur in everyday decision-making situations. There, emotional and logical mechanisms get mixed with one another, frequently making it hard to tell how much of our commitment to a course of action is "objective" and "logical," and how much of it is emotionally self-protective.

Managers must not think of human emotions as noise, weakness, or trouble. Rather, they are natural and powerful human attributes that can, properly managed, drive toward dedication, loyalty, and extraordinary effort.

4

Thinking, learning, problem solving: People are also reasoning creatures

The main purpose of this chapter is to counterbalance the general impression of human irrationality and emotion we have built up thus far. In the preceding chapters we emphasized the driven, often "illogical" character of much human behavior. But it's obvious that that isn't the whole story. Children learn to keep clear of hot stoves. Students learn to type and to solve arithmetic problems. Junior executives think about ways to add to their incomes and their job security. Architects think creatively about their designs. Managers use their heads to choose the most effective ways of budgeting their capital and marketing their products.

A couple of decades ago, this chapter would probably not have been included in a book like this. Psychologists and social scientists were so deeply focused on the emotional life of people that they largely ignored the reasoning and thinking life.

That emphasis on emotions was itself partly a reaction against still earlier entirely rational approaches. Around the turn of the century and on into the 1920s, for instance, our model of human beings was largely a rational one; we assumed that people worked only to earn money, and that managers, in turn, sought only to maximize their profits. We built theories of economic behavior and industrial organization around such rational models. Humans reasoned, and some reasoned better than others. Thus, industrial engineering grew up as a logical, "scientific" process, treating issues such as worker hostility and resistance as irrational quirks, attributable largely to stupidity. Those people didn't know how to think straight. Later, with the emergence of such odd bedfellows as Freud and the Western Electric studies, attitudes turned toward the opposite direction. In many intellectual quarters, rather foggy conceptions of human emotions took precedence over reason. Workers now were seen to be trying to satisfy ephemeral motives for "belonging," and managers were not managing but unconsciously coping with childhood images of their fathers. Words such as *motivation, morale,* and *industrial democracy* entered our managerial vocabularies.

42

Only recently have social scientists from many fields set about to integrate and modify these two perspectives, trying to deal with the undeniable whole human being—the manager who may indeed unconsciously feel competitive with Dad, but who also spends a fair portion of time trying to collect and process information in order to decide what materials to buy and what marketing strategies to deploy. This chapter, then, is about those more conscious efforts to think, learn, reason, and solve problems—abilities that are just as much part of the human picture as emotionality.

What does it take to learn?

Our three basics—motivation, cognition, and reinforcement from outside—provide the framework that makes learning possible. Earlier chapters have said that people learn continuously, that they learn their personalities, as well as many of their motives, attitudes, and habitual ways of behaving. People also learn to speak, walk, read, build airplanes, and make managerial decisions. They have learned whenever they modify their behavior at time 2 as a consequence of experience at time 1.

The questions now before us are these: How do people do those things? What does it take for someone to be able to learn? If we set about to build a "thing" capable of learning, what would we have to build into it? And just how would the thing work?

This thing we are trying to build must demonstrate that it is a learning thing by behaving more effectively—perhaps more quickly and with fewer mistakes—the second or third time it encounters a problem than it did the first time. What characteristics do we have to build into it to permit it to pass such a test?

Our thing will surely need at least two quite different mechanisms. It will need some hardware, some gadgets, some devices that will "allow" it to do certain things. But it will also need some software, some "rules"; it will need a program that will permit it to select among alternative possibilities.

On the hardware side, our thing will first require some *input mechanisms* so that it can have those "experiences" for it to learn from. It will need, that is, some ways of getting information into itself from outside itself, something like human eyes or ears. (Some photoelectric cells might do.)

Second, it will need some *output mechanisms,* some ways of acting and searching. It will have to be capable of moving through the world or sending signals out into the world. It will need some equivalents to human muscles or the human voice, such as wheels or a printer. How can it modify its behavior if it cannot behave? How can it search for easier paths if it cannot explore?

We aren't through yet. If this machine is to improve performance as a consequence of experience, it will need to remember its experience. It needs a *memory mechanism* for storing its experiences so that it can "keep them in mind" when faced again with similar problems. Lacking such a memory storehouse, or lacking access to it, each experience will be a brand-new experience.

Besides those external mechanisms, it will need several inside gadgets. It will need an *associative device* to connect its inputs to its outputs. The device may be a simple one that makes only one choice—to connect or not to connect a given input with a given output. But without such a device the thing won't be able to close the circuit between what comes in and what goes out; hence, it will be unable to profit behaviorally from its experience.

Besides all this hardware, which allows the thing to receive, process, and put out information, the thing still needs some software—a program, a set of rules so that it doesn't just connect any old input to any old output completely at random.

One of these rules could be a *stinginess rule*. If the selective device has to make a choice among alternative outputs, it can be built either to select the most "efficient" of all outputs—perhaps the simplest and shortest one—or to try out parts and select the first one it comes across that works, or to use some other specified decision rule.

It will also need a *response rule*. It cannot be allowed to sit still and ignore all inputs. It has to be built so that it is *on* when inputs are coming in and stays on until it gets an answer.

Our thing also needs a *motivation* rule, doesn't it? It has to have some basis for evaluating inputs. Is this input good or bad? Pleasant or unpleasant? Should it try to get rid of the input or get more of it?

The thing had also better have a *reinforcement* rule, such as this: If the output works (eliminates, for example, a noxious input), do it again in similar situations. And perhaps our learning thing also needs an *attribution* rule, a notion of causality. So if it "wants" B, it can try to make sure that it does A first. Notice that such attribution rules, as we shall see later, can be tricky. Sometimes our thing may mistakenly attribute outcome B to cause A, just because they happened close together, when in fact the two may have no connection at all.

One final requirement: the thing will need some way of getting *inputs about its own outputs*. It has to know whether its own actions worked or didn't. If you're using a bow and arrow and can not see that you've missed the target, you can never know how to modify your aim. If managers could not know about the effects of their past changes in plant layout, for instance, they could not know how to improve the layout. But this means that the input mechanisms have to be somehow related to the output mechanisms. If the only input device in our gadget is a buzzer that signals with sound, and the only output device is a gadget that signals with lights, then

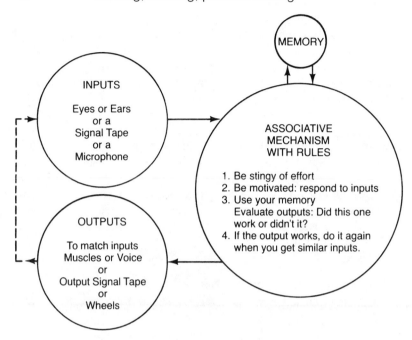

Fig. 4.1.   A hypothetical learning mechanism

our thing might have a tough time learning. So there has to be some kind of common "language" between input and output. If our thing can input and output in the same language, then it can learn about the effects of what it has done.

Given all these characteristics, our learning thing begins to look like figure 4.1.

Notice that the thing is full of closed loops, with the arrows completing full circles. It is also a relatively elaborate system; it is not a cellulose sponge. Notice, too, that it looks a little like the design of a control system that one might find in many engineering situations.

Theoretically then, if we could build a thing like that, it could learn. If any of those characteristics were missing, it could not learn—nor theoretically, could people. If, for instance, we were to knock out all of your input senses—your sight, hearing, touch, taste, smell—you won't be able to improve your performance as a result of experience over time because you can't find out how you did the first time. If we knock out your memory, you can't learn because each new try is your first try. If we knock out your outputs—your voice and your muscles—you can't try at all. If you have no brain to make choices, you can't improve because you can't change. If we knock out the stinginess principle or the motivation rule, you won't improve because you don't give a damn; the hard way is as good for you as the easy way, and no behavior at all is as good as anything else. And if you don't have a reinforcement rule, you won't care whether you get more or less of that input. And if you can't see or feel your own hand—that is, if you can't determine the effects of your own outputs—you have no way of deciding which way to change your outputs.

If we put all these requirements together, we come out with an essentially mechanical but nevertheless dynamic view of what it takes to learn. Learning becomes a process of doing things, finding out and evaluating what happened, figuring out what probably *caused* what happened to happen, storing that experience, and trying again—using past experiences as a jumping-off place. Psychologically speaking, one can say that (1) we act, (2) we perceive the effects of our actions, (3) we attribute causation, (4) we reorganize and remember our perceptions, and (5) we act again on the basis of our reorganized perceptions.

Artificial intelligence and machines that learn

Technologists have been able, in the last couple of decades, to design machine or software equivalents for most of these requirements for learning, trying to build machines that can learn. Using such machines—computers are the best example—psychologists, mathematicians, and others are able to program them not only to solve problems but to *learn* to solve similar problems faster after experience.

Sometimes computer programs that learn behave very differently from human beings, working in a routine, mechanical way, checking out every possible choice no matter how patently foolish it may be. But other programs show quite human attributes. Those *heuristic* programs (as distinct from more mechanical *algorithmic* ones) are designed to behave like people. They are built by observing how people solve problems and then programming the computer to do likewise. And heuristically programmed computers, therefore, sometimes make mistakes and draw wrong conclusions just as we humans do when we're learning new games or solving new puzzles.

Some of us remember, for instance, the way our geometry teachers used to trap us by giving us a series of similar-looking problems and then springing a new one on us that looked just like the rest. We would have generated a little rule about how to solve the first lot, and then try to apply that rule to the new problem because it looked just like the old ones. After hitting dead ends half a dozen times, we would finally realize that our rule simply didn't apply this time, and we would have to search in another direction.

Heuristically programmed computers behave in much the same way. They do not behave as machines "normally" do. They do not just try everything whether it looks sensible or not, nor do they forever keep banging their heads against walls. They use strategies of the sort that people use. For example, "If the problem is complex, try to reduce it to a simpler form first," or, "If this problem looks like another problem you have already solved, first try the method you used to solve that other problem."

While these artificially intelligent programs often simulate human methods, they do not simulate the human brain. The simulation is not of neurons and synapses; but of information-processing tactics.

Several questions about these man-machine comparisons have stirred up considerable emotional heat. It seems clear that by usual definitions of learning, machines really can learn to solve difficult, nonroutine problems. They can do much more than arithmetic. It is not clear that machines are necessarily going to end up smarter or dumber or more important than people, although robotization, one form of applied artificial intelligence, is clearly moving in on many manufacturing jobs. And many observers, including these authors, are convinced that many present-day management jobs will ultimately be filled by programmed problem-solving machines—after an intervening period of programmed problem-solving people.

But the most important issue that needs to be stressed here is the critical importance of the closable loops of feedback systems for both human and machine learning. *It is only by obtaining information about the effects of behavior that we can correct and tune that behavior.*

The social side of learning

Feedback—the flow of return information about our own outputs—is not only important in learning to solve intellectual problems; it is also critical in social problems. To learn to be skillful in our relationships with other people, we must rely on the feedback we get from other people about our impact on them. And therein lies a conundrum we shall be discussing at much greater length in later sections of this book. The problem is this: It is *relatively* easy to get feedback about the effects of our actions on *things*. We can see whether or not the ball has gone down the fairway or off into the rough. And we can then make efforts to correct our stroke on our next drive. We can try to put a piece into a jigsaw puzzle and see whether or not it fits. We can sing a note and (some of us) can hear whether or not it is off pitch. But when we say something to other people, we do not necessarily or automatically get immediate feedback to tell us whether or not they heard what we intended. For now we are working through the perceptual filters of people. And their outputs in response to our inputs are subject to great distortion.

While we *know* that the golf ball sank into the water hazard, we do not always know whether or not the bright idea we just offered our boss sank into his brain. So, in social situations (and other situations in which feedback is slow or easily distorted), we become especially vulnerable to our own attribution rules. We attribute causality, almost by nature, but in a world of distorted feedback, those attributions can be way off the mark.

Behavior modification

Teaching machines and other programmed learning techniques are applications of a general feedback principle to human learning. The essence of the teaching machine idea is to provide students with immediate feedback about the effects of their own performance. The students fill in the blanks and immediately learn whether or not they were right. But in much regular, nonprogrammed teaching there are long intervals between learning and feedback—between lectures and examination grades, for example. And in many areas no clear evaluative feedback is ever forthcoming.

In the last few years, another more far-reaching effort to apply that feedback principle has taken place. It operates under the general label of behavior modification and, as the name suggests, it is concerned with changing human behavior. If people behave, and then get quick feedback about the effects of their behavior, then they can modify their behavior in search of better effects. Thus, if someone is afraid of snakes and we want to help that person to eliminate that fear, we can set up situations associated with snakes that provide immediate positive, rather than negative, feedback. By carefully controlling both incremental exposure to such situations and the feedback that follows, perhaps we can eliminate the fear. And since managers are often in positions to generate reinforcements for particular kinds of behavior, they should be able to modify other people's behavior by generating reinforcements that are quick and appropriate (from their point of view).

Of course, the implications of behavior modification go much further than the treatment of fears. The implications extend into the shaping of all human behavior. So the behavior modification movement carries theoretical and ethical implications, too. For it takes the position that one needs to know relatively little about the internal dynamics of the human being or about what caused the present behavior of an individual. It is essentially a behavioristic point of view, arguing that what needs to be changed is behavior and that what changes behavior is feedback that appropriately reinforces desired behavioral changes. So your behavior and mine can be "shaped" by our world of reinforcements. We shall say more about these issues in later chapters on the manager's role as a changer of human behavior.

Are people really more complicated than machines?

People's decision rules about what is relevant to a problem are usually broader and more diffuse than those thus far programmed into machines.

Human rules reflect the complexity of memories and motives that exist within us at any one moment. Humans think. We ascribe causes; we notice relationships; we observe what happens to others. As a result, we are likely to learn more from an experience than anyone out there intended us to learn. Suppose you are a new management trainee. Not only do you learn about the company's finances; you also learn that the financial vice-president likes to push people around. As a student, you learn not only about geometry but about the characteristics of the geometry teacher, and you also learn attitudes toward geometry. It's great, or it's a load of nonsense. And you think about the whole show. You perceive all sorts of things as parts of the problem-to-be-solved because your own satisfactions are tied up with all of them at the same time. Learning to solve the geometry problem is only one of several potential reinforcements out there for the student at that moment. Learning to please the teacher is another, as is learning that geometry is something to stay near, or to escape from. Learning to impress that cute girl or boy is another.

Certainly one difficult task for teachers, whose *sole* objective is to teach geometry (or management, for that matter), is to make sure that it is geometry and not themselves or other "irrelevant" parts of the situation that students see as the important problem-to-be-solved. In fact, one of the major advantages (or is it a disadvantage?) of the movement toward impersonal teaching machines may turn out to lie precisely in that area. By eliminating the human teacher, we also eliminate many special and sometimes irrelevant learning problems that the human teacher creates for the student. With the machine as teacher, almost all that students need (or are allowed) to learn is the naked subject matter. In the classroom they need to learn about both the subject matter as well as people in an inextricably interrelated way. Which way, thoughtful reader, is likely to generate broader learning or better learning?

Another complexity stems from people's limited storage capacity. We cannot hold many raw bits of information in our memories unless we classify and categorize them. It is as though we have only a limited number of file folders to work with but can label them in any way we choose. If we insist on putting just one piece of information in one folder, we soon run out of space. But if we can find useful ways of grouping information, the same set of folders can hold an almost limitless quantity of information.

The problem of finding appropriate categories becomes a key issue in improving our ability to learn. Managers who insist on classifying each bit of information about their organizations separately will soon be overwhelmed by detail, as some managers are. But if they can set up an efficient system of categories, they can handle all they need to remember.

Unfortunately, categorizing systems, once set up, are difficult to break down. Clerks often have difficulty giving up their clerical categories even though they have now been promoted into managerial jobs. They go on "thinking like a clerk." As a later chapter on management development will point out, one weakness in up-through-the-ranks training is that it demands difficult recategorizations at each step up the ladder. Why, one may ask, teach people to think like clerks if we later want them to unlearn all that so they can act like managers?

A third source of complexity in human learning lies in the fact that mistakes can be both costly and valuable. We often (being stingy) want to learn only the "right" way of doing things. But learning only what is right means that all the other possibilities are unknown, uncharted, and unstored; hence, they cannot be categorized for dealing with similar but not identical problems in the future.

Suppose, for instance, that you are in a hotel in a strange city. You want to drive over to plant X. The hotel clerk gives you directions, and you follow them successfully and memorize them. What have you learned? And what haven't you learned?

Suppose, instead, that you just got into your car and started out, stopping to ask for help, noticing landmarks, and finally, after many mistakes, arriving at plant X. Then you try again the next day, and the next, until you end up on the same route the clerk had given you. Isn't that a waste of time? Or is it?

By the first method you learned one efficient path through an otherwise unknown jungle. By the second you learned a lot about the jungle and alternative ways of getting through it.

Now suppose one day the clerk's route gets dug up for road repairs; you must detour. The advantage of those earlier costly explorations now becomes obvious: you have a mental map from which to work. You can "feel" your way through the city; those mistakes you made now help you solve this new problem.

Insofar as the world of the manager is a world of new problems, one must worry about balancing what the fledgling manager learns through costly experiment and exploration against the high cost of such exploration. If managing were nothing but a series of repeatable routines, the choice would be easy. But if most present problems in management are a little different from past problems, breadth and richness of experience look very valuable.

Problem solving as a multistage process

Learning, thinking, and problem solving are inseparable processes. When we solve problems, we learn about them and we also think about what we have learned. But for convenience let's shift our attention now to the problem-solving part of the learning–thinking–problem-solving process.

One interesting issue to begin with is this one: Just what constitutes a "best solution" to a problem? What is *the* best solution to the problem of college for the children? Or *the* best solution to the problem of allocating our capital budget?

We could assume, and we often do, that *a* best solution exists and that humans should and will look for it. We could assume that people will rationally select the very best alternative from an array of all possible alternatives that they somehow lay out before them.

There are three things wrong with that assumption. First, we do not usually have anything like a complete array of alternatives to lay out before us. Managers do not know all the equipment available on the market or all possible marketing strategies from which to choose, and *it would cost them a great deal to find out*. Second, it is wrong to assume that only the best does or should satisfy most people most of the time. In practice, people often save themselves a great deal of time and effort by searching only until they find something that works well enough to meet their own level of aspiration. In fact (as the preceding chapter pointed out), it is precisely when people feel impelled to find the very best method, when their levels of aspiration are set (usually by others) far above their abilities, that they are likely to be inefficient problem solvers, unable to decide and act because every available decision and course of action looks less than satisfactory.

Third, the one "best" solution idea ignores a central aspect of human thinking, *creativity*. Often the most interesting alternatives aren't to be found out there, but in here—inside oneself—such as a new design for a boat or a new vision for a company. Some alternatives lie within ourselves. And even more important, some of us find and make our own problems. They aren't just thrown at us by the world. That problem-finding or problem-making aspect of thinking and learning is one we shall emphasize again and again in the pages that follow. Managers don't just *re*act; they *pro*act. They assertively attack problems instead of waiting for problems to find them.

But to get back to problem solving, notice that we have mostly been talking about it as a sort of two-stage process. Usually, when we think of solving a problem, we think mostly of finding the right answer. But we have tried to consider problem solving here in a broader sense, to include not only the decision part of the process but also the *search* part that must precede it. It is very seldom, indeed, that the real world supplies us with free road maps describing all possible routes, all possible choices. Before we can solve a problem, we must do our own search for the best routes. Such search costs time and energy, and often costs money and other resources, too. Part of the problem of deciding which car to buy is how much time and effort we are willing to spend searching, shopping around, and fending off car salespeople. That search can be costly; dealers, options, deals, and finance charges all vary from place to place.

And if we should dare to enter the private used-car market, things get worse. How many classified ads shall we respond to? How many miles will we travel to see a car? Can we ever know all the potentially satisfactory used cars in full detail, so that we can make a choice among them? No way. The market, after all, is dynamic; while we are searching for the last car, the first ones have already been sold. Few of us are foolish enough to pay the price of such a thorough search. Instead we search until we have some idea of the comparative advantages of different kinds of cars and then go on until we find a satisfactory one. From there on, with any luck at all, our thinking processes go to work to help us support the decision we have just made. But we will know perfectly well that there may still have been a better car out there, at a better price, but we never found it. So the search and the costs associated with it play a big part in problem solving.

Another big part of problem solving lies, of course, in the decision itself. Having gathered as much information as we can afford, having arrayed as many alternatives as we are willing to, what then? Then, apparently, we combine some of our emotional balancing processes with our rational thinking processes. We use *heuristics*.

Heuristics are rules of thumb, strategies for making complex decisions. Sometimes our heuristics are not very good. Sometimes they aren't bad. We kick the tire of the used car. We start the engine and look at the exhaust to see if it's burning oil. We try to figure out whether or not the car has been repainted. And on the basis of these less than perfect tests (plus our emotional reactions—we just love the color), we make a decision. Some of us have longer checklists than others. Some of us find a mechanic we can trust who will come along with us to help make the decision. We don't optimize; we "satisfice"! We choose a car that is "good enough" and meets our minimum requirements.

Humans as satisficers

Whether selecting a job or a used car, deciding which of several package designs to adopt, or trying to choose among several applicants for a job, we usually follow a *satisficing* model. We indulge, that is to say, in a limited amount of search, until we reach a *satisfactory* rather than an optimal alternative.

That model of people as satisficing problem solvers—as individuals using both their heads and their guts, with a limited degree of reasoning and with large elements of strategic guesswork to back it up—is quite a different model from others that have existed in the past. Some earlier conceptions of problem solving, laid almost exclusive emphasis on reasoning—full search, full test, and rational choice of the best alternatives, largely ignoring the impulsive and emotional aspects of behavior.

Human emotions are not central to the satisficing model, but they are not neglected either. They are simply placed in a different setting. When one talks about the "cost" of search, one must take into account the *psycholog-*

ical cost. And the locus of search—the segment of the world in which we choose to search—can be very much determined emotionally. Some car buyers may choose to look only at used Lincolns and Cadillacs; others will look only at used sports cars. And their front-end selection of those areas for search is quite likely to be related to front-end emotional aspects of their personalities. Clearly, the satisficing view is rather different from the more traditional rational views of problem solving.

The rational view began as a description of how people *ought* to solve problems rather than as a description of how they actually do solve them. Somewhere along the line that distinction became blurred. Researchers, and even industrial problem solvers, now often treat the rational model as though it were a description of typical behavior. It seldom is, though some people clearly learn to use it. To borrow an apt example, consider the problem of looking for a needle in a haystack. "Rational" people search carefully through the haystack collecting all the needles they can find there. They then measure the sharpness of each needle and select the sharpest one. Satisficers search through the haystack until they find a needle; then they try it, and if it's sharp enough to sew with they get on with their sewing, and that's the end of it. If not, they search some more, but only until they find a needle that works.

It seems quite clear that most of us do behave more like the second person than the first, whether we ought to or not. If we satisfice too much, we probably come up with lousy answers. If we search too hard for excellence, we may never get anything done.

Notice, too, that the satisficing idea drives toward an incremental view of problem solving. Try something. If it works, go on from there, and so on; a very different approach from a preplanned, carefully worked-out course of action.

Can some people satisfice better than others?
Or why should we all learn mathematics?

If humans are really satisficers, and if we often use heuristic rules for solving problems, then we are rather closely bound by our earlier experiences. Faced with a new problem, we call on heuristic rules that we have developed out of our earlier problem-solving experiences. It is as though most of us carry a rule in our heads that says, "If it worked before, try it again in similar situations; if it didn't work, try something else." That is a kind of *local* problem-solving process. In the television industry, a network tries a comedy series about doctors; if it works, other people pick it up and try the same theme next year. When the ratings begin to drop off, the producers search for new themes. Similarly, if our company has been lucky with engineering graduates from Barleycorn College, we are apt to go on recruiting from that school. We keep our ears and eyes open to see whether or not this year's recruits are doing all right, and only if there's trouble do we begin to search in other schools.

It's possible, of course, that somewhere in the world there are potential employees who could do the job a good deal better than the ones we are getting. Or that there are better television themes. But as long as present results are *satisfactory,* our search for new solutions is likely to stay minimal. Or so it will be *unless we have better analytic tools than the next guy*—unless, for example, we can use an X-ray on the haystack.

Consider this example:

Suppose I have a big box in which I tell you truthfully there are a thousand marbles, 750 black and 250 white. I tell you I am going to select 25 marbles, one at a time, and I want you to predict what color the next marble will be.

I am now ready to reach into the box and pull out the first marble. What color do you think it will be? Black or white? Write the answer down before I pull the marble out.

In fact, the first marble was *black.*

Now predict the second marble.

In fact, the second was *black.*

Now predict the third.

In fact, the third was *white.*

Now predict the fourth.

In fact, the fourth was *black.*

Now predict the fifth.

In fact, the fifth was *black.*

Now predict the sixth.

How did you go about working on this problem?

If you are like most of us, you begin to develop *local* hypotheses. You notice that there were two blacks followed by a white and then two blacks, so you begin, perhaps, to generate a hypothesis like this: "There should be more blacks than whites because there are more blacks than whites in the box; and there were two blacks and then a white and then two blacks. Maybe there is a pattern of two blacks and a white. So I guess that the next one will be white." If the next one was in fact white, then you might feel more sure of your "theory" about two blacks and a white. But if that pattern broke, and a string of six whites followed, you would search for a new theory. Indeed if six whites came up in a row, you would probably even bet that a black one was "due."

But a statistician would not use that approach at all. He would say something like this: Three-quarters of the marbles in the box are black; one quarter are white. So on any try the probability is three out of four that a black will come up. I shall, therefore, *always* predict black. And that trained analyst would beat you most of the time, *because he had a better analytic tool than you did.*

Billing Address:
Joseph F. Norton
41 W097 Bridle Creek Dr
Saint Charles, IL 60175-7677
USA

Shipping Address:
Joseph F. Norton
41 W097 Bridle Creek Dr
Saint Charles, IL 60175-7677
USA

Returns Are Easy!
Visit http://www.amazon.com/returns to return any item—including gifts- in unopened or original
condition within 30 days for a full refund (other restrictions apply)

Qty	Item	Item Price	Total
	IN THIS SHIPMENT		
1	**Managerial Psychology: Managing Behavior in Organizations**	$35.20	$35.20
	0226469735 : 0226469735		
	Hardcover		

SDsRtvqBR

SubTotal		$35.20
Order Total		$35.20
Paid via Amex		$35.20
Balance due		$0.00

This shipment completes your order.

1010 (1 of 1)

The point is that there may be methods in the world for solving problems that are unknown to some of us. Often they seem almost contrary to common sense. Some of us learn some of these tools and apply them quite naturally. Some readers, we are sure, were not for a moment trapped by the marbles problem, because they were armed with a tool that they were not likely to have developed for themselves. Someone else developed it, and they were taught it.

In human history, great numbers of tools have been developed and have passed eventually into the realm of common sense. None of us has to figure out anymore how to add two and two. Other people have long since worked out rules, and we learned them in the second grade. But in more complex problem areas, where very few tools have existed, new ones are being developed all the time. And especially in management, the competitive advantage may often lie with that manager who is expert with such tools, or who is expert enough to realize that other people are expert with such tools. Managers do not always take easily to the notion that other methods, better than their longtime favorites, may be available. They resist the staff analyst's or the operations researcher's complex formulations for solving commonsense problems. Yet in many cases (*not* in all cases) their own local methods simply do not work as well. But there ain't no free lunch. While those new analytic tools can offer huge pluses for some classes of problems, they often inhibit more imaginative problem finding.

Learning as an active process

Learning and problem solving, as we have been looking at them, are *active* rather than *passive* processes. People don't learn much just by absorption. They have to work at learning. They have to search for information, make tough choices, and act on those choices. Certainly, people can and do learn from experience and from observing the experience of others. In this context, however, experience means doing things to the world as well as letting the world do things to you. For example, we observe other people's successes when they behave in particular ways. But the learning process isn't complete until we take the active step of trying to imitate that behavior and encounter the consequences for ourselves.

This distinction between active and passive learning is important for the manager. If we take the passive view, it follows that the way to train new recruits is to pump them full of knowledge. So we probably invest heavily in classrooms, lectures, and unsupervised job rotation. If we take the active view, we invest in projects, problems, and coaching staffs. If we take the passive view, we assume that learning should *precede* action—that we should first learn potentially useful things and *then* try to apply them. If we take the active view, we, in effect, encourage learners to get themselves stymied first, and then to search for useful ways out.

If we take the passive view, we go on to count heavily on the wisdom and instruction of seniors. If we take the action view, the wisdom and experience of seniors is relegated to a supportive, behind-the-scene role, available when juniors need it. We encourage juniors to learn first from working on hard problems, with all their pain and frustration, and secondarily from their seniors as helpers in that search.

Moreover, if we generalize a little, the passive view would probably support the sequence of school first and job experience afterward. It suggests that business school ought to (as it often does) precede the real world of work. The active view would prefer a back-and-forth sequence; one that started with the job, then went *back* to school, and so on, back and forth as, and if, required by the problems encountered on the job.

In defense of schools of business, however, even the most assiduous activist must face up to one dilemma. If we start with active problem solving, how does the problem solver know *where* to search for solutions? How can we know what better tools may be available?

One answer might be that motivated business problem solvers are probably highly accessible to new tools and ideas because they have competitors and because their level of aspiration doesn't ever quite settle down. But to get to those new tools, they, or their inventors, must open up channels of communication with educators and researchers. This is to say that the organization, with its host of challenging problems, is an ideal active learning ground for managers—a better one, in many ways, than any school can hope to be—but only if the organization maintains close and solid communication with that other tool-developing world outside.

Learning and motivation

Active learning gets moving, we said earlier, when people feel motivated; and when people are motivated, they are *not* satisfied. So we come up against another curiosity. On the one hand, many psychologists, the authors of the book included, argue that stability, security, objectivity, and many other lovely things begin to emerge when people feel secure and satisfied. But motivated people are uncomfortable and dissatisfied. What's the escape from that dilemma?

One possible but questionable answer is that there need be no escape. If the purpose of business is to get things done at a profit, and if things get done by discontented people, then let's keep people discontented. Keep their bellies empty and jobs scarce, and then they'll work very hard.

But even if we were to argue (which we won't) that human stability and security are not the business of business, objectivity is. We want our people to learn effective ways of doing things. We want problems to be solved reasonably, sensibly. Discontented people are often not reasonable, or sensible. They may learn to hate their managers rather than to work hard at their jobs. So we are still in a box.

Another way out can be derived from the distinction made in the preceding chapter between frustration and deprivation. People can be dissatisfied without feeling frustrated. They can want to solve problems without getting into an emotional uproar, *if they feel reasonably confident about themselves*. So the trick (if that's a fair word) would be to let people develop their own dissatisfactions about job problems—about making the sale or designing the package—while staying comfortable about more basic issues, like feeling competent and appreciated. Then they can concentrate their energies on the job to be done and do it with some degree of objectivity.

Note that the idea of active learning is not the same as the idea of learning from experience. Experience often has little effect on learning. Repeated experience, without appropriate motivation or feedback, may teach us almost nothing. Pulling dollar bills out of our wallets for years has not taught most of us much about dollar bills as such. We have learned a good deal about their use, but whose picture is on them? How many signatures? Whose? How many times does the number 1 appear? Where? But of course those things aren't important to us, so why bother to learn them? Exactly!

Repetition of an act may help people to perform the act more skillfully, not *because* of the repetition but because the repetition gives them a chance to try out different methods frequently enough to find a good one. So let's not assume that years of selling experience have *necessarily* taught veterans to be better salespeople than novices. All their experience has indeed given them the *opportunity* to learn; but whether they took that opportunity and what they learned from it are quite separate questions.

In summary

People are not perfectly rational, but neither are they incapable of thinking and learning reasonably. They are endowed with all the equipment they need: input senses, output mechanisms, memories, motivations, and information processors. Only recently have we come even close to equipping machines with like endowments so that they can perform a few intellectual acts as well as competent people can.

On the other hand, people seem to use their endowments with considerable inefficiency. Partly because their equipment is too good, they can and do learn too much. They learn feelings and attitudes that often interfere with other aspects of learning.

People's capacities for learning are in one sense limited, in another almost unlimited. By devising categories—systems by which they can classify and remember things that are appropriate to the levels of problems they are dealing with—they can store and use huge amounts of information.

If capable people are not lured by the rest of the world into seeking "perfect" solutions for their problems, but search instead for satisfactory solutions (as most people do naturally), they can operate with considerable savings in effort and considerable effectiveness. Finding a *good* product design usually costs far less, in terms of both money and mental energy, than finding *the best* product design. The danger is that what looks good enough may not be.

Clearly, however, some man-made tools for searching and deciding are better than others. And better analytic tools are being invented every day. They are likely to be very different from the commonsense methods of today—though our children may use them as we now use addition and subtraction.

It is useful to consider thinking and learning as active processes that begin with motivation. People learn more by doing something than by being told about it. And they try to do it when they are motivated.

5

The turbulent marriage of reason and emotion: Attitudes, beliefs and values

Managers manage whole persons, not just their reasoning sides, and not just their emotional sides. And managers are themselves whole persons. They're usually reasonable, but they're also emotional.

That mix seems obvious and "natural" to most of us now. But it was neither obvious nor natural to managerial theorists even as late as the 1950s. The prevailing emphasis then was on a person as a rational actor, one "factor of production," contracting to do prescribed work in exchange for prescribed pay. Emotions were out of order—irrelevant noise in a rational system.

In recent years we have come not only to understand much more about the nature of emotions but also about their importance and utility in effective managing. And we have also come to understand more (but there's much more yet to be understood) about how human beings mix and blend the yin of emotions with the yang of reasoning.

This chapter is about those mixtures of passion and reason, love and logic, anxiety and common sense, and about managing them in ourselves and in others.

The feeling/thinking mix and the modern manager

It's where feeling and thinking come together that fuzzy but critical human attributes are born—attributes such as attitudes, opinion, beliefs, and values. Attitudes toward communism, birth control, war, or the company one works for are all complex compounds of reason and emotion. Prejudices of all sorts are part of this set, too; so are values about honesty, spirituality, innovation, individual dignity, materialism, and much more. Those too are compounds of learned feelings coupled with a good deal of more or less reasonable thought.

Are attitudes and values important to the manager? Of course they are. Attitudes drive behavior (sometimes!), and values set limits (moral and ethical as well as pragmatic) on behavior. They set the directions of behavior. What effect does one's attitude toward the company have on the quality of one's work, on accuracy, on effort, on absenteeism? It's not easy to measure the effects of attitudes and values, but clearly they are critical controllers of our behavior. If you doubt their importance, try the question another way: How good a job would you expect from an engineer who believes an assignment is stupid, the company immoral, the boss a fool, and colleagues not to be trusted?

Of course, those attitudes and values have been learned, out of motivation, via reinforcement. So they can also be modified and changed. Enemies can become friends, and vice versa. Good workers can become goof-offs, and vice versa. Trust can become suspicion. Today's beauty can become tomorrow's ugliness.

Managers are, among other things, necessarily managers of attitudes, beliefs, and values. Morale is a matter of attitude, as is commitment to the organization and its products; so is trust among the organization's members. Managers also play a key part in shaping the core values of the organization. So managing attitudes and values is part of managing the whole organizational culture.

Notice that there are certain prerequisites to this business of managing attitudes. One oft-neglected prerequisite occurs at the front end: managers must know first which attitudes and values they want to develop. Another is that managers must have their own ethical and moral values clear before they try to manage anyone else's.

We'll discuss questions of managing organizational culture in later chapters, but now let's look at a few relevant rules of thumb about the nature and shaping of human attitudes and values.

1. Since we are dealing here with both emotion and reason, *don't expect the rules of reason to explain all we find.* Reason—logic, rationality—is characterized by consistency and transitivity. Patterns of attitudes and values are often internally inconsistent and intransitive. Rationally, if someone espoused free enterprise yesterday, we should not expect that person to espouse socialism today. And if one espouses free enterprise, we should also expect advocacy of fewer government regulations and more free trade, and so on. We should expect consistent, more or less logical patterns—but only if people were just reasoning creatures and nothing more. Often we do get such internally consistent patterns. Much of the time, if we know one attitude, we can predict others with some (but far from perfect) certainty. If we know a person is a feminist, we can predict a favorable attitude toward the Equal Rights Amendment, equal pay, abortion, and much more.

But those predictions are often wrong. We *may* encounter a practicing pro-life Catholic who is also a feminist. And although we might expect that feminists—all things equal—will take a liberal posture toward sexuality, should we also expect a positive or even tolerant attitude toward pornography? And shouldn't entrepreneurial managers also believe in free trade? But what if those imports are coming in at half your company's manufacturing cost? Isn't that cheating? Isn't that a threat to the American way of life?

In general, the reasoning side of us pushes toward patterns of consistency in our beliefs and attitudes. But sometimes the emotional side drives against it or drives us to rationalize our inconsistencies. And our emotional side does not include a consistency rule—only a motivation reduction rule.

Implications for the manager: Don't expect consistency from human beings. When you encounter inconsistency, don't treat it as stupidity or punish it because it is irrational. Inquire into it. Understand the psycho-logic of it. Those points of inconsistency, the ones that drive us to rationalize, are often the birthplace of new ways of looking at old things.

2. *People are wonderful rationalizers.* Outsiders often see logical inconsistencies in our patterns of attitudes and values. It is also true that human beings *try* to move toward a kind of internal logical consistency, to seek ways of bringing inconsistent thoughts and feelings together. If we encounter new information that is inconsistent with some of our existing attitudes and beliefs, we are likely to feel uncomfortable until we have managed to deal with it. That discomfort is motivating. It makes us try to deal with the discovery that the politician we campaigned for last year was later proven to be a crook; or after we have denounced homosexuality as sinful and immoral, our son proclaims his homosexuality; or after spending millions of our company's dollars to champion and develop a new product, we discover that nobody wants to buy it. But how do we deal with such inconsistencies? Answer: most of the time we rationalize.

Humans are extraordinarily skillful rationalizers. We can find all kinds of ways to justify our holding on to inconsistent positions. That politician wasn't really a crook; his enemies framed him. That kid isn't really gay; it's just a phase. He'll get over it. That product is great; it just hasn't gotten the advertising budget it deserves. We can *reject* the inconsistent information ("there is not really *good* evidence that smoking causes cancer"). We can demand more (and more and more) evidence. We can keep adding bells and whistles (let's repackage that product in cellophane with a pink bow on it, then it will sell), and so on. People, you and we included, are rationalizers.

But such rationalizations are not necessarily foolish. They are often quite functional. They can be thought of as part of a great balancing act between our emotional side and our rational side. We search for consonance, consistency, and balance, in business decisions and in the choices of everyday life. When we have invested a large amount in a course of action—such as a new line of products—we find it hard to accept reports showing that the products aren't selling. To maintain internal balance, to reduce psychological dissonance, we often do "irrational" things—such as blaming the sales force or investing *more* in promotion and advertising, on the grounds that we haven't given our ideas a fair test.

Suppose you are a scientist who has put a year's work into a problem, and your hypotheses don't check out; you're in a state of dissonance, too. You can either give up the hypotheses—to which you have given much of yourself—or you can seek a larger grant to develop finer instruments that will give your ideas a "really" fair test.

And so on. An old, well-known study of an offbeat sect that predicted the end of the world is a good example. The leaders predicted the end would occur at a special hour on a special date. The members disposed of their worldy goods and gathered at an appointed place to await the end. When the critical hour had passed and nothing had happened, did they abandon their beliefs, quit, and go home? Not at all. Too much imbalance, too much dissonance. Instead they "received" a late message from outer space telling them that this had only been a test run to check their readiness and their faith. A new hour was then duly set, but it too passed without apocalypse. And now how could the imbalance be handled? Ingeniously! A new message arrived. It declared that the faithfulness of this little group had convinced the Great Powers that some hope was still left for mankind. So the earth would be spared for a few centuries more.

You are a salesperson in company A who moves to competitor company B and begins to sell B's products after many years of espousing A's products. How can you sell B's razor blades if you think A's are better? Dissonance again. So you look into B "more carefully" and "discover" that it is a far better blade than you had ever realized. How could you have been so blind in your callow youth? Now you can get back into balance.

You are an ambitious executive who is clearly shunted aside by your company. Dissonance. How to resolve it? Either by admitting that you aren't as good as you thought—which is difficult and will create greater dissonance elsewhere in your makeup—or by beginning to look at the company differently. You begin to mobilize a list of your company's ethical weaknesses and economic stupidities. You soon prove that they don't deserve people of your integrity. That's the likely course. You make yourself ready to leave by searching hard for the negative side of what you are leaving. By so doing, of course, you may actually speed up the divorce, irritating your colleagues even further. And in their turn they can assuage their guilt and uncertainty by treating your present negative behavior as further evidence that they were right in unloading you.

Maybe it is because we often sense just this rationalizing propensity in ourselves and our organizations that we sometimes sensibly seek help from uncommitted outsiders. Because they are uncommitted, they can examine some areas in which our involvement has created psychological blind spots. On the other hand, though outsiders may be more objective in their judgments, they may have a tough time communicating these judgments to us when we are in a rationalizing mood. If the effect of truth, as outside judges define it, is only to aggravate further the emotional imbalance, we will have a strong inclination to reject both it and the judges. The consultant who shows us that our decision was wrong becomes just another bit of dissonance. And one easy way to cope is to find reasons for believing that someone hired the wrong consultant—unless, of course, this is a very expensive consultant, in which case dismissal after we have paid so much may create more dissonance than sticking with the consultant.

These balancing and rationalizing mechanisms provide people with a way, albeit often tortuous and unsuccessful, of trying to pull the psychological pieces together. In effect they try to solve the dilemma by modifying the psycho-logic of their position, and then bending rational logic to fit it. It is, after all, the whole person who makes choices, not just the reasoning part.

The father of one of the authors, for example, was both an active atheist and an active Republican—and a right-wing Republican at that. He used to be chided by friends about the logical inconsistency of holding both positions. Good Republicans, others argued, had to be God-fearing people. It was the left-wingers who were supposed to be the atheists. But the discrepancy didn't bother him at all. He could argue for hours about how the two positions were perfectly consistent with one another. No one could have argued him out of his position on *logical* grounds.

Perhaps his particular pattern of beliefs emerged because he had been an immigrant into the United States. He wanted to make it on the American scene—to be a real American. That meant giving up his traditional, old-country ways and really joining up with America. So he started a business and became, naturally enough, a Republican businessman. But he was also, when he got here, something of a Talmudic scholar and an orthodox Jew. How could he be a real American that way? Hence, the discovery and embracing of atheism. Perhaps the same problem would not have arisen if he had been a Scottish Presbyterian. That could have been consistent with both business and Republicanism. But traditional European Judaism seemed to him old-fashioned, unprogressive, and irrelevant to this new world of his. In its own way, his pattern makes sense.

One more critical point: Would we really do better work if we didn't rationalize? If we didn't deny facts? If we faced dissonant information fairly and coolly? Not always. Isn't it often the stubborn, the unreasonable, or the committed who push just a little harder even against long odds, who refuse to give up though the "evidence" is overwhelmingly against them? And aren't those often the people who make the big breakthroughs? Were Jesus Christ or Abraham Lincoln or Martin Luther King, Jr., entirely rational? Or did they rationalize enough to stay committed to their beliefs even when "rational" people would have backed off? People who believe passionately are seldom objective.

3. *People are always trying to explain things, even the unexplainable.* This is the attribution idea. People think and reason, and they want to know

why. There has probably never been a society that has not "explained" for itself the rising and setting of the sun, the seasons, the existence of moon and stars, or why the fish are less abundant than they used to be. And people then use their explanations to try to do something about what is happening to them. They try to control their worlds. In some societies they try to assuage the gods by praying, dancing, and sacrificing goats. In others, they conduct research, write treatises, and believe that physicians can cure the sick.

That pervasive human tendency to attribute causality can be attributed to a marriage of emotional motivation and cognitive skills. The motivation is to reduce anxiety, to reassure ourselves that we control our volatile worlds. The skill that we then apply (and often misapply) is our capacity to imagine and to reason.

Note how pervasive that attribution tendency is in each of us, how often we are motivated to explain ourselves and our world to ourselves and to others. Note, too, how seldom we feel absolutely sure of our answers. "Why did he say that?" "What did she mean by that?" "Why did this happen to me?" "What made my kids go wrong?" "Why did this marriage collapse? "Why did the Russians go into Afghanistan?" "How could Bhopal have happened?" "Why did IBM succeed?" "How did that fool Joe get to be CEO?" Those are all questions to which we give ourselves causal answers. And note how often television news shows bring on psychiatrists to tell us, after the fact, why that guy went berserk with his automatic weapon; and economists to tell us, after the fact, why the stock market dropped 30 points.

The *positive* consequence of all that effort to attribute cause is the development of *theories,* and theories are useful tools for managers and everyone else, too. If we have a theory of why people buy our kind of products, we can make judgments about how to modify those products. If we have a theory of why people work, we can better design jobs and working conditions that we hope will elicit more and better work. Unfortunately, of course, theories often turn out to be wrong. Then we're back in cognitive imbalance until we have made a few modifications.

But not all incorrect explanatory attributions are proved wrong, even over very long periods. Then we have what has been called "superstitious learning." Remember the example of the black and white marbles, in the preceding chapter. Try that experiment yourself. You will find yourself, even against your own will, developing "explanatory" themes and patterns that grow ever more elaborate. "Ah, they alternate. First black and white then black." But then you pull out two blacks, so you add, "except for every third time when two blacks in a row come up." And so forth. It's almost impossible for us to ignore our attributional tendencies in favor of the more rational concept of randomness.

In organizations, where many complex forces often come together to generate an event, superstitious learning occurs very frequently. That old loser, Division X, came up with a very profitable year after Joe Jones got fired and Sam Smith took over. Therefore, Joe Jones must have been a lousy manager. And Sam Smith *now* looks like a hero—real presidential material. After all he *caused* it to happen. But did he? Or in that market, at that time, would the profitability increase have shown up even if old Joe Jones were still running the show?

4. *Most people commit "the fundamental attribution error."* Unfortunately, managers are both blessed and cursed by that tendency to ascribe causality, because the causality—either way—is often ascribed to them rather than to other aspects of the situation. Hence the notion so common in the politics of organizational life: the important thing is to be in the right place at the right time.

Indeed, the tendency to attribute responsibility to people rather than to situations is called "the fundamental attribution error." If our team loses five games in a row right after the new coach comes on board, what do you think the prominent causal attribution will be? Surely it's the new coach's fault. But are we sure? Wouldn't statistical laws suggest that strings of losses will occur periodically and will tend to be balanced, over time, by winning streaks? All managers have to watch out for that error—the tendency to ascribe the cause of trouble to the person, and not to the situation. If we have a bad quarter, we begin to worry about the CEO, even if new government regulations have trebled our costs and halved them for our competitors. We carry a strong bias toward blaming the *person* when situations go wrong. So if you want to look good in your organization, make sure you never get into the middle of a bad situation. Bad situations make good people look bad.

5. *Attitudes and behavior are like chickens and eggs.* Changing attitudes generates changes in behavior, which generates changes in attitudes, which generates changes in behavior, which generates changes in attitudes, which generates . . . That's roughly the way we now believe it works. It is not suprising to most of us that changes in attitudes are often followed by changes in behavior. If I can convince you that the Republicans are right, then you will *probably* go forth and vote Republican. It's a bit more surprising to most of us that the converse is also often true: If I can get you to vote Republican, then you will begin to believe the Republicans are right.

Changes in attitudes are not always followed by changes in behavior. We may change our attitude toward smoking, but we may also go on smoking. But there is a gross connection, isn't there? Over the long pull, we tend to bring our behavior into line with our attitudes. That's what advertising tries to develop. And, to a considerable extent, that's what education also tries to help along.

So, one way, less than ideal, to change behavior is to start by trying to change attitudes. The ways we try to change attitudes are legion: peer-group pressures, propaganda, simple reward for expressing the attitudes we want, introducing cognitive imbalance. They are all ways of pushing the individual to reassess and modify existing attitudes.

But the reverse process is generally even more true. To change attitudes, try changing behavior first. Not only does behavior usually eventually line up with attitudes; attitudes usually line up with behavior!

For example, if I can get you to debate in favor of X, even though you don't like X, you will probably hold a more positive attitude toward X after the debate than before. If I can get you to sing my commercials, you will probably feel more favorable toward the product after your performance than before. If I can get you to throw a rock at a cop, your attitudes toward the police will become more negative. If I can get you, the union steward, to argue on the company's behalf, you will feel more positive toward the company.

And if I can get you to take small behavioral steps now, my foot will be in the door. You will be much more likely to take large steps in my direction later.

Once again, notice that changing attitudes and values is both an emotional and rational process. Perhaps the biggest mistake many of us make in our efforts to change others is implicitly to treat others as though they were *only* rational, reasoning beings. Indeed, it may be because we in the West value rationality so highly that that value shapes our approach to trying to change the values of others. We believe that we can (and should) argue people out of things, that reason and logic will (and should) prevail. In the long run we may be right. But we tend to ignore the huge and immediate emotional components that accompany the change process.

We all know that even as we argue some point with our colleagues, even as we calmly present our carefully reasoned arguments, our own emotions are building up. I want to convince you that trade barriers are both morally wrong and don't work. But even as I offer you my reasons, and you counter them with equal arguments of your own, I can feel my heart beginning to pound and my voice beginning to rise—and you are experiencing the same thing.

It may soon become obvious to both of us that we are getting ourselves caught in a hopeless rational/emotional trap; the spiral of argument will lead inevitably downward, with each of us becoming more emotionally resistant to the other, while we clothe that emotion in the now convoluted trappings of logic. And neither has any chance at all of changing the other's view. It is at that emotional level that the heart of the issue of attitude change lies. I am not likely to get you to think differently until I can get you to feel differently, which is most likely to happen if I can first get you to behave differently.

Notice, too, that we often denigrate those people who try to change attitudes via largely emotional means. Because we value reason, we tend to deride salesmen, advertisers, evangelists, and all those other passionate persuaders who rely heavily on emotions.

Perhaps the central message of this chapter is that, though we may wish for a rational world, we are not likely to achieve one by exclusively rational means.

In summary

Humans are emotional creatures, but they also use their heads. Attitudes, beliefs, opinions, and values are the progeny of the marriage of emotion and reason. Although the patterns of attitudes and values that develop in a person are usually more or less consistent, don't count on it. Humans have a fascinating capacity to rationalize inconsistent beliefs in unique ways. Those rationalizations do not reflect weakness or supidity. Rather they are efforts to maintain internal balance, to reduce dissonance in a world of complex, cross-cutting, nonharmonious forces.

So don't expect that reason is likely to prevail. Expect rationalization. Watch out for the tendency to attribute some cause to everything that happens, whether the "cause" really was the cause or not; and watch out for the bias toward blaming the person rather than the situation when things go wrong. Remember also that, while changing someone's attitudes may lead to changes in behavior, the converse is also true and often easier to accomplish. Get me to go a little way in your direction and my attitudes will swing toward support, which will encourage me to move a little more, and so on. Does that sound manipulative? It can be; there will be more about that issue in part 2.

6 Managerial styles of thinking: Is orderly thinking always good thinking?

We said in an earlier chapter that people are all alike and yet people are all different. We were referring then to the emotional sides of people—to their motives, their conflicts, their feelings. But people are alike and different in another important dimension, too—in their thinking styles. We all think, but we think differently. Some kids grow up with a "natural" skill at numbers, for instance. Others are "intuitive" or "good with words." Women, some men like to say, tend to think "impulsively." Men, some women like to say, tend to think "insensitively." We may say of one person, "He has a clear orderly mind. He reasons things out." And of another, we say, "He's tremendously imaginative. He comes up with ideas that would never have occurred to me." Or of another, "He gets things done. He knows how to get what he wants."

Such differences in the ways that people think about the world are both real and important. Some of these differences are probably inborn. But it is also quite clear by now that the whole process of formal and informal education strongly influences our particular "style" of thinking, if not its quality. At the extremes, those effects of education aren't hard to see. The engineer's professional education teaches not only facts but ways of thinking, analytic ways of approaching problems. A liberal arts education teaches ways of thinking, too, but probably quite different ones; and those styles are likely to carry over into other parts of life. Moreover, such differences in styles may lead to interesting and significant organizational dilemmas. For instance, individuals in an organization who think in one style may have trouble communicating with individuals who think in other styles. The sales manager complains of not being able to understand those whiz kids in strategic planning. The account executive in the advertising agency handles the creative people on the staff with kid gloves, because "they think in peculiar ways," which the rest of us simple folk cannot comprehend.

In this chapter we shall consider some categories of thinking styles, and then talk about the normative question of whether (or when) some styles are "better" than others for solving organizational problems. Finally, we'll consider how such differences in thinking styles can help or hurt large organizations in which many people with many different styles have to co-ordinate their efforts.

Some different kinds of styles

I ask you to throw six dice. You throw them, and they come up as shown in figure 6.1.

I now tell you that, in the set you have just thrown, there are *three* wind-blown daisies and *six* petals. You ask, "What the hell is a 'windblown daisy'?" I reply, "That's the name of the game. Your job is tell me what a windblown daisy is and what petals are. Throw your dice again, and see if you can guess how many daisies and how many petals there are this time."

So you throw again, and this time the dice fall as shown in figure 6.2. Now how many daisies are there? How many petals? The right answer this time is that there are *two* windblown daisies and *four* petals.

Have you caught on yet? Have you developed a decision rule? Do you know what a windblown daisy and a petal are? If you think you do, or if you think you don't, figure 6.3. provides three more samples. In this figure, the first row has five daisies and eight petals; the second, two daisies and two petals; and the third, four daisies and eight petals. Now have you got it?

Here's the answer, or more properly, here is an answer. First, the only relevant dice are the odd-numbered ones. Every odd-numbered die has one daisy, because the daisy is the dot in the middle. The number of petals is the number of dots other than the center one on those odd-numbered dice. So the die with the face showing one is a daisy with no petals. A three is a daisy with two petals; a five is a daisy with four petals.

But that's only one way to express the answer or to think about the prob-lem. And indeed it's a very difficult problem to solve if you do think about it that way; that is, if you think about it as a *numbers* problem. If you don't think of it that way, if you forget about numbers, and if you think about the phrase "windblown daisy" and imagine a *picture* of a daisy, the problem becomes much easier to solve. What does a windblown daisy look like? A real windblown daisy? It's a daisy blown by the wind with just a few petals or no petals at all left on it. Now the face of each die becomes, not a num-ber, but a picture, a kind of skeletonized picture. The dot in the center is the center of the daisy; the dots around it are petals.

The windblown daisies problem is solved more quickly by people who think in pictures than by people who think more with numerical or other symbols. Children do pretty well at the game; so do artists. Accountants and many engineers have a lot of trouble with it.

Let's elaborate on that idea of *iconic* (or pictorial) thinking versus *sym-bolic* thinking.

In recent years developmental psychologists have tried to observe the

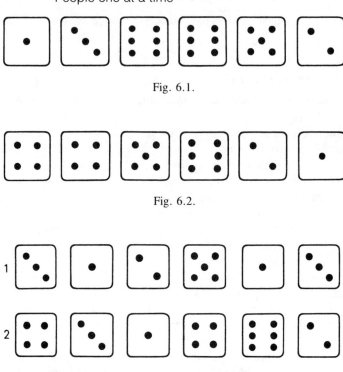

Fig. 6.1.

Fig. 6.2.

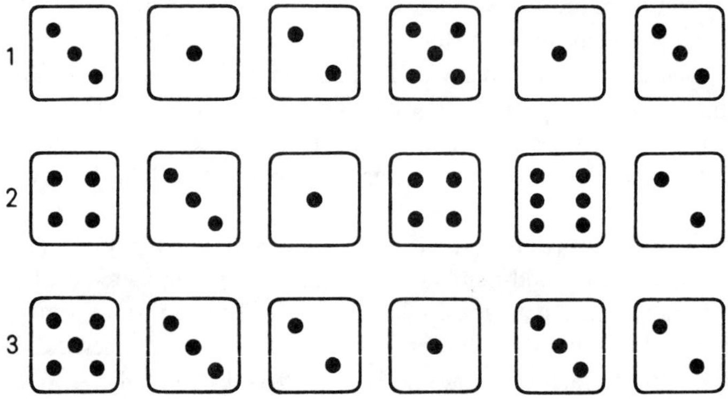

Fig. 6.3.

ways that children go about finding meaning in things. The way such understanding seems to evolve is through three gross stages. Very young children tend to find meaning in things *enactively.* Enactive here means acting upon the thing, touching it, feeling it, biting it, handling it. An apple then becomes something to bite or to rub. It is what it feels like.

Later, around the age of five or so, children begin, by some unclear maturing process, to think in images. They begin to understand things *iconically.* Now an apple becomes an internal mental picture of an apple, an almost one-for-one representation of the real object.

Later still, children go to another stage in their thinking. An apple can be understood *symbolically,* using abstract symbols to define it. Thus, an apple is an edible fruit, of about three inches or so in diameter usually red but sometimes green or yellow, and so on. It is understood with symbols, with words, or perhaps with numbers. Reasonably enough, the rate and extent of the development of symbolic thinking is closely related to education, since most of the symbols we think with are man-made and taught to us by other humans. Thus some children and some societies develop symbolic vocabularies more quickly or over a wider range than others.

This whole developmental idea provides one way of thinking about thinking styles. Now we have three "languages" of thought. Some of us develop large vocabularies in one while continuing to speak in basic English in others. It may be, for example, that particular kinds of occupations or education encourage people to develop more elaborate and skillful *enactive* thinking. Others generate more *iconic* thinking. Still others generate more *symbolic* thinking. A mathematician or an accountant couldn't get very far without skill in manipulating abstract symbols called numbers. But perhaps a painter or a photographer or (if we allow for sound images) certain musicians might develop their highest degrees of skill in the iconic realm. And perhaps a ballerina or a good mechanic might develop a large enactive "vocabulary," developing ability to sense very small differences in muscle movements that the rest of us might miss entirely.

But we should consider one other quite separate dimension of the issue of thinking styles—not the *languages* of thought but the *processes* by which we use them. Not only are some people more skillful than others at manipulating images, or muscle movement, or symbols, but some people also think more *analytically* than others, and some think more *imaginatively* than others. The words *analytic* and *imaginative* are rather difficult to pin down in fine detail; but the reader can sense their flavor. An analytic thinker is one who can take a complex problem apart, break it down into its logically interconnected pieces, and then put it together again. An imaginative thinker is one who might be quick in generating ideas and multiple solutions to problems or who can move through a problem in a "local," trial-and-error way, taking step 1 and then assessing the situation, and then trying for step 2 and assessing the situation, and so on. Contrast this person with a more analytic type who lays the whole problem-map out and then selects the best route.

As most of us learned early on, psychologists and educators try to measure our *analytic ability* with instruments like logic tests and arithmetic reasoning tests—the kind of things we struggled through in school. The fuzzier concept of *imagination* has been tested by giving people problems like this: "In the next three minutes write down all the uses you can think of for a brick." Thus, many tests of analytic ability tend to require convergence—that is, finding the right answer or the right method. Many imagination tests tend toward divergence—thinking up many possibilities and ideas.

So now we can, analytically, draw a little three-by-two table as one way to characterize some different thinking styles (table 6.1).

As the reader might guess, certain occupational groups—engineers and accountants, for example—do in fact tend to score relatively higher on

"Languages" of Thinking	Processes of Thinking	
	Analytic	Imaginative
Symbolic	1	2
Iconic	3	4
Enactive	5	6

analytic tests than on imaginative tests, whereas art students and salesmen tend to score higher on imaginative tests. In fact, in one study that compared freshman engineering and fine arts students with their senior counterparts, the following results emerged. The senior engineers scored much higher on analytic tests than did freshman engineers, but significantly *lower* on tests of imagination. The seniors in fine arts made higher scores on imaginative tests, while they fared worse then their freshman counterparts on analytic tests. The four years of professional education had succeeded, it seemed, in spreading the two groups apart, increasing the engineers' analytic skill, apparently at the expense of their imaginative powers, and increasing the fine arts students' imaginative powers at the expense of their analytic skill.

That finding may be important. If one unexplained outcome of professional education in those different fields is to cause the thinking styles of the two groups to diverge, a follow-on effect may be increased difficulty in later communication between members of those two professions.

This binary distinction between two ways of understanding, (here labeled "analytic" and "imaginative") has been noted under different labels for hundreds of years, by philosophers, theologians, psychologists, and others in many cultures. But in the last couple of decades, as most readers may know, some seminal work at the neurophysiological level has found what looks like a parallel binary specialization in the two hemispheres of the human brain. For example, experiments with people who have had the "cable" connecting the two major hemispheres of the brain surgically severed (for quite independent medical reasons) seem to show consistent differences between the specialized capabilities of the left and right hemispheres. The left hemisphere (controlling mostly the right side of the body) seems to be the primary home of verbal, serial, and logical skills. The right hemisphere (controlling mostly the left side of the body) seems to be more imaginative, holistic, and emotional. It seems to deal with wholes more than parts.

Those studies of the brain seem to support the analytic/imaginative distinction. But let's not push that idea too far. Things aren't that clear yet, either in the behavioral or neurophysiological research.

The reader may now want to take a shot at filling in some boxes in the above three-by-two grid. Can you, for example, think of occupations or professions that ought to be good in box 1, the symbolic/analytic thinking

box? Or box 2, the symbolic (using words and numbers) but also imaginative box? Poets, perhaps, or others who play skillfully with words? Where
would classical ballet dancers belong? How about box 5? And the Beatles?
Box 4, perhaps, if we include music composition as iconic skill, because
the Beatles played it first and then wrote it down afterward. In contrast,
where does one place Beethoven, who is supposed to have composed
by the numbers, because he was deaf, never even hearing what he had
written?

Are there better and worse styles of thinking?

We come now to the normative issue: Is imaginative thinking "better" or
"worse" than analytic thinking? Is symbolic thinking "better" or "worse"
than iconic or enactive thinking?

Clearly, the thrust of most formal education has favored symbolic and
analytic thought. Western education puts much less effort into developing
imaginative or iconic skills. Consider, for example, your own conception
of a *good* thinker? Isn't it the disciplined, orderly thinker, skillful with symbolic tools, analytic in process? And don't we tend to denigrate people
whose thinking is impulsive or intuitive? And don't most of us also feel that
it's a little simpleminded and childish for people to think in pictures?

Clearly, too, human progress as we usually define it, especially material
progress, has emerged largely from our skillful use of symbolic languages
and analytic processes. For it is by those means that knowledge has been
communicated and the uncontrollable has been controlled. To carry that
idea further, suppose we made this comment to a group of senior engineers:
"What do you think of the following interesting finding? Engineering students, after four years of engineering education, score better on analytic
tests than freshmen do." They might well reply that the finding didn't seem
interesting at all; that it was not in any way surprising. What, after all, was
engineering education all about if not to teach analytic methodology?

If, on the other hand, we added, "But after four years of engineering education, engineering students are *less* capable of solving intuitive-
imaginative problems than their freshman counterparts," that might indeed
both surprise and concern them. Most engineers, one assumes, are not so
much anti-imagination as they are just pro-analysis. Engineers (and many
others) are pro-analysis for at least two reasons. First, it works. Second,
the buildup of analytically derived knowledge is the foundation on which
the next generation of the profession can add further knowledge.

If we turn now from the engineer to the artist or the humanist, we may
arrive at a different posture about "good" thinking and "bad." The artist
may be much more interested in uniqueness than in shared knowledge. The
education of artists tends to reflect that difference. Certainly one key idea
in education for artists is to encourage *individuality*, with the hoped-for

consequence that every work produced will be a unique reflection of that artist. Can you imagine an engineer whose training aims for *uniqueness*, whose professor criticizes a solution to a problem because "That isn't *you!* That isn't unique!"? But such criticism is common for the artist.

Another aspect of the normative problem: The analytic-symbolic orientation not only places a positive value on "objective" thinking; it often implicitly places a negative value on "emotional" thinking. Some observers have argued that one important cost of our society's tilt in favor of symbolic-analytic thinking is impoverished emotional development. We have not educated ourselves to attend to, to understand, and to express feelings and other kinds of awareness that are not easily symbolized or analyzed.

Another normative issue: Considering only the quality of problem solving itself, is it true that symbolic-analytic approach is always the most appropriate one? In many realms and many times, clearly, it is. But curiously enough, people less competent in the analytic-symbolic mode, but more competent in imaginative-iconic thinking, sometimes discover solutions that analysts miss, usually because those analysts limit their search to those segments of the world predefined by their thinking style. We refer our reader, for example, back to the windblown daisies game, but one can find many other examples of "better" solutions by nonanalysts, even when "better" is defined by analytic criteria. One can legitimately ask whether a world run exclusively by "the best and the brightest," by highly analytic but not very imaginative or intuitive thinkers, will necessarily turn out better, by any standards, than one run by more diverse types.

Let's get back now to the managerial problems. As a manager, what kind of thinking styles would you like to have in the people working in your organization? Do you want sharp, cutting-edge, logical folk? Or would you like to have a few dreamers and individualists around? Or all dreamers? All individualists? Visionaries? Mystics? . . .

For a couple of decades, in the 1960s and 1970s, American managers and American management educators carried on a lively affair with the symbolic-analytic mode of thinking. The then-new computer and new methods of systems analysis, modeling, and simulation all offered seductive possibilities for advancing the field of management. Indeed, much of that promise was and is being fulfilled. But our intense preoccupation with our beloved analytic style also led us to ignore or even to denigrate other ways of defining and solving problems—more intuitive, imaginative, and entrepreneurial ways.

In the past few years we have matured a bit, moving back toward a more balanced perspective—adding people who can create, who can innovate, who can champion new ideas, as well as seeking ways to design modern organizations that will be both analytically solid and encourage diverse styles of thinking.

What's "intelligence"?

In the West, we equate intelligence mostly with IQ. IQ tests, in turn, have been composed mostly of analytic components. We tend, don't we, to equate intelligence with symbolic skills (facility with words and numbers) and analytic abilities (logic, orderliness, internal consistency). But the concept of human intelligence has always been a slippery one. Measurements are easily distorted by social and cultural biases. And the more basic question keeps coming up: Is any analytically oriented conception of human intelligence sufficient or appropriate? Notice that this is not just a semantic matter. Once we define intelligence as that which is measured by IQ tests, very important consequences follow. Students are selected on the basis of their IQ scores; better jobs go to higher scorers; parents try to teach their kids the abilities measured by those tests; status and prestige become attached to high scores; and on and on.

Much of the debate about intelligence focuses on the nature versus nurture issue. Can better education raise IQ points? Or is it all in the genes? But some of that debate is about broadening the concept of intelligence. One recent offering, for example, proposes a "triarchic" theory of intelligence. IQ-type intelligence is seen as only one of at least three kinds of intelligence, the theory argues. One must also consider a creative/imaginative kind of intelligence. And a third kind is what the researcher calls "street smarts"; it is intelligence that shows itself in skill in getting things done in the real world, in playing the game of life, in dealing with one's social environment. If someone is creative and imaginative, but scores poorly on an IQ test, is it sensible to consider that person "unintelligent"? And if somebody can get out there and get the desired results, influence people, or "manage" the environment, can we still say that that person's low IQ points are proof of low intelligence? Not likely. Intelligence, one must surely agree, takes many forms. Since organizations need it all—innovation, pathfinding, analysis, and implementation, too—managers need a broader-than-IQ model of intelligence to work with.

On blending thinking styles within the organization

If you and I think differently, how can we communicate? Our organizations need both analytic and imaginative thinking, don't they? We need different kinds of people with many kinds of specialized education and thinking propensities. But beyond all that, we also need some way to bring them together, to blend them into smoothly working units that will carry us on to that best of all possible organizational worlds.

But bringing all those styles together isn't easy. Greater specialization drives toward greater separation, making it harder to reintegrate all those specialists. Thus, the fine arts and engineering students we talked about earlier tended to move away from one another over their four years at college. Their differences showed up in their dress, in where they chose to live, in their haircuts, in their attitudes and values, and most of all in their ways of thinking about the world.

Several years ago one British author pointed to a variant on that problem, but on a much larger scale. He argued that the entire culture of science, on the one hand, and the nonscientific world on the other, had grown apart in Western societies. Scientists deal with critical problems in ways that are simply not comprehended by less scientific types. Yet it is the less scientific politicians and managers who must try to govern and manage in a world that the scientists are reshaping rapidly and quite independently.

Within any organization, real dangers stem from poor communication between specialists. The frequent failures of technical people in large organizations to implement their analytic solutions provide a case in point. In our view, integrating the many thinking styles of different specialists into some kind of organizational whole has now become a major task for modern, differentiated organizations.

Although no one can offer easy ways to integrate diverse thinkers, we do know a few things that *don't* work. It is not enough, for instance, to "bring people together." The engineers and art students we talked about earlier occupy buildings within fifty yards of one another, but the two groups have nevertheless moved apart psychologically. Nor is it enough to teach common courses to all groups, such as courses in history, psychology, or economics. Those courses tend to be ignored, or else they are modified toward the special interests of the professions. So the courses are pulled apart more than the specialists are brought together. Even joint projects and task forces won't usually work, unless they're backed up with considerable pretraining.

One better solution may be to develop a new breed of interpreters, generalists with feet in all camps, who can translate one thought-language into another. In some ways the modern MBA was intended to perform that function. But it hasn't always worked. Instead, the MBA has come to be seen as one more analytic specialist. Another suggestion (offered, of course, by analytic types) is to devise computer programs that will serve as interpreters, converting symbolic data into iconic form, for example, or vice versa.

Probably the most valuable thing managers (and everyone else) can do at this point is to *appreciate* differences in thinking styles and to encourage others to do likewise by demonstrating that different styles are valued in our organization.

At this point we don't know very much about how to *un*educate people who have been so educated into one style that they cannot think in others. But we can find ways to get such people to begin to appreciate, rather than denigrate, the styles of others. Meanwhile, simply expecting people to communicate with one another in mutually foreign tongues will not in itself breed understanding.

Thinking styles and the whole managing process
Is there a right way for managers to think?

Later in this book we shall describe a three-part model of the managing process. We shall be talking about *(1) pathfinding, (2) problem solving,* and *(3) implementing.*

Issues of human emotion are closely tied in to the third part of managing, *implementing.* One major chunk of managing, after all, involves social influence—persuading, challenging, and motivating people. The second part of managing, *problem solving,* on the other hand, calls for competence in analysis, in planned, orderly, systematic thinking. But the first part of the managing process, *pathfinding,* makes still a third demand on the managerial mind; that part requires much more of an imaginative style of thinking, a creative, visionary style.

Pathfinding is not primarily concerned with either social influence or orderly analysis. Pathfinding occurs at the front end of the whole managerial process. It is about choosing the right problems rather than the right answers. It is, therefore, about issues of creativity and purpose. Imaginative processes and iconic languages of thinking become important for that part of managing. Pathfinding questions are tough, open-ended questions. For example, what do we want this organization to look like five years from now? Or, more personally, what do I want to be when I grow up?

The difference between pathfinding and problem solving is something like the difference between the architect and the engineer. The construction engineer tries to figure out how to build a building given a basic design, a budget, and some other constraints. What the architect adds is the element of creative design. Even given a fixed budget, a site, and many other requirements for a new building, an infinite number of different designs can still be created. The criterion for the "right" design is not cost per square foot but some personal standard of beauty. It's a great design because it's dramatic, or we just love it, or it sends a message we want to send.

But more about pathfinding in later chapters.

In summary

People differ in their "languages" and processes of thinking, just as they differ in other aspects of their personalities. Education, particularly professional and vocational education, tends to emphasize particular thought-languages, especially symbolic languages, and to pay less attention to iconic (pictorial) and enactive (touch-and-feel) languages. Thinking *processes* also differ; it is useful to divide those processes into two subclasses, *analytic* and *imaginative*.

No particular combination of these languages or processes is in itself "better" for the manager than another. But it is clear that people trained in and connected to one style often find it difficult to use another or to communicate effectively with those committed to another. Hence, as organizations use more specialists, we might expect a greater need to find ways to bridge this communication gap by introducing "thought interpreters" or other means of increasing understanding.

The issues here are not only those of communication but also concern how we think about the concept of human intelligence. It is only in recent years that we have broadened our conception to include more than the narrow analytic abilities. In today's world, organizations would find it useful to pay more attention to imaginative styles of thinking, along with already highly valued analytic styles.

7

Assessing people: Dilemmas of the evaluation process

One pioneer of organizational psychology once defined managing as "the process of getting things done through people." That's no longer a sufficient definition. Yet every manager knows that much of success in managing still hangs on two people issues: (1) the manager's own skills in dealing with people, and (2) the "quality" of the people in the unit. Finding "good" people is a critical and continuing problem in any organization; and identifying the "best" ones for reward and promotion is a close and difficult relative.

That set of evaluation problems keeps most managers hopping. How do we decide which of these candidates to hire? How shall we evaluate our people's performance after we get them? Is Mary Smith performing better than Joe Blow? Which one is the "better" person for the promotion that's coming up? And both Mary and Joe want feedback; they want to be told how well or badly their managers think they are doing. They want to know, quite concretely, just what they need to do to improve their evaluations next time.

And still another related problem: You've just spent half an hour talking to Henry Brown. (He may be a new customer, or job applicant, or consultant the company is thinking about hiring.) Your boss then drops by to ask, "What do you think of Brown?" How do you *say* what you think of him? How do you say it accurately and succinctly?

This chapter is about those questions—"assessing," "selecting," and "evaluating" human beings. That means it's about deciding who's good and who's bad, who's worthy and who's unworthy. So this chapter is partly about formal tools for doing those jobs, such as selection tests and other measuring devices that have been developed to help out on those problems; but it's mostly about *in*formal working tools, such as talking with people to try to find out what they're like. It's about judging people, comparing people, getting a fix on people in a limited time, in real time, in the real world, without the help of professionals or elaborate measuring devices.

There are, the reader will have noted, many evaluative words in the paragraph you have just read. They are intentional in order to highlight a fundamental moral problem in all this. For this chapter is about some human beings making judgments about the worth of other human beings, deciding whether one is "better" than another, at least for some specific purpose. That whole process stirs up issues of democracy, tolerance, ethics, and our willingness to accept one another as human beings, regardless of race, creed, sex, or test scores. Those are real problems, not yet resolved in modern organizations. We shall talk about them more as they arise in the pages that follow. For the most part, however, we shall have to ask our readers to take account of their own attitudes and values as they go through this chapter.

The scope of the assessment problem

Both professionals and laypeople frequently fail miserably in forecasting how people will behave in specific jobs. It's a very tough task. If our earlier chapters were right, forecasting the behavior of one individual is much like trying to predict exactly what pattern of cracks will result when a particular thrower throws a particular baseball against a particular pane of glass. We can be fairly certain that the glass will crack. But we seldom know enough about the ball, the air currents, the thrower, the angle of impact, and the particular pane to be sure about the numbers, directions, or lengths of the cracks that will result.

Nevertheless, organizations have to assess people for tasks. Every contact with customers, with new members of our own organization, with those individuals who are relevant to our work, includes some need for assessment—some evaluation of how this or that person will behave when faced with this or that suggestion, this or that kind of job, or this or that bit of bad news.

So, assessment is not limited to "formal" problems such as selecting new employees or rating the performance of old ones. It must necessarily involve day-to-day assessment of other people's knowledge, experience, skill, motivation, emotional stability, and much more. Indeed, we are often required to do multiple assessment. How will Joe get along working for Susan? How will Sam fit into that particular group of characters? Trying to assess how several people will work together complicates the assessment problem by orders of magnitude.

A good deal of research and experience is available on the formal phases of personnel selection and performance appraisal. These days every executive is aware of personality tests, patterned interviews, performance evaluation forms, and all the rest. Underlying each of those is a large (but not large enough) body of theory and empirical research. Unfortunately, no comparable amount of work has been done on the day-to-day problems of assessment to help the executive make increasingly accurate spot judgments about other people. Even so, some useful things are coming to be known. So, when the boss asks, "Well, what did you think of him?" one can honestly say something more meaningful than "He's a nice guy" or "I don't like him."

Formal methods of selection and evaluation

One can single out at least three separable formal approaches to the problem of organizational selection and evaluation. Looked at right now, the separations among the three are not perfectly distinct, for they have been coming together more and more. But historically, each has made its entry over a different route.

Pencil-and-paper tests and the empirical method. The first approach, one largely American in origin, can be roughly labeled the "pencil-and-paper test approach." These tests fall into two major classes. The great bulk of short intelligence tests, aptitude tests, and so forth belong to a set we'll call type 1 behavior instruments. So, too, for the most part, do standard interview forms, most performance appraisal scales, fitness reports, and the like.

These are typically American products in the sense that they derive from our American behavioristic tradition in psychology, with its emphasis on things analytic, on quantification and measurement, and on empirical data gathering, as well as with its corresponding de-emphasis on unquantified, introspective judgments and opinions. As a consequence, pencil-and-paper tests try to improve the empirical reliability and validity of their procedures, at least as much as they try to improve the rationale or depth of the material being sought. Such methods mostly apply to the measurement of specific aptitudes, attitudes, or abilities. They are not often used to get an overall assessment of the whole person.

The advocates of type 1 pencil-and-paper tests present their position something like this. Selection of people for jobs requires us to predict in advance how particular people will perform some set of tasks at some future time. Clearly, then, what is first required is some prior measurements on which to base predictions, followed up by some corresponding measurement of actual performance at some later time. If the before and after measures correlate highly, the predictive instrument must be a good one; if not, back to the drawing board. If, for example, our task were to try to select retail store managers, these might become the appropriate procedural steps:

1. Let's gather—in a standard way—information about the people who are possible candidates for the job of store manager. We can do this by collecting standard information about issues that seem relevant, such as level of education, and/or by interviewing job applicants to learn about related experience and personal style. Then we code our answers into several categories. We can also collect test scores on IQ, vocabulary, and anything else that looks relevant. We can do the same with questions about home

ownership and applicants' preferences for one kind of occupation or another; we can measure the time required by applicants to solve selected puzzles and problems; and so on.

2. In the best of all worlds (for the tester), we will next lock up all those interview and test answers in the nearest safe and allow *all* applicants to go to work managing equivalent stores.

3. Now we just wait a predetermined time, perhaps a year.

4. During that time we set up some clear standards for just what constitutes "success" in managing our stores. What is needed is an unequivocal, quantifiable set of criteria of success. That's never as easy as it sounds. In store management, a theoretically ideal approach would be to permit all test subjects to manage stores in exactly comparable locations, with precisely the same amount of training, the same personnel, and precisely the same budgets. One might then use dollar sales at the end of the year, number of sales, percentage increases, or some combination of all of them as a criterion. But note that reasonable people might want to select other criteria, such as personnel turnover, employee morale, or customer satisfaction.

5. The tester now has (*a*) the scores of all test subjects on all the tests they took a year ago, and (*b*) a measure of their subsequent, actual job performance. The next move is statistical: measure the relationship between predictions and performance to estimate the reliability of that relationship (i.e., to guess how frequently we could expect the same relationship to occur in the future); then to decide which, if any, of the measuring instruments are worth keeping.

We may discover that a standard IQ test actually predicted performance somewhat better than chance. The tester would then consider that IQ test useful for selection. Strictly speaking, it would not matter which direction the test-performance relationship might take. That is, it would not matter if more successful managers were significantly more intelligent or significantly *less* intelligent than the less successful ones. The question is not whether the predictions make sense, but whether they predict. Sensible or not, if they predict, they are useful; if they do not predict, they are not useful.

The connection point between that rigorous type 1 behavioral, pencil-and-paper approach and any theory of the nature of human behavior lies in how particular tests are constructed and chosen. This is because the pencil-and-paper approach is mostly a method of measurement, rather than a theory of human behavior. Any theorist of any persuasion may use it. Some test items may be based on a theory of physiognomy, some on Freudian psychodynamics, some on a theory about the color of people's shoes.

This type 1 method has many advantages and some practical disadvantages. It has the advantage of quantification and empiricism. It also has dollar advantages. Pencil-and-paper tests, once standardized, can be easy to produce, administer, and score. Professional testers are often needed only in the developmental stages; later administration and scoring can usually be turned over to quickly trained technicians. Those tests are usually not very time-consuming either, so that large numbers of people can be tested, frequently in groups of indefinite size, at reasonable cost.

Type 1 tests are most useful for making statistical predictions about the performance of large numbers of people. They are not usually very good for predicting how a particular individual will perform. Thus, a pencil-and-paper tester may be able to tell a manager, "Of every fifty applicants who pass my tests, you can expect successful job performance from thirty of them. If that is good enough, you ought to use my package." The tester can not go on, however, to say whether or not Joe Doaks, test subject number 23, who received passing test scores, will be among the successful thirty or the unsuccessful twenty. Furthermore, the tester would also admit that some *rejected* applicants would turn out to be "false positives"— people who would have been successful, but who nevertheless failed the tests. He could not predict who those unlucky individuals would be.

However, some pencil-and-paper tests—let's call them type 2—can indeed help in predicting how a particular person will behave, and they can also help the person do a self-assessment. Although many other factors affect such predictions, some tests have, over the years, proven helpful even at the individual level. Those are usually "personality"-type tests based on some theoretical, usually multidimensional, model of human behavior. Those tests may contain several scales on variables such as introversion/extroversion or competitiveness/cooperativeness. The ones that are most useful are those for which a large data base has been built up over time, so the tester can compare the subject's pattern of scores with information about the patterns of thousands of other people.

Using pencil-and-paper methods of either kind to select or promote people raises two other broad questions. The first is ethical. Is it "right" to turn any job applicant away, even if only one in a hundred, who was one of those false positives, someone who would have performed perfectly competently if hired? Is it "fair" to so depersonalize people that they become simply scores among hundreds of scores, their individual fates inexorably tied to statistical trends? Or is it somehow more fair to tie an applicant's fate to the rose-colored perceptions of a particular interviewer? It would seem that this particular ethical issue should be properly attached to the whole evaluation problem, not just to the issue of selection by tests.

Second, most pencil-and-paper tests are, it has been argued, "culture-bound." They are tests built mostly by and for WASP (White Anglo-Saxon Protestant) males. That deficiency has been partially corrected by now, though the debate about "standards" versus racial or gender bias is by no means over. And selection testing has lost much ground over the last decade, partially because of those moral and, of course, political issues.

Projective tests and other clinical methods
for selection and evaluation

A second general approach to formal selection puts more emphasis on the dynamics of personality, and less on empirical validity. We have labeled it the "projective approach," but only for the sake of labeling. Projective tests are much more "head doctor" techniques than pencil-and-paper tests. They are largely European in origin, springing conceptually from Freud and Jung, and technically from the Swiss psychiatrist Rorschach. They are built on the assumption that one can develop a reasonably valid picture of the deeper structure of another person quickly from how that person projects personal concerns on to some standard but ambiguous stimuli. All projectives contain that element of standardized but ambiguous stimuli. Thus the "questions" on the original Rorschach test are a set of standardized inkblots. Respondents are asked to say what they see in each blot. From the nature, number, and variety of subjects' responses, the tester interprets each person's motives and tensions, in the context of the tester's theory of personality as well as the responses of many other subjects to the same blots.

Similarly, in another widely used projective test, the Thematic Apperception Test, the respondent is asked to tell stories about a standard but ambiguous series of pictures, about which any number of stories could be developed. The tester records the stories and the respondent's behavior, then interprets motivations in the light of the themes that characterize that subject's stories.

The end result of a battery of projective tests, then, is not a set of numerical scores comparing subject X with other subjects. It's a verbal report, assessing subject X's dominant motives and concerns, tolerance for frustration, attitudes toward authority, major personality conflicts that seem to be operating, and so on. Given such a report, managers must then decide for themselves whether a tester's judgment deserves heavy weighting in any final decision.

One organizational advantage of projectives is also one of their scientific weaknesses. They are essentially individualistic, and they cannot easily be "proved" right or wrong, even by their proponents. Projectives, therefore, push decision making back to where it belongs, into the hands of the manager. The projective tester says to the manager, in effect, "Here is my expert opinion about John Jones. You have your opinion about him, and you can now add mine to it. I have tried to add information to your reservoir of relevant information, but I cannot guarantee that my judgment will be right. *You* make the decision."

When one considers the history of projective tests, it is reasonable that they should be used in this way. Projectives were born in clinical psychology, in the climate of psychopathology, rather than in education or management. In the clinic and the hospital, their primary function was to help the therapist diagnose the meanings of the psychological pains of a new patient. Perhaps, if the therapist had known a new patient intimately for five or ten years, the projective tester would not be needed. But each patient is an individual, and it is in this individuality that the causes of the illness are probably to be found. So the therapist can use a highly individualized and relatively detailed picture of this unknown personality. That's what the original projective testers tried to provide.

Unlike pencil-and-paper tests, projectives are seldom standardized enough to be scorable by amateurs. The judgment, sensitivity, and wisdom of the tester remain a large factor. When managers buy pencil-and-paper tests, they buy a quantitative tool from which most subjective elements of interpretation have already been eliminated. Any honest technician counting up the yeses and noes on an interest inventory will come up with the same score as any other honest technician. Not so with honest projective testers. In effect, when managers buy projective tests, they buy the tester, just as when one buys an X ray, one buys the judgment and experience of the interpreting physician much more than the plate itself.

Projectives are also expensive. Because they are mostly one-subject-at-a-time tests, a professional tester may spend eight hours or more working with a single respondent. Consequently, projectives have entered organizations at those levels where they are most likely to be both useful and worth the money—at higher executive levels, where type 1, statistically based, pencil-and-paper tests are relatively useless.

Managers can determine whether projectives are worth the investment along two dimensions: (1) their own assessment of the tester hired to assess others, and (2) *their experiences over time in comparing the actual behavior of applicants with the predictions that the tester has made.*

In the face of such difficulties, one wonders how projectives have made any headway into supposedly hardheaded business circles. One reason may be that projective reports seem to catch the subtle realities of executive behavior better than most pencil-and-paper tests. Another is that assessment is so important and so difficult that managers are willing to incur the costs and take the risks in order to get the complicated, qualified, yet rich reports that emerge.

Here is a typical excerpt from a projective test report on an applicant for an executive position:

> Mr. X is of superior intelligence. Problem situations, even those for which he is momentarily unprepared, do not throw him. He usually does not become emotionally involved when he has to work on a problem but adheres to a strict formula that forces him into an intellectual and rational approach. . . . [For him] the problem is uppermost and feelings are disregarded. More specifically, the feelings of others are

disregarded, for when his own personal satisfaction is involved, then his approach to problems is somewhat less systematic. For example, he wants others to think that he is a very capable individual and tries hard to maintain this impression because of the satisfaction that this gives him. However, because of this attitude, he is apt to become too self-confident or "cocky," and thus makes errors in very simple situations or problems that he usually would not make under such circumstances. . . .

The job is paramount in his mind and he believes that he and others should subjugate themselves to it. Consequently, he is highly critical of the performance of others who work for him—but he demands as much of them as he demands of himself. Furthermore, because the job is so important to him, he does not take sufficient time out to realize the nature of the personalities working with him. He does not accomplish a job by the "human approach" but by insisting that there is a job to be done and all must do it regardless of their personal needs. . . .

Being a competitive individual with a high level of aspiration, Mr. X may be a member of a group with whom he is associated, but he will not feel a part of them or share with them all that he knows, etc. To some extent he feels superior to those with whom he is associated; he feels that he could direct and lead them. But he does not win their confidence, since he is too forward in this regard, and they may resent his attempts to be in the limelight. . . .

And so on. Managers sometimes react against all these qualifications, wishing for more "practical," definitive decisions. Should this guy get the job or shouldn't he? But it is not usually true that people are simply good or bad. They succeed or fail "if," or they would have succeeded or failed "but." They might have succeeded if they had worked for another kind of boss, or if the manager had given them a little looser or tighter rein, or if they had been provided with a high-powered assistant, or if the job description had been rewritten so that they were given more responsibility in area A and less in area B.

Success on a job, especially a decision-making managerial job, after all, is not just a function of the person alone but of the person-in-situation. Any testing procedure that describes the complexity of the person provides extra data for relating that person to the relevant situation. And if the person is relatively unchangeable, the situation often is not. The manager, much more than the tester, has to decide which to change and how.

This may be the best place to point to another major dilemma. Remember our discussion of the "fundamental attribution error?" How much does any person's behavior in one particular situation tell us about that person? If a military recruit cracks up under the pressure of basic training, can we safely attribute that crack-up to that person's "weakness" or "incompetence?" Might we not argue that the recruit's failure indicates that superiors were "incompetent" by exerting too much pressure too quickly? But if only one recruit out of fifty cracks up, isn't that "proof" that that one is the weakest of the recruits? On the other hand, does a recruit's failure in that military situation mean that becoming a heroic accountant is impossible? Yet, if the recruit gets some kind of questionable discharge, won't the world always remember that military failure and treat it as a sign of *general* inadequacy, even much later, when being considered for quite a different situation?

The difficulty is that we only see persons-in-situations. In the past, we probably overemphasized the person part of the combination. In recent years, in our attempts to match the person to the situation, managers and psychologists alike try to put much more emphasis, properly, on the *interaction* between the person and the situation. Projective tests, if used well, can contribute to our understanding of that interaction. Such tests do not ask, "How good a person is Joe Blow?" but rather, "How is Joe Blow likely to behave in situations like this or that?" And each of us, as we do informal assessment, without tests, probably ought to be doing much the same thing; we should always ask, "How would this person be likely to behave in job X or crisis Y?"

Therefore, if projective tests can start the manager worrying about whether it would be wiser to put somebody like Brown to work for systematic department head Smith or for loose, easygoing department head Jones, that in itself may constitute a considerable service.

Sociometric methods

Sociometric methods try to assess people by collecting the judgments of other people, organizational peers, or subordinates. The "buddy rating" systems used by the military are classic sociometric devices. A platoon of potential officer candidates, for example, trains together for several weeks. Then all members are asked to nominate the three candidates they think would make the best combat officers and the three they think would make the worst combat officers. Members might be asked, too, to rate their buddies on honesty, intelligence, sense of humor, or any of a number of other characteristics. Positive and negative votes received by members are totaled and scores assigned. The scores represent a collective estimate of their buddies' beliefs about their aptitude for a particular role.

Sociometric techniques usually do not require the judges (usually peers) to provide a rationale for their judgment. Each individual is simply asked to express overall estimates about every other individual in the group. The sociometric method thereby finesses one very difficult area, the area of verbal communication. Both our language and our capacity to communicate our images of people are, after all, woefully inadequate. Moreover, what we do know about human beings suggests that they are not things to be decomposed into a large set of separate elements and then reassembled. People are better assessed by other people, all things being equal, in a kind of all-at-once, whole-person way. When, sociometrically, one asks people to make an overall gut judgment of another, one is, to an extent, automatically taking both the wholeness of personality and the wisdom of that marvelous human computer into account.

The reader will surely sense the impressionistic, intuitive flavor of the paragraph above. It's not sloppiness. It is important not to underestimate (nor to overestimate) the value of our own intuition. "Intuition" in this context simply means that we are very rapid processors of large amounts of current information against the background of our rich past experience in other similar situations. And there is good evidence that such intuitive judgments of other people are often quite valid—especially when several observers pool their intuitions. It is when we try to specify *why* we make such judgments that most trouble starts. Feelings such as "I'd like to work for that guy!" are quite useful, especially if aggregated. But be careful about destroying their value by asking too many questions about *why* we feel we'd like to work for him. Then we often come up with answers like "Well, he's very honest, honorable, and clever." Total judgments, when decomposed and itemized, often lose their essence.

This coin has another side. When data consist of the intuitive, unsubstantiated feelings of some people about other people, the dangers of distortion are many. Maybe I just don't like that guy because of what he did to my sister 20 years ago. Such distortions may be partially eliminated by combining the intuitions of many observers. Although the judgment made by one platoon member about Private X may be far off base, the judgments of fifty platoon members will be reasonably valid predictors of performance—more valid, as World War II experience showed, than paper-and-pencil tests, rating scales, and even military-school grades.

Sociometric methods have been used in a variety of ways for a variety of purposes. Sometimes one asks several judges to observe and listen to a group of applicants discussing some issue (like a case study) with one another. The judges sit on the periphery and observe the applicants. They then decide individually which one of the applicants they believe would best perform a particular job. Then those individual judgments are discussed and combined.

Sociometric methods have only made their way slowly into modern organizations despite evidence of their relatively high validity. It has been slow in part because of the "political" implications they generate. Sociometric methods, especially buddy ratings, are something like the voting process. Voting-style democracy doesn't fit well with ideas of authority and obedience in organizations. Many real or imagined dangers to traditional managerial power and "prerogatives" stand in the way. If operators are allowed to select their own foremen, some managers argue, political plots and fixed elections would not be far behind. Selection by popularity, they add, will replace selection by ability, despite the fact that research to date has shown that such ratings seldom turn into popularity contests.

Day-to-day assessment of people

Men and women directing organized human efforts must necessarily spend some of their time making judgments about other people—about customers, bosses, employees, suppliers, recruits, and many others. Some judgments can be formalized, but it is at the informal, day-to-day level that most assessments are made. Top managers—informally, gradually, often imperceptibly, perhaps even unconsciously—decide that Jones looks like presidential timber and Smith is likely never to go anywhere.

The professional psychologist has surprisingly little help to offer the manager in this broad realm. We can provide tests, questionnaires, and individual experts to help with formal screening and selecting. But we have done little to help managers improve their accuracy in making quick and dirty judgments about the people they encounter in day-to-day business life. Skill in judging other people is not easily passed from one person to another.

Probably the most useful first step toward increasing the accuracy of our assessments is to make ourselves quite conscious of what we are doing. Often we assess unconsciously, while our conscious concern revolves around other things, like giving instructions or evaluating the proposal.

But even with a conscious purpose, how should we go about ordering the information we hope to get? The scheme that follows is a crude one, but perhaps it will be useful. It is made up of three categories. First, we try to get a fix on the *givens*—the more or less durable characteristics of the person we are assessing. Second, we look at the *motives*. What does that person seem to want most? And third, we consider *achieving styles,* the methods by which one uses one's givens to try to achieve one's goals. Put another way, we can say that the accuracy of our assessment will increase to the degree that we can better answer this question: How does this person characteristically use the givens to get what's wanted? That question—coupled with the question "What are we assessing this person for?"—is one rough framework for the informal assessment process.

The givens. By the time we have become adults, all of us show some relatively durable characteristics. Some of those characteristics are givens in the sense that they were inherited; others are givens in the sense that we learned them early and intensely and they have stayed with us. The general energy level of a person is one such characteristic; so are particular skills, educational background, styles of thinking, general sensitivity to and sympathy for others, and certainly physical makeup and appearance. We can find out about those things directly or indirectly.

Motivational patterns. To a considerable extent, people are known by their motives: "Mary is ambitious. She wants to be number 1 in any situation. She's infuriated when she doesn't come out on top"; "Joe needs people. He just has to be with people. He'd go crazy if he didn't have lots of friends and a busy social life"; "Sam has to figure everything out. Give him a puzzle and he won't let it go until he's solved it." Those are descriptions of motivational patterns that we believe we perceive in other people. If we have known those people for awhile, and if we can maintain reasonable objectivity, those descriptions can carry real meaning. Something imprecise, but nevertheless meaningful, is achieved, for example, by saying of another person that he has a strong need for neatness and order, or that he is unusually affiliative, or that he seems to have a strong desire for power and control over others.

Achieving styles, characteristic ways of trying to get what we want. "Even at a cocktail party, Joe always acts as though he's in a big competition." Some people do that, don't they? They turn noncompetitive situations into competitions. And some people seem to want to take over and run things, no matter where or when. Remember General Haig, after President Reagan was shot? "I'm in charge," he said, and many of us felt that said more about him than about the situation.

People vary, that is to say, in the means they typically use to achieve whatever it is they go after. Some people tend to be *direct* achievers, taking direct action to get what they want, usually feeling personally responsible for getting things done. Others are more *relational,* taking pleasure in helping others or preferring to collaborate with others to get things done. Some prefer mostly *instrumental* methods, using their relationships with others as their primary route to getting whatever they want; they follow a who-you-know rather than what-you-know policy.

Each of these styles may, of course, be appropriate in some settings and inappropriate in others. Direct achieving styles may work well for a bench technologist or an entrepreneur, but most supervisory and managerial jobs require more "relational" behaviors.

One can spell out each of those three broad categories in more detail by making a checklist of givens, another of motives, and a third of achieving styles. But that much detail would not be useful here. Perhaps what is most useful is simply to suggest that assessors compress the information that they obtain about another personality into a few (very few) broad categories like those three, and then compare what they find with the purpose for which they are judging. Keep the categories broad and the number small, for the greater danger lies in too much fragmentation, too many narrow categories. The panorama of the forest is lost when we only count the trees.

The role of intuition

Evaluations derived from face-to-face meetings always mean that information about the other person has been filtered through the screen of the evaluator's own perceptual biases, through the evaluator's own history of learning. So personal judgments are double-edged swords, very dangerous, very rich, and also inescapable. Indeed, all of us form strong impressions of other people (whether we intend to or not) in the first minute or two of our initial encounter. Often we form those impressions before any words have been said, deriving our information from clothes, bearing, body language, and a collection of other inputs, all of which are processed very rapidly through our incredible human computers. Often those impressions, while clear to us, are hard to put into words. They occur mostly in iconic language. Often, too, these impressions are quite accurate. Our computers have almost instantaneously compared what we are seeing against a mass of past experiences, using cues we did not even consciously recognize.

The point is that we often build rather elaborate, albeit nonverbal, evaluations of others, mostly semiconsciously or intuitively and usually well before any formal information has been gathered. It has been argued, in fact, that most of our interviews actually consist largely of checking out hypotheses that the interviewer has made about the person in the first few minutes of contact. If subsequent questions clearly disprove the hypotheses, the good interviewer may reject them. Bad interviewers treat those hypotheses as facts, cast them in concrete, and make sure that selectively collected later data don't contradict them.

The wise assessor does not keep personal feelings out of it in favor of entirely objective methods. Ignoring one's feelings would not be desirable even if it were possible. The experienced human computer is a wondrous instrument. It is not a machine to be ignored or denied. Using it well is where the skill comes in.

But we really do not have a choice. Whether we try to or not, we listen to other people on at least two levels: at the level of the speaker's words and the information they carry, and at the level of the listener's own feelings about the speaker's words, movements, and manners, and the feelings all those things convey. Most of us, for example, can tell rather quickly whether or not another person seems to be afraid of us, angry at us, or comfortable or uncomfortable with us. We swiftly determine whether that person talks too much for our liking or has what we consider a sense of humor. Yet, in formal evaluation situations, we often try consciously to block out and ignore those impressions, preferring to deal instead with what we like to think of as "the cold facts."

This effort to discard our own impressions derives, of course, from justifiable caution about our own subjectivity and bias. Certainly such self-doubt is warranted. Most of us would like to have something more solid to

lean on than our own amorphous judgments. We prefer to draw our in-
ferences from school grades, test scores, kinds of jobs the applicant has
held, and any other piece of objective, factual information that we can
find. Yet, paradoxically, especially outside the office, only the most insen-
sitive of us would try to estimate another's friendliness by asking whether
he has read Dale Carnegie. Instead, our data about friendliness are obtained directly, by socializing and then filtering the results through our own
conception of what "friendly" means. In effect, we listen with our third
ear. Of course, the third ear is only as good as the degree to which we use it
objectively about ourselves. But can't the same be said about the other two
"factual" ears?

In organizations, going the "subjective" personal-assessment route carries great dangers, both for accuracy and for justice. "Good" people may
become the people that today's manager likes. And the people today's
manager likes may well be people like today's manager. Subjective, person-
alized assessment, with little reference to the question of assessment for
what, may indeed ultimately yield an in group of "all-alike" people. But
since all-alike groups may be able to work together on some tasks better
than all-different groups, an organization may, under certain conditions,
profit from just such prejudice. For example, one can argue that, in a period of growth and youth, an all-alike team has many advantages. Later in
an organization's life, the same subjective prejudices may be stifling to the
birth of new ideas.

On gathering information via interviews

When we are being assessed and we know it, we behave in ways we think
will evoke the best assessment; we put on an act. Suppose a personnel interviewer asks Mr. X, "How do you get along with people?" His answer
might be, "Oh, just fine. I like people." But if Mr. X's psychiatrist asked
him the same question an hour later, his answer might be quite different:
"Well, Doc, that's just the problem. Most people don't seem to pay any attention to me."

One widely used technique for getting around people's acts is to evaluate
in disguised situations: "Let's go have a couple of drinks"; "I just wanted to
chat with you." This alternative immediately introduces procedural as well
as ethical questions. A second technique is to have assessors turn themselves into inkblots. The assessor does not ask, "How do you get along
with people?" but, "What are the kinds of people you like best?" By
broadening the questions, by modifying them so that "right" answers are
not at all obvious, the interviewer provides a projective-type stimulus so
subjects' answers can be their own and not the interviewer's. Even so,
people who are being assessed through interviews often make good guesses
about what the "right" answers are. As long as they remain guesses, how-

ever, they represent a valid projection of the personality being interviewed. The major assumption underlying what has come to be called "nondirective" interviewing is precisely that one. The interviewer tries to become an ambiguous stimulus, a human inkblot, requiring interviewees to "project" their own attitudes into the interview. In contrast, unambiguous interviewers, whose demeanor makes the "right" answers obvious, are apt to generate only a reflection of themselves.

The inkblot idea is simple and sensible. The purpose of an interview is to gather information about the other person, not about the interviewer. It is appropriate also that the interviewer provide a situation free enough so that interviewees can talk about themselves and be themselves, without feeling impeded. In practice, the application of this principle suggests that an information-gathering interview should be designed like a series of inverted triangles. The interviewer opens each area of search with big, broadside queries so that interviewees can structure and describe their perceptions of the whole question, raising points in the order that seems significant to them, with varying intensities and degrees of passion. If the interviewer still feels the need for more specific detail, the questions can later be narrowed down to greater and greater specificity. Then a new area is ready for opening up with a new open-ended, ambiguous question.

Ultimately, an evaluation of one person by another is a judgment and nothing more. Good judges need all the information they can get from all the sources they can find. Scales, forms, and patterned interviews can be helpful. But no "system" obviates the need for sensitivity and understanding. There are no formulas that can rule the judge out of the judging equation.

On telling other people what you think of Harry

Our internal computers are often rather good as assessors, giving us a clear and quite comprehensive sense of another person. But communicating that gestalt, that total picture, to a third party is another ballgame. We don't do it very well. For most of us, words never quite seem to catch it all. Indeed, we admire and wonder at those few great writers who do manage to communicate to us, in words, a full portrait of a character.

But we have to communicate our assessments to others as best we can, and here are a few tips that might help:

1. Use metaphors, similes, and comparisons: "You know Harry? Well, Joe is just like Harry." "He's much quicker than Sam, but he has the same kind of warm easy way about him." "He's always like a coiled snake, ready to strike."

2. Keep it specific and simple. Try not to use too many global words, such as *integrity* or *honesty*. Use, instead, incidents and examples of what the person did or said.

3. To escape partially our inadequacy as communicators, give several colleagues a chance to spend time with the person and then pool everybody's overall reactions. Does this person look to us like someone who would do well in that situation we're thinking about?

4. Build up your symbolic vocabulary. Read good writing. Make lists of relevant adjectives. None of us communicates our assessments very well, but we can improve by working at it.

Performance evaluation
Fear and loathing inside the organization

Assessment to select new employees, tricky as it is, is a much less treacherous process than assessment of present employees. Performance appraisal, often tied to salary increases and promotions, is a real organizational killer. It can destroy morale and decimate teamwork.

All of us carry mixed and strong feelings about being evaluated by others. We are a little schizophrenic about it, both resenting and seeking out such evaluations. We resent negative assessments because they threaten our egos and our autonomy. But we also want to know where we stand and how much we are loved by those on whom we depend.

From the managerial point of view, then, the problem of assessment is much more than a problem of finding the right tests and questionnaires. The tests, interviews, appraisal forms, and other ritualistic paraphernalia of assessment are only a small part of the problem. The bigger parts raise questions such as these: Do we want to (or have to) consciously and regularly evaluate individual members of this organization? If we do, shall we formalize the process? Written evaluations? Every six months? Shall we report back results to each person? *All* results? Who shall evaluate whom? Superiors evaluating subordinates? Or peers? Or shall subordinates evaluate their bosses? What is to be evaluated? What's *good* performance? Do we emphasize short-term results or long-term promise? Is being liked by colleagues important? Or being cooperative? Or being imaginative? Shall we evaluate all of them in a great hodgepodge of detail? Can we quantify "cooperation" or "imagination"? Shall we build a work environment permeated with an atmosphere of evaluation? One in which people are forever generating games and gimmicks to get high ratings, even at the cost of good work? What about teamwork? Can we expect cooperation and mutual trust when each of us knows that each of us is being evaluated? By one another? On a curve? So that we will be ranked from best to worse? But if there is no ranking, won't everyone end up with the same marks?

Organizations in some other societies are much less preoccupied (once selections have been made) with evaluations of individuals than Americans are. They conduct performance appraisals less frequently (in the United

States, we tend to do formal assessments annually or even every six months) and less formally (looking for some general consensus over time rather than numerical scores on rating forms) than we do. They put more emphasis on evaluating the performance of groups than individuals, treating the group as the relevant unit and leaving individual assessment and adjustment to the group members. We in the United States, perhaps because we value individual merit, often overkill in our enthusiasm for individual evaluation.

Is there a right answer to all this? Is there a direction in which we ought to be pointing our performance evaluation policies? Probably yes—*away* from our number crunching efforts to grade every person on everything we can imagine. We are certainly sensible enough not to play such foolish games within our families. We know that if we did regular performance appraisals on our spouses, children, and parents the tensions generated would be enormously costly. And at this juncture, we ought to be doing less of it in our organizations. Why? Because in this period in our history we need loyalty, commitment, and trust from our people much more than we need point scores to justify raises or promotions. The manager had better be aware that evaluation of individual human beings is a treacherous process. Game playing, political manipulation, and divisiveness typically accompany it. The costs (including emotional costs) often far outweigh the benefits. Indeed, these authors have never met a company using a formalized performance evaluation scheme that was also happy about it.

The chapters that follow are devoted, in large part, to considering the implications of issues like evaluation for effective team behavior.

In summary

The most widely used approaches to formal assessment of people in organizations include pencil-and-paper tests, projective tests, and sociometric methods. Each has its advantages and costs. Many pencil-and-paper devices are quite standardized and economical to apply, but their use is largely limited to problems of mass selection. Projectives go deep into personality and are rich in the material they dredge up, but are more subjective, expensive, and poorly validated. Sociometrics are easy to use and relatively valid, but carry serious implications for the power relationships in the organization.

Day-to-day informal assessement of people is a much more difficult problem. It can be helped by a set of categories for thinking about personality, by using modern interviewing techniques, by increasing one's insight into oneself, and by communicating examples and incidents to third parties.

The larger questions of evaluation and assessment are not "How?" questions, but "Why?" "How much?" and "At what cost?" In general, American organizations spend much more time and money on individual performance-evaluation schemes than do organizations in some other countries. Results in the United States have not always been very good, often generating an "atmosphere of evaluation" that unintentionally drives cooperative team members toward interpersonal competition and turns task-oriented people into manipulative game players.

2

People two at a time: Communicating, influencing, commanding, challenging

Introductory note

Our focus shifts now from the singular to the plural, from individuals to relationships between people, and especially to the methods one person may use to change the behavior of another.

The minute we begin to talk about ideas like persuading or influencing others, however, a major ethical consideration comes up: When is it right and when is it wrong for A to try to change B's behavior? And then come all the questions associated with the uses of power and authority: When is it right and when is it wrong to order people to do things? to use blackmail? coercion? Is it ever right to con people, to manipulate them in order to get them to do what you want them to do? What about "brainwashing"? Is that ever ethical? Those are all proper questions in a free society.

Notice that such questions are by no means limited to business organizations. They are pervasive questions, arising continuously in the family, in education, in politics, in international relations, and in every other phase of human interaction.

Indeed, those ethical problems, along with the technical problems of changing human behavior, grow more complex every year. Our technological society and our shrinking world have increased our dependency on one another. It's no longer just the infant who is dependent on others for survival. Very few adults could last long all alone.

Our dependency is not just physical, either. Some years ago an astute observer called Americans an "other-directed" people—a people who need others not only for bread and warmth but to justify our existence and to provide us with standards of value. Young executives find it hard to separate good work from their boss's approval of it. Authors cannot feel sure they have written a good book until the critics laud it. In a world of massive interdependence, we had better watch our ethics.

This part 2 of our book emphasizes three central ideas about influence in human relationships:

First comes the idea of *communicating,* because communicating is the prerequisite to any attempt to change human behavior. Our current understanding of the communication process has evolved as much from engineering and science as it has from the behavioral sciences. Many of the following pages, therefore, can trace their origins as much to the natural sciences as to psychology or sociology.

The second idea is a sharply contrasting and more psychological one. It is the idea that *emotionality* is more a key to success in influencing than rationality. Although we can rationally analyze the process of transmitting information, we would be foolish indeed to think that the transmission of information is all there is to communication. Information has to be accepted and internalized. People are seldom influenced just by clear, rational, well-communicated argument. We are influenced much more because we have been touched in our hearts than in our heads. No matter how much we pride ourselves on our objectivity and rationality, our fears and fantasies become critical when it comes to influence.

To say, however, that we are influenced emotionally more than rationally is not to denigrate either us or reason. Emotionality is by no means equivalent to stupidity. The emotional, nonintellectual, feeling parts of our beings can be wise, sophisticated, and truth-seeking, too!

The third idea in part 2 is about *relationships between people*. When we communicate, we communicate with other people. And they communicate back to us. We try to change one another. The focal unit is the *pair* rather than the individual. And the space between the two (or more) members is the territory we call the relationship. Relationships are generally characterized by some degrees of mutual dependency; and, as the reader will remember from part 1, dependency situations are likely, even among adults, to generate strong and usually ambivalent emotions.

All of us who are members of organizations are living in an atmosphere of dependency. We should therefore feel some love and some hate toward that organization. The intensity and direction of those feelings should, in turn, vary with the ups and downs of our individual organizational lives.

The morals of this tale are simple but important. Don't look for psychological equilibrium in the individual/organization relationship (or in marriage or any other relationship, for that matter). Look for variability and change. Don't look for statics; look for dynamics. Don't look for a permanently "happy" connection between you and your company. Look for one that has the capacity for self-correction.

The organization is frustrating as well as satisfying. And the organization (or any manager) fools itself if it thinks it can be otherwise. But what the organization and the individual can do is to limit the duration and buildup of frustration by providing mechanisms for expressing it, releasing it, and doing something about it. But the organization had better also be satisfying and not just frustrating, because the dependency is mutual.

Those issues bring us to a big old question in the field of organizational behavior, the question of the tension between the individual and the organization. Endless debate has gone on about whether or not human beings can

live complete, fulfilled lives in the constricting, dependent environments of large organizations. Indeed, one senior executive who had spent many years in both the public and private sectors told a class taught by one of the authors that he had concluded that all contemporary organizations are essentially prisons, that the differences between the best and the worst are small at best. In the better ones, he argued, the food in the cafeteria is a little better and the prison cells may be a little larger or decorated a little better; but no organization, almost by definition, can provide anything approaching full human freedom.

That seems a cynical, embittered view. But suppose we carry it further. Couldn't we say the same thing (and haven't many people said it?) about marital relationships? about family life? about small towns? or about any long-term human relationship? That is, isn't it true that any ongoing interaction between people always involves some degree of mutual dependency and mutual constraint? And can't it also be argued that, to the degree that B is dependent on A, B is always less than fully free?

But that's the negative side of it. How about the positive side? Isn't it fair to argue that life without mutually dependent relationships would be unbelievably barren? Can't we say that, if most organizations and most relationships imprison us, then nonorganizational and nonrelational life condemn us to solitary banishment into outer space? All of which is to reiterate the yang-yin theme of oriental thought, and its flip Western equivalent. "There ain't no free lunch!" Relationships everywhere involve responsibility.

Chapter 8, the first chapter in part 2, goes directly to the communicating process, the basic mechanism through which relationships become possible. Chapter 9 hits the influencing problem head-on, describing several dimensions of influence and their implications. Then we devote four chapters to four different ways of influencing people: the first considers the use of authority as a tool for influence; the second examines coercive power; the third looks at manipulative tools for influence; and the fourth examines motivational and collaborative methods for influence. Then the last chapter, chapter 14, looks at the changing world of *incentives*—money incentives and other incentives—which organizations use to try to influence the behavior of their members.

8

Communicating:
Getting the word
from A to B

People begin, modify, and end relationships by communicating with one another. Communication is the channel through which influence flows. It has become popular in recent years to communicate about communicating—to talk and write about the importance of communication in organizational life. The increasing talk about communicating itself reflects the growing complexity of the problem in the modern, interdependent human organization.

Unfortunately, the word *communication* has, in recent years, been used to mean everything from public speaking to mass advertising. Unfortunately, too, most of the talk has been more hortatory than explanatory. Managers are urged to use "two-way" communication, because it is "better" (what does "better" mean?) than one-way communication. And by labeling difficult human problems as "communication problems," we seem often to feel that we have solved them or at least absolved ourselves from solving them.

The purpose of this chapter is to describe some major dimensions of the communicating process as it occurs between people, to examine what can be meant by "better" or "worse" communication, and to connect the process of communicating to processes of interpersonal influence and behavior change.

Some dimensions of communicating

Sometimes seemingly simpleminded questions turn out to be rather useful. They can help strip away some of the confusion surrounding an idea so that we can see it more objectively.

Suppose we ask, simplemindedly, what are the things that go on when A talks to B? What is involved when two people talk to one another?

First of all, A usually talks to B *about something*. A doesn't just babble. The process carries *content*. A talks to B about yesterday's ballgame or next week's advertising schedule. The content is what usually hits us first when we tune in on someone else's conversation. The content of communications, in fact, is what psychologists and businessmen alike are usually thinking about when they think about human communication.

We can see subclasses within content, too. We can differentiate categories of content, like *factual* content and *feelings* or emotional content.

Other things, quite independent of content, also can happen when A talks to B. Some conversations are carried on in the presence of a great deal of *noise;* others are relatively noiseless. In this context, of course, "noise" means things that interfere with clear transmission of the intended content. We can encounter channel noise, like the static on a telephone line, that may make it hard for B to hear what A says. We can also usefully think of psychological "noise," like B's thinking about something else, so that it is hard to hear what A is saying; or B may be so afraid of A that it is once again hard to hear what A is saying. Language or code noise may also make it hard for B to hear. B doesn't understand the words A is using in the way A understands them; or A is speaking in Spanish and B only understands English.

All sorts of noise can occur independently of content. We can find noisy or noiseless communications with any content. We can also usually observe that A, if aware that noise is present, usually communicates more redundantly, repeating the message or shouting it, in the hope that B will be able to hear it better; or A may say the same thing in different words, again hoping that that will help get the message through.

Redundancy is one of our best and most common weapons for combating noise. It is "efficient" in the sense that, so long as noise exists, redundancy helps to push the content through.

Besides the *content* and *noise* dimensions of communication between A and B, there is a third dimension worth noting, especially in organizations—the *communication net.* Usually we think of A-to-B conversation as direct; but many such communications, especially in organizations, are mediated through other people. One thing an organization chart is supposed to define is the channel or channels over which A can legitimately get a message through to B, and often that may be only through C and D. As a later chapter will show, the structure of the networks that a particular organization uses can have a lot to do with the speed and accuracy of all members' communications with one another.

One more dimension of the communicating process is worth noting, especially since it has been ridden so hard in managerial literature. It is the *direction* of communication—its "one-wayness" or "two-wayness." Again, that's an independent dimension. Whatever A and B may be talking about, however much static may be involved, whatever the network, A may talk to B this way, A→B, or this way, A⇄B, or somewhere in between. Putting these diagrams in words, A can talk and B can only listen—that is, one-way communication; or A can talk and B can talk back—that is, two-way communication.

This last aspect of the process, one-wayness versus two-wayness, gets special attention in the remainder of this chapter. Is two-way communicating really better? What does "better" mean? Better for what and for whom? When?

One-way versus two-way communicating

Essentially our problem is to clarify the differences between the following simple situations: (1) one person, A, talks to another, B, *without* an opportunity for return talk from B to A; versus (2) A talks to B *with* return talk from B to A. The differences can be clarified best by testing one method against the other. Here is such a test situation:

The pattern of rectangles shown on page 106 is an idea you would like to tell a B about. Suppose you want to communicate it, in words, to a half dozen of your friends who are sitting around your living room. The arrangement is presented in figure 8.1.

Assume that the rectangles touch each other at "sensible" places—at corners or at midpoints along the lines. There are no touch points at any unusual places. All the angles are either 90° or 45° angles; there are no odd ones. This pattern of rectangles is an idea comparable perhaps to a complicated set of instructions you may have to give to a subordinate, or to the definition of a policy that you would like to pass along, or to the task of explaining linear programming to a sales manager. Let's now try to communicate this idea under (1) one-way, and then (2) two-way conditions.

If you are the communicator, these are your instructions for one-way communicating:

1. Turn your back on your audience so that you cannot get visual communication back.

2. Give the audience blank sheets of paper, so that they can listen and draw exactly what you are communicating. Ask them to try to draw as accurate a picture of the pattern of rectangles as possible.

3. Describe the pattern of rectangles to them in words as fast as you comfortably can. The audience is not permitted to ask questions, laugh, sigh, or in any other way to communicate back to you any information about what they are receiving.

This exercise makes a good parlor game. If you can find some people to try it on, try it, time it, and then, afterward, check the accuracy of your communication by seeing whether or not your audience has drawn the pattern you thought you were communicating. If they received what you tried to send, so their pictures match the test picture, then you have communicated very well. To the extent that their pictures do not match the one in your drawing, you have not communicated.

Two-way communicating can be tested, for contrast, in the same way. Figure 8.2 presents an equivalent test pattern. For this figure the basic job

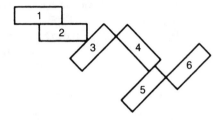

Fig. 8.1.

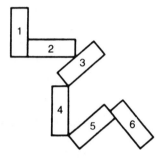

Fig. 8.2.

is the same, to describe the pattern verbally so that the people who are listening can draw it. But here are the differences:

(1) This time you may face your audience; (2) now they are allowed to talk back and ask you any questions they want to at any time.

Now try it again and time it. The differences between what happened the first time and what happened the second time are the differences between one- and two-way communicating. (The order in which the two methods are tried does matter, but not a great deal.)

Under experimental conditions, these findings have emerged from this game: First, one-way communication is considerably *faster* than two-way communication. Second, two-way communicating is *more accurate* than one-way. That is, more people in the audience correctly reproduce the drawing under two-way conditions. Third, the receivers are *more sure* of where they are and make more correct judgments of how right or wrong their patterns are in the two-way system. Fourth, the sender usually ends up feeling psychologically *under attack* in the two-way system, because the receivers pick up mistakes and oversights and say so. The receivers may make snide remarks about the sender's intelligence and skill, and, if the receivers are trying very hard and taking the task quite seriously, they often actually get angry at the sender, and vice versa. Finally, the two-way method is relatively *noisy and disorderly*. People interrupt the sender and one another, the slowest person holds up the rest, and so on. The one-way method, on the other hand, appears neat and efficient to an outside observer, but, as noted already, the communication is less accurate.

Such a demonstration points out both the advantages and the costs of one-way and two-way communicating. If speed alone is what is important, then one-way communication has the edge. If appearance is of prime importance, if one wishes to look orderly and businesslike, then the one-way method again is preferable. If one doesn't want one's mistakes to be recognized, then again one-way communicating is preferable. Then senders will not have to hear people implying or saying that they are stupid or that there is an easier way to say what they are trying to say. Of course, such comments may be made about them whether they use one-way or two-way communication, but under one-way conditions they will not have to hear what is said, and it will be harder for anyone to prove that mistakes were made by A rather than B. If one wants to protect one's power, so that senders can blame receivers instead of taking blame themselves, then one-way communicating is again preferable. The sender can say, "I told you what to do; you just weren't bright enough to get the word." If two-way communication is used, the sender will have to accept much of what blame there is, and it will be apparent to all that some of it is deserved; but the message will also get across.

If one wants to simplify managerial life, so that even a rank amateur can handle it, one-way communication helps. It tightens and structures the situation so that A only has to make decisions about one issue, the content of the problem. When opening up two-way communication, A has to be professional. Now A must make many kinds of decisions at once, content decisions as well as decisions about people (Whom will I recognize? How long should I work to make sure Joe understands while everybody else waits?), about personal strategies (When should I cut off the discussion? Should I accept sarcasm or fight it?), and about many other things. Like some formations in football, two-way communicating is too powerful a device for safe use by amateur managers. But skillful use by a competent professional can be as beautiful and impressive as the work of a good quarterback.

Those are the major differences between one- and two-way communicating. They are differences that most people are aware of implicitly. If people get a chance to ask questions, to double-check what they might have missed, then they can make sure they have received exactly what they expected. On the other hand, if they must only sit and listen, they may or may not get the word, and they are likely to feel frustrated and uncertain about what they do get. Moreover, that frustration and uncertainty is likely to grow because there is no way of making sure of things they aren't sure of. They are, in effect, helpless.

To put it another way, one-way communicating is not likely to communicate the intended content very well. It is more likely to be empty talk, sending words into the air. Those words don't become communication until they enter meaningfully into somebody else's head.

Of course, it is simple for communicators in an organizational network to claim that their responsibility is only to pass the message along, that it is the receivers' responsibility to make sure that they understand it. But that's not a very adequate claim. If one really were to argue through the question of who is most responsible for the success of a communication, one would certainly conclude that communicating is largely the communicator's responsibility. If your job is to communicate—and if to communicate you must get your message through to the receiver—then your job isn't done until the receiver has received. And you cannot be sure that the receiver has received until you get confirming feedback from the receiver. On the other hand, the location of responsibility becomes a far less significant issue when one perceives communication as a two-way process to begin with.

A partial definition of communicating is now possible. First, to communicate is to shoot information and to hit a target with it. Shooting alone is not communicating. Second, to have more than a chance probability of hitting a target requires that the sender get some degree of feedback from the target about the accuracy of his shots.

If an artilleryman had to fire over a hill at an invisible target, he would have to fire blind and hope that by luck one of his shells would land on the target. He would spray the area with shells and go away, never being certain whether he had or had not destroyed his objective. But by the simple addition of a spotter, human or electronic, feeding back results, the likelihood of accurate shooting is increased tremendously. The spotter can feed back to the gunner information about the effects of the gunner's own shots. "Your last shot was a hundred yards short. The second was fifty yards over." The advantage is obvious, and it is precisely the advantage of two-way over one-way communication—the communicator can learn the effects of his attempts to communicate and can adjust his behavior accordingly.

One-way and two-way communicating are really different methods

By this definition, two-way communicating is not just different in degree from one-way; it is different in kind. For when one switches from one-way to two-way, a great many changes take place, changes not only in the outcomes but in the inputs. For example, one-way communicating usually calls for and gets much more planning than two-way. When you tell senders in these experiments that they are to send one-way and you show them the diagram and tell them they can take a few minutes to get ready, it is almost always true that they use more minutes getting ready to start than they do in the two-way system. The reason is probably obvious. Senders need to choose carefully the code they will use, even the precise words they will use. But in two-way communicating, they are apt to start out much more quickly, not worrying too much about a general plan or the right words because they know that the feedback will give them a chance to correct themselves. The first system is like a phonograph record. Once it starts, it must be played through. Hence, it must be planned very carefully. Two-way communicating generates a different kind of "local" strategy, in which senders start down one path, go a little way, and then discover they are on the wrong track, make a turn, discover they are off a little again, make another turn, and so on. They don't need to plan so much as they need to listen and to be sensitive to feedback.

There are important differences associated with these two approaches. Planning, orderliness, systematization, are associated with one-way communication. The two-way method has much more a trial-and-error, "let's make a stab at it and see what happens" kind of flavor. It is understandable, therefore, that people with more analytic thinking styles find one-way methods more agreeable, whereas people with more interactive styles of thinking tend to favor two-way approaches.

Given our definition of communicating, the issue of one- and two-way communication inside organizations can be cast in a somewhat unusual way. For now one encounters apparent conflict between the short-run effectiveness of two-way communicating and the long-run need to maintain power and authority at various levels of the hierarchy. Two-way communicating makes for more valid communicating, and it appears that more valid communicating not only means more accurate transmission of facts; it also generates different attitudes. Authority, for example, may, under ideal conditions of two-way communication, cease to serve as a sufficient protection for inadequacy. The dictum that a well-informed citizenry is democracy's best protection against autocracy may also be applicable to the well-informed staff or the well-informed employee.

Barriers to effective communicating

In our experiment, we set up two-way communicating simply by telling our subjects that we wanted them to talk back to the sender, to ask any questions they wanted to at any time they wanted to. Moreover, the experiment was just an experiment, and nothing really rode on it. So people should have felt free to talk back until the right answer was clear. Yet in almost every case it turned out that some people in the two-way situation did *not* come up with completely right answers. And it was also true that most of those people knew as they went along that they were wrong—*yet they did not ask questions.*

When we asked those people why not, we got a variety of answers. Some of them didn't ask questions because they were bored; they didn't think much of the experiment. Some of them didn't ask questions because they didn't want to take up the group's time. Sometimes they just got plain mad at the sender because of the way the material was presented. They wouldn't give the sender the satisfaction of asking a question. Sometimes they were scared. They had noticed that when Joe Blow asked a question earlier, the sender had given a curt and nasty answer. So they just quit asking questions. Some people said that they had wanted to ask questions, but so many other people were talking all at once that they couldn't get in.

So, even in this gamelike little experiment, where nothing much rode on what was going on, where the sender had no authority at all, there were many things that kept people from saying what they should have said. Many barriers to two-way communicating remained even after we had tried to set up a situation in which no such barriers would exist.

In the real world, of course, such subtle barriers are likely to be much stronger and more numerous. In the real world, the boss's statement that his office door is always open is much *less* likely to bring people in than the experimenter's statement that people should feel free to ask any questions they want to at any time they want to.

There is, then, an important moral to this tale. The moral is that if you want two-way communication in your organization you must figure that you will have to work for it. It doesn't happen naturally or by issuing a proclamation. If you, as a sender, want to make sure that two-way communication will in fact occur, you will need to be extremely sensitive to what the people in your group are thinking and feeling. You will have to have your eye open for the person who wants to talk but doesn't dare. You will have to be alert lest your own behavior deters people from raising the questions and comments that need to be made. You will have to worry about keeping enough order and discipline in the group so that people can get in to ask the questions they want to ask. You will even have to worry about the interpersonal relations among the members of the group, for sometimes people do not ask questions from the sender because they may be afraid of one of their colleagues. To get two-way communication, in other words, the manager has to accept many new kinds of responsibility.

Communicating about novel and routine problems

Earlier in part 1, when our focus was on individual learning and problem solving, we talked about how people learn by using their memories of past problems to solve similar present ones.

Correspondingly, it is also true that, if the task we had used in our communicating experiment had been a familiar one instead of an unfamiliar set of rectangles, the results might have been quite different. A, for instance, could probably have communicated the English alphabet accurately and rapidly using just one-way communicating. In fact, if we use two-way communicating on these rectangle problems again and again with the same group, it would soon become one-way de facto. After a few runs, people stop asking questions. They don't have to. They have learned the code. So A and B understand one another.

From the viewpoint of speed and accuracy, then, one could make this tentative generalization: Two-way communicating improves the accurate communication of previously uncoded or insufficiently coded ideas. But two-way communicating contributes considerably less to accuracy *after* the code has been clarified—after new problems have been programmed into old familiar ones. Coupling this generalization with the notion that new, unprogrammed problems occur more frequently in today's organizational world than in yesterday's, we can also conclude that two-way communicating may be generally more important for managers now than it was in organizations of the past.

What gets communicated?

One aspect of the content problem deserves mention here, although it will be dealt with more fully later. The problem is that people usually communicate more than information; they communicate feelings as well as facts. Suppose the artillery spotter, instead of simply announcing where the last shell had landed, decided to add a few typically human comments of his own. Suppose the spotter said to the gunner, "Look, you stupid s.o.b., your last shot was three hundred yards over. Where the hell did you learn to shoot?" That kind of communication of unsolicited information will, to say the least, complicate the picture, just as communication of inaccurate information would do. It might, mightn't it, cause the now frustrated gunner to change his aim from that old farmhouse to the spotter.

Such problems of the content of communications are the subject matter of the next few chapters of this book—the chapters on (communicating as a tool for) influencing human behavior.

In summary

Communicating is our primary tool for effecting behavior change. We can isolate at least four independent dimensions of the communicating process: content, noise, network characteristics, and direction.

One-way communicating has some clear advantages over two-way. It is faster and has the advantage of protecting the sender from having to recognize his own faults, as well as protecting him from having to confront some complex problems of managing. Two-way communicating carries advantages of greater accuracy and greater feelings of certainty for the receiver. But two-way communicating involves some psychological risks to the defenses of the sender. Two-way communicating also means less *planning* for the sender as far as the message itself is concerned, but opens up a whole new series of managerial problems in maintaining and expanding the two-way system. In general, it would be fair to say that two-way communicating is more effective in dealing with novel, unprogrammable problems, whereas one-way communicating is more efficient when dealing with familiar preprogrammed problems.

9

Influencing other people: Dimensions and dilemmas

The purpose of this chapter is to consider what happens when one person, A, sets out to communicate with another person, B, for the specific purpose of changing B's behavior.

Some of the important problems here are largely tactical ones, such as these: A sets out to get B to quit smoking; or A sets out to "discipline" B, who has again shown up late for work; or A sets out to stimulate a passive staff into more energetic activity; or A tries to get B to accept a great idea; or A sets out to gain B's friendship or respect. When we watch A undertake such tasks, several common denominators become noticeable. Some seem to center on A, others center on B, and still others are apparent in the relationship between the two. Let's begin with a clear code: A is the chang*er,* B is the chang*ee.*

Influence and emotion

Perhaps the most important idea in all this is that, when A sets out to influence B, A must realize that the task is an emotional as much as an intellectual one; significant change—in individuals, and organizations—always involves elements of emotionality. Of course, most of our education has taught us to believe that we influence people through reason, or at least that we ought to. People *should* be persuaded by facts, evidence, and truth. But any careful observation of reality will show us that reason plays, in most cases, only a small role in the total process. Most of us accept or reject new ideas or change our behavior more in response to feelings than to facts. We change because we are terrified, flattered, loved, or threatened.

The reader who is deeply committed to logic and reason may reluctantly admit that some (other) people are more emotional than reasonable, but that only offers one more reason to work toward a more rational world. It is important, however, even for the most rational reader to consider the positive, even desirable, side of emotionality. Surely there are times in our lives when it is appropriate to change out of loyalty, or out of love for people close to us, or out of commitment to a moral cause, even if pure reason might lead us elsewhere.

So, when we argue that change and influence are largely emotional processes, we do so neither regretfully nor cynically. Love, commitment, and loyalty need not be treated as imperfections in the human condition.

The changer's motivation

In the next few pages let's look at the three key elements in this behavior-change picture—the changer, whom we call A; the changee, whom we call B; and the relationships between them, which we shall call (with considerable originality) "the relationship" (fig. 9.1).

One oddity about people who seek to change others is their readiness to undertake the job without thinking much about their own objectives or motives. A friend once told a story about his extended efforts to get his baby daughter to stop sucking her thumb. He had been worried about it for a long time and had seen the family doctor about it. The doctor had examined the child, found no physical damage, and advised the father to forget about the problem.

But when the child got to be about three years old, Papa began to worry about it again. He was worried, he said, about what thumb sucking would do to her teeth and jaws. This time he took her to a psychiatrist, who talked to the child at some length and came up with the same advice the family physician had given: Forget about it; it would take care of itself.

Six months later Papa decided on his own to try some of the popular methods for stopping thumb sucking. He put some nasty-tasting stuff on the thumb; he spanked her; and he made her wear mittens. But those methods didn't work either.

Later we talked about it together. His objective *seemed* clear enough: Stop the child from sucking her thumb. But when pressed, he agreed that there were some secondary objectives that were perhaps not so secondary when he thought about them. He wanted the child to stop sucking her thumb, but he was not willing to pay any price to accomplish it. He was not willing, for instance, to exchange thumb sucking for stuttering or even for nose picking. Moreover, when we talked more generally about what he was trying to accomplish, he finally admitted that what he really wanted was to start making an adult out of his daughter, to start socializing her. He was disturbed because this three-and-a-half-year-old extension of himself was behaving in a way that he considered childish and shameful. He thought that other people disapproved of children who sucked their thumbs and that their disapproval reflected on his capability as a parent. He finally decided, after thinking a good deal about himself, simply to stop the whole attempt.

Such confusion of motives is not at all unusual, even among managers. A sales manager, under pressure from his superiors, starts pushing his

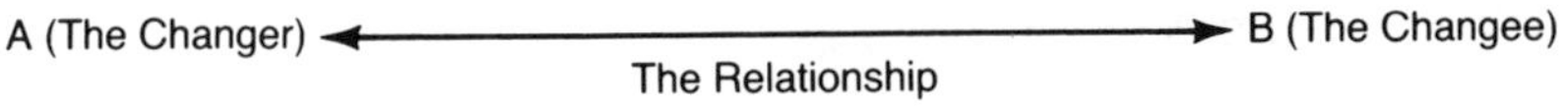

A (The Changer) ◄──────────────────────────► B (The Changee)

The Relationship

Fig. 9.1.

people to make 20 percent more calls each day. If an observer asks why he is suddenly demanding so much more from his people, he may well argue that his goal is to get more sales, purely and simply. But the whole situation may suggest that the motives involved are mostly personal and emotional—for example, to gain the approval of his boss.

A human resources manager tries to get his staff working hard on a new incentive system. His objective is to build a system that will help the company. But a careful look might show other motives that the manager may not admit very readily. He received a copy of *Business Week* from the president the other day, with one of those little yellow stick-on notes attached; "Joe, please let me know what we are doing about incentive programs like those described on page 128."

Perhaps the most common form of confusion about motives for changing others stems from conflicts between short-term and long-term priorities. In most managerial change settings, no matter how simple, specific, and immediate a problem may be, a secondary, long-term factor is likely to be lurking in the background. It is the factor of the continuing relationship. Anytime a manager performs some specific act to get more or better work on a specific job at a specific time, he is acting like the big brother in part 1. He is shaping, incrementally, his long-term relationship with his employees. Unlike the big brother's, the manager's acts are almost always played before a large audience. And every specific incident in his handling of every one of his people can be thought of as another frame in the long movie that shapes his people's attitudes toward work, their optimism or pessimism, their approval or resentment. The difficulty is that everyday pressures tend to push executives, like parents, toward short-term solutions and toward the satisfaction of short-term personal and egoistic motives, often at the expense of the long-term relationship.

So, if any generalized rule of thumb exists for the prospective behavior changer, it might be this one: Let him examine his own reasons for wanting to effect a particular change before plunging into the effort. Let him first examine his own motives. He may then be more likely to effect change successfully because he will be more clearheaded about what he wants to do. He may even abandon the effort altogether should such an examination bring the realization that changing other people would hurt the long-term objectives he wants to achieve.

The changee is in the saddle

No matter how much power a changer may possess, no matter how "superior" he may be, it is the changee who controls the final change decision. It is the employee, even the lowest paid one, who ultimately decides whether to show up for work or not. It is the child who ultimately decides whether to obey or not. It is the changee who changes. It's true that A can exert more or less influence on the situation, that A can cut capers before B; he can cajole, threaten, or punish. But B (and he may be an irrational and unreasonable B) makes the ultimate decision about whether or not he will change. Moreover, it is not just B but also A who feels tension, whose needs are unsatisfied. So A is always at least partially dependent on B.

B, after all, is a whole person; and A's activities in trying to get B to change constitute just one set of forces in the multitude of forces that determine B's behavior. B, in effect, sits behind the solid fortifications of his own history and personality, integrating A's activities into all the other forces that act upon him, and then comes up with a new behavioral pattern that may, or may not, constitute what A wants.

So, greater power in A's hands is not necessarily a better weapon for control over B's attitudes or behavior. B is never *completely* dependent. The shop-floor worker and the middle manager can find all kinds of ingenious ways to evade, avoid, or retaliate against changes imposed by their superiors.

Moral: Never underestimate the strength of the weak!

Change is uncomfortable

Often, during the process of behavior change, changees become disturbed. B, during the course of a significant change in his own behavior (whether the change results from A's actions or not), gets upset and anxious. A, the changer, may mistakenly interpret such action by B as a sign that his change efforts are failing, that he has gone too far.

However, disturbance almost invariably accompanies behavior change. The absence of signs of disturbance, therefore, may be more a sign of trouble than their presence.

Signs of disturbance during the process of change occur in many situations. The child is likely to become upset when switching from diapers to the toilet. The bachelor suffers from sleeplessness and loss of appetite as he approaches his wedding day. The manager somehow feels anxious and upset, as well as happy, when he learns of his promotion to greater responsibilities.

Moreover, such anxiety is likely to lead the changee toward aggression and hostility or into moodiness and withdrawal. A is often the nearest target for the tensions created by such disturbances; so B is very likely to go after A.

A's effort to change B usually generates some degree of conflict into B's situation. People change when their present behavior begins to appear inadequate, either because they have been frustrated—something in the world has thrown a block across a previously open path—or because some new path has become visible and looks as if it *might* (the conflict) be a better one. In either case, a way of behaving that had been adequate in the past has now become less adequate. But if I now find that my old behavior is no good, but no alternatives are immediately available, I am in a classic frustration situation; hence, you should expect manifestations of aggression from me. If my present direction doesn't look good any more because another has begun to look much better, then I am in conflict between continuing along the safe and secure old path and taking a chance on trying an uncertain new one. Once again you should expect me to show some emotion, and its particular nature should be fairly predictable.

What does A need to know about B?

Different A's in different change situations have different ideas about the importance of "diagnosis," of knowing all about B, before trying to change B.

An A who uses force as a prime tool for effecting change doesn't usually worry much about diagnosis. The effects of a whip, after all, are fairly predictable, even if one doesn't know much about the psyche of the particular person being whipped. But at the other extreme one can find the A (and many therapists are among them) who devotes a large portion of effort to finding out a great deal about B—about B's background, current situation, and history of successes and failures.

A great deal can be said here, as elsewhere, in favor of gathering information about a problem before trying to solve it. But three easily overlooked points are worth considering. First, who most needs the information thus gathered, A or B? Second, what kind of information does A (or B) need? Third, how much information is worth chasing after, especially if the process costs time and effort?

Behavior-change problems, however, are somewhat different from most other problems. Often it is more important for B to understand the problem than for A to understand it. If the ultimate control for change lies with B, and if it is for B to integrate new behavior into the framework of personal perceptions, then B can best make decisions when B, not A, understands what is going on. Although A may understand B inside out, A may not be able to communicate that understanding to B or even to plot a very effective course of action. Somewhere along the way, B has to line things up into a form B can understand and utilize. That's the problem with giving advice. A looks over B's situation, thinks (often correctly) that B sees it less clearly, and says, "What you ought to do is . . . " B thereupon feels that A's advice represents poor understanding; or B takes the advice literally, uses it poorly and finally rejects both advice and adviser. Perhaps if A spent less time diagnosing B and more time helping B at self-diagnosis, the likelihood of successful change would be enhanced.

A second problem involves the two kinds of information available to both A and B—information about facts and about feelings. Facts, in the usual sense of observable phenomena, are likely to be much less important than feelings in change situations. Fears, doubts, low self-confidence, and ambition are much more likely to constitute useful bits of information for behavior changers than the cold facts of duties or salary bracket. Moreover, those feelings may be hard for A to get at, even if they are needed. That's so partly because our language and culture make verbal communication of feelings difficult and partly because probing into private feelings raises psychological defenses.

An A who wants to know how B feels needs to have a sharp third ear, able to pick up information from cues such as the tone of B's voice, the raising and lowering of B's eyebrows, or the secondary emotional connotations of B's words. Any A who sets out to find out reasons for a B doing something had best think of the job as something considerably more than a simple fact-finding expedition. A had better recognize that he will have to listen for some subtle and indirect cues that can easily be misinterpreted.

One of the many good things to be said for a serious effort by A to understand B's feelings is that an A who undertakes such diagnosis often ends up changing personal objectives. An A who takes time to find out about an employee before imposing discipline may end up changing his own attitudes toward the employee and hence changing his own behavior more than B's. "That guy isn't really lazy after all. There were good reasons for what happened."

The location of responsibility in change situations

In watching an A trying to change a B, one may also notice that the responsibility for effecting the change seems to settle in different locations on different occasions. Sometimes A takes all the responsibility, and B none of it. Both A and B tend to see A as the person in charge and B only as an actor. On a road crew, for example, or in an office, each worker often seems to be thinking, "It is not my responsibility to work; it is the boss's responsibility to make me work. Therefore, it is perfectly proper for me to do as little as possible, to do only what the boss can directly coerce me into doing."

Ascribing all responsibility to A is not limited to chain gangs and office staffs, and it doesn't always happen against A's wishes. If anything, an A will often assume the responsibility for changing B and for seeing that B stays changed. Sales managers sometimes take this view in an extreme form. Quite properly, they consider it their job to stimulate their sales-people; but mistakenly, they assume that what is their job cannot be the salesperson's job, too. Since the effects of such extrinsic stimulation tend to wear off, they try periodically to reinforce it. Hence, many sales managers focus on incentive gimmicks, on "inspirational" sales meetings, and so on. Very often even managers who talk a lot about "delegation" actually take all the psychological responsibility. Their people often end up taking the same view—that is, that it is not their responsibility to sell so much as it is the job of managers to use their gadgetry to get them to sell.

Clearly, the responsibility for change does not have to lie solely with the changer. It can be shared by changer and changee, or it can even be taken over altogether by the changee. From the changee's viewpoint, change is equivalent to learning, and learning, as we proposed in part 1, is an *active* process. If teachers want to motivate their students to learn, one thing they can do is try to get their students to take the main responsibility for their own education, to come to want to learn on their own rather than to sit passively while the teacher pumps learning into their heads. Many psychia-trists and counselors will even argue that there is no real hope for effecting much "deep" change in clients unless the clients take such responsibility. But in business, organizational pressures and ideas about authority tend to make A feel personally responsible. He may then inadvertently encourage B to adopt pawnlike, nonresponsible behaviors.

The advantages of shared responsibility are great for both A and B. For one thing, a B who wants to change is more likely to change effectively and lastingly than a B who feels no such internal tension. Moreover, no A is likely really to understand the subtleties of B's position better than B. No matter how successful A's communication with B, there are probably sig-nificant things left uncommunicated. If A takes sole responsibility, with less information than is available to B, A may be trying to solve the wrong problem. If, on the other hand, B takes some of the responsibility for changing, B can take more personal peculiarities into account, and perhaps A and B can find a new behavior that deals with the needs of both.

In summary

In this chapter the spotlight has been on a few common aspects of many behavior-change situations. First, we urged the reader to remember that behavior change is an emotional process. That should lead the changer to treat logic as a useful but very limited tool for influencing the behavior of others.

Often the changers, A's, face a serious problem of understanding what they are doing. Often A's literally do not know what they are doing or why they are doing it. Their real motives and objectives may be both unconscious and unclear. By thinking through their inner motives, changers can help to reorient and clarify objectives, even to the point of prompting A to give up the project entirely.

The changee, B, ultimately controls the decision about whether or not to change. Although A can influence that decision, A cannot make it. The decision that B makes represents the integration of the forces imposed by A, along with a multitude of other forces over which A has no control.

An A will often try to understand B's reason for present behavior before attempting to change that behavior. Or A will make no such effort but depend instead on observed similarities in all people. While there are clear advantages to a moderate degree of diagnosis of B, it is more important that B make a self-diagnosis than that A make it of B. B ultimately controls the decision to change. Moreover, the diagnostic process can be conceived of as a fact-finding and feeling-finding process. Feelings are as important as, if not more important than, facts in behavior-change problems.

Final responsibility for changing can rest with A or B, or it can be shared. Behavior changers, expecially when they sit in managerially superior positions, tend to feel that the responsibility for change lies exclusively with them. But if B can be made to accept some of the responsibility for personal change, the resulting change is likely to be more lasting and more effective.

10 Authority: What is it, and when does it work?

We turn now to the means and tools of influence, to models for changing behavior, looking at them against the background of chapter 9.

This chapter and the next are largely concerned with the role of power as a tool of influence. This chapter focuses on one "legitimate" form of power, authority; the next considers more extreme forms, like pressure and coercion.

Perhaps it's important to start with a few generalizations. First, one way to define power is simply to treat it as influence that has worked. Thus, all successful influence attempts would be considered (after the fact) to have been manifestations of power. If you have succeeded in getting me to do something you wanted me to do, then you have demonstrated your power over me. Then, of course, we would want to look at what means you used to get me to go your way. That would lead us into different categories, different kinds of power.

Another entirely different way of looking at power is from the input side, in motivational terms. The person who is strongly motivated to influence or control the behavior of other people is said to be *power motivated*. He wants power.

In addition to the question of defining what power is, there is a large set of moral issues here. When should or shouldn't one try to exercise power over another? When is it "legitimate"? Power, after all, is often thought of pejoratively. We talk about "power plays," "power-hungry people," "power politics," and "power tactics." All of those carry connotations, if not of evil, at least of inequity or gamesmanship. All of them stand in sharp contrast to virtuous notions like "fair play," "teamwork," and "merit." And yet it is obvious to any executive (or any parent for that matter) that, if we weren't sophisticated, skillful, and effective users of power, neither the organization nor the family would survive for long. That is not to avoid or deny the huge ethical problems that center around the power question. But it does seem important to recognize from the start that power is here to stay; we influence, or try to influence, other people every day under all sorts of conditions. Although each of must be continuously concerned

121

about using power ethically and justly, it would be nonsensical to deny its central role in human relationships.

What is "authority"?

Consider the kind of power we call "authority." It's only one kind. There are other kinds, too. Some of us can exert "expert" power, like physicians when we're sick. Sometimes we try to use "referent" power, which derives from our instrumental exploitation of our relationships with other powerful people. A good example is the chairman's secretary. Some of us hold "coercive" and "reward" power, the power to punish or reward other people by withholding, withdrawing, or giving resources that we control and that they need, like teachers' use of grades.

Most organizational structures are designed with formal authority in mind. We build organizations in the shape of pyramids in part because that shape makes the exercise of authority easier. In pyramids, we can differentiate among ranks and roles; permitting the people in higher ranks to use the authority of that rank to influence lower ranks. Managers in organizations almost "naturally" turn to authority whenever they want to influence people in subordinate ranks. The very idea of *delegating* authority rests on the assumption that authority can help people who have more of it to change the behavior of those who have less of it. In fact, we often even define the "superior" in an organizational relationship as the person in the role with more authority.

Like other tools, authority can be used expertly or blunderingly. And like other tools, it is used by fallible human beings. Top managers have long since recognized that the delegation of large amounts of authority to middle and lower echelons does not by itself guarantee effective influence over subordinates. Indeed, many executives seem to influence more effectively with less authority than with more, using other more personal methods of influence. And contrarily, some supervisors function better with more authority than with less. The issue is not only how much authority but how it is used and by whom.

There are, however, a few general tips that managers' might want to keep in mind: Don't count on your formal authority to get things done; others may have less authority, but they may also have other kinds of countervailing power that could overwhelm your authority; you'll need more than rank and role to influence your people.

And a related tip, when you do use your formal authority, remember that you can use it effectively only with the consent, tacit or explicit, of the people you are trying to influence.

Let's try some definitions of *authority,* not to be academic but to try to clarify an important though fuzzy concept. Generally, when we talk about authority in organizations, we are thinking about something formal, like *rank.* Authority can be defined by one's military rank, for example. Captains may not know exactly how much authority they have or even what it is, but they know they have more than lieutenants and less than majors.

Formal authority is intended, as we said, to convey power to its holders. Again, like military rank, it conveys power that can be formally given and taken away. "They," the "top brass," somebody up above can change one's rank and thereby one's authority and thereby perhaps one's power over certain others.

Sometimes, however, we relate the words *authority* and *power* differently. We talk about someone with an "authoritative" (synonymous with "powerful") personality. Here we mean something like "influential" or "respect-evoking," but we do not mean formally delegable. We mean something people carry around *inside* themselves, like wisdom or expertise, not something they wear on their shoulders.

Besides this mix-up between formal and personal authority, another confusion results from the word. We can also look at authority from the perspective of those on whom it is used. When we identify with the user, authority looks like a mechanism for coordination and control. But when we take the perspective of the subordinate, authority looks more psychological. It becomes a mechanism by which "they" try to reward or punish us for our behavior.

Here's how we would define *authority:* Authority is one of many kinds of potential power. We use the word here to mean formal, delegable, worn-on-the-shoulders power. Authority is power that enters the two-party relationship through the organization. It is an institutional mechanism that aims to define which of the two members of a relationship, A or B, will be the superior. Authority is potential extra power, given by a third party (the organization) to some of its members in order to guarantee an *un*equal distribution of power; in other words, it makes sure that some people are chiefs and others braves. Sometimes authority has nothing to do with relationships. For example, the organization may assign to A the authority to spend X dollars of its money for supplies. But for managerial purposes, we use the word *authority* to include potential power over other people, power to restrict or punish, and power to reward. For example, the president announces to the superintendent, in the presence of the supervisors, "You are permitted to decide to fire supervisors or to keep them; you are permitted to decide to raise supervisor's pay to this limit or not to raise it." Now the superintendent has some authority—some additional, formal, control over resources beyond and above any other power that he may have carried into the relationship with supervisors.

A difficulty arises at this point. An organization (or a powerful person) cannot delegate all the power it possesses, even if it wants to. A chief executive officer can delegate only certain kinds of potential power by calling it "authority." The forms of power to satisfy or frustrate another person are legion. In organizations, power may take the form of control over concrete resources, like income—a form delegable as authority. Or it may take the form of control over the terms of the relationship. That, too, is delegable as authority. It may be power to provide perquisites that are symbols of status or prestige. That, too, may be partly delegable.

Other kinds of power are not so readily transferred—for example, the power deriving from an individual's competence and skill or from a member's sensitivity to the needs of others. Sensitivity cannot be delegated. One's name, one's social standing in a community, or one's whole personality can be significant forms of power in a relationship, but they too are nontransferable. In fact, only a fraction of the ways one person can control what another may want or need are readily delegable as authority. The delegable forms include mostly external, nonpersonal kinds of power.

This assessment suggests that superiors who turn immediately and exclusively to their authority may either be ignoring many other, often more effective kinds of power, or else they derive their only power from their authority. In either case, their effective range of control over other people's behavior will be narrow.

Authority as seen from the top

If we ask managers whether authority is useful to them, they will surely have some ready and reasonable answers, these among them:

Authority is indeed useful because authority is a mechanism for coordination and control in organizations. People have to be made to come to work on time; and they have to spend their time working, rather than telling stories. They have to carry out company policies and make appropriate decisions. They have to do all those things in regular and predictable ways if the organization is to move forward. Thus, authority is a powerful tool for helping managers implement their decisions and achieve their goals.

When authority is used as a tool for influencing behavior, a good manager might add, it is not just for the hell of it, nor to show people who's boss; it's used to help achieve the organization's goals. Moreover, if the effect of its use is mostly restrictive and limiting for the individual—if it is used mostly to block or to frustrate—that is because organizations are what they are. In large organizations, people cannot just do as they please. Each of us agrees, when we accept a job, to submit to certain restrictive rules and standards. If members of organizations finished projects when they felt like it or always said what they felt like saying, no large organization could survive for long.

From that reasonable perspective, authority becomes a tool with which to restrict behavior (even if restriction frustrates) and to create necessary conformity and homogeneity by leveling out individual variations. It is an important and efficient tool because it has the advantages of the shotgun over the rifle. We can broadcast restrictions and rules, and then use our authority to back up those restrictions when someone steps beyond the bounds. The mere presence of authority (precisely because it can be used to deter nonconformists) will keep most people within the rules most of the time.

The legal structure seems a fair analogy. Laws provide a threat of punishment for anyone in the population who steps outside the bounds. We need that threat even though most people would obey most laws without threat. However, to carry the legal analogy a little further, even the threat of punishment can become insufficient when a specific law comes to be seen by too many people to be too restrictive. The issue here is much like the issue of frustration versus deprivation. Restriction that only deprives is tolerable, especially if it has accompanying rewards. Restriction that frustrates can backfire, especially when many are frustrated by the behavior of a few.

Authority as seen from the underside

We can't see the entire spectrum of authority in action if we just watch the boss using it. Whether A has or has not effectively blocked or controlled B is determined almost entirely by B's interpretation of A's actions. The perceived world, after all, is the world that determines how we behave. Thus the mere appearance of the CEO in a department may be seen as a threat by some people in that department. Or if we are extremely insecure and distrustful of all people in positions of authority, we may interpret *any* act by someone of higher rank as a threat even when that higher-ranking person is busy patting us on the head. In fact, those in a superior role almost always have to work harder than peers or subordinates if they want to be seen as rewarding and nonrestrictive. The reason again is the dependency of the subordinate on the superior. No matter how nice Papa may be, he is still Papa, and the belt of authority around his middle *could* be used as a whip.

Even though the boss's position carries continual implications of potential restriction, the intensity of such implications depends on the boss's own behavior. Certainly many organizational superiors use their authority in ways that generate much more confidence than fear from their subordinates. Limited and consistent restrictions on our behavior can be seen by most of us as quite "reasonable," and only a little depriving, especially if the atmosphere in our unit is generally satisfying to our interests and motives.

Most organizational subordinates, then, probably see authority in the same way their superiors do—as a tool to be used by those upstairs to restrict and control their activities. But, though they may see the same thing, they usually attach different meanings to it. Whereas the boss interprets restriction in cool organizational terms, as control and coordination, the subordinates' interpretation may be far more personal and emotional.

The propensity to obey authority

In the 1960s some impressive research was carried out demonstrating just how much many of us have come to accept authority and to obey it almost without question. The reader may remember those "obedience" studies. The experiments were typical psychological ones in which volunteers were paid to serve as subjects. They were asked to help as "teachers" in an experiment designed to test the effects of punishment on learning. They were given an electric shocking device and told to push the shock buttons every time the "learner" in the next room gave a wrong answer to a memory question. They were also told to increase the intensity of shock with each wrong answer, up to a point on the shock machine marked with dramatic danger warnings. The "learner" in the next room was actually a shill who was part of the experimental team; no shocks were actually delivered. His job was to groan and, on occasion, to scream in pain as the shocks apparently grew stronger. He would, in late stages of the experiment, beg to be released and complain that he was suffering from a heart ailment.

The results came as an unwelcome surprise both to the researchers themselves and to many other presumably sophisticated observers. Most experts had forecast that very few subjects would push the shock buttons all the way to the maximum. In fact, about 50 percent followed orders to the hilt, even while believing that they were inflicting very severe electric shocks on a screaming middle-aged man with heart disease. (Something close to that figure holds up for many different kinds of people.) And the person giving the orders had no "real" power. He was just a guy in a white coat running the experiment.

What those experiments suggest is that there is a strong propensity for people to obey even very minimal authority. It is not, it seems, just because we fear sanctions—like getting fired—that most of us obey orders. We seem to obey anybody who wears even the simplest trappings of authority (in this case, a white lab coat), even if it is obvious that no significant sanctions can be imposed on us for refusal to obey. We may fuss and complain, but to a disturbing and frightening extent, we also obey.

Perhaps, then, we must be careful as managers in assuming that our organizations run smoothly because we are such great managers, such effective users of authority. Rather, they run because our subordinates were taught, long before they came to work for us, to obey authority. Mama and Papa did a great job of socializing them. Maybe we aren't as masterfully authoritative as we would like to believe. Those people don't just obey *us*. They obey anybody!

And if that is true, perhaps we should be more concerned about how *not* to use authority than how to use it. Perhaps we should worry more, that is, about getting our subordinates to question our authority and to think for themselves before they obey that order.

The advantages of authority

From the manager's viewpoint, the advantages of authority, especially restrictively used authority, are huge. We have already cited two of them—the control-and-coordination advantage and the easy-because-any-damn-fool-can-use-it advantage. There are many others.

For one thing, one doesn't have to know much about any particular Joe Doaks to be fairly certain that firing him or cutting his pay or demoting him will strike at some important needs and thereby keep him in line. But one might have to know a good deal about the same employee to find out how to make work more fun for him.

A corollary advantage, then, is simplicity. Authority as a restrictive tool does not require much subtlety or much understanding of people's motives. How simple it is to spank a child who misbehaves, and how difficult and complicated to distract the child, provide substitute satisfactions, or "explain" the situation. Given a hundred children, how much easier it is to keep them in line by punishing a few recalcitrants than by teaching them all to feel "responsible."

And we cannot ignore the fact that exerting authority is often personally gratifying to superiors, and therefore attractive. The exercise of discipline over others can be reassuring to those who need reassurance about themselves. Moreover, authority fits neatly with organizational superiors' needs, if they have any, to blow off aggression deriving from their own frustration. When parents spank children they don't just change the child's behavior but provide themselves with an outlet for tensions built up in them, by their boss, or spouse, or the irritating, troublesome child.

Similarly, authority is sometimes seen, perhaps properly, as a way for organizational superiors to guarantee their superiority. If your subordinates know that you can and will punish readily, they are likely to behave respectfully and submissively, at least in your presence. The reassurance derived from these visible demonstrations of respect may represent a great distortion of true feelings, but it can be helpful to the superior's own uncertain psyche. Bosses who take an essentially supportive approach seldom receive such simple reassurance. Like the good big brother of part 1, they may be complained to or complained against. They may get accurate feedback, even if it is unpleasant. They may have to tolerate emotionally upset people telling them stupid, even insulting things. If managers want shelter from unpleasant realities, let them use their authority restrictively.

Restrictive authority has another kind of advantage: speed. A do-it-or-else order eliminates the time-consuming dillydallying of feedback. But speed may cost both accuracy and morale. Where those issues are not critical, speed may be worth its costs.

Restrictive authority, we have said, also has the advantage of imposing orderliness and conformity on an organization. Large numbers of people can be made to conform to fundamental regulations. A manager *must* make sure that his people stay through the required eight hours of the day. Even though the great majority may conform without external threat, the superior has to guarantee minimum conformity by all employees. The job of obtaining willing or self-imposed conformity without threat may just look too big to handle. Moreover, such restrictive authority looks efficient because it can be used on large numbers of people at the same time, even when one doesn't know much about those people.

If those are the pros, here are some cons worth thinking about:

First, restrictive authority carries some by-products. When A's activity interferes with B's efforts, B may not sit still very long. A often has caught crabs instead of lobsters. A has changed behavior not intended to be changed as well as (or instead of) behavior intended to be changed. Children who are spanked every time they put a hand into the cookie jar *may* learn to keep their hands out of the cookie jar, but they also may learn to go to the jar only when grownups aren't looking. They may also learn (irrationally) that their parents are out to keep them from getting what they want. Employees who expect to be censured whenever they are caught loafing may learn to *act* busy (and *when* to act busy) and also learn that the boss is an enemy. They are thereby provided with a challenging game to play against the boss: Who can think up the most creative ways of loafing without getting caught? That sort of game, in which they can feel that justice is on their side, is a game they can usually win.

Restriction, then, can be effective in changing specific *actions* in the direction A wants (e.g., B will *act* busy), but often only to the minimum that B can get away with. Such restriction is less likely to change B's attitudes in the desired direction. When it does change attitudes, it may change them in the general direction of distrust and hostility.

Moreover, another negative element may enter the scene when restrictive authority is called on. Restriction by A often produces an unintended downward spiraling relationship between A and B. A begins by trying to change B through the exercise of threatening authority. B changes to the extent that seems necessary, but because of frustration also feels aggressive, and in one way or another may retaliate. A then uses more restriction, this time to control the retaliation. Again, B is frustrated, and wants even more to retaliate. And so it goes.

It might seem that such a serious downward spiral can occur only in relationships between equals. In a subordinate role, B should not have enough power to retaliate effectively. But subordinates do have power in relationships, even though the power may be different from and less than the superior's. So long as B has any power, and so long as the relationship exists, B can retaliate. Sometimes this is accomplished by joining together with colleagues, perhaps to form a union. Sometimes B does it by cutting down or distorting the flow of feedback on which the superior depends so heavily. Often, B and several colleagues work together, informally. For instance, a group of middle managers may succeed in defeating a superior they dislike and fear by using passive resistance; they simply do everything the superior asks them to do—*and no more.*

The tenuousness and self-defeating weakness of reliance on restrictive authority become apparent right here. When their authority has been "undermined" by the "sabotage" of subordinates, superiors who have depended on authority are likely to assume that what they need is *more authority,* because authority is the only tool they know how to use. But is it possible for the CEO or the board, in fact, to delegate authority that will guarantee that superiors will be able successfully to coerce their subordinates into doing more than they are told? More likely the CEO will simply begin to view the superiors as the people on whom it is now appropriate for the CEO to exert restrictive authority.

It is therefore a serious error to assume that the *greater* power in a relationship equals the *only* power. As parents, we may start out feeling that power lies exclusively in our hands, only to change our minds radically when one of the children runs away from home or gets hurt. It is also a serious error to think that delegable power—authority—is a useful weapon in *all* hierarchical conflicts.

Still another difficulty with restrictive authority is its relative irreversibility. It is just not as easy to pat subordinates on the head after spanking them as it is to spank them after patting. Human beings have memories. Since restriction tends to reduce feedback rather than increase it, a series of restrictive experiences for B may destroy the possibility of further communication between A and B. Once A has lost communicational contact, *no* tools of influence are likely to work very well.

In fact, the irreversibility of such methods sometimes creates difficulties even for those who preach a supportive, "human-relations" approach to superior/subordinate relationships. Restrictive managers, exposed to human-relations propaganda, will sometimes see the light and change methods completely. Overnight the scowl becomes a smile; the office door is thrown open. Then comes the rude awakening. Subordinates don't behave right. They don't dance in the aisles. They "take advantage" of their new freedom. At that point the managers decide they were taken in by those "soft" ideas. They revert to the "right" way—the way they had been using to begin with.

Obviously, that kind of sudden reversal from restrictive to satisfying behavior is unwise, just as it is unwise to leave a candy-starved child alone with five pounds of chocolates. The child is likely to gorge. That behavior may then be taken as "proof" that letting children have their own way doesn't work.

Added together, the pros and cons of restrictive authority lead toward the following general conclusions: Restrictive methods can be effective in situations that meet some or all of these conditions: (1) the change that A is trying to bring about is a change in a specific overt activity, rather than in generalized action or attitude; (2) the restrictions are seen by B as depriving rather than frustrating; (3) the balance of power is such that B's power is minimal and A's maximal; (4) restriction can be effective when speed and/ or uniformity are of the essence.

Many organizations have long since learned some of these lessons, mostly the hard way. Authority as a direct and openly restrictive weapon is used more consciously at lower levels than at higher ones. Lower organizational levels are (or once were) the levels at which B's actions, more than attitudes, become the targets of influence. They are also usually the levels at which employees have already retaliated by organizing, so that restrictions, openly imposed, have often become more depriving than frustrating. And lower levels also used to be the levels at which the power difference between A and B was greatest, though that too is less clear today than in the past.

At higher levels we have tended to be more interested in changing attitudes than actions, and we have learned that a B can wield power, too. So, broadly speaking, we lean less heavily on restrictive authority as we move up the pyramid. A vice-president who shows up a half-hour late is not likely to be "disciplined." We use more subtle weapons to shape the behavior of higher-level executives.

Key ideas in the authoritarian model

Consider now the relationships between this discussion of authority and our discussion in the preceding chapter of the dimensions of the influence problem.

First, what kinds of motives is the user of authority likely to be working from? Toward what objectives? Usually when we label someone "authoritarian," we intend to connote domineering, power-seeking motives. And certainly many of us, when we order our subordinates around, are motivated by our needs for power and dominance. But many of us also use authority for less emotional, more rational reasons. Authority, in any complex social system, is a means to orderliness. We use authority as a mechanism to coordinate complex, multiperson activities, as well as a mechanism of control.

Second, what kinds of assumptions about B's motives are made when we take such authoritarian positions? One may be the old white-man's-burden assumption, that other people, like our children or our subordinates, are too dull or naive to understand anything but the direct application of authority; they are too lazy to work without a push. But a very different assumption that may also underlie the use of authority is that B perceives the world as we do, at least as far as authority is concerned, that B perceives our use of authority in this situation as reasonable and legitimate. Perhaps B isn't a dummy at all but quite intelligent—intelligent enough, in fact, to recognize the need for legitimate authority. By the first view, the commanding officer gives the orders because the troops can't or won't make their own decisions. By the second view, the officer gives the orders because the situation demands some single center of control; the officer's role is legitimate and necessary.

Third, what assumption does the authoritarian model make about the relationship between A and B? First, it usually assumes that the responsibility for change lies with A rather than B. In fact, it is precisely out of authoritarian models that the "principle" that "authority should be commensurate with responsibility" emerged. When I give an instruction, by this view, its outcome is *my* responsibility. Responsibility is the burdensome but legitimate price I must pay for the right to give such orders.

Clearly, then, the motives behind the use of authority may range from needs for self-aggrandizement, to protection of the status quo, to efficiency and orderliness. Notice, however, that those motives do *not* include more social and affiliative motivations; notions about love aren't included here, nor even is much emphasis given to A's motives to achieve. These social and achievement motives in B are taken more into account by other approaches to influencing behavior in organizations.

One good thing to be said about authority is that its use is usually quite direct, open, and aboveboard. No slipperiness, no circumlocution, and no game playing exist when your boss is a plain old authoritarian type. Orders come straight, clean, and perhaps nasty, too. Moreover, there is an impersonal quality to authoritarian influence. It is rules, laws, and contracts that justify its application, not personal feelings like affection or hatred. The authoritarian father takes his son to the woodshed—or he believes he does—because the boy has broken known rules or because the boy "has to learn." He does not consciously take him there out of dislike or vindictiveness. Conversely, he does not offer rewards out of love or personal esteem, but rather because his son has lived up to the rules, accomplished the agreed goal, carried out his "duties."

These ideas, then, prevail in the authoritarian model: order and efficiency, in a perceived world full of people who are most interested in goofing off; the legitimate "right" to use authority; and impersonal, rational "contracts" between employer and employee.

In the next chapters we contrast some of those ideas with the beliefs underlying other approaches to influencing behavior in organizations.

In summary

Formal authority is intended as a delegable kind of power. Power to influence behavior may also derive from other sources, largely from the skills, personality, and possessions of the changer.

Restrictive authority is seen by managers as a tool for coordination and control. It has advantages in simplicity, speed, and personal gratification to powerful changers who feel unsure of themselves. It also helps to establish a minimum level of conformity by all subordinates to the superior's standards.

A major difficulty inherent in restrictive authority is the probability of unintended second-order changes accompanying the desired changes. Restriction may generate frustration and may consequently be followed by aggression toward the changer. Restriction may then incur only a minimal amount of the desired behavior change while incurring significant increases in hostility and decreases in accurate feedback. Restriction may thereby destroy A-B relationships.

One reason authority often works quite effectively lies with the subordinate, rather than the organizational superior. Bosses can give most orders successfully, not because they are inspiring or persuasive leaders but because most of us have been taught—from a very early age—to obey *anybody* who wears any trappings of authority.

Authority, as a restrictive mechanism, seems to be most useful in short-term, specific situations, where B's retaliatory power is minimal, where the change sought is change in specific overt action, and where the restrictions are perceived as depriving rather than frustrating.

The authoritarian view of influence is likely to be motivated in part by needs for order, efficiency, and control. It assumes either that B is less competent than A or that A's role legitimizes A's use of authority on B. It also assumes a kind of B who is willing to accept and live by impersonal rules and contracts.

11

Power tactics:
Pressure, brainwashing,
blackmail, and more

The authority we considered in the last chapter was mostly a formal kind of power, organized into a quasi-legal system of rules and roles. Everybody knows that company presidents can tell junior executives what to do. Indeed, the extent of that president's authority may even be quite clearly specified. But the kind of power we consider in this chapter isn't that bounded kind, nor even always a legitimate kind. It's the power that one picks up when one finds it and uses for personal or group ends only so long as it works. In this chapter we focus on other varieties of power—especially coercive varieties like blackmail, pressure, and threat—the power tactics almost all of us profess to despise, but which, unfortunately, almost all of us use from time to time.

Power as reduction

We need not remind any modern reader that much of the influencing going on in our world uses the tools of terror and threat. Such coercive power tactics usually depend on the reduction (or threat of reduction) of other people's opportunities to get what they want, accompanied by a demand for behavior change.

The powerful nation masses its troops at the border of the weak one and says, "Unless you return the territory (which is, of course, historically rightfully ours), we will invade you." The gunman demands, "If you want your life, give me your money."

But notice. The supervisor saying, "Come to work on time or you'll be fired," is a reductive use of power, too. Yet for a supervisor, to threaten to fire an employee is a *legitimate* use of authority, isn't it?

One of the big issues that arises here is the issue of social *legitimacy*. When is such reductive power considered by the relevant group, by the larger society, or by the world to be legitimate or illegitimate? When is such behavior within the rules and when isn't it? Who makes the rules, and how are they changed? That supervisor could have "legitimately" fired a worker for a minor offense in 1920; but since then workers have used some power tactics of their own, so they have been able to change some of the rules. That supervisor's behavior might look arbitrary and illegitimate today.

We are dealing, then, with a floating crap game in this chapter, with ever changing boundaries of social rules and social values. We are dealing with the "social construction of reality." But we are also examining the psychological issue of the reductive uses of power.

Let's consider the psychological issue a little more before returning to the broader social issue.

Notice that attempts to influence by reduction don't always work. Supervisor A may have misjudged the relevance of a threat to fire B. This week, B may just be starting on a far-out new life-style that doesn't call for a job at all. The supervisor may then have misjudged B's vulnerability. Or perhaps our B has enough support from buddies to be willing to test the supervisor's ability to carry out the threat. B organizes colleagues and discovers that the supervisor is scared to death of having the whole department aligned against him. Now carry that same idea along to areas not quite covered by the rules of the legitimate game and we enter into the realm of this chapter. "Give me an exclusive interview," demands the columnist of the senator, "or I will publish a story about your weekend with your assistant." "Give up those investments in firms doing business in South Africa," demand the students of the college president, "or we'll boycott all our classes."

Power and dependency

Power is closely associated with that old troublemaker, dependency. If B is more dependent on A than A is on B, then A has the potential for exerting power over B.

But we come now to a difficult question: How does one decide which member of a relationship is the more dependent? Most of the time the answer to that question appears more obvious than it really is. It is obvious that the lieutenant has power over the sergeant. Or is it obvious? Suppose it's a new, young second lieutenant and a seasoned, old sergeant. It is obvious that the teacher has power over a student. The teacher can fail or discipline the student. But is the teacher really more powerful? If you lived around an American university in the late 1960s and early 1970s, the balance of power in the teacher-student relationship would have seemed much less clear. And students fill out faculty rating forms these days, and the dean reads them! Or they write nasty letters to the campus paper about this faculty member or that one. Who's really in charge? Who's influencing whom? The reader surely can go on and cite other examples from personal experience. They may range from the father's discovery that his teenage son is no longer willing to do what he's told (and may be able to back up his unwillingness with his fists) to the panic of the young officer who discovers that the troops are just going to stand there deadpan and not accept what they are ordered to do.

There is another kind of dependency that for most of us has been so implicit and so pervasive that we are seldom even conscious of it. It is the dependency involved in our relationship with the aggregate of people we call society. It is our dependency, in effect, on law and order, our expectation that other people on the street, *all* other people, will obey minimal social rules in their interactions with us. When that dependency is violated, when one of us is mugged, when someone smashes our windows, or when terrorists hijack a plane, we begin to appreciate both the extent of our dependency on societal rules and the fragility of those rules. If we consider the other side of that same coin, we can empathize with what must be the exhilarating discovery of power that comes with a successful breaking of the social rules. What a thrill it must have been for students to discover the vulnerability of their university administrations back in the 1960s, to discover, as it were, their own muscle.

Power and the rules of the game

The important point is that A may appear more powerful than B, but may in fact be more powerful *only so long as both A and B play the game within a particular system of social rules*. Those rules, implicit or explicit, may range from the acceptance of the hierarchy of authority in an organization, to mutual respect for private property, to a mutual agreement not to use physical force. One important way to try to influence other people, then, is unexpectedly to violate the rules of the relationship. The captors torture the prisoner, despite the Geneva Convention; the terrorist drops the bomb in the department store; the politician broadcasts a big lie about an opposing candidate. Notice that rule breaking is not the property of underdogs alone. It can be done by those at the top of the relationship or by a peer, as well as by those at the bottom. In the short run it is an infuriating, often terrifying, and frequently effective method and a most difficult tactic to defend oneself against.

In the late 1960s, for instance, blacks and other protest groups learned the value of "mau-mauing" and other rule-breaking (not necessarily lawbreaking) techniques. Most college administrators, most executives, and most government officials expect and can deal with (which may mean "stall" or prevaricate throughout) "normal" across-the-table negotiations. But they are likely to be flustered and, therefore, put in a weaker bargaining position when they are confronted by a hundred men, women, and children crowding the office, shouting approval of their leader's statements, and booing at everything the official tries to say.

Notice that such power tactics (or better, counterpower tactics) need not be illegal, though they are often seen by their victims as "illegitimate" or "unfair." And notice that the utility of any particular surprise tactic is probably short-lived. Once the other side learns to expect them, defenses against them can usually be improvised. But the process is dynamic. If my defense against crowd pressure is to get a law passed forbidding gatherings of more than five people on the steps of public buildings, two things are likely to follow: (1) the creative invention of brand-new surprise tactics to outgame the new regulations, and (2) the psychological "freeing" of the other side, which now can feel justified in going outside the law into guerrilla or terrorist tactics. In such downhill spirals, "legitimate" defenses, such as new laws, then become quite useless.

Some sources of coercive power

People's skill at coercive persuasion is as old as human kind. We've been extraordinarily creative in developing everything from torture racks to isolation cells. Humans are expert in the techniques of extortion and blackmail, riot and political pressure. But this chapter is not intended as a treatise on the tactics of coercion. It is intended rather to alert managers to the importance of such tactics in the life of contemporary organizations.

Most of the sources of power we have discussed so far supply the manager with "legitimate" power, but they can also be used for coercion. Clearly, one such source of power is ownership of resources. If I have the Bomb and you don't, I can coerce you. If I have money and you don't, I can coerce you—if your needs are susceptible to manipulations by money. That last qualification brings up the issue of relativity again. I can coerce you only if the resources I control are important to you. If your needs are irrelevant to my resources, I have no power over you. If your needs change so that they are no longer relevant to my resources, I no longer have power over you.

Another traditional source of coercive power lies in collective action by large numbers of people. Throughout human history, from the uprisings of the slaves to the organization of workers and the massing of armies, large numbers have been one of the great sources of coercive power, modifying the behavior of kings, college presidents, and, on occasion, of generals. But let us remember that numbers are not always used in the interest of the good guys. Crowds also lynch people.

We must not forget still another extremely important source of power, albeit a very different and a much more direct one: anonymity. Anonymity is almost never considered legitimate in any society, and it is almost always directly coercive. If you have ever received an anonymous threatening phone call or have had a cross burned on your lawn, you have been exposed to this source. Once again, that kind of coercive behavior is not limited to the underdog in desperate search for some kind of retaliatory power. It is often used by those in authority—from leaking anonymous stories to the press to using agents surreptitiously to start revolutions. Although such coercive behavior is almost never officially sanctioned, it is a form of control that is nevertheless widely used, secretly, by many "legitimate" organizations.

Brainwashing

Since the Korean War, the word *brainwashing* has become well known in American society. It first achieved notoriety during that war as a characterization of the "illegitimate" methods used by the Chinese to convert American prisoners to the Chinese ideology. The phrase has since been used again and again in relation to issues such as Patty Hearst's apparent collusion with her captors, or the Reverend Moon's methods for converting young people to his church.

Brainwashing is a loose concept with many shades of meaning. Mostly it refers to a form of coercive persuasion that is *not* based primarily on threat. People are not "brainwashed" by do-it-or-else methods. No threats of solitary confinement or physical torture are used here. Brainwashing involves the rather subtle exploitation of some now well-known truths about the rationalizing nature of human beings, and the principles of attitude and behavior change. We know, for example, that most people are much more vulnerable to influence when their social support systems are removed, and they feel they are all alone. If we can isolate you from your traditional group memberships, from the people who reinforced your old behavior, you become more susceptible to influence. Obviously, with prisoners of war, we have the direct coercive power to remove individuals from their support groups or to control the information they get. We can set up conditions that can cause an individual to believe that his buddies, his officers, or indeed his whole society can no longer be trusted. Thus isolated, you become more susceptible to influence. Now, in your lonely state, we can urge you, cajole you, almost seduce you into taking small steps in the directions we choose. And small steps are enough. If we can now get you to agree to even a small piece of our ideology, we can go on to reinforce that choice and make the next steps easier. For example, we can now place you, having been isolated, into a new group composed of people who will actively support your changed attitudes, reassuring you that your small movements in our direction are right and proper. Your new group not only helps convince you that your new behavior is legitimate; they also promise you full membership if you go further.

The process of brainwashing is essentially no more than the process once described by a famous social psychologist as "freezing, unfreezing, and refreezing." It is a process, if one thinks about it, that we use widely in education when we take students from their homes and put them on a college campus. We isolate them from most of their previous groups and then provide them with new paths that are locally reinforced by faculty and peers. And we use rituals, examinations, and cheerleaders to reinforce the changes. Companies, armies, and fraternities do much the same things.

Where does one draw the line between legitimate "socialization" and "education," on the one hand, and illegitimate "brainwashing" on the other? Is it "brainwashing" when parents try to educate their children into high moral standards? What if the moral standards favor sexual promiscuity, or stealing, or using hard drugs? Or what if they favor wearing uniforms, carrying guns, and beating up blacks or Irishmen or other ethnic or racial groups?

Do managers need to use power tactics?

Of course they do. Changing others, persuading, and negotiating all necessarily require the use of one's available resources to influence behavior. Managers promise people promotions, set up attractive situations for new recruits, selectively withhold information, and personally use their dramatic skills to get other people to do what they want them to do. And they also threaten people.

Managers have power. They control resources that other people need. Skillful and ethical managers use that power to move their organizations ahead. Unskillful managers use that power ineffectively or are so modest or unaware that they don't use as much of it as they should. Unethical managers use it to aggrandize themselves at the expense of their employees and their organizations.

What are some of the resources most managers control? Some use their rights to hire, to fire, to promote, and to pay. Other less obvious resources are perhaps even more important. For instance, they may use control over something other executives must depend on to get their work done. "If you don't give me what I want, colleague, your project goes to the bottom of my department's priority list." Or they may use control—psychological control—over a subordinate's access and support. One senior executive we knew was a master at cutting off communication selectively and periodically with certain subordinates. Suddenly one would find that the boss was simply not available—no answers to phone messages, no more drop-in visits, no listening to great ideas. It was a powerful power tool that sent some subordinates into anxiety and depression—and often brought them into line.

Then there was the senior civil servant we knew, a personnel officer, who referred to his cabinet-level boss as "Christmas help." The civil servant controlled all the key appointments and, moreover, he told us, he also had friends on the Hill. Cabinet members came and went, he said, but *he* decided who they could hire and who they couldn't.

Sometimes the resources an executive controls are only temporarily important to others. The surgeon controls resources we need when our appendix is about to rupture. At other times the surgeon may not carry much clout with us. The organization's lawyers become powerful when that antitrust suit is filed. So alert executives are aware of the current state of their resource control and are aware that their power may be fleeting.

You can surely add, from your own experience, to a list of various kinds of power that managers can exercise. And any reader can probably cite examples of the misuse of power by executives, either clumsy, ineffectual misuses or unethical ones.

The central point is a simple one. Managers have power. They would be foolish to be unaware of what kinds and how much power they have, foolish to deny it on some vague egalitarian grounds, foolish to misuse it for selfish rather than organizational ends, and foolish to be seduced by their power or by those around them into immoral and unethical uses of that most important managerial tool.

Power—the control of resources needed by others—can take many forms—from sitting on the money, to knowing the right people, to occupying a key position in a production or communication network, to having the skills the organization needs the most right now, to taking hostages.

Power and legitimacy

Perhaps most outside-the-rules, illegitimate uses of power tactics are practiced by groups or individuals who are also outside the society. What most of us consider "illegitimate" attempts to exert power—blackmail, terrorism, revolution—often (but not always) come from people who see themselves as outside the mainstream, members of minorities or other protesting subgroups or disaffected civil servants.

It's not that the "in" group people are good guys, clean and legal in their power tactics. Rather, they use legitimate means mostly because they are the "in" groups. That usually means that they have written the rules of the game. When we set up the rules, it is not surprising that those rules tend to favor our beliefs, values, and abilities.

So it is understandable that groups that are excluded, or exclude themselves, often turn to what the "in" group considers illegitimate power tactics, like Gandhi's passive resistance, or the burning of draft cards by young people during the Vietnam years, or the theft of the Pentagon papers.

In companies, comparable events also occur. Subgroups that feel ignored or mistreated pack up and go to work for a competitor or start a competitive business of their own; or individuals go to the press with scandalous (often true) stories about illegitimate company practices. Managers, therefore, have still another good reason to keep in close touch with their people, even with the people they don't like or trust. By learning about disaffection early, managers can often eliminate its causes or absorb it.

On the other side, "in" groups have been known to use illegitimate tactics, too. Sometimes it's naked greed or ambition that drives it. But often it's something more subtle, like pressure on the manager from superiors. Top management expects us to beat last year's performance, but the market has gone sour and competitors are cutting prices. So we fudge a little, or do a little price-fixing deal with our counterparts in competitive companies, or play some tricky accounting games.

The probability of that kind of illegitimate behavior can be sharply reduced if top management is clean and strong about its values, as well as sensitive to the pressures it is exerting on the people in the organization. Many of the crimes of organizational subordinates can properly be blamed on the practices of their organizational "superiors."

One more point on the legitimacy issue. A legitimate tactic today can become illegal tomorrow. Organizations do not control all their own rules. Society gets its fingers into the pie, too. Organizational behaviors considered legitimate by society change over time. Certainly, businesses are one set of institutions for which the societal definition of legitimacy has changed radically in recent years. In the 1960s and 1970s, more and more of what had previously been considered unquestionably legitimate in business practice came under fire. Societal controls over business behavior increased, from what the company had to print on the labels of its products, to how much information the company could withhold from its employees, to where the company could dump its toxic waste. In the '80s, with deregulation as the byword, we began to shift in the other direction, freeing up advertisers, manufacturers, and transportation services from many of those regulations.

Yet the general perspective of this chapter is correct. We should expect that more time and effort will be spent by CEOs to try to confirm their organization's legitimacy and, at the same time, to fight the constraining regulations that have been imposed on them. The organization, regulated or not, is under public scrutiny. We are in a time when "strategies of legitimating" are more critical than ever in the lives of American organizations. And that probably also means more difficult moral choices for the manager than ever before.

In summary

This chapter is about power tactics as mechanisms of influence. Such tactics, ranging from coercive tools like torture to more subtle brainwashing, have been around for a long time. A major protection against the now coercive tactics has been the evolution of social rules and humanitarian values. Those rules and values, of course, depend heavily on changing social consensus. Coercive tactics are periodically used, however, by deviant groups or individuals who hold little other power or by legitimate organized authority to keep those deviant subgroups in line. Both sides are likely to justify such outside-the-rules tactics as the only feasible means to the ends that they desperately seek. No society in history has ever developed foolproof protection against terror or other coercive tactics, whether the tactics are applied by other societies, by recalcitrant members of their own society, or by their own institutions under threat. Our society is no exception. It behooves business managers, even now, to look to their organizations' defenses against such tactics and even more to the capacity of their organizations to deal with such tactics or with changing societal pressure without responding in kind.

Within the organization, managers had better keep in touch with all subgroups to catch disaffection early. They had also better be aware of the pressures on them, from above, to meet standards that can only be met by violating the rules. Moreover, it is important to realize that the line between "coercive" and "legitimate" persuasive tactics often becomes very fuzzy. The "brainwashing" that most of us deplore is, in principle, not very different from the "education" that most of us positively value.

This is a red-alert chapter. Its message: Managers are powerful and should acknowledge and use their power. But watch out! Coercive power is alive and well, in organizations and in society at large. Managers need to worry constantly about their own morality as they use their power to modify their people's behavior.

12

Manipulation:
Slippery styles for
influencing behavior

If we were to ask a military officer how to get subordinates to do things, we would probably hear a lecture on issuing orders. That's authority. If we were to ask a loan shark how to get clients to repay debts, we would probably be shown a couple of large, dour characters lounging in the shadows. That's power. But if we were to ask salespeople how they get customers to buy things, or politicians how they get people to vote for them, we would hear somewhat different kinds of answers. The common elements would include notions like these: "You've got to make them think it's their idea"; "You've got to make them like you"; "You've got to sell yourself"; "You've got to act sincere"; "You have to make them believe that you're in favor of the things that are really important to them." That's manipulation.

How are those answers different—as they obviously are—from the kinds of authoritarian ideas we talked about in chapter 10 and the power tactics of chapter 11?

One of the biggest differences, of course, is that what we are calling "manipulative models" pay a great deal of rather sophisticated attention to human emotions and human relationships. They acknowledge that they want to influence people in specific directions, that human beings are driven by multiple, often unconscious motives, and that they usually want support, approval, recognition, and all the rest. In that respect, these approaches contrast sharply with the authoritarian methods, which assume rational, objective beings who obey rules and understand contracts. And they contrast with most power approaches—which concentrate largely on only a few human motives—notably fear, greed, and ambition.

Those manipulative ideas carry another distinct flavor, too. They carry a quality of surreptitiousness, or slipperiness, at least in their implications. "You've got to make them think it's their idea" implies, of course, that the idea is really yours, not theirs.

We notice a third quality, too. These are the kinds of ideas that might come to mind when thinking about how to influence organizational peers or superiors; but we would be less likely to consider them seriously when dealing with our subordinates.

They differ from authoritarian approaches in another way, too. The person using an authoritarian model can be fairly open and direct. If I am your boss and tell you to do something *right now,* there's nothing very hidden about my intent or my objectives. Even blackmailers and stickup men usually communicate their purposes quite clearly! But when the insurance salesman or the politician sidles up to you at a cocktail party, you begin to suspect some devious, unannounced motives, some *hidden* purposes.

This point probably gets at the heart of the manipulative problem. It is the reason that so many of us want to reject it and retaliate against it. That kind of attitude—that I will make you think it's your idea—is seen by most of us as denigrating, as an attempt to play us for suckers. If A succeeds, then B is never aware of having been manipulated, and A wins. But if A fails, if B suddenly becomes aware of being manipulated, then B is apt to retaliate rather violently.

The growth of manipulative models

Manipulative models have been with us for a long, long time. They show themselves to a fare-thee-well in the writings of Machiavelli, and even earlier. From about 1930 onward, newer versions became especially popular in sales training, an understandable phenomenon. For salespeople enter into relationships often at their own initiative with customers who are usually at least as powerful as they are. Authority isn't a very useful tool for them. On the other hand, salespeople have a rather clear and precise objective, which varies little from day to day or customer to customer. The salespeople at a Ford dealership don't want customers to buy an automobile; they want them to buy a Ford, and to buy it from them. So the task for salespeople is very clear. It is to get those people to take a specific action, but they have to do it without authority and usually without coercion.

Out of this specific problem—the problem of trying to get B to do precisely what A wants B to do, without using authority or other direct power—has emerged a series of sophisticated manipulative models for influence. Those models all share six key ideas, although they may vary considerably in other respects:

1. A's motives are not to be made fully known to B. A wants to sell magazine subscriptions, but starts out to convince B that A is really not selling anything at all, just offering free samples. The gigolo really wants a white Mercedes, but the motives he communicates are love and affection.

2. The manipulative models usually use the relationship between A and B as a tool for influence. Most of the manipulative approaches are essentially two-step processes: (1) develop the relationship with B so that B comes to value it; (2) use the now-valuable relationship itself as a resource, a bargaining weapon to effect change. The magazine salesperson tries to develop in a customer feelings of sympathy and support. "I'm working my

way through night school," the salesperson may say, thus touching the householder's heart, offering the magazines as a means for that householder to show support. The politician offers favors, little services to the people of the ward, and then asks of them the little personal favor of their votes. The paternalistic manager takes a deep personal interest in subordinates, buys them gifts at Christmas and in other ways develops personal rapport with employees; then, consciously or unconsciously, the manager uses those relationships, with their implications of loyalty and friendship, to get desired results.

Just for contrast, it is worth pointing out that the complete authoritarian we described in an earlier chapter does not move in that direction at all. The personal relationship is consciously set aside. The complete authoritarian focuses on the rules, not the relationship; the manipulator works with relationships.

Such manipulation of the A-B relationship can be thought of as an effort to create a kind of dissonance. First, we make you feel love and loyalty toward us. Then, we demand that you change the beliefs you hold dear. Thus we set up an imbalance. For you to love us and yet keep your contrary beliefs places you in a dissonant state. So you must bend either your beliefs or your feelings toward us. If we're clever, you will change your beliefs, not your feelings. But if we fail, that failure understandably, can be followed by an explosion, with the possibility of you shifting from extreme love to extreme hatred.

3. A third and related characteristic of skillful, manipulative A's is that they exploit B's dependency on them. Whereas authoritarians exploit dependency, too, they do so directly and always downward in the hierarchy, demanding that subordinates perform or get fired, that children obey or get punished. But the complete manipulator exploits dependency differently. They exploit it in both directions, upward and downward in the hierarchy, using psychological devices rather than authority. Manipulative executives, for example, may make their way upward in their organization by forming close relationships with some higher-level executive and by trying to make that dependency reciprocal. They search for sponsors, someone with whom they can develop a parent-child kind of intimate relationship. If they can be successfully dependent on some superior, then the superior will be reciprocally dependent on them. It is not surprising that we attribute to women, in Western society, a greater ability than men to manipulate dependency skillfully, for women have historically had to work largely from subordinate, or, at best, peer roles.

Manipulative executives are likely to exploit dependencies downward, too. They will not count on their impersonal role as boss, but rather on their subordinates' personal relationship with them as individuals. They may seek close personal relationships with their people, and then use those deep personal attachments as a base for effecting change.

If they are really consistent manipulators, they will try to have superior and/or subordinates develop very strong attachments toward them, but they will always hold back on the reciprocal end of the deal. Good manipulators never expose themselves completely. Some of their personal motives always remain undisclosed. They must never become so entangled either with subordinates or superiors that they cannot abandon them and move when they need to do so.

4. Users of manipulative methods demonstrate extreme sensitivity to the emotions of B. Good manipulators exploit B's needs for approval, support, recognition, and participation. Aware of the potency of those motives in their two-step process, they make great efforts to sell themselves by offering satisfactions of other people's hungers. This awareness and exploitation of widespread emotional starvation is, of course, precisely what the out-of-bounds manipulators—the con artists—use so effectively. But within the law, it can be these same kinds of wants that manipulative spouses can exploit in their partners, currying favor, flattering, or providing satisfactions that may be hard to come by elsewhere in the world. Thus, manipulative partners increase the value of the relationship and the extent to which they can go on to use it as a bargaining weapon. But manipulators are also fulfilling the partner's emotional needs.

5. Another characteristic of these models is really just an extension of the two-step process. It is the idea of incrementalism. Manipulators do not move precipitously, nor directly, nor completely. They influence in bits and pieces. They use foot-in-the-door tactics, letting B win the first few hands, and then gradually moving B along to the vulnerable position. If they are good con artists, they even "cool out the mark" after B has been taken. They take steps to make sure the widow gets her first dividend after she has been bilked of her savings, so that she will not run off to the police.

6. Finally, it is worth pointing out that manipulative models not only exploit the relationship between A and B but also the relationships between B and other people. There is a step beyond the process of developing a relationship between you and me so that I can later press you to do what I want you to do. That next step is the exploitation of group pressures in your interest, pressures by other people.

The early and primitive stages of the human-relations movement represented such a transfer from the exploitation of the A-B relationship to the exploitation by A's of the relationship between B and others. Much of the early talk about group participation and many of the early experiments on group decisions were seen later as unintentional extensions of those manipulative models. A's still wanted to get people to do what they wanted them to do. And A's still kept some of their motives unexpressed. But now, using group discussion as a tool, A's did not work only to develop the relationship with the group. They also tried to develop cohesiveness and rapport *within the group*. Then, when the group began to move in a particular direction, the individual member would be pressed *by the group* to conform, to move in the same direction. That device was not new, of course, even several decades ago. Any good, rabble-rousing politician knows how easy it is to keep someone from saying "no" in a public meeting once 99 percent of the crowd has already shouted "yes."

So group participation as a tool for influencing behavior had its problems, too, especially in its earlier years. One got workers to accept a change in their methods of working (a *predetermined* methods change) by holding group discussions and by trying to get group members to commit publicly to the change. But in our next chapter we will consider more recent developments on the participative side: collaborative methods for trying to effect change, methods that make intense use of groups, but that try to escape from some of the ethical and technical difficulties of manipulation. As we shall see, that fourth model differs quite sharply from the authoritarian, coercive, and manipulative approaches to influencing behavior.

When is it "helping"?
When it is "manipulating"?

The line between manipulating people and helping them can often get foggy. Psychiatrists score high on manipulation scales, whereas surgeons score low. But is your local psychiatrist, nondirective counselor, or sensitivity group leader trying to manipulate you or trying to help you? In fact, such people probably come a lot closer to manipulating you than does, say, a top sergeant in the army. Almost all of the "helping professions"—teachers, therapists, clergy, physicians, nurses—must worry about the extent to which their efforts to change other people may be more manipulative than they want them to be. One criterion, of course, is whether or not the changer's motives are exposed and open. But is it always sensible for the physician to tell you exactly what each procedure is and why it's done? Might it not be an honest judgment that it is better to withhold some information while building trust, with smiles and small talk? Isn't it often wiser for a therapist to let clients discover the truth for themselves, instead of blurting it out to them?

The point is that manipulation, as we have tried to describe it, is by no means always selfish or unethical. Manipulation is a method. One of the critical considerations involved in the choice of any method is the user's own values.

In summary

The manipulative models for effecting change show up mostly in settings where the use of authority is inappropriate, settings in which A is a peer or subordinate to B. The manipulative approaches share some basic ideas. A manipulative A withholds some private motives from public exposure. An A often uses foot-in-the-door tactics on a B, asking only for little bits, then demanding more. A manipulative A tends to develop close relationships with B, often dependent relationships, and then uses those relationships as tools. The manipulative models tend to take two steps in the influence process—the relationship step followed by the influence step.

For most of us, *manipulation* is a word loaded with deplorable connotations. But in many situations the method can be both useful and, by most standards, also ethical.

13 Collaborative models: Influencing softly, by supporting, helping, and trusting

Authority is an impersonal, formal tool. Coercive power seems a cruel, often inhuman tool. In many situations, manipulation is an ethically questionable and demeaning tool. What, then, are other alternatives?

Some readers may already have discerned, and perhaps been disappointed by, the absence of rules of thumb in this section. The absence will continue, not willfully, but because the nature of the influence process obviates magical, tidy rules. The means of influencing behavior do not reside exclusively in one person. They reside in the *relationship*. If B stood still, A could indeed devise fixed rules for influencing B. But B moves, responds, retaliates, and changes. If we're to come up with any rules at all, they must be rules governing the behavior of the A-B relationship, over time, not just the behavior of one of the elements.

It is true that we could play the probability game. We could say to our salesperson, "This is your spiel. Run it off like a phonograph record. Eighty-five percent of the people you call on will throw you out. Fifteen percent might be influenced." But if managers take that view about influencing subordinates, peers, or superiors, they are in for trouble.

Without expecting rules for answers, then, we can ask, What are the alternatives to the use of authority, power, or manipulation?

The A.A. model

Consider Alcoholics Anonymous. For decades that organization has influenced people in very difficult situations with considerable success. Their objective is to cause drinkers to stop drinking. By what methods can one hope to reach that objective?

People have tried many methods to change alcoholics. Wives have threatened to leave their drinking husbands. Bosses have threatened to fire employees with drinking problems. Churches have warned drinkers of everlasting punishment for their sins. Alcoholics have been isolated from alcohol and forced into "cold turkey" withdrawals. Those are essentially restrictive methods, using power tools to punish. They are concerned with

symptoms rather than causes. They aim at changing overt behavior rather than more fundamental motives or attitudes. Some of them work some of the time. Often they don't work at all.

Direct, negative reinforcement methods have also been used, with mixed success. Put something in B's drinks to cause throwing up with every drink, or give B an electric shock with each drink.

A.A. approaches the problem quite differently. Their procedures work something like this:

- They make the availability of their services (and their motives) known to the alcoholic (who may choose not to use the services).
- If the alcoholic chooses to attend a meeting, he listens to testimonials from ex-alcoholics (which may leave no impression at all—in which case the alcoholic is, again, free to leave).
- If the alcoholic decides that they seem to know what they are talking about, he asks for help (that's not required either).
- The alcoholic is assigned one or more "buddies"—who were once alcoholics, too. The buddies make themselves available (calling on them is voluntary) to talk over the problem or just to hold a hand.

If the alcoholic decides to try to quit drinking, these buddies say what all alcholics already know: it will not be easy. So the alcoholic calls on faith in God, if he has any, and on those buddies. They provide help with support, hand-holding, and a supply of knowledge of the future—for example, "Sure it's tough, but if you hold on a while longer, you begin to feel different, and then it gets easier, and *we know.*" They also provide the knowledge that real changes require a really new way of looking at the world.

When A.A. is successful, the alcoholic stops drinking. But usually it doesn't end there. Often the alcoholic then helps others to stop drinking, as one way of maintaining control and dealing with the new void within.

One finds no threat, no command, and no surreptitiousness in those influence processes. Alcoholics stop drinking; they are not stopped. They are helped to change themselves, helped by being shown alternative means and being supported and coached in learning to use them. The process is augmentative, rather than reductive, and major responsibility never leaves the changee.

Is management different from A.A.?

Managers will point out several differences between the problems they face and the Alcoholics Anonymous problem. First, A.A. can afford to wait for people to recognize their own problems and to seek help. Managers often cannot. They must change people even when those people don't come to them seeking to be changed. Second, A.A. can let people solve their own problems in their own way at their own pace. The business organization requires conformity to certain standard behaviors and to pressures of time.

Finally, the manager will complain of the risks in this A.A. method, the lack of control by A over B. In A.A.'s approach, any alcoholic can just walk out the door any time he feels like it, without changing at all. In business, we have to be sure that people will do what needs doing; we cannot always allow them to decide for themselves whether they would like to or not.

The alert reader will add still another objection: Where is the diagnosis, the understanding of causes in the A.A. approach? A.A. seems to bring about effective behavior change without any attempt to look into the source of alcoholism—the frustrations and conflicts that probably led to it.

These are partially valid objections, both to A.A.'s method and to the whole-hog applications of the A.A. model to managerial problems. But before considering the modifications that need to be made to fit organizational requirements, it might be useful to consider the similarities between the A.A. method and those used by some other behavior changers.

Similarities between A.A. and other approaches

The A.A. pattern, in its broadest outline, is a pattern that has independently taken hold—for good or evil—in a great many segments of modern American life. It shares with the manipulative models a strong sensitivity to human feelings. But at that point most of the similarity stops. It shows up in educational thinking, when educators argue that education is an active function of students as well as teachers. The teacher's role is to provide help and knowledge as students require it and as they can integrate it. The teacher's job is not to treat students as passive sponges, soaking in a pool of pedagogical wisdom. The job is to help them to help themselves.

Counseling and psychotherapy have moved rapidly in the same direction. Both "nondirective" therapeutic approaches and most other present-day models play a helping role and encourage people to work through their own problems.

Some may argue that such methods indicate precisely what is wrong with contemporary society. They make us weak and soft. Perhaps they do. But if any managers feel that those methods will be our ruination, they had better look over their shoulders at their own organizations. Related ideas, in modest disguise, have probably crept into their own operations. First-line supervisors are probably practicing participative, collaborative methods all over the place. Market-research people have gone psychological. They are using in-depth interviews and projective methods in dealing with consumers. The same applies to the employment interviewers. Industrial-relations people are probably trying to apply essentially the same ideas to resolving conflicts with the union. And the advertising people certainly are not using whips on the customers. Even the old chairman is probably saying things like, "You just can't order people around any more. They've got to want to do it." These are all ways of saying that we must all help to change ourselves; others cannot do it all for us.

The A.A. model and the managing process
Getting people to see a problem

We said earlier that three major obstacles block the use of the A.A. approach in managerial problems. Let's examine those difficulties one at a time to see whether or not they really are difficulties and, if they are, to see how they might be dealt with in the managerial setting.

Here is a simple, but perhaps typical, behavior-change problem in a managerial context. A new manager of a staff department grows increasingly concerned about the "weakness" of many subordinates. They seem stolid, inflexible, unimaginative, and uncreative. They go on doing things as they have always been done, though it is obvious to the manager that many procedures could be simplified and many new and more useful services could be rendered to line people. How can the manager make them less resistant to new ideas? How can they be made to adopt a new outlook toward their jobs?

Alcoholics Anonymous, for the most part, simply waits for alcoholics to become unhappy with their alcoholism. Only then do they undertake to cause change. Similarly, therapists mostly sit in their offices waiting for the client to feel bad enough to initiate an appointment. But the social inefficiencies of that process are obvious. Many people may be psychologically sick for a long time before the sickness becomes painful or crippling enough to make them look for help. And it doesn't make much sense, in educational settings, for teachers just to wait for children to want to learn arithmetic, or in business for executives just to wait for secretaries to want to come to work on time.

Yet, although managers cannot always wait for people to recognize a problem, theoretically their people will not change very significantly unless they do feel and acknowledge that tension. So a manager's first task becomes this: How do I make these people realize they have a problem? How can I make them feel dissatisfied with their present behavior?

Just waiting, we suggested, is one way to do it, and we should not discount it too quickly. Certainly many a person in an organization will quickly notice that a new boss holds different standards from the old one and, apparently out of the clear blue sky, will come voluntarily in search of help, say, in improving the quality of his work. The employee may already have felt uncomfortably inadequate when he compared his work with other people's work. Now he has his first opportunity to try to do something about it. The manager who had been wondering how to get a subordinate to improve then finds himself in a superb position for influencing behavior. So, just waiting for B to encounter problems, recognize inadequacies, and get enough courage to ask for help is one alternative that should not be discounted altogether. Moreover, the very act of *not* acting precipitously, of waiting, especially by a new boss, may be interpreted by subordinates as a sign of tolerance and hence of accessibility.

But there are other possibilities besides waiting. One is to throw subordinates into situations that will make some inadequacy obvious to them. The superior takes an active, but impersonal, part here. Subordinates begin to see a problem in themselves because they have screwed up an assignment. The boss has simply set up a situation that caused that problem to occur. Thus, a manager may cause a subordinate to recognize problems by *increasing* that employee's responsibility, by assigning difficult assignments, or by setting up meetings with people who make no bones about their attitudes toward the employee's work. Such behavior by managers is unusual, for managers are wont to *reduce* the responsibilities of "ineffective" people much more frequently than they are to increase them, thereby reducing the risk but also reducing the opportunity for learning.

Again, a superior can get a subordinate to recognize a problem simply by asserting that a problem exists. Thus, a group that has been perfectly happy about the way things are going can be made to recognize a problem, if the manager simply announces that the group's work is not quite up to standard. The teacher can do the same for students by giving them low grades on an exam. The difficulty here is obvious. The manager will probably not only succeed in getting the group to recognize a problem but succeed (though not by intention) in having the group blame the manager for it. The group may decide that its work doesn't need to be changed; the boss needs to be changed. And sometimes they can do it. But a little anger or disturbance is to be expected in change situations, and it's usually temporary.

To get people to see a problem by threatening, directly or by innuendo, that if they don't change they will endanger their bread and butter is, of course, straight restriction and carries with it all the dangers inherent in reactions to frustration. The danger is especially great when the source of the threat is the same individual who later wants to "improve" B's behavior.

That's the point at which a third party becomes useful. Parents are often abashed at how easily a new teacher can accomplish what they themselves have been unable to accomplish. Some of the credit given the teacher, or the family doctor, or Uncle Joe, does not belong to them as individuals so much as it does to their roles in the relationship. Anomalous as it may seem, a position of lesser power may often be a better position from which to effect a behavior change than a position of greater power. Our manager may try to start a change with a threat, but may then have to turn over the rest of the job to someone from the human resources group. The third party can often do much more to effect change from then on than the manager can do. In a sense, the manager's action has made the third party's job easy.

Now the human resources staffer, like A.A., receives a knock on the door from a B who has already recognized the need for help.

There is something paradoxical in this line of reasoning. This chapter is about methods for effecting change without authority. And yet it seems that one cannot effect change unless some outside, often authoritarian, pressure has been applied, so that employees come to feel dissatisfied with their present behavior.

But that's only half the picture. It is true that people are likely to start wanting help after they find out that their present behavior isn't as effective as they thought it was. But there is a second, more positive possibility, too, People may also want to change because they learn to want more or better or higher goals; because their level of aspiration rises. We may start looking for a new car when the old one stops performing. We may also start looking because Detroit or Japan has put out some shiny new ones. Managers can add new information to their staff's picture of the world; they can open new promotional avenues, new opportunities for learning, or new responsibilities that might well stir even the most stolid of old-timers into activity.

The problem then is how to raise the levels of aspiration. It is a difficult problem. It requires the changer to keep opportunities for growth and development open—always new ones, always better ones. As long as employees can foresee new, better, and achievable means for moving forward, they will be ready to change their behavior in the direction of those better means.

Once again, the reader will notice that many of these techniques for getting B to see a problem are not very easily distinguished from some of the techniques labeled "manipulative" in the last chapter. A's motives aren't always fully disclosed, for example. And many of our suggestions call for indirection, if not surreptitiousness. In this respect, as in the case of sensitivity to human needs, it is just plain true that manipulative models parallel part of the collaborative approaches. The differences between the two become clearer when one moves on to the way A uses the relationship with B and when one looks at the locus of control over what will happen.

All this is to say that people usually begin to change when they begin to feel uncomfortable with what they're doing now. One may use A.A.'s method of standing by until the world makes the person uncomfortable; one may needle people into discomfort; one may do it by trying to raise levels of aspiration so that employees themselves find their present behavior inadequate or awkward; or one may get third parties to use their power to make employees uncomfortable. Some of these methods or a combination of them are necessary for getting employees to think seriously about taking some responsibility for changing their behavior.

What does a changer need to know?

We're back to a question raised earlier in this part of the book: Who must know what about whom? In one-on-one counseling situations, it is more important for B to understand the nature of his personal behavior than for A to understand its causes. In the A.A. model, the buddy provides the alcoholic with an opportunity to communicate any facts or feelings that may be relevant. If they are communicated aloud, it is true that the buddy may also come to understand them, but it is much more important that the alcoholic can come to understand them. And if you already want to change, then it is far more important for you to understand what you are gaining or losing from your present behavior than for anyone else to understand it.

This is not to say that A needs no understanding of the situation being confronted. But what A needs most is to understand what's going on here and now, and not a full history of B's childhood.

Let's return here to the example of the new manager of an ineffective department. The job is to revitalize the department—without replacing any of the people. How much does he have to know about why subordinates are unimaginative, unenthusiastic, and unproductive?

He has to know about the how and the why of subordinates' current feelings much more than their deeper fears and motives. He doesn't need a case history on every employee so much as he needs enough understanding of what's going on now, so he can estimate the meanings his actions might evoke. He has to know whether the people have just been waiting for a break and are all ready to grab it or have settled firmly into a path of safe stolidity. It would help the new manager to know how subordinates felt about the previous manager. It would help to understand those things in order to know how to communicate his picture of the problem. And how can he find out about them? He can listen, "wander around," and communicate two-way.

To set great, new challenges for people who are already very fearful may not encourage enthusiastic readiness to change. It may only lead to denial and avoidance. But if those people have been put down and are held back, then those same challenges and opportunities may be just the right medicine. The present feelings, more than their causes and origins, are the most important working materials for managers trying to change the behavior of their people.

Perhaps even thoughtful managers would do well to encourage periodic sessions to talk about how things are going, how people feel about how they're doing, and what those people think they could do to improve the situation.

Who controls the change situation?

A third difference between the A.A. situation and management is that A.A. has little control (and little need for control) over the alcoholic's behavior. At any step along the way, B is free to reject the whole process and leave the situation without changing. Managerial situations aren't like that. Managers have deadlines to meet and responsibilities to carry out. But does that really make that much difference?

Consider again the new department manager. First, as manager, he can always veto what his people may decide to do. He can give subordinates opportunities to change themselves, and, finding that the change fails to occur, he can still resort to authority. So the major risk added by giving B more leeway is the possible loss of time, if the method fails.

On the other hand, if the manager only seeks changes in overt behavior, then there might be a good case for tight control. If all the manager wants is that his people show up before 9 A.M. every morning, and depart after 5 P.M., he could probably stand at the entrance, watch in hand, to make sure they carried out the daily ritual, rewarding the prompt and punishing the laggards. But the changes most managers usually seek are changes in attitude and style. They want their people to think and implement differently than they did before. And they know perfectly well that many of those thoughts, decisions, and actions will have to be made in their absence. Though the manager can watch to see that a clerk is at his desk, he often cannot watch to see whether the clerk is doing effective work. Since that is the usual case, is it actually more risky to let subordinates decide for themselves that they want to change and then to make the decisions that fit their changed perceptions of the world? Or is it more risky to force them to change, so that when they face a new decision they face it with a mixed feeling of wanting to do it and resenting having to do it?

The answer seems clear. The manager's control, in the sense of the ability to predict subordinates' behavior, is far greater if the opportunity exists for them to decide for themselves (and the manager knows where they stand) than trying to impose change on them.

Even self-imposed change is uncomfortable

A.A. does not have an easy time changing people. And people do not even have an easy time changing themselves. Since any behavior change usually means abandoning some previously adequate behavior in favor of some new and untested behavior, almost all behavior changes are accompanied by some degree of tension and anxiety. It's like that, for example, when we switch from one job to another—butterflies in the stomach on the day before starting the new job.

Even if they use an A.A.-like, augmentative approach in trying to effect a change in subordinates, managers cannot expect smooth sailing. They must still expect B to show tension and anxiety. Changers cannot prevent anxiety in B, but they can help to ease it by encouraging and supporting B's efforts to change.

A generalized pattern of collaborative influence

The A.A. method, then, has some limitations when we try to transfer it to managerial use. But perhaps by making a few modifications we can set up a general set of ideal conditions for effecting behavior change in continuing relationships, including managerial relationships. Try this set:

1. *B perceives a problem.* A.A. waits for people to perceive that they have a problem. In organizations, managers must often take action to make people aware that a problem exists and that change is necessary. One can think of all sorts of ways to do that, ranging from simply telling B that present behavior is inadequate to manipulating the environment so that B runs into trouble on the job. But the changer must always beware lest B begin to perceive the changer as the major problem.

2. *B takes responsibility for considering alternative ways of behaving (and if possible seeks A's help in discovering additional alternatives).* After B has decided a problem exists and that a change is desired, B then begins to consider new possibilities for change and, ideally, asks A to provide help.

3. *A and B mutually communicate the implications (for both A and B) of one new alternative versus others.* Now B wants to change. But remember that manager A is involved, too. B's change will affect A's world. The choice of change that B wants to try can be important to A. A therefore needs an opportunity to feed back to B the implications for A of one alternative or another. B, for example, may decide to change to a new behavior, but one that is *still* unacceptable to A. The responsibility now becomes more mutual.

4. *B selects an alternative that A can accept.* The major responsibility for deciding what B will do, and how, still remains with B. But if A is an organizational superior, B's selection will have to be acceptable to A, although *acceptable* may not mean *ideal*. The situation is a little like a discussion between husband and wife about where they want to take their vacation. If a location can be found that is entirely acceptable to both, well and good. If the location is only a compromise satisfactory to both, that is still good. If no compromise is possible, then A, if in a superior power position, can always revert to the simple use of the veto.

5. *B tries to change; A supports.* It is at this point that A's role shifts from that of the provider of information to the helper and supporter. It is here that tension and anxiety begin to show up in B. After taking a few initial steps, B may decide that changing to new behavior is hopeless or

ridiculous. Then A can help by (1) providing knowledge of the future, (2) reassuring, and (3) reinforcing even small signs of progress. It is here, too, that A can expect to come under overt or covert attack from B. It is A, after all, who has "forced" B to try this new, awkward, and inefficient way of behaving. The great mistake that A can make is to meet attack with counterattack, to deny all blame and to argue the facts of the case. The issue is emotional, not rational. What B needs is help, not argument.

6. *B finds the new method successful and integrates it into his patterns of behavior, or finds the new method unsuccessful and abandons it.* After being nursed along in an attempt to behave differently, B's skill usually increases; the new style serves B's own purposes better than the old. B can then be said to have changed. But if B finds that the new is not as good as the old, reversion to the earlier method may occur, if that is still possible, or a third method may be found. If the latter is B's choice, then the whole process begins again.

Those six steps constitute a crude and incomplete set of conditions for collaborative behavior change in continuing relationships. It is a difficult set of conditions to bring about. But the important question is whether it is more difficult and more time-consuming than the beguilingly simple use of authority, other kinds of power, or carefully planned manipulation. If the time and energy devoted to the unforeseen by-products of those other methods are added to the total, they often turn out to be even more costly than collaborative processes. And one of the important advantages of collaborative methods is that they tend to become easier over time. B, who has "been changed" by this method is likely to develop trust and confidence in A, feelings that make future changes easier. Such feelings may even allow A to use authoritative methods effectively, when they seem appropriate, because they will no longer be seen as arbitrary and frustrating.

In summary

Alcoholics Anonymous seems to do a good job of changing people without much call on power or authority and without the guile of manipulation. Its method may seem to managers to be uncontrolled and uncertain, but, with modifications, it may be much more applicable to organizational problems than one might imagine.

The basic assumption underlying the A.A. approach is that people must take most of the responsibility for changing themselves, and that changers must be helpers rather than coercers or manipulators. A superior's authority can become a warehouse of means by which to help subordinates see and experience their problems themselves rather than an ammunition dump with which to overwhelm them. The collaboration process then becomes a much more shared, mutual "win-win" activity and much less one in which one person simply acts to change the behavior of another.

14 From monetary incentives to career development: Efforts to influence human productivity

In the preceding chapters we looked at four models of influence. These were four general approaches that one person might use to try to influence the behavior of another person. In this chapter we take a managerial perspective, looking into some tangible ways managers can and do influence the behavior of their people. First, we take a look at that most classical and ubiquitous of all organizational incentives—pay. Then we'll examine some more recent and innovative approaches to motivating and influencing an increasingly professional and expectant work force.

Perhaps the first thing to keep in mind in this chapter is that pay is as much a psychological symbol, a surrogate for many other things, as it is just plain money to help feed the kids. When any of us gets a hefty raise, we think about what it might buy—the sports car or the Christmas turkey—but we also think about what signal it is sending about us, about how the boss values our work. A big raise means they love us, unless Joe got an even bigger one, in which case that same raise means they don't love me. Similarly, we mull over the implications of a smaller raise than expected, a pay cut, a smaller bonus this year than last year, and on and on. In organizations the paycheck always carries much more than a dollars-and-cents meaning. And it often means much *less* than managers intend it to mean.

The second thing to keep in mind is that the word *incentive* was not coined by psychologists. It's a rather mechanical, nonhuman word with connotations of carrots tied just beyond donkeys' noses. It came into organizational use in the days when most jobs were so designed that they were either physically exhausting, dangerous, or excruciatingly boring. Then, of course, managers really needed to find "incentives" to induce reluctant people to work at lousy jobs. But most jobs in developed countries aren't quite like that anymore, or at least they needn't be. So the idea of incentives has by now been mostly folded into broader concepts such as "motivation," "career development," and "participation." That doesn't mean that we are now willing to work without getting paid for it. In almost every organization people get paid for working, and some people receive more

158

pay than others. (But that's not always true. In universities, students at least, pay for the privilege of working.) And some people are promoted to higher-paying jobs more quickly than others. Traditionally, most managers have used both pay and promotion as reinforcers to influence people's behavior because they believe, usually correctly, that most people always want more money and more promotions. They try, therefore, to get people to work harder, faster, or more effectively by offering the carrot of more pay or better-paying jobs. But monetary reinforcers can be very tricky. Consider the following statements:

■ Managers pay people *in exchange for specific work.*
■ Managers pay people *as a reward for good work already done.*
■ Managers pay people *to motivate them to work more effectively in the future.*

All three generalizations are based on several reasonable but different beliefs. One is that people will tend to repeat behaviors that have already been rewarded. Hence, if we pay people who have done just the "right" things, they will tend to do those right things again. Another belief is that people should be paid for work performed. This is a contractual belief: if you do *X,* I will pay you *Y.* A third belief is that, if we pay them, people will work; otherwise they won't. Those beliefs carry different implications.

Back in part 1 we discussed a related issue—performance appraisal. Notice that the generalizations about pay are close to underlying assumptions about performance appraisal, but performance appraisal adds in the question of *differential* rewards:

■ Managers appraise people's performance in order to identify better workers from worse ones.
■ Managers appraise performance so that they can then better reward the better performers.
■ Managers appraise people in order to motivate people to do better work.

Those three generalizations assume that the feedback people get from their appraisals will help motivate them and help them learn where they went right and where they went wrong. The more accurate and rapid the feedback they receive, the more quickly they will learn. The assumptions also suggest that bigger rewards to *better* workers will be more motivating than bigger rewards to *worse* workers. All in all, those seem to be reasonable assumptions. They recognize the importance of money as an "incentive" and the importance of differential money rewards and differential appraisals in the managerial tool kit of influence.

But they also generate certain managerial problems. For instance, although we believe that doing better work deserves greater reward, we also believe in teamwork, cooperation, and mutual trust. If we pay some team members more than others or give some better appraisals than others, what happens to teamwork? Won't new tensions arise? And does more pay *after* doing good work necessarily generate better work in the future? If the pay follows the completed work, how can it motivate in the future? If worse workers get less reward, why should they become more motivated?

Tying pay to performance
Incentive schemes for individuals

The history of individual money incentive systems dates back to the early days of cottage industries and take-home work. The underlying notion has always been the same quite logical notion that people should be paid only in return for what they produce. For every unit of work that you perform, I agree to pay you one unit of money. If you don't produce, you don't get paid. If you produce more, you get paid more. If you want more, all you have to do is produce more. And the other assumption we usually make, of course, is that everybody always wants more.

Individual incentive programs take many mixed forms on the shop floors of modern factories and service organizations. Usually employees receive a basic hourly rate, with incentive bonuses for units produced above some standard. Similar systems are often used for salespeople, with incentive commissions paid for sales produced. Versions of the same system also show up among executive ranks, where bonuses are often paid for outstanding performance, usually once a year.

Notice that the time that passes between performance and pay can vary enormously. Given the general rule that reinforcements work best when they follow very closely after the actions we want to reinforce, that time difference can be critical. But the major problem associated with all such incentive schemes, regardless of time gaps between action and reinforcement, is its tendency to generate organizational game playing among employees and among managers. The history of individual incentives on factory floors, for example, is fraught with accusations by workers that managers reduce incentive rates as soon as people become skillful and efficient enough to take home large paychecks. On the managerial side, the argument has been that workers often secretly hold down the pace of their work or develop private tools for beating the system. Instead of generating more and better work, such systems have often generated suspicion and distrust.

Understandably, too, individual incentives drive people to do what they are directly paid for and not to do what they are not being paid for. As a result, people at all levels may take the short-term pay advantage over the long-term good. Over the long term, problems arise around issues like maintaining equipment, helping others in emergencies, or taking initiatives in unusual situations.

Game playing with incentive schemes is not limited to blue-collar workers. It often shows up among salespeople who may push the highest commission products over all others, or who load up customers unnecessarily in order to make their bonus. Nor are managers immune. Plant managers, for example, can often keep short-term costs down so they can demonstrate outstanding performance while actually letting equipment, quality, and inventories deteriorate.

Let's also remember that money isn't all that people want all the time. Even as early as the 1920s, researchers at Western Electric were pointing out that the introduction of individual money incentives could create unhealthy psychological conflict by forcing people to choose between money and cooperative social relationships with team members. Is money more important than membership? Monetary incentive schemes sometimes force people to make that unhappy choice.

The simple logic of individual incentive pay has its benefits, but it also has serious costs. It offers the advantage of tying meaningful rewards to the performance that the rewarder wants. But it's big costs lie in two directions.

First, by rewarding behavior X, such methods often unintentionally draw attention and interest *away* from Y and Z. Most jobs, especially in modern organizations, require much more than just the nose to the grindstone, followed by rewards. Managers also want their people to apply a little intelligence, adaptiveness, and even creativity in their work. If the incentive system fails to reinforce such behaviors, they will quickly dry up.

Second, the logic of many individual incentive programs does not take account of the interdependencies among organizational members, nor of the fact that people learn from other people. It assumes that the total tasks of a company can be broken down into individual subparts, each just the right size for one individual. But the organizational whole is far more than the sum of its parts, because the parts are interdependent. In real organizations, individuals have to trade off and coordinate all those individual little pieces, and most individual incentive systems don't deal well with those problems. Indeed, as one moves up the hierarchy in the organization, such interaction becomes even more critical, because at higher levels there is not only more interdependency but also more ambiguity. At the end of each day, the individual executive may have real trouble deciding whether a good day's work has really been done today.

Groups and unit-wide reward systems

Other methods try to compensate for some of the problems of individual incentive schemes. One set of alternatives shifts the unit of thinking from the individual to the group. The underlying assumption is that organizations will be more effective if people who must work together share a common reward.

Group-based plans define each individual's job differently than most individual incentive plans. The job is no longer seen as an independent undivided activity like punching that press X times a minute. It is now seen as punching the press in a social context, as one part of a large team activity, such as building a subassembly. And the reward is associated with the number, quality, and costs of those subassemblies, not its individual pieces. It then behooves all members of the team to search for ways to improve the performance of the whole unit and to work in whatever way may be needed to improve the total efficiency of that unit.

One early example of such a group-based incentive was the Scanlon Plan, developed back in the '50s but still alive today. It is a joint union-management endeavor involving money rewards for everyone in a unit. The amount of those rewards is calculated against an agreed-upon index of increases in the overall productivity of that unit. The bonus, if any, shows up in everyone's paycheck *on every payday*. Productivity committees, made up of small groups from all levels and all departments, are the major mechanisms for tying everyone's efforts into the overall goal of improved organizational productivity.

More recent versions of such group methods are showing up in employee profit-sharing plans and many other employee involvement programs. Although most derive from the same reasoning as the Scanlon Plan, seeking to provide every employee with a share of overall improvements, many of them calculate and pay their bonuses only once a year. That means that the work and its later reward are separated in time, with a consequent loss of much of the intended incentive effect.

One intent of group and unit plans is that employees develop a sense of responsibility and ownership. When that actually happens, however, many managers treat it as a mixed blessing. An "ownership" attitude usually means that Joe Doaks now takes a serious interest in how other employees and departments do their jobs and how managers are managing. Indeed, Joe Doaks may now want to question some of the marketing vice-president's decisions, or even the CEO's. Manufacturing people now become interested in sales programs, questioning some, urging others. Prerogatives of one group or another are likely to be challenged and widely scrutinized, making the organization both more open and more political.

Recent outgrowths of such group or organization-based systems have paid much more attention to nonmonetary motivation, like providing more opportunities for participation in planning and decision making, enriching jobs and building closer relationships among unit members. Such plans try to open more channels of communication and to create settings in which some common goals operate meaningfully throughout the organization. They try to move people toward greater "efficiency" by the simple expedient of providing a sense of ownership.

But once again, there is no free lunch. Such programs can also generate those pervasive and ubiquitous problems always associated with continuing small groups. It is one thing to develop a sense of common purpose. It is another to cause people to work together smoothly and cooperatively toward those goals. Conflict and debate are characteristic of hardworking groups. But that's an appropriate part of the manager's job, isn't it—to see to it that individuals in a group work effectively together in the common interest?

Straight salaries
From the hourly wage to the monthly paycheck

Most people who work in organizations don't get paid via some incentive scheme; they just get paid by the hour, the week, or the month. They get "straight wages" or "straight salaries." That method of paying people has been around even longer than individual incentive schemes. Of course, straight pay *is* an individual incentive scheme. It rewards you for showing up at work and staying there until closing time. In recent years, straight salaries have spread more and more to lower organizational levels, replacing hourly wages even among blue-collar workers, where individual piece rate incentive systems used to be widespread. The underlying new hypotheses are (1) that people, given the right working conditions, will be positively motivated by a variety of things other than money; (2) that pay should be treated as a basic contract rather than as a source of active motivation; and (3) that a "two-tier" system, hourly and salaried, generates conflict between lower and higher levels. It is rewards other than money that will cause people to work harder; "rewards" such as intrinsic interest in the work itself or a chance to learn new skills, move ahead in the organization, be recognized with a gold watch, or be accepted as a group member. It is to escape from both the negative impacts of incentive schemes and the stigma that has come to be attached to hourly rates that many companies have turned to straight salaries as a more mature way to treat all employees.

A new challenge then emerges. Once we have removed incentive pay, what do managers have left in their motivational tool boxes? They must now think of other ways to motivate and challenge their people. They must worry about creating the right environment and the right working conditions. They must make people's jobs more interesting. They must provide opportunities for people to learn, grow, and develop. Those may be more difficult conditions to generate than monetary incentives, but they are also more important tools for influencing an increasingly professional and educated work force—people with high expectations for their own careers. Besides, what are managers getting paid for?

Developing people as another way of looking at the manager's tools for motivating

Monetary incentive programs were based on the assumption that the manager can influence behavior *directly* by providing the right kind of reinforcement for the right kind of behavior. If employees do their jobs properly in the desired way, they will be rewarded by higher pay or promotions to better jobs. They will also be more likely to repeat that desired behavior, which will make them good at their present jobs. But will it prepare them for other jobs?

In recent years, organizations have broadened the whole conception of incentives, thinking more collaboratively and relying far less on simple reinforcement. Broader, cognitive aspects of human behavior are being brought into play. The older, more mechanical notion of more work/more pay is fading away and is being replaced by a more sophisticated view of conditions that generate productivity. Human beings, after all, think, observe, and learn from their environments. One can therefore affect human behavior by affecting attitudes, thinking styles, and relationships. The rather simplistic and narrow idea of "incentives" is being expanded to include the broader idea of "development"—management development, career development, organizational development. These days, when one looks for ways of "motivating" people, one had better take the whole work environment into account.

Among the pioneers in these more comprehensive approaches have been several emerging young companies, in lively environments like California's Silicon Valley. Small high-tech companies usually have to deal with a continuing stream of rapid changes in their volatile worlds, and they have to worry about motivating a professional, highly educated, and mobile work force. Most jobs in such companies cannot be predefined neatly because the rate of change requires that they be continuously redefined and because ambiguity and uncertainty abound. Such companies must try to develop people who can deal with whatever problem may come along and who can also *cause* new ones to come along. They must develop people who can treat the unexpected as routine, who will take initiatives in coping with new situations, who have flexible mindsets, and who need to think of themselves as self-adjusting, continuous learners.

To influence people toward those difficult behaviors drives toward experiments with methods that go far beyond monetary incentives. Here are a few examples of reward systems that are showing up more and more in such organizations:

■ *Sabbaticals*. One method for rewarding executives, for restimulating them, and for getting fresh ideas into the organization, is to provide them periodically with some time off, often on full pay, to go back to school, or to explore a new environment. This "unfreezes" some of their own and their organization's established ways of thinking. The practice is modeled after academic sabbatical systems. For many professionals, time off can be as important a motivator as money, both rejuvenating the employee and restimulating the whole organization.

■ *Fellowships and other forms of special recognition*. Many companies in which technical expertise and scientific know-how are at a premium recognize and reward outstanding contributors in special ways. IBM, for example, elects a small number of its people as IBM Fellows, both to recognize outstanding scientists and engineers and to signal the company's support for excellence. Other companies set up special clubs that elect members on the basis of their tangible contributions. Such elite groups are sometimes also rewarded financially, through special bonuses and stock options, and also enjoy the recognition and status that membership bestows. The purpose of all these is more than to offer reward for excellent performance. It is also to challenge others to try to reach the heights. Some companies are now beginning a long overdue extension of such programs to other nontechnical groups, accountants, marketing staff, and others.

■ *Job rotation.* Rotation is one of the most commonly used ways of trying to develop and motivate executives, especially in larger organizations. It is based on the assumption that a variety of job experiences provide the employee with many opportunities for continuous learning about the business and with situations that make creative contributions more likely. It is also a way of influencing attitudes by exposing young managers to new work settings, new challenges, and new tasks. The target individual is periodically rotated through different jobs at different organizational levels.

■ *Training programs and seminars.* Educational programs, both in-house and at universities, have become an important and widely used method of developing and rewarding executives at all levels. In-house programs often use outside faculty, emphasizing leading-edge ideas; they also serve as important mechanisms for socializing employees—that is, for inculcating company cultures and values. University programs, like short sabbaticals, also provide time away from the job, in the company of other executives from other organizations and other parts of the world. They serve to broaden, refresh, and recharge middle and senior executives, as well as to prepare them for more responsible positions.

■ *Job enrichment, flexible working hours, and much more.* Many organizations seek new ways to expand and enrich jobs, so that there is always more to be learned. Some try to improve the physical and social environments of the work place, to make the whole work scene more attractive and more interesting. Many companies are moving to flexible working hours, provision of child-care facilities, and multifaceted health and recreational programs. They are finding that such programs can generate a sense of community and a sense of confidence in the company's commitment to its people—feelings that can pay off in more effective work. Some companies try such methods for solely economic reasons. Wiser ones just do them because they feel right.

All those examples share some common characteristics. They all provide opportunities for people to learn, to develop themselves, to think about new ideas, to practice new skills, and to treat their working time as something more than an exchange of punishing toil and sweat for a few pieces of silver.

So modern applications of the incentive idea are becoming far less mechanical and simplistic than older views. They treat motivation and influence as part of a large problem of making the work situation more attractive, more challenging, and more rewarding for its members.

In summary

Managers can use many methods to influence the behavior of their people in organizationally desirable ways. The traditional method is through pay, which is related to one or another form of individual performance appraisal. Traditional individual incentive systems are most appropriate when employees can sensibly operate independently of one another. Difficulties begin to arise when individual incentives are applied to interdependent people working on interdependent and overlapping activities.

Group-based reward systems address the problems of interdependency by focusing groups of people on common group or organizational goals and by rewarding individuals in relation to their whole unit's performance. Although such programs help generate a sense of ownership, they also blur traditional lines of authority and control, a phenomenon that carries with it both rewards and challenges for the manager.

To overcome the problems associated both with individual and group systems, many organizations have moved toward straight salaries for most employees, developing other kinds of broad packages to influence and motivate their people. Nonmonetary methods for stimulating and educating members of the work force have grown rapidly in recent years, as more organizations are confronted with the challenge of managing more professional and better-educated employees. Instead of relying exclusively on pay, managers are tending to use other more indirect methods to influence the behavior of their people and to provide opportunities for growth and development. Innovative companies have pioneered a wide range of such methods, including paid sabbaticals, fellowships, job rotation schemes, educational programs, and flexible working conditions. In general, managerial conceptions of incentives have moved away from mechanical work/pay reinforcements to a more encompassing search for collaborative ways to make working situations challenging and enriching for both the employee and the organization.

3

People in threes to twenties: Efficiency and influence in groups

Introductory note

The third part of this book is about groups, about those committees, task forces, and meetings that occupy such a large part of the manager's working days. Managers (most people, in fact) not only spend time working in groups, they also spend a lot of time complaining about them. Groups are inefficient; they are places for people to flex their muscles and show their power; they are the abominations of managerial life. And having vented a whole string of such feelings after a long day of meetings, many of us then proceed to do a really curious thing: we march right back, on the very next day, into another set of meetings. We curse meetings, yet we go on having them. This suggests that either we are very stupid or that somehow groups, committees, and meetings are in fact useful tools for performing important managerial functions.

We prefer the second explanation. So, the general thrust of part 3 is to try to make the reader worry, not about whether groups are good or bad but about the *conditions* under which groups work well or badly; we try to consider how groups affect people, how meetings can be improved, and how groups can be used more effectively in managing organizations.

Groups are important because they are the major intermediaries between large organizations and the individual people who compose them. One of the really misleading things about most organization charts is that they picture the organization as an orderly collection of *individual* positions. Each box on the chart represents a job for one person, so that if we added up all those jobs, we would appear to have a picture of "the organization." That, of course, is not at all the case. Among other things, most charts ignore the ever-present small groups that intervene between the individual and the organization. Whether the organization likes it or not, people form groups. Those informal groups that people organize for themselves and the more formal groups the organization sets up both play very important roles in shaping the organization's behavior.

The group, formal or informal, affects the behavior of both individuals and large organizations in at least these five ways:

1. Groups discipline, mold, and change the behavior of their individual

members. Both common sense and research results show that the groups individuals belong to are powerful determinants of behavior, attitudes, and values. Whether it be gangs or university departments, groups influence their members. They reward and punish, motivate and challenge, and provide role models. Chapter 17 is specifically concerned with the ways that groups press, form, shape, and control their individual members.

2. Groups can generate commitment and loyalty in their members, with members frequently feeling far more loyal to their group than to their organization. Groups also make decisions in modern organizations. Despite the protest that camels are horses designed by a committee, despite the fact that some organizations have even flatly forbidden committees, a great many decisions in organizations are made in groups, whether they are called committees or not. Two of the chapters in this next section are about decision making by groups. One is concerned with the conditions that make for good or bad group decisions; the other examines ways of improving group processes in general.

3. By looking toward the whole organization, instead of toward the individual, groups turn out to be important in still another way. They are major contributors to the decisions made by the entire organization. The many groups within an organization bargain, negotiate, form coalitions, and compete with one another. Those active intergroup activities drive much of the corporate decision-making process. Chapter 18 is about conflict and cooperation among groups within the organization, about group politics in organizations.

4. Chapter 19 deals with communication networks in groups. Groups can be set up in many different ways. By understanding networks, we can learn a good deal about the costs and benefits of alternative ways of designing structures and large groups.

5. Groups are important for morale, learning, and development of people in organizations, from assembly-line workers to senior executives. Chapter 20 is about how groups can be used to improve managerial and organizational effectiveness.

15　Group decisions: Monsters or miracles?

Some readers may have encountered one or more of the interesting exercises that simulate survival situations.* Sometimes the simulation is about a group lost on the surface of the moon; sometimes the group has crash-landed in the desert or in a subarctic region. The exercises always require six or seven people, isolated and in danger of death, to make decisions as a group. If they're lost in the desert, they must decide, for example, whether it is more important to keep a few quarts of water than to keep a loaded gun or a compass. As a group they must rank order the importance of several such items. The exercise is usually set up so that the members first get a chance to make their own individual decisions. Then the group sits down for forty-five minutes or so to talk the situation over and to make a group decision about those same items.

Those are useful exercises for two reasons. First, people learn a good deal about their own and others' behavior in a tightly constrained task situation. But they're even more useful because they demonstrate, in most cases, that the group decision comes out a good deal better (when compared with a survival expert's ranking) than the average of the individual decisions. Moroever, in many cases the group's decision turns out to be better than *any* individual member's decision. In those cases, the group is "synergistic," yielding a net improvement over the performance of anybody in it. But sometimes, the reverse is true. The group decision turns out to be worse than the average decision of its members. Often, members would have had a better chance of surviving if they had stuck with their own decision and ignored the group decision. But *most* of the time, the group decision is the best one.

---

*Some excellent ones were developed by J. C. Lafferty and P. M. Eady and published by Human Synergistics of Plymouth, Michigan.

171

Why and when are group decisions better or worse than individual decisions?

Group discussion in the survival experiments is a little like some kinds of military intelligence work. If six of us get together and collect all our bits and pieces of information about the desert, the total information available is likely to be much more than any one of us had before. More and better information obviously can help us make better decisions.

But another reason those group decisions are usually good is probably equally important. When groups talk things over, the logical strengths and weaknesses of certain opinions become clearer to all concerned. Wheat is separated from chaff. It isn't only information that people share; it's also a critical evaluation of the arguments that contribute to the quality of any group decision. Notice that this critical faculty of groups is not guaranteed to work. Some groups are scared or shy and don't dare question one another's beliefs. Some are "snowed" by self-styled experts or authority figures. Therefore, that critical faculty is something groups often need to train themselves to use well.

There is a third reason that these simulations so often show the superiority of group over individual decisions. In these survival exercises, the groups always exist in isolation, all by themselves. The group is not part of a larger set of groups. The members have only one overwhelming purpose—to survive. But in most real organizational situations, the members of a given group are much less "pure." They are usually also members of other groups. They are not just motivated to do what is good for their present group and for themselves. They may have other important motives. They may be acting as representatives of other groups. Members from the marketing department may not be interested solely in making the best decision for the whole organization. They are also interested in getting a fat piece of the action for their marketing group. Or they may want to use this group as a platform for getting themselves promoted. In the real world, that is to say, group decisions do not occur in an isolated vacuum but in a world of other motives, other commitments, and other loyalties. That's when groups often do create camels when they're trying to build a horse.

Nevertheless, these survival cases point to the fact that groups, when the conditions are right, often make high-quality decisions. Moreover, groups that have been *trained* to work together improve their decisions more than those groups that have never had any training. So, group decisions can be good, and they can be made better if the group members are willing to do a little work toward making them better. Those facts are inescapable, regardless of the complications that take place in larger organizational settings.

Groups and commitment

The reader will note that we have dived headfirst into the issue of decision quality. But groups are not called together solely to try for better-quality decisions. They are often called together for another very important reason: to gain commitment to a decision. The I-love-my-own-baby proposition holds true over a wide range of situations. If we have participated in making a group decision, we are likely to become more committed to that decision. That proposition can become very important in organizational life. It underlies the whole concept of "participative management," and it works in a wide variety of cultural settings. It contributes to the effective implementation of decisions, after the decisions have been taken. Most decisions, after all, no matter how good their quality, are not worth much if they don't get implemented. One of the most powerful drivers of effective implementation is the commitment to that decision that derives from prior participation in making it.

On leadership and group decision making
Contingency models

We have said so far that groups are often effective decision makers because (1) they can bring many pieces of information together, (2) they can analyze information critically, and (3) they can generate commitment in their members.

But there are situations in which managers (1) already have all the information they need, (2) are perfectly capable of processing it alone (or with the help of a computer), and (3) do not require the commitment of others for implementation purposes. So they might not need to involve a group at all. If we take such a contingency view—the view that different types of decision-making situations may require different degrees of group participation—we can then identify a whole variety of group-relevant or group-irrelevant decision problems. For some, group decisions may look most sensible, whereas others can probably be made faster and better by one person alone.

In the past two decades, much interesting research has been done in an attempt to look into this contingent view of leadership behavior, trying to specify the conditions under which a leader might use one decision method or another. To give the reader a feeling for one of the more useful models, consider the following case:

> You are supervising the work of twelve engineers. Their formal training and work experience is very similar, permitting you to use them interchangeably on projects. During the last few months the backlog of new projects assigned to your unit has decreased, causing

you and your engineers to worry about possible layoffs unless business picks up.

Yesterday, your manager informed you that a request had been received from an overseas affiliate for four engineers to go abroad on extended loan for six to eight months. For a number of reasons, the manager argued (and you agreed) that this request should be met by your group.

All of your engineers are capable of handling this assignment and, from the standpoint of present and future projects, there is no particular reason any one should be retained over any other. The problem is somewhat complicated by the fact that the overseas assignment is in what is generally regarded in the company as a highly undesirable location.*

If you were the manager in this situation, how would you go about making the decision? Remember that the question is *not* what is the best decision but how you would go about making the decision. Will you sit at your desk and make the decision yourself? Will you call each of the engineers in and talk to them, then make the decision yourself? Will you call a meeting of all the engineers, listen to them, and then make the decision yourself? Or will you set up a group meeting, in which you would participate, aimed at reaching one decision satisfactory to all?

If you give this case to a number of managers, you will find a lot of disagreement about the appropriate way to approach the problem.

The contingency model we referred to earlier tries to make sense out of problems like that one by reasoning in the following way:

The model starts by emphasizing two important issues: (1) decision quality and (2) commitment to the decision. To make a good-quality decision, we need good information; to make a decision to which people will become committed, we need participation. The model then reasons: If in problem X only the quality of decision counts, and commitment is unimportant, the leader should gather the information needed and make the decision. And that would be the end of it. But if commitment is also important, because implementation requires willing work from group members, then the decision-making process must be more participative.

If you now review that little case, you can ask yourself questions such as these:

Is the quality of the decision important? The answer seems to be that it is not. Almost any four engineers can do the job perfectly well, as long as they are willing to do it.

*Borrowed with permission, from Professor Victor Vroom of Yale University. See V. Vroom and P. Yetton, *Leadership and Decision Making* (University of Pittsburgh Press, 1973), © 1973, University of Pittsburgh Press.

Is the commitment of the employees important? The answer has to be yes. The job will not be done very well if the people who are sent out to do it do so under protest, or if everyone feels it was "unfair." In this case, then, the contingency model recommends a group decision-making process aimed primarily at building commitment and not much concerned with decision quality.

But, of course, one can find a whole collection of other cases in which quality is critical and commitment unimportant. And in some of those cases one might find that meeting with subordinates can contribute nothing to the quality of the decision. In those cases, the model's recommended solution is that the manager make the decision alone.

Notice that that kind of contingency model does not put much emphasis on the information-processing part of decision-making activity. It assumes that, if the manager has all the information needed, a good-quality decision can be made. Some students of small groups argue that that is an oversight; even given good information to each head, several heads are still better than one.

There are other problems with such models. Is participation the only route to willing implementation by team members? How about *socialization* as an alternative? If, like the Marine Corps or the Church, we can train people not only to do their jobs but also to *believe* in the importance of willing obedience to superiors, won't that generate effective implementation? And what about the personal philosophy of the leader? Should leaders of groups always behave contingently? Or should they demonstrate certain ways of behaving that apply in *all* situations because those ways represent the long-run *values* of the organization? But the idea that effective decision making requires concern for both quality and human willingness to carry out decisions is a good basic idea, one that you might want to keep in mind the next time you are trying to decide whether or not to call a meeting of your people.

Brainstorming and group creativity

We have not yet mentioned still another function of groups in organizations: groups as stimulators of creativity. Sometimes we bring people together not so much to make decisions but to generate ideas, offer alternatives, or provide counsel. Sometimes groups "brainstorm," associating freely without constraint to find creative solutions to problems. Whether "brainstorming" really works is a subject of some debate. Some studies suggest that the same group of individuals working independently in separate rooms would turn up as many or more creative ideas in the same amount of time as they would brainstorming in a room together. Whatever definition of creativity we use, that elusive concept seems to be largely the property of individuals, not groups. Nevertheless, most of us would probably agree that our own creative ideas are often sparked by interactions with others.

And therein lies the notion behind brainstorming and several other related techniques. Get people together in a loose, nonevaluative setting simply to think out loud about anything that might be even remotely relevant to the problem at hand. The process is both useful and fun when divergence seems more important than convergence—when we need new possibilities or new alternatives, rather than conventional solutions. And one of the greatest weaknesses of contemporary styles of managing may lie in our frequent failure to choose the right problems rather than the right answers.

A good deal can be said in favor of occasional opportunities for members of an organization to hang loose and spin off ideas, dreams, and fancies no matter how odd they may seem. Sometimes, for the sake of both the individual and the organization, it is useful to quit working and do a little playing.

In summary

This chapter has tried to encourage the skeptical reader to adopt more positive attitudes toward group decision making. But this chapter is by no means an all-out pitch for group decision making. It has tried to describe the conditions under which group decisions can be better in quality and implementability than several alternative forms of decision making. It has also tried to specify some conditions under which they can be worse.

But groups are important for more than decision-making purposes. They can also generate commitment and loyalty from their members. These two factors, quality and commitment, are perhaps the key pragmatic questions to consider when evaluating the usefulness of groups. Of course, other questions remain concerning the leader's style, morality, human development, and creativity, which you may also want to think about as you approach the question of how group-oriented you want your unit to be.

We have not said very much in this chapter about how to improve the working machinery of groups. In matched-problem situations, some groups will still make better decisions than others, usually because they are more skillful users of the machinery of group process. The next chapter looks at the problems of developing effective group process.

16

Group process:
What was really going
on in that meeting?

Suppose we put several small groups of comparable people to work on the same task. Some will surely do a much better job than others. Perhaps one group has "better" people than the others. Or perhaps some groups' members work together more effectively than others. Maybe the people in one group feel so competitive with one another that they concentrate more on winning points than on doing the job. Or perhaps one group is so dominated by one person that the others just aren't motivated. This chapter is about those kinds of issues—the working processes that increase or decrease the effectiveness of task groups.

In earlier chapters on face-to-face communication, we made a distinction between "factual" and "emotional" communication, between facts and feelings. We argued that effective influence in most cases requires communication about feelings as well as about facts. If we now switch our thinking from individuals to larger units, such as groups, a comparable binary distinction turns out to be useful. This time the distinction is between *task* and *process*. *Task* is analogous to *facts*. Most groups in organizations are there to perform some specific tasks, such as to set next month's production targets or to determine next year's vacation policy. But all groups, no matter what their tasks, also go through some working *processes* to complete that task. Their members communicate with one another, assemble and process information, and make decisions. The manner in which group members go about their task we shall call *group process*. *Task* is about deciding where you want to go in your car. *Process* is about how the car itself operates—whether the oil pressure is up, the spark plugs are firing, and the whole vehicle is well maintained.

It's task issues we usually talk about when we go to meetings. Process is what we usually talk about over a drink after the group meeting. Task is about whether or not we ought to hire twelve more technicians. Process is about that department manager who never agrees with anything the rest of us want to do, or the way that decision was pushed through by the chair.

177

We are all process experts

All of us have developed considerable expertise on many matters of group process. However, we seldom use that knowledge to try to improve the operations of our groups. We are expert in the sense that we can go home after a meeting and describe the group's dynamics and social structure in considerable detail, and we can spot particular acts that were dysfunctional to the group. We detect quite easily the undercover fighting going on between Joe and Susan. Or we usually know that when Sam said what he said he really meant something else. And we know that the boss acted as if everybody's opinion was wanted, but that the decision had really been made before the meeting even started.

All those are *process* observations. Most of us are highly sensitive to them, but usually we either simply lock them up in the backs of our minds or we talk about them over coffee after the event. We don't use that knowledge to improve the next meeting. Yet those are, of course, highly relevant, valuable bits of information that could potentially help to improve performance. Certainly, if you're a basketball coach and see a couple of the team's players tripping each other up, you would consider that very much part of your business. And yet many of us sit in groups and watch our colleagues tripping each other up and just keep quiet about it.

Why don't we talk out loud more about process issues? The reasons tend to be social, don't they? "It would be embarrassing," we might say, "to call attention to someone talking too much," or "People just don't go around announcing that Mary and Sam are always on opposite sides of the fence, no matter what the issue is. It just isn't done!" But isn't it? It's often done in the family and among close friends, and with increasing frequency, it is being done in organizations.

One process problem:
Dealing with emotional "noise"

Consider two almost extreme approaches to the way one might handle emotions in group meetings. One common procedure is simply to set up rules to disallow the direct expression of such feelings. The rules may be formal parliamentary ones or informal norms. The chairperson says, "We will stick to the facts in this meeting. We will keep personalities out of this. We will cut off people who talk too much or for too long." The purpose of this announcement is to eliminate the expression of feelings, and the chairperson's weapon is personal authority to enforce organizational rules. That seems like a sensible, businesslike approach to problem solving, but it is usually quite foolish.

Another not-so-businesslike and quite different method for handling process is to assume that feelings should not be kept out of meetings but let in and identified. Here the chair says, "If you're angry, say so. If you think what we're talking about is nonsense, say so. If you feel that nobody is listening to your great idea, get in there and make sure we know it." This second method also has its costs, but in most ongoing small groups, it has many advantages.

Emotional behavior in groups, like other behavior, can be viewed functionally. People have reasons for feeling angry, isolated, put down, hurt, or whatever.

When several of us join together to try to solve a problem, we remain human. There may be one central problem of common concern to all of us, but our own individual problems also come along to the meeting—attitudes, fears, private motives. If other members are, for example, in a position to help or hurt me, I am likely to keep one eye on that person throughout the meeting. Therefore, the emotional "noise" in a group may consist, to a large extent, of efforts by individuals to deal with their personal motives in the presence of the group. That kind of "noisiness" is natural. If we try to deal with it by ruling it out, it will go underground and show up in the guise of reason. If we try to surface and deal with it, perhaps we can then go on to something more like true rationality.

Often, authority or parliamentary procedure or social pressure, either intentionally or unintentionally, drives such individual feelings and motives underground, but such methods do not typically eliminate them. Everyone who has served on a committee has seen that kind of velvet-glove activity many times. It may take the "It's an excellent idea, but . . ." form or, "Well, of course we could go about it your way, but. . .". Such tactics divert much more energy and are much less likely to contribute to honest unanimity (or honest disagreement) than an open haggle. If we want a good decision, we may have to put up with human emotions.

Hence the other choice: Let the communication channels carry both task and process information. Such a policy need not be as chaotic as it may sound. The question is not anarchy versus governance so much as the orderly handling of anarchistic factors in a group.

But even if we like the open-channels policy, implementing it isn't easy. Getting group members to say what they feel takes both skill and time. Patience and some respect for people's ultimate willingness to accept responsibility can help a good deal. Postmortems and bull sessions devoted to what was right or wrong about the last meeting also are useful techniques, especially if the group meets regularly.

Take, for instance, this true example of a group of six men working on a research project full-time. The project called for the six to break up into pairs and travel to some field locations for a few days. The group, to its own surprise, spent several hours trying to decide who would go where with whom. Afterward, in a bull-session review of the day's progress, someone said aloud what everybody knew—that it had been foolish to take so long over such a trivial issue. The next question: Why did we do it? Why did we waste so much time? That brought a previously hidden issue out into the open. Everyone, it turned out, really liked Joe, and everyone wanted to be the one to travel with Joe. But no one would admit it; so they had used all sorts of "rational" arguments about why one pairing arrangement or another wouldn't work. Of course, that recognition came several hours too late, but it helped to prevent similar stalemates later. Postmortems like that one become easier with time. Better still, they can be worked in as ongoing parts of the meeting itself, so that people are always watching for and pointing out underlying feelings at the same time as they discuss content problems.

Groups that operate with fairly free expression and recognition of feelings follow a different pattern from more carefully controlled groups. Tightly controlled groups seem to progress in an orderly linear way. Open groups tend to start slowly, often with considerable hodgepodge and disturbance and little measurable progress. Then they accelerate fast once the air is cleared.

Barriers to communication in groups

It may be useful to examine the same problem from another side. Instead of asking, "What causes noise?" one can ask, "What blocks the communication of relevant information? What blocks feedback?"

Looking at the problem from that perspective can be useful, for, although it is true that too much is often said in groups, too much may also be left unsaid. The subordinate asserts, "Yes, sir, I understand your instructions," but it turns out later that they were not understood. The salesman does not tell the sales manager about the customer's recent complaint. The production worker does not report that his machine is acting oddly. The patient says, "You're the doctor; you tell *me* where it hurts." Relevant information is often left uncommunicated, especially in groups. Indeed, there is one good rule of thumb: never trust a group that operates very quietly. It may look smooth and efficient, but it may be completely missing the point.

The most significant barriers to communication in groups are the ephemeral psychological ones, such as these:

- The *status barrier* between superior and subordinate. That one limits communication in the upward direction because of fear of disapproval. It can also happen in the downward direction, for fear (by superiors) that if they say what they feel they may lose status or be seen as weak: "If I admit that to the boss, he'll be wild. He'll think I've lost my touch"; "If I ask that question, those people will think I don't know enough to be boss, so I'll act like I know the answer already."

- The *low assertiveness* barrier. This sometimes takes the following form: "I can't speak until I'm recognized by the chair; and if the chair never recognizes me, my information will never come out. If the chair does recognize me later, I'll still say what should be said now—even if it's irrelevant later."

We need not elaborate on the way parliamentary procedures, originally designed to promote and simplify communication, have been used in social and political affairs selectively to prevent and complicate communication.

■ The *rookies-don't-talk* barrier. If you're a newcomer to a group, you may feel (and the group may feel) that you have not yet earned your spurs. Therefore, you should shut up—whether you have a good idea or not.

■ The *self-deprecating* barrier. "All these people seem so knowledgeable and so sure of themselves. My little idea can't be worth bringing up. I'll just look like a fool."

And the reader can surely add many more such psychological barriers to the list.

The answers to such barriers may be the same as the answers to too much emotional noise. They could be more easily circumvented if they could just be communicated. If people, for example, can reach the point where they can say that they are scared to death to express ideas in their groups, that may be enough to get such issues out on the table, and could well lead to more open communication henceforth. But ordinarily we do not communicate such feelings—especially in organizations. Instead, we say, "Stick to the facts! Don't get emotional! Let's be businesslike!" That cultural attitude is probably the biggest barrier of all.

Group process and group objectives: What are we trying to do here?

Suppose a task force of executives starts out to decide whether or not to institute a program of selection tests for salespeople. Their objective seems, at first, perfectly unambiguous. Then someone discovers that one member's conception of selection tests is quite different from other members'. Ten minutes later someone raises these questions: "Is our objective to decide on selection tests only? Or are we really here to revise all our selection procedures?" And half an hour later: "Wait just a minute! Are interviews and application blanks selection tests? If not, why are we discussing them?" And still later, someone with an irate tone of voice asks, "What are we trying to decide anyhow? Is it whether or not tests are a good idea? Or is it which tests to use?"

And so on, at intervals throughout the meeting. What seemed at first to be an unambiguous objective turns out to be diffuse and shadowy.

Rule of thumb: Don't let it throw you. Objectives are never what they seem. They need reassessment and redefinition. That's not wasted time. Clarifying the objective often takes us a long way toward reaching it.

But there's a further related issue: Whose objectives? Groups in organizations are often composed of representatives of other groups. A task force has a marketing person on it, and someone from research, from human resources, and so on. Although all share an interest in one common objective, all also represent the interests of their own groups. Hence, pulls and tugs and political deals result.

Once again, what's the best route through that minefield? Maybe it's the same one: get those private agendas out in the open.

A third level of objectives and problems also exists, the individual level: What can I get out of this group? What behavior will help my career? What might hurt it? How do I come out of this a personal winner?

That's a more difficult problem. In the long run we can perhaps encourage enough mutual trust so that people will open up about such personal issues. But the rule here, for the short run, is a weaker one: Be alert! Listen with the third ear! Be tolerant, but don't get snowed!

Indeed, there is a whole set of techniques for consciously keeping groups from doing their jobs, if it is in one's own interest to do so. Sometimes an individual or subgroup can profit most by blocking the definition of objectives. One can hardly find a better way to keep a meeting from going anywhere than to raise a new objection every time the group gets close to clarifying its broader purpose. One can also obfuscate a meeting by overemphasizing objectives—especially if a member chooses to broaden and complicate them so as to take the meeting altogether out of the range of possible accomplishment. The problem is that objectives create difficulties for groups so long as they are understood differently by different people in the group and so long as some of them are not out on the table. Once everyone in the group has a reasonably good feel for the limits of the problem and the variety of objectives present, something positive can usually be done about them.

For instance, one can help to clarify group objectives by restating someone else's statements. That can help a group get started and can also put the restater, the clarifier, in a position of strength in the group. Similarly, conscious efforts to talk (nonevaluatingly) about covert individual or subgroup objectives, if one suspects their presence, can help a committee to function more efficiently, although the person who does that job takes some risks in so doing.

A census of ideas about the group's objectives, taken early in a meeting, can also help get that issue out on the table quickly. Often, in meetings, the first idea raised becomes the takeoff point for discussion, thereby eliminating expression of some other possibilities. Since the first highway may not be the best one, it can be useful to map out several alternatives before starting the trip.

From the perspective of the whole group instead of any individual member, the problems to be solved are these: (1) to make sure every person in the group knows where the group is going; (2) to have everyone in the group either want to go where the group is going or say where each wants to get off; (3) if there are people who want to get off early, either to change objectives so these people can go along or to let them off and start over; and (4) to take another look every once in a while to see whether objectives need to be changed or modified.

"Personality" and interpersonal problems in groups

Another class of problems that often inhibits effective small-group process centers on the personalities of the participants. Such "people problems" include characteristics carried into the group by members, like the leader's tendencies to dominate or a member's strong desire to be liked. They also include individual members' styles—their talkativeness, shyness, argumentativeness, and defensiveness.

There are problems of communication, too, stemming from differences in rank, age, sex, expertise, and prestige in the organization. And many problems may arise from within the group itself. Somebody's idea is ignored; somebody else's is laughed at; somebody else says absolutely nothing and just smiles, thereby frightening some colleagues and encouraging others. Finally, this general personal/interpersonal category includes problems of group mood: elation, depression, and regression into dirty jokes, golf or baseball scores, or anything except the subject at hand.

There is no way of avoiding such problems, but there are many ways of dealing with them. From the group point of view, they are problems only if relevant ideas and information are omitted or distorted or if time is wasted because of them. Often, of course, such problems do affect both kind and degree of communication. The quiet man who sits and smokes his pipe may seriously affect the rate and even the nature of the ideas contributed by others. Out of the corner of an eye each member may be watching that man for some sign of approval or disapproval. Depending primarily on any member's own feelings of security or insecurity, this point or that may be modified, withheld, or overemphasized just because of that quiet one in the corner.

Or shy person A offers a suggestion that is ignored. Then A offers it again, and it is still ignored. Gradually, A withdraws into a shell, to come out only infrequently and only to jab at someone else's ideas.

What, then, can be done, not so much to prevent such problems as to deal with them? Again, the answer seems to lie mostly in the communication process. If a group can sense such problems and also talk about them, the problems may be resolved. But they are unlikely to be resolved so long as they remain hidden. If a group chooses to ignore them, fearing they are too "sensitive," then the group is ignoring data relevant to its own operation. And data about itself are as important to the solution of a group's problem as they are to the solution of any individual's problem.

Discussion of such personnel issues need not mean that the group has to examine the remote origins of people's feelings. Just as in the case of A trying to influence B, in an earlier chapter, the original causes of B's feelings are often irrelevant, but the feelings themselves need airing. Thus, when some members of a group leave the field by going off into gossip or fantasy, it is not absolutely necessary to find out why they are doing that. It is necessary, however, to recognize that such digressions are not accidental. They represent attempts to get rid of tension or avoid tense issues. Therefore, it may be wise to permit time to be "wasted" in the release of such tensions, instead of forcing them to find their outlets through later distortion of "rational" discussion. Recognition and acceptance of people's feelings and encouragement of an atmosphere of permissiveness seem to be sensible directions for most groups to take.

As it is for problems of objective, the periodic census of reactions is a handy device for getting personnel problems out on the table. It is useful for a group to stop once in a while, just so that people can say how they feel—about the group's progress, the methods the group is using, and things in general.

A third method for coping with personnel problems is, surprisingly, to deemphasize premeeting preparation. It would seem to make sense to urge group members to think about a meeting's agenda in advance and to come "prepared." But preplanning can also be a source of serious difficulties. "Preparation" may mean that each person works out an individual position before the meeting, and then comes into the group to try to sell that position to the rest. If that is what members mean by preparation, each now comes in with a position to be defended. If the position is rejected, it may be considered a personal defeat.

Group leaders, especially, are given to overpreparation. They often feel that the responsibility for success rests solely with them. Consequently, a new chairperson is likely to go home and think out alternative answers to problems before the meeting and to select the answer that seems best. The chairperson then comes into the meeting with the wrong expectations about the right answers, whereupon a whole host of reactive personnel problems arises.

"Preparation" can and should have another more useful meaning. Leaders can preplan group meetings in a way that will be helpful to them and their groups. They, or any member, can gather all the relevant information to feed into the common hopper. But watch out for drawing your conclusions in advance of the meeting. Moreover, to be prepared with a general procedural plan for a meeting can be very useful—and very different from coming with a specific structured step-by-step outline to be imposed on the group. Group members are likely to accept information or a general plan but to resist the imposition of conclusions or tight, inflexible procedures. Besides, if a problem is big enough to call for a meeting, a chairperson who has the answer in advance is often incorrectly prejudging the complexity of the issue.

This group leadership question raises one of the issues we discussed earlier—the location of responsibility. Groups are likely to function with a minimum of personnel difficulty when the responsibility for action and procedure belongs, psychologically, to every member rather than to the leader or to any other single person. The responsibility then remaining for the chair is to help provide and police a communication system that will evoke all the valid information the group can get to make its decisions.

Problems of navigation

Groups often get lost on the way to where they want to go. They sometimes have difficulty locating their current position after they have been exploring some strange territory for a while. Groups get lost with respect to timing, allocating priorities, and sequencing their work. Group members then begin to feel uncertain and anxious. Or they may feel they have made no progress when in fact they have. Or they may feel that they are drifting purposelessly. These feelings are often direct consequences of poor navigation.

Skillful navigation is something of an art. If you, as a leader (or any member of a group), begin to feel that your group is getting lost, you have several options for trying to do something about it. You can just wait and hope the group will find itself. You can ask the members to stop going in that direction and go somewhere else. Or you can ask them to stop and decide where they are (in time as well as content) and where they want to go from there. If they then decide they approve of where they are and want to go on, they can pick up where they left off; if they don't like it, they can change.

This third alternative is sensible for several reasons. Failure to do anything includes the possibility that people who begin to feel lost may also begin to withdraw from the scene. Simply vetoing the present course is bound to create some kind of debilitating emotional reaction, either further withdrawal or aggression. But just asking for a pause to reconsider is likely to yield few side effects and may actually save time and enhance the group's progress.

Decision making in groups

Groups, as every reader knows, also have trouble in making decisions. Often they end up with compromises. Sometimes they just can't decide. And sometimes the decisions that groups do make aren't real decisions. People don't pay much attention to them, or they don't follow up on them once they leave the meeting.

The problem is to get decisions made when they are ready to be made and in a way that will lead to follow-up action by the people in the group after they leave the group.

Group leaders may approach this problem in one of two extreme ways. Sometimes leaders will push hard for a decision, allowing a specified period for discussion and then asking immediately for a vote. At the other end of the scale are leaders who never get to decision-making points, either because they don't recognize those points or because the discussion of an issue just never seems to be fully completed. Like the individual problem solvers discussed earlier, groups, too, may fail to search for alternatives long enough or may demand an optimum solution well beyond their realistic capacity.

Many managers favor the limited discussion and vote method of the parliamentary variety. They recognize that the best is too hard to get, so they satisfice with a brief search. But when a decision is forced quickly and the method of deciding is by vote, two problems arise. First, those decisions are often bad decisions. Too little information is processed. There is too much "group think." Conclusions are not subjected to the healthy rasps of deviant positions. Second, minorities left over from that process will have almost no alternative but to mentally reject the decision. If they (or any of us) were "rational" beings, of course, they would accept the majority wish and carry out their part in it. But most of us, even though we may try consciously to accept a decision with which we disagree, have trouble getting very enthusiastic about it. Indeed, people holding minority positions often feel challenged to prove the majority wrong. Such a challenge is easy to meet when the time comes for individual action, simply by acting in ways that "prove" the decision won't work.

Moreover, if decisions come too early, before people feel that they have contributed what they have to contribute, before they have organized and clarified the issues for themselves, then the decisions reached may be superficial and unsatisfactory by any standards. Therefore, they are likely to be forgotten quickly or passed over lightly once the meeting is over. Vague feelings of hostility and resistance may also follow, feelings that may lead consciously or unconsciously to sabotage or denial of the decision.

A good deal of research evidence shows that decisions are carried into action most effectively when they approximate group-consensus decisions, when all members of a group can somehow settle, by their own efforts, on a choice with which they all more or less agree. On the other hand, decisions imposed from the outside, imposed on a minority by a majority, or imposed by the leader are less likely to be lasting or effective, for the same reasons that restrictive authority is a poor tool for effecting important changes in attitude.

Consensus decisions, however, are hard to achieve. Group members have a tendency to disagree with one another, either overtly or covertly. Yet, if the group's problems require that every member later take positive action on the group's decisions, then it is imperative that everyone at least accept, both consciously and unconsciously, the decisions reached in the group.

Often, we must fall short of ideal decision-making procedures. Deadlines and other immediate pressures force us to make majority or individual-leader decisions. But in ongoing groups, that should occur less and less as we build an atmosphere that makes meetings of the minds easier. Open two-way communication, clarification of people's feelings, and freedom to object contribute to the ease with which a considerable degree of consensus can be reached. Sometimes even the most efficient group will run into a problem on which consensus seems impossible to achieve. Someone just cannot agree with the position being taken. Here again, however, even if total agreement on the issue cannot be reached, it can often be reached on the need for some kind of decision. Then, at least, the minority has expressed its position, has announced that it is not ready to change that position, has had a chance to express its own feelings, and has agreed that some decision short of unanimity is necessary and tolerable.

Techniques for improving group process

Over the last thirty years, many methods have been developed for trying to train group members to improve group performance. The sensitivity-training movement represented one such important effort. In effect, what people are asked to do in a sensitivity-training group is to pay attention to process rather than task. They are groups set up *without* extrinsic tasks in order to caricature and highlight intrinsic process. It is probably fair to say that most people who participate in sensitivity training come away feeling they have a better grasp of the importance of underlying feelings and emotions in groups. They may also feel that they have a little more skill in expressing how they feel—and in getting others to do so.

Sensitivity training has concentrated on teaching individuals to be generally more sensitive to group and interpersonal processes. Other related techniques, such as team-building programs, now widely used in large organizations, also emphasize the training of groups rather than individual members. In team building, real teams—groups of people whose work is interconnected—are the relevant units. The method is also process centered; group members are encouraged to talk about their job-related feelings in order to improve task performance.

Although team building and other forms of organizational development are frequently helpful, much of their essence can be and is often achieved more informally on a day-to-day basis. For example, if a particular work group meets frequently, one way to try to improve its performance (if you are the leader or a member) is to try to save a few minutes at the end of every meeting for "process analysis." This involves switching the discussion from task to process and briefly reviewing the process that has taken place in the preceding meeting. The questions for discussion can be simple: What was good and what was bad (in our opinions) about today's meeting? Let's identify the problems and then think up ways to solve them. Initially such discussions are usually quite "sanitary." People will suggest the meetings be scheduled in the afternoon instead of mornings, or on Wednesdays instead of Fridays. Or couldn't we serve coffee? But if the atmosphere stays open, after a few such sessions, more important issues will surface: Can we propose our own agenda items? Or, can we ask Joe to stop bringing outsiders in, because that makes it more difficult for us to speak freely? Focusing on group process is not magic, nor is it amateur psychiatry. It's just a fairly commonsense way of encouraging people to improve the way they work together by trying it, reassessing what they've tried, and trying it again.

In summary

Group process is about how groups work, rather than what they work on. It is, among other things, about people problems, styles of decision making, and methods of group leadership. Here are some conclusions about group process:

The "emotional noise" generated by people in groups usually represents attempts by members to address personal objectives. If that noise is forbidden expression, it may go underground and thereby distort the group's operation.

Conversely, there may be too little noise in a group; that is, available relevant information may not be forthcoming because of barriers to open communication. Some barriers may be mechanical, but most of them are psychological, such as barriers created by status differences, interpersonal jealousies, or fear of embarrassment.

In either case—too much emotional noise or too little—the preferred course would seem to be to promote rather than limit communication, to accept and deal with information about personal feelings and personal objectives as well as with information about pertinent facts.

Problems involving objectives are a major category of process problems. Objectives often seem more clear at first than they turn out to be later. Some ways to deal with that problem are to include objectives as an agenda item, to take an early census of members' views of the objective, and to periodically reexamine and modify objectives.

"People problems" constitute another major set of process issues. These include problems of mood, interpersonal hostility, individual personality clashes, and the like. Again, open, permissive communication seems to encourage consideration of these second-order but essential questions.

Navigational problems also plague groups. Groups can get so involved in content matters that they may lose direction. Periodic stops to shift from content to process can alleviate these difficulties.

Decision making raises additional problems in groups. Broad participation in a search for consensus is in order if later initiative by members are sought, but there are also costs involved.

Sensitivity training and its relatives, such as team building, make up a diverse package of techniques aimed at helping group members understand process issues and improve the validity and quality of communication in groups.

17

Group pressure and the individual: Conformity and deviation

The preceding chapters in this section were concerned with issues like effective performance and high-quality decision making in groups. But groups also shape people. They influence and train us. They scare us, punish us, or make us feel great. Groups also shape and socialize their members. They teach standards, values, and beliefs, often so deeply internalized by their members that they will make great personal sacrifices because of them. Groups can exert extraordinary power. They can "educate" and "brainwash" people.

This chapter is mostly about how groups shape people, and a little about how people shape groups.

Group pressure on the individual

Here is a problem:

You are a member of a committee. It doesn't matter what sort of committee; you may be trying to select new products, working out a strategy for upcoming negotiations with the union, allocating space in the new laboratory, or surreptitiously plotting an attack on the enemy. It is a committee made up mostly of people at about your own level, chaired by a man who is intelligent, reasonable, and rather well liked by all of you. He has circulated an agenda in advance of your next meeting. You have thought a good deal about it and arrived at a position on the very first item—a position you feel rather strongly about.

You arrive at the meeting room on time, but a few of the eight members have not yet shown up, so you and others make small talk until things get under way. The late arrivals show up, a few pleasantries are exchanged, and the chairman gets things started. Gradually, the members successively express their views about the first item on the agenda. By the time you get into the act, it has become pretty clear that most members seem to agree on one position—a position very different from yours. Most people are nodding their heads and saying, "Yes, method X certainly looks like the best way to go."

Then you speak up rather strongly for method Y. Nobody seems very upset. Everybody listens. Some people ask you questions and make comments that are partially supportive and partially in disagreement. And the discussion goes on.

After a while the chairman says, "Well, we've been at this for a while; let's see where we stand," and tries to summarize the two positions that have been taken, position X and your position Y. He polls the group informally, and one after another, the members, all in their own style, go along with X rather than Y. As each of the other members lines up with X, you begin to feel some discomfort. The others seem to be turning toward you, psychologically if not physically; the chairman casts an inquiring look your way. This is a committee that likes to operate informally, and you approve of this informality. You know that the chairman doesn't want to go to a formal vote. He doesn't want to have to say, "We have decided seven to one in favor of X over Y." On the other hand, you feel strongly that Y is right and X is wrong.

So the pressure begins to build, and the spotlight begins to focus on you. The chairman says, "Look, ladies and gentlemen, we've got a little time. Why don't we talk a little longer." And turning to you, he says, "Why don't you give us a rundown on the reasons for your position?" So you do. You lay it out in a way that sounds (to you) forceful, reasonable, and correct.

The rest of the group, which is now focusing rather intently on you, asks questions. It's as though you are on center stage. Everybody is turning toward you and talking to you. They are not shouting at you; they are not angry at you; they are simply asking you "rationally" to justify your position.

This goes on for a while, and then people begin to get a little fidgety. Finally, one of the members turns to you and says, "Perhaps our differences aren't as big as they look. Perhaps it's all really just a matter of words. Sometimes differences that are really small begin to blow up and look like something bigger than they are." The chairman adds, "Well, it is getting rather late. In order to get the job done, I think we have to arrive at some kind of conclusion pretty fast." Then somebody laughs, turns to you, and says, "Why don't you just come along for the ride, and then we can all go out and have a cup of coffee?" You're no fool. You can really feel the pressure now. You know what these people are really saying is, "You are one of us. We like you, but we also need to get going. Don't hold us up any longer."

But you're a tough and rugged individualist. You're a person of principle. Position Y is right, by golly, and you say so again rather forcefully. There is a long silence. Then one of the members says something forceful in reply: "For Chris'sakes! You've been riding that horse for about three-quarters of an hour now, and you haven't come up with a single new reason. It isn't like you to be so stubborn." As though this first opening is a signal, others join the attack. People go at you from all sides. They point out that you've been wrong before when you've held out in situations like this. They attack your loyalty to the group. After all, you know this group likes to operate by consensus and that it is important to all the rest that you all agree. They hit you with everything they've got. Even the chairman seems to be joining in.

But still you hold out. You just can't bring yourself to accept position X when it is so patently clear to you that Y is the only reasonable answer. So there you sit, feeling a little like you're being interrogated by the Gestapo. Your mouth is dry, and you seem to be curled up all alone inside your own thin skin. But you've been raised right! You also think of duty, God, and honor. And so you grit your teeth and fight back. And the clock ticks along.

What comes next?

Fairly far down inside you, you know what will come next. The spotlights focused on you will be turned off, and the real action will begin. Finally (and rather suddenly), one of the members turns to the chairman and says, "We've been at this for almost an hour and a half. We have other business at hand. I think we should adopt position X, and then go on to the next item." And other people turn their chairs, facing one another and the chairman, but no longer facing you. They summarize the arguments for position X, and someone says, "Okay, we've decided to do X; now let's move on."

You've been quiet for the last few minutes because people haven't been talking to you. You've listened to the reasons for accepting position X, and since one of them is clearly absurd, you open your mouth to say something about it. A couple of people in the group turn and look at you as you talk, but they don't say anything in return. The others don't even look, and the chairman finally says, "Let's go on to the next problem on the agenda." And the group goes ahead—without you.

You know what's happened. You have been psychologically sealed off. As far as the group is concerned, you are no longer there. When you speak, no one hears you. Your influence is now zero. You have reached the final stage in the multistage process by which groups deal with nonconforming members. You have been amputated.

The stages of group pressure

In one version or another, that sad story is probably familiar to almost all of us. It is not limited to committees of executives. We encountered the same pressures when we were kids, in the family, in streetcorner gangs, and in school groups. We met it again as teenagers, when we were pressed to conform to group standards of dress and deportment—standards we often tried to resist. And we will continue to encounter it throughout our lives.

But the fact that we have often encountered group pressure doesn't always reduce the pain. In fact, our experience has taught us that we can usually foresee early in the process what is in store if we buck the group. We know they are likely to start out being reasonable, discussing the pros and cons of the issue. But even at that stage, it is implicitly clear that the deviant, not the group, is expected to change.

We can sense what will come next, too. We know the seductive, pat-on-the-back routine. We know that some members of the group will be friendly, smile, and joke with us. They will, in effect, tell us how much they love us and remind us of how valuable the group is to us. They will chuck us under the chin and make up to us in order to pacify us.

We also know what is likely to happen if we don't come across.

Groups of adults, like children, tire of playing games rather quickly. They will decide that they have wasted enough time on that tactic. Then the silken glove will come off to expose the iron fist. If reason won't work, and seduction won't work, then the group moves to stage 3—attack. Now they try to beat us into submission. They pull out all stops; the gloves are off.

But even that isn't the last stage in the process of exerting pressure on the deviant individual. The last stage is amputation. It's as though the members of the group were saying, "Let's reason with you; if that doesn't work, let's try to tease you by emotional seduction; and if even that doesn't work, let's beat you over the head until you have to give up. Failing that, we'll excommunicate you; we'll amputate you from the group; we'll disown you."

This final stage is for most of us a very serious and frightening possibility; the more we value the group, the more frightening it is. The threat of isolation, physical or psychological, is a very grave threat indeed. We don't want to be abandoned by our families, nor by our friends, nor by our business associates.

Perhaps it is because we can foresee this ultimate stage that even mild and early pressure often causes us to change positions, beliefs, or attitudes. Most of us don't get all the way through meetings like the one we described at the beginning of this chapter. We (or the group) give in earlier in the game. We "work things out" when we are still at the reasoning level or the emotional seduction level. The paradox in this process is that the greater the pressure that the group exerts on the deviant, the more difficult it becomes for the deviant to give in. The stage at which we can give in most easily (and still save face) is the first stage—the reasonable, rational stage. If we say yes at the second stage, in response to emotional seduction, we will probably feel a little sheepish, but that isn't terribly embarrassing. To give in under a beating is a lot more painful and a lot more shameful. And to give in after we have been amputated is almost impossible because nobody is there to accept our surrender.

Is the group being cruel and capricious?

So far we have been viewing the group's pressures on the deviant from the deviant's perspective. For most of us individuals who hold out are the heroes, whether they win or lose. We value individuality and nonconformity in our society, or at least we say we do. We identify with the underdog, with the deer attacked by wolves. But consider this same problem from the other perspective, the group's. We may ask, Why are these people doing this? Why are they reasoning, seducing, attacking, and amputating? Is it just a malicious, devilish kind of behavior to satisfy some sadistic motives of the group members? Not usually. If we think of the times we ourselves have been members of the majority, we can begin to see the other side of the picture.

Here is a group that is trying to get a job done. To get the job done well depends in large part on getting wholehearted agreement and cooperation from all members of the group. But there is a deadline, as well as other constraints imposed by the world.

We go about the problem in good spirit, trying to cooperate, understand, and work out a solution that we can all accept in a reasonable time. Here we come very close to an answer. Everybody seems to be in perfect agreement except for that one character there.

Then what shall we do? As reasonable people, we do not just ignore someone just because he thinks differently from us. We listen to him and we ask him to listen to us. So we go through that ritual. We reason with him. But that doesn't work. He just doesn't seem to be able to see it our way. The clock is ticking away.

What next? We try to appeal to him on emotional grounds, on grounds of loyalty or decency. We almost beg him to agree. This is difficult for us to do, but we want to get the job done and don't want to hurt anyone. We appeal to him to join up, to go along, to maintain a solid front. But he refuses stubbornly.

Now what? Now we really are mad, so we let him have it. Maybe if we all jump up and down on him, he will have sense enough to come around. And the clock ticks on. But the stubborn character still holds out.

What then? Well, then we must take a step that is as painful for us as it is for him. We must dismember our group. We must amputate one of our own members, leaving us less than whole, less than intact, but at least capable of coming to a conclusion. With this recalcitrant, stubborn, impossible member, this group cannot remain a group. To preserve it, we have no choice but to cut him out.

Viewed this way, the deviant individual is not such a hero. Much of the world's complex work is done by groups. When a group exerts pressure on an individual, it may not constitute an arbitrary imposition of naked power but rather a set of increasingly desperate efforts to try to hold the group together in order to get the work done.

Does the deviant do anybody any good?

Besides the argument that it is wholesome, and healthy for individuals to be independent thinkers—an argument that is not always as sensible as it sounds—is there any other good argument for encouraging individuals to take deviant positions if they believe in them, and for encouraging groups not to clobber people who deviate?

The answer, of course, is that there is at least one very good practical reason, in addition to all the moral reasons. Deviants stimulate groups to think about what they are doing. Deviants, whether they are themselves creative or not, generate both creativity and thoroughness in groups.

The process is simple and understandable enough. When like-minded people get together to talk over an issue, they are likely to come to agreement pretty quickly, then pat one another on the back and go out and drink beer. When the same people get together in the presence of someone with quite different ideas, they are forced to reexamine their own beliefs, go over them in more detail, and consider aspects of the problem that they never had to consider before. They must do that in order to argue effectively with the deviant, attack him, and reason with him. As a consequence, they end up knowing more about their own problem than they would have had the deviant not been there. It costs the group time and effort. But what they earn is a greater understanding, a broader search, and more knowledge of their own subject matter.

Can the deviant ever win?

We now come to the next question in this logical sequence: Suppose the deviant is right. Does he have a chance? Or will his presence simply cause the group that is already wrong to believe more strongly but more sophisticatedly in its wrong position?

The answer to this one is, unfortunately, complicated. Research evidence shows that people can and will distinguish better answers from worse ones. And a deviant who comes up with a clearly better answer, even in the face of a large group that has agreed on another answer, has a good chance of getting his answer accepted. Such is the case, at least, for problems with a clear logical structure. If I can demonstrate to you a clearly easier way to add a column of figures than the way all of you are adding them now, it will not be too hard for me to convince you to change over to my method. So the deviant who comes up with a new solution to a well-defined problem—one that other people had not even thought of—is likely to have little trouble getting it through.

Unfortunately, *most* problems that are tackled by groups aren't that clear-cut. They are fuzzy judgmental problems with no clearly, unequivocally right solutions. The normal problems require decisions about promoting one candidate from a set of five, or allocating a fixed fund among several departments, or deciding on one of many sales promotions. On those kinds of judgmental issues, the deviant is likely to have a hard time swinging the group.

And that leads to another paradox. The person with the different ideas, the deviant, has a better chance of getting his ideas accepted by a group that isn't very cohesive and doesn't work together very well than by a group whose members know how to work together effectively. So managers are faced with what looks like an odd dilemma. On the one hand, they want solidity, loyalty, and high morale in a team. On the other hand, they want the creativity they can get from deviant thinkers, people who march to a different drummer. And yet it is precisely the high-morale, cohesive group that will go after deviants hard and fast, clobbering them even more quickly than the new group or the unsure group.

But that dilemma may be more apparent than real. True, we are suggesting that those with different ideas may be better able to influence a group of people who feel uncertain with one another than they could a solid group. They are likely to get their ideas through, however, not because the less cohesive group will examine and consider those ideas more carefully than a cohesive group but because its members are constrained, uncertain, and unwilling to open themselves up. So the aggressive deviant, the one who talks loudest and fastest, may be able to snow them.

On the other hand, when faced with a solid, self-assured group, the deviant will have to prove a case and prove it rather thoroughly. Of course, the probability of being able to prove it to a group that is solid and self-assured is not very great. But if they accept the deviant's idea, it will be because it is incontrovertible. They are not likely to break ranks unless the logic of the case is so clear, so rational, and so obviously better than their own solution that only a fool could reject it.

What kind of deviant can survive?

Interestingly enough, even powerful deviants don't have much of a chance against a strong and solid group. And the chances drop almost to zero for the group member who is new or peripheral—the new, young member of a street gang, for example. Such members are poorly positioned to try to push a new idea through. Note, however, that even strong, old members can have a tough time changing a group's mind. We are apt to think that a person central to a group, like the leader of the street gang, should be almost omnipotent, capable of getting the group to accept even extremely deviant ideas. Not so. The fact of the matter is that even members with much authority and much personal power can have a very tough time pushing a group very far from its own standards. Even the kingpin has to move slowly, by bits and pieces, to get the gang to stop stealing apples and start playing basketball. The leader who doesn't move slowly will get the same treatment as any other deviant, eventually being amputated.

The same is true in organizations. Even the powerful boss will meet a good deal of trouble in pushing a very different idea through a solid group of subordinates. If a real Machiavellian manipulator, the boss will work first on individuals when trying to bring about a radical change, rather than confronting the whole group face to face.

The lonely executive

Most of the research and commonsense analysis of conformity leads one to the conclusion that the heart of the matter is loneliness. Group pressures can be exerted on one individual—a lone individual—much more effectively than they can be exerted on pairs or groups of people. It is when the deviant finds himself alone, without a twig of support, without even another deviant (even one who deviates in a quite different direction), that the pressures of the group are apt to become overpowering. It may be a pervasive anxiety about isolation that permits the group to press the individual to conform, even if that individual has authority or other kinds of power. Even CEOs want and need some sources of support, some assurance and reassurance of backing from subordinates. They need not to be all alone. In fact, much of the effect of group pressure can be washed out by the simple expedient of having just one other member of the group provide support for the deviant member.

Once again we encounter a paradox. Now we are proposing that fear of loneliness will force a member to conform to the group's wishes, and that implies that he will feel less pressure to conform (and therefore feel more independent) if he is in the group—a full member of it—and thus not at all lonely. How are we to answer our earlier question? Does a group force its members to fit into its mold, thereby reducing individuality and brainwashing them? Or is it only when we are psychologically secure members of a group that we can express our individuality without feeling pressure and restraint?

There is an answer. People need psychological support, an environment free from the fear of loneliness. But if that support is bought at the price of constricting conformity, the individual loses his individuality no matter which way he goes. So the critical focal point becomes the nature of this group. On which dimensions of behavior, and how many of them, does it demand conformity? Does it demand, as the price of support, that we dress as they dress, that we believe as they believe? Or does it set more open standards, requiring conformity in fewer dimensions and perhaps less critical ones? Does it only require, perhaps, that everyone conform to certain time demands and certain demands of procedure, while consciously avoiding requirements of conformity in opinion or belief? Indeed, can a group set a positive standard of *nonconformity?*

Since the individual needs the group, the group can exploit the individual, forcing him to bend to its demands. But individuals make groups, and it is possible to have groups that exert tolerable pressures on procedure yet do not constrain diversity of ideas.

In summary

Groups put pressure on members who deviate. Usually the pressure moves through several stages—from rational argument, through emotional seduction, to attack, and finally to amputation of the deviant member. But the process is seldom capricious or sadistic. From the group's side, they exert pressure in an effort to survive intact and to get the job done.

Group pressures work best when the deviant individual feels all alone. Given any kind of minimal support, one can hold out much more effectively. And though a powerful deviant has a better chance than a weak one, no deviant can try to push a solid group very far and very fast and expect to get away with it.

Clearly, deviants make groups think, even when they don't change the group's mind. But we need to temper two prevalent notions about deviants. The first is the mostly American notion that nonconformists are somehow always good guys. We must remember that much of the world's work can only be done by conforming to agreed-on standards and rules of conduct. That's called teamwork, isn't it? The second is the notion that groups always kill individuality by exerting pressures to conform. We need to remember that most of us feel more free to be our imaginative selves in groups where our position and membership are secure than in settings in which we feel alone and unsupported.

18 Conflict and competition among groups: My team can beat your team

Suppose that you are the progressive manager of a large manufacturing and consumer marketing operation. You want to get the best possible ideas out of your people. It is clear that you will need a new design for one of your key products. So you ask the heads of three different groups to submit proposals for the redesign. The heads are to get together with their people and develop what they think would be an optimal design.

But you don't want to get into the position of having to select the one design you think is best, especially since you are not a designer. Moreover, you want to open up discussion and communication. So you inform them that, after all three designs are in, you would like each group to circulate its design to the members of the other two groups. Then, when everyone has had a chance to look over all three possibilities, representatives of the three groups will meet together and decide which of the three designs is, in their joint opinion, the best one for the company to develop.

Thus, by keeping everyone informed of everything, by giving all groups a chance to consider all three alternative designs, you figure that you should be able to get (1) the best of the three designs and (2) understanding and agreement among all three groups. Do you think that plan will work?

The experimental evidence suggests it won't work at all. That scheme of having several groups work out a problem and then resolve their differences among themselves is almost doomed to failure. Most of us know it, but we don't really believe we can't make it work, even when we're right in the middle of it. Perhaps the best way to describe what does happen is to quote an insurance company executive who once joined an experimental version of the same kind of problem, and then wrote the following letter to a magazine:

> We were divided at random into four teams. The instructor then asked us to draft a statement of policy for our Company in answer to a certain hypothetical situation. Each group, working separately, was to draft its version. It took each group about two hours to hammer out its statement. Each group elected a representative to meet with one another to

select one of the four statements. I was elected to represent my group. The members of my group, though naturally proud of their effort (they had reviewed the other three drafts in the interim), were confident that reaching agreement with the others would be easy.

The four representatives sat at a card table in the center of the room; behind each man, breathing down his neck, sat the group he represented. It soon emerged that the over-all objectives of the four groups were quite close; it merely remained to choose one of the drafts. At the end of an hour we were further apart than ever. I asked my group for permission to vote for one of the other drafts. My request was indignantly turned down. Feelings had begun to run high. Logic had been tried; gamesmanship had been tried.

Notes were passed forward by each group to its representative. These notes were not helpful at all; they merely urged us to "get" the other man on some point or other. All had failed—the results were shattering.

Four judges, previously elected by their groups, were now called in. They had not participated in drafting the policy statements at all. During the time we had been working out our policy statement, they had drawn up criteria for evaluating the four drafts. The drafts were then submitted to them anonymously. In just one half hour and in a separate room in calm deliberation they had reached a unanimous decision. The experiment was over.

Most of the events that that insurance executive describes were highly predictable. They were predictable because emotional and psychological elements drove them, elements we tend to overlook when we concentrate on getting a task done. Those uniform and predictable events include these:

1. As each group begins to develop its own solution, it will become more internally cohesive and solid. Morale within groups will tend to go up as their design takes shape. When they have finally produced something together, they will usually feel quite good about themselves. Sometimes, of course, a deviant or two can disturb the happy solidarity of the group.

2. When each group sees the comparable work of the other groups, the initial reaction will be a momentary letdown, followed by a quick recovery and continued increase in group morale. Usually, after group members have seen the others' solutions, someone will say, "I didn't feel very happy about our group's design until I saw those others. But if those are the best other groups have to offer, it's clear that ours is the only one worth a damn." That means that deviant members now have a face-saving means of reentering their groups.

3. In each group this same solidifying, balancing process will go on. By the time the representatives come together, they have each, in effect, convinced themselves that the design being offered by their group is the best of all designs—honestly the best. Moreover, each representative will by now

feel charged by the group to convince the other two that their group's design is the one they should all buy.

4. Initially, the representatives, when they meet together, are likely to behave like the majority dealing with the deviant in the preceding chapter. They all provide reasons to support their own group's design over the designs of the other two. But, especially if this is a public meeting with others watching, this rational discussion soon turns into a duel. The representatives will try to cut one another to pieces. They will try to top one another in their cleverness and wit. The goal of finding a single best design will soon fade in favor of trying to be a hero/winner in the eyes of one's own group. And if the representative cannot appear a hero, at least there will surely be no appearance of being a traitor. The representative must not give in. So the representatives almost never become a functioning group. They become gladiators, battling for the approval of their constituents, trying not to be publicly destroyed by the others.

5. The representatives will then try to form coalitions, two or three against one; but they all know that those coalitions are opportunistic. They cannot count on their allies, who will desert them if they see an opportunity to advance their own causes. Sometimes the representatives will manage to come to some kind of half-baked decision. Two of them will outvote a third, or one representative will be weak enough (or the representative's group divided enough) to give in. But most of the time they will reach a deadlock and finally give up in favor of a decision from some higher authority (if a higher authority exists).

6. Suppose at this point we argue that the difficulty is obvious; the social pressure of the groups on their members is really preventing a decision. Somehow, if we could get to the private opinions of the individual members—if we could get to the people—they, in their wisdom, would recognize and admit to the design that is really the best one.

So now we decide to take a secret ballot among all members of all groups. They have all had a chance to see and discuss all three designs, and they all have some expertise about design.

That won't work either. In almost every case the group members will vote nearly 100 percent in favor of the design submitted by their own group. Even privately, one's own group's design will look best to almost all members. Occasionally there will be a break in the pattern. One or two members of a team may decide that another design looks better. Usually those are deviant members of their teams, who were "troublesome" from the beginning.

7. If the groups can't decide, and if the individual members can't decide, we can now throw the decision to authority—to the boss. Or if we wished, we could throw it to a board of arbitrators who would sit down impartially and look at all designs independently, perhaps without knowing which design was presented by which group. In most cases, the boss or the arbitra-

tors will then have no trouble at all. They will come to a decision quickly and quite easily.

8. Now we have a decision. We have taken it to the top, and the top has decided. Isn't that the way we should have done it in the first place? Perhaps so, but what does that "decision" mean? The design submitted by group X has now been chosen; group Y's is the alternate; and group Z's is considered completely inadequate. Now what will happen? In experimental runs of this sort, what happens is quite uniform. The winning group becomes elated. It feels great and thinks highly of the board of arbitrators that has chosen its design. The losing group feels hostile, frustrated, and depressed. Privately, and sometimes publicly, they will insist that the arbitrators really didn't know what they were doing and that any really imaginative expert in the field would recognize the superiority of their (losing) design. The decision being from above does not completely solve the problem. It certainly has not solved it in the sense of developing commitment by all groups to the new design.

9. We can follow this experiment one step further, putting the groups to work again on a new problem. Then we will encounter some interesting results. The group that has just won will probably be self-satisfied, comfortable, and "frozen." Though its organization and social structure may be less than perfect, nobody will dare to change it. The people who were powerful in the development of the first design remain powerful on the next problem, whether they are qualified or not. Even though some members may want some changes, no one dares disturb the winning combination.

The third team, the losing one, may be in serious internal trouble. They may feel their representative has let them down. Individuals who took minority or deviant positions may now come back with I-told-you-so comments that engender further bickering and interpersonal stress. Usually such groups recover from this internecine warfare; but sometimes they collapse entirely. If winning teams freeze, losing teams melt. The loser abandons its original organization so fully that it will have a great deal of trouble holding it together.

The second team is a lot better off. They have lost, but they have not been decimated. They are apt to be thoughtful in reexamining what happened in the first round. They are unfrozen in a sense, but they have not completely melted. Other things being equal, they are a good team on which to place a bet for the future.

Psychologists have conducted experiments of this kind to demonstrate issues that seem obvious and simple: people develop great loyalty to what they produce themselves, and loyalty to one another when they produce something together; this in-group loyalty may be so overwhelming as to make it effectively impossible (at least within the structure set up in these experiments) for the groups to come to agreement with other groups.

Some morals

Let's turn now to the morals of this tale. Most of these conclusions seem rather depressing. They demonstrate how agreement can*not* be reached, rather than how it can. They also show how easy it is to start a war, even among reasonable people. They reiterate the old truism that it is easy to build a solid group by providing them with an outside enemy. They tell us—as we all know—that representatives of groups are often much more concerned (and understandably so) about the groups at their backs than about the problem before them.

But those conclusions also offer a few larger, if tentative, morals. As we begin to realize how easy it can be to create conflict between groups, two worrisome, related thoughts arise.

First, one begins to appreciate the wonder of the existence of large societies. The pressure toward fragmentation is so great, and fragmentation itself so easy, that the development of large groups such as tribes or nations or even large companies looks very impressive indeed. One wonders why they don't all break into little bits.

Second, if social dikes are really as easily rupturable as it appears, perhaps it is time for more of us to learn how to hold them together.

Perhaps a third generalization is worth noting: Although most of us are properly proud of our uniqueness and individuality, we should stay conscious of the fact that we are shaped by our social structures. We are, in effect, prisoners of structure. Although psychologists would not find it easy to predict the precise behavior of any single individual in the experiment we described above, it's easy to predict the overall behavior of the groups. Once we have set up the structure, the overall human outcomes appear to be almost guaranteed. Autonomous and free though we may appear, we live in social structures, and our collective behavior is largely an outcome of those structural characteristics. If we had been raised in the USSR, we would not only speak Russian; we would probably think Russian, perceive Russian, and fight Russian.

The positive side

How about the positive side? How can we increase the probability of a good decision in that design problem? One thing we can try is to reduce the pressure on the representatives from their groups; another is to make the representatives a sufficiently cohesive group so that membership in the *representatives group* is something meaningful and important in its own right. By doing that we will be squeezing all of the representatives, requiring each to owe loyalty to two groups, even though those two groups are in partial conflict. But we will also increase the probability that each will indeed represent both points of view to both groups and thus increase the level of objectivity.

There are several other things we could do to increase the probability of an acceptable solution. Readers may want to note their own lists of possibilities. We could, for example, search for some "superordinate" goal, an objective so important to every group that differences will largely disappear. They could be superordinate enemies—as in the case of the attack on Pearl Harbor—that bring subgroups together by threatening all of them; or better still—but harder—they might be positive superordinate goals, such as the collaboration of many groups in a depressed community to get it out of the doldrums.

There is another possibility—education. Perhaps if we all become more aware of structural traps, we can avoid them more successfully.

Another note should be sounded here. Organizations can almost be said to have their own *styles* of conflict management. In some, for example, direct conflict is avoided at almost any cost. The culture demands that people be polite in meetings, that underlying differences not be discussed openly. In other organizations conflict tends to be confronted more directly. People express disagreemnt and argue for positions. It may seem easy for most of us to prefer the first to the second. It looks civilized, courteous, and comfortable. But it may be wise at this point to take a closer look at the second. When the world is changing fast, it may behoove organizations to face internal conflicts openly and to welcome argument and debate.

Some varieties of conflict and some tactics that accompany them

We haven't said much yet about the different kinds of conflict that can occur in organizations. In our example, the conflict was among peer groups of about equal size, status, and power. But that isn't the way things always line up. Sometimes a small group finds itself up against a much larger group or coalition of groups. Sometimes power differences arise—employees versus management, for example. And sometimes a small, subordinate group takes on a larger group with more power and authority, such as a dissident subgroup in the larger church or a small group of radical students in a large, conservative university.

There are several, quite different methods that groups use to resolve these different classes of conflicts.

The first is war—coercive power, as we called it earlier. If you're the big powerful group, you clobber the little group. You kill them, jail them, excommunicate them, banish them. You hoist their heads on poles.

If you're the little group in a power war, you may count on other forms of power: hit-and-run guerrilla tactics, terrorism, blackmail; and, of course, you seek alliances to increase your power. You curry public favor. You try to prevail on other big groups to back you up.

Obviously, all of those kinds of tactics are alive and well, largely unchanged from the days of the caveman. But we have added a few new, somewhat more moderate and civilized tactics to the conflict scene, haven't we? Indeed, isn't one measure of civilization the degree to which conflicts, even between more and less powerful groups, are resolved by less coercive means? We have set up governments, legal systems, and organizations, all of which try to move methods of conflict resolution away from raw power tactics and toward . . . what?

How about toward *negotiation* and *trade-offs?* From the bread-and-butter bargains made by representatives in Congress who vote for one another's favorite bills, to the informal (and sometimes illegal) coalitions among business competitors to fix prices or define territories, to union-management bargaining, society rides on negotiations, trade-offs, compromises, and accommodations to conflicts. Most of them are legal; many aren't. Most don't truly resolve conflicts; they just keep them within bounds. But surely that's better than war.

Sometimes we inch a step beyond that, especially in the relations between large, powerful groups and small rebellious ones in their midst. Traditionally, the resolution of such conflicts was simple: the big one steps on the little one. But sometimes, because the big groups are unsure of themselves, or sometimes because the big ones are very sure of themselves, they have moved from direct coercive power toward *absorption* as a method for ending conflict with little groups.

All that absorption means in this context is that large group A tries to deal with dissident little group B by behaving like a big pillow. University Administration A, for example, says to its protesting students B, "Okay. We'll do some of the things you ask. But you must take a large part of the responsibility for doing them. You want to participate; we'll let you participate, partway. We'll put three students on the fifteen-person search committee for a new president."

The big organization bends and backs off, but in bits and pieces. The little one gets some of what it wants, but at a price—the price of partial collaboration, of partial reentry into membership in the parent organization.

This process may at first seem indistinguishable from slaughter, at least to the dedicated and rebellious members of the smaller group, for its effect may well be the ultimate demise of that group. Certainly it can be viewed as emasculation, for protesting groups, founded on protest, cannot easily survive after they get most of what they want. But sometimes, depending on motives and intent, the process can represent a considerable degree of civilized effort by the large group to acknowledge the need for change and to bring it about at a price. The large group pays a price in the absorption process, too. Although it remains the establishment, it is a slightly changed establishment, modified by its absorption of the small group.

Does it happen in business organizations?

The reader may well point out that the kind of experiment we described at the beginning of this chapter seems more typical of governments or political groups than business organizations. Intelligent managers, they might argue, would never set up a situation like the one described. They wouldn't put three groups to work doing the same thing, and even if they did, they wouldn't let the groups decide among themselves which of the outcomes was best.

Let's grant that one. But can't we think of large organizations, at least in part, as collections of smaller groups engaged in negotiation and power plays with one another? The problem may not be a new product design. It may be the location and size of a new warehouse. And the groups may not be three parallel design groups, but a regional sales force that wants something very different from what a staff group thinks would be optimal. Or the issue may be the allocation of the capital budget. And the members of the capital budgeting committee may be, partially at least, representatives of one subgroup or another. Or sales groups vie for the same classes of accounts; or maintenance people want control of a process the engineering people claim is theirs. And so on and on. These cases may be less pure than our experiment, but their essence is the same.

Confrontation techniques for managing intergroup conflict

Traditionally, organizations have tried to handle conflict, we said, by coercive measures, through negotiation and compromise, or by "absorption" of protesting groups. They have also called on higher authority to settle the question. But since, in companies, both warring groups know that they will look bad if they take their dispute upstairs, conflicts are often "handled" simply by going underground. Nobody ever admits there's a war going on.

The dangers of such phony resolutions are very great in organizations. Conflicts between groups nefariously eat away at the organization's health.

Are there alternatives? One that has been experimented with widely is the technique of *confrontation*. It is partially based on some of the beliefs about the nature of human groups that we discussed earlier. When groups are in conflict, the argument goes, the conflict will necessarily involve feelings as well as facts, process as well as content. Although the groups may only argue about the facts of their positions, they also tend to develop stereotypes and prejudices about one another. We see ourselves more and more as the good guys, and the other groups become more and more the bad guys. They are selfish, power-mad, and wicked; we are just trying to do a job. This process of valuing one's own group positively and increasingly denigrating the other, derives, as the reader will see, from the tendency of group members to support one another and to overvalue their own position in the presence of outsiders.

Even if this emotional separation accompanies conflicts that may have been started over factual issues, it will have to be dealt with. Hence the notion of confrontation. Let's bring the groups together, usually with a third-party process manager, and let's have them talk, not about the factual issues but about feelings and attitudes. If we can get those stereotypes and distortions of feeling straightened out, perhaps we can then go back to the factual differences and work on them, this time with a problem-solving attitude rather than a game-playing or warlike one.

In summary

It is very easy to set up situations in which groups compete with one another. In such settings the solidarity and morale of members *within* groups tends to increase steadily as competition progresses. But between groups, bickering and hostility also grows. In such situations the naive use of intergroup meetings may simply aggravate the problem. What starts out as an honest effort to reach a resolution can quickly become a public display of each representative's capacity to outtalk and outwit the others.

Members of groups identify so closely with their own product and with their own groups that the likelihood of resolution decreases as the morale of each group increases. Yet outsiders, not identified with any group, find it easy to evaluate and choose from among the different groups' products. But if these outsiders then try to impose their choice on the groups (even though the groups have invited it) the result will be less than ideal. "Losing" groups will feel recalcitrant and generally dissatisfied with the situation and with themselves, often degenerating into internal bickering. Winning groups on the other hand, may sit on their hands, fearful of changing anything lest it destroy the winning lineup.

This chapter offers no clear solutions to problems of intergroup competition. It suggests, however, that greater understanding of the power of the larger structure may contribute to more objectivity. It suggests that compromise and building cohesion among representatives of different groups are both useful. Finally, if we can all develop stronger identification with some larger "superordinate" goals, then, perhaps, our local conflicts can be set aside.

Experiments in trying to resolve conflicts by confrontational methods are under way in many different settings. Their aim is to help conflicting groups share their feelings about one another, as a precursor to resolving more factual differences.

19

Communication nets in groups and organizations: Who can talk to whom about what?

The relationships among members of a group—like the one between two people—are limited by the kinds of communication that occur. In an earlier chapter, we also pointed out that the communication process has several dimensions, only one of which is its *content*. The same holds for groups. Group members can talk about all sorts of ideas, but they can also use either one-way or two-way communication no matter what they talk about. They can, moreover, carry on more or less noisy and redundant conversations. And group members can communicate over different *networks*.

A network, for our purposes, is a structure, a system of connections among the people who make up any group or organization. Sometimes, in larger organizations, we find formal networks, "official" communication structures. First-level people can talk to second-level people, who can carry the word to third-level people, and so on. In smaller groups, networks tend to evolve more informally, often unknowingly created by the person leading the group. Some group leaders tend to encourage everyone-can-talk-to-everyone networks, and some set up structures in which each member speaks only to the leader.

Those networks are important, both for small groups and for larger organizations. They can seriously affect productivity as well as morale, attitudes, and even creativity.

This chapter summarizes the findings of research studies on communication networks in small groups. Those experiments may strike the reader at first as somewhat abstract, but try to stay with them, because the underlying ideas have important implications for the way we design and manage organizations and small groups.

What we mean by communication nets

A communication net is a group *structure*. The net defines how the group is hung together. Consider, for instance, the difference between bosses who set themselves up to communicate with their staffs as drawn in figure 19.1 and those who prefer to divide their four staff people into two seniors and

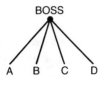

Fig. 19.1.

Fig. 19.2.

two juniors, as drawn in figure 19.2. The lines in these diagrams represent lines of normal communication. They are structural diagrams. They tell us nothing about the people involved—just something about the "system." What differences might such different systems make in the boss's information about what's going on in the shop? In the boss's flexibility? In the number of ideas received from subordinates?

Consider also the effects on subordinates of being in one communicational position or another—such as B in the two figures. In one case, B can talk to the boss directly. In the other, B must go through channels.

Suppose, further, that for a group of five people every channel is a two-way channel. Then this question still remains: What system of channels will be the most effective for those five people trying to do a particular job? Will they work best when everyone has an open two-way channel to everyone else, as in figure 19.3? Or is the system in figure 19.4 better? Or in figure 19.5? And which of those nets will be the most fun to work in?

Fig. 19.3.

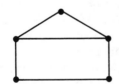

Fig. 19.4.

Fig. 19.5.

Even though each of these networks provides enough communication channels to *permit* everyone to know what's going on, the arrangements and numbers of channels differ. Also, the effectiveness of the group as a problem-solving body may differ. Moreover, some of those networks fit better with the usual company organization chart than others; some would look very strange indeed on an organization chart.

In practical terms the question now is this one: How does the communication network affect both the efficiency of a group's performance and the morale of the group's members?

Testing communication networks

The best way to answer such questions may be to strip away temporarily the complications found in real life. Then one can set up small experimental committees and put them to work in one or another of these networks. By providing each experimental group with some standard tasks and then measuring performance, one can get some ideas about the relative efficiency of one of these networks versus another. Many such experiments have been carried out, and the results have been quite consistent and somewhat surprising.

You might like to try to decide for yourself, on a commonsense basis, just what results one should get with one of these networks or another. For illustrative purposes, consider the two networks of five people each given in figure 19.6.

Such groups might be analogous to groups of field people, each located in a different branch or district but all reporting eventually to the same person up at headquarters. Let's say all communication has to be by telephone. In both networks, A, E, B, and D are district people, and C is someone back at the central office.

In an experimental setup, one can give each of these groups the identical problem, which requires some information from each person before it can be solved. In most experiments it is some sort of puzzle, in many ways analogous to a pricing problem in a rapidly changing supply-and-demand situation.

Which of these two groups will solve that kind of problem faster? Which group will, over time, develop higher morale? Will a leader emerge in group 1? In group 2? Which particular positions in group 1 or 2 will be high-morale positions? Which will be low-morale positions?

Here are some answers that have come out of experiments like these:

- Network no. 1 will be the faster of the two.
- At the end of the experiment, the morale of group 2 will be higher than that of group 1. People will feel more enthusiastic in group 2.
- Only one person in group 1 is likely to feel really good about the job, and that is the person in position C. The others, A, B, D, and E, will probably feel bored and left out of things.
- Person C in group 1 will probably be seen as the leader. Everyone in the group will be likely to turn to C for decisions. In group 2 the leader (the one who gets the answer first and sends it out to the others) can be almost anybody. In fact, there may be a different leader each time the group runs through a problem, or else no identifiable leader at all.

Another finding from these experiments carries intriguing implications for organizations. Two groups are put to work, one in the circle (group 2), the other in the star (group 1) pattern. This is the job they are given: Each person is given five marbles of five different colors. Only one color is com-

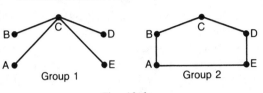

Fig. 19.6.

mon to all five. The group must then discover the one color common to everyone. They try to do so by sending written notes to one another over the available channels. The notes say things like this: "I'm B, and I have red, green, yellow, blue, and brown marbles. What do you have?" Eventually they discover that all have a red marble in common. After playing that game several times, the groups in both networks become proficient at it. But at this point, we pull a dirty trick. We change the colors. Instead of simple solid colors, the players are given mottled marbles, of odd shades, difficult to describe. Now two people looking at identical marbles may describe them quite differently. One may write, "I have a greenish yellow one." Another may describe it as "aqua." Semantic noise, in other words, has now been injected into the task.

Now which team performs better? The interesting finding is that these two networks perform quite differently when they meet this changed situation. The circle (group 2) handles it well, so that after a number of tries it has figured out how to do it and is back to high efficiency. The star (group 1) can't seem to cope with the new problem, still making large numbers of errors even after many trials. That result suggests that the structure of an organization influences its adaptability, as well as other aspects of efficiency. And adaptability is a critical factor in real-world organizations.

Communication structures, then, do affect group performance, at least in these experiments. But notice that performance, even in these little experiments can mean many things. Some communication networks perform *faster* than others, but that advantage is often gained at the cost of accuracy and/or morale. People feel happier in some networks than they do in others. Therefore, some networks are more likely to perform longer than others without blowing up. But those networks may also work more slowly than some others. In some nets, creative new ideas are more readily accepted than in others. Is that a measure of performance? Some networks make fewer errors than others. Some are more flexible and adaptable than others. So let's be sure we know what kind of "performance" we most want. Deciding that is a big problem for the thoughtful manager.

Why different networks cause people to behave differently

If we look at these results in the light of parts 1 and 2 of this book, they are not hard to understand. Why is network 1 faster than network 2? For one thing, network 1 is like a one-way communication system. Although people can talk back individually to the central person, they cannot talk to one another. Network 1 imposes an orderliness on the group that wipes out extra messages. In network 2, no such clear organization is imposed. Each person can send messages to two other people. Therefore, they can and do send more messages and use up more time.

But in sending more messages, members of network 2 are also taking advantage of more checkpoints of the kind provided by two-way communication. Thus, they can locate and correct more of their errors more easily than network 1.

Players in network 2 also have more chance to participate and take responsibility. They are less dependent on one person since they can check with another person. So they are more satisfied and happy, just as people were in an earlier two-way communication example.

On the other hand, the central person in network 1 is quite happy—and for the same reasons. That person has responsibility, has several sources of information and several checkpoints, and is independent and powerful.

In such ways, then, the mere mechanical *structure* can act on individuals to make them feel more or less dependent, more or less certain of where they stand, and more or less responsible. That same structure can also act on the total operational efficiency of the group, permitting it to work faster or slower, more or less accurately, and more or less adaptably.

Once again, though, it is worth pointing out, as we did earlier, that structure seems to affect people's feelings in one direction and their speed and accuracy in another. We have yet to find a structure that generated high speed and accuracy and, at the same time, high morale and flexibility. Perhaps modern information technology will help us deal with that problem. We may be getting closer to achieving speed, accuracy, and creativity, all at the same time!

Networks in larger organizations

One may argue that these laboratory findings, though interesting, are not particularly relevant to the problems actually encountered in organizations. In most real face-to-face small groups, only one communication network seems possible, and that is a fully connected network in which everyone can communicate directly with everyone else.

But the argument that that is the only actual network does not hold very well. A clear, albeit informal, notion about who can talk to whom exists in most groups. In fact, in face-to-face small groups, although the *official* network may be a fully connected one, the *actual* network may be some other one altogether. Communication networks are much like organization charts; there is likely to be a formal, officially charted organization, as well as an informal, uncharted organization that plays the more significant role in practice.

In a committee meeting, for example, a chairperson can usually manipulate the communication setup so that each member talks only to the chair and not directly to other people. Even if the chair tries to be "democratic," the same result may occur unintentionally because of differences in rank or power among members of the committee. Privates don't interrupt generals whenever they feel like it, no matter what the official communication network.

In continuing work groups, the possibilities for changing communication nets are better than in periodic or one-shot meetings. Almost any network becomes possible if the group in question stays together for an extended period.

"Good" and "bad" networks

What, then, are the characteristics of the "best" communication networks? That question demands another: Best for what? If we mean "best" for small meetings and conferences, where everyone's ideas can make a contribution and where the same people will probably get together again next week, then the answer seems clear. The best networks are likely to be the ones with at least two related characteristics:

First, more egalitarian networks are probably preferable to more hierarchical networks. That is, networks like the circle, where everyone has access to about the same number of channels, are preferable to networks like the star, where one person has many neighbors and the rest none. Second, those networks that provide everyone with more than one direct communication channel are probably better than those that give some people only one channel to other members of the group.

Several different networks meet these criteria. And there are real differences even among these. But in general, networks that meet those standards do indeed—in experimental situations—yield higher morale, greater involvement in the work, and a series of other advantages over networks that do not meet them.

But if by "efficient" we mean fast in getting started and fast in its operations, our conclusions about the best network must be quite different. Then, more differentiated, hierarchical networks like the star may work more "efficiently." They impose a clear-cut organization on the group, defining each person's job and leaving little leeway for wandering away from that job. As a consequence, such groups get started faster and work faster once they have started.

Similarly, the experimental findings would lead to other predictions. For instance, consider a manager, A, who creates the situation shown in figure

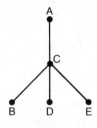

Fig. 19.7.

19.7. Managers who do that put themselves in serious danger because subordinate C may end up in a very powerful spot. For the subordinate has greater and faster access to all others than the boss or anyone else, and by being a little selective in what is transmitted (purposely or by oversight), C can end up controlling the organization. Sometimes one sees such a situation with the private secretary to the boss. Since that person is in a position to screen all incoming and many outgoing messages, the private secretary can become a formidable personage.

Preferential access to information, after all, is a major source of power in any organization. In experiments with the star network, anyone in the central position, C, is likely to become the functioning boss. Personal characteristics do not matter much. C gets to know more, faster, than anyone else. In real life, of course, C's communication power may be counterbalanced by someone else's authoritative power. Curiously, one will often find organizations so structured that the position of greatest authority is *not* located at the center of the communication structure, even where one objective is to maximize the power of the person in a position of authority. That means trouble.

These ideas are related to some ideas about feedback talked about earlier. Information is transmitted more broadly and more accurately, and the people involved feel more willing to send and receive it, when they have some degree of control over what is happening—that is, when they get fairly rapid feedback, when they have checkpoints to help them increase their certainty about the information they are receiving, or when they have opportunities to contribute to what is going on. Fuller feedback clearly helps in that direction, and now one can add that "democratic," "multichannel" communication networks also seem to help toward the same end.

A word of warning may be appropriate here. It may seem to follow from what has been said that the very best network is necessarily the fully connected one, in which every member can communicate directly with everyone else. Although that's probably true for certain types of problems in relatively small groups, it becomes less valid as groups grow larger. Purely practical considerations, such as how much one person can send or receive or digest in one time period, might require limitations in the number of

Fig. 19.8.

channels used in larger meetings, or even in small meetings for special kinds of problems.

Another warning: The research on communication has not dealt much with "real" situations. Problems of authority and responsibility that exist in business organizations clearly complicate real-life situations. So we must necessarily be cautious about jumping too quickly into generalizations from such experimental findings.

Although it is probably true that many of these results would hold up if we could test them on large groups, some would not. We would soon run into the problem of oversupply of information, for example, if we expanded the star network to even twenty-five people with only one central person in position C. We would probably need some intermediate people to absorb irrelevant information and organize the remainder for C. Similarly, if we had a hundred people in a fully connected network, we would get chaotic results for a long time, until a good many channels had been voluntarily closed off. And we cannot even draw some networks for larger groups. Some, such as the one shown in figure 19.8, are unique to a particular number of people. How does one draw that *same* structure for ten people? Shall we connect new people to A and E? Or to D and B? Will it still be the same network?

Self-defense and the design of networks

If these notions hold, one may ask why real working groups are not egalitarian and multichannel more often in organizations. One good reason is that those designs come into conflict, as do many aspects of small-group operations, with the pyramidal, highly individualized structure of most business organizations. Another good reason is that short-run speed and control are often *thought* to be more critical than longer-run morale or even creativity.

There is also a not-so-good reason that may be worth special mention. Two-way communication in egalitarian networks often seems dangerous and threatening to some people in the group. For instance, people in higher positions in an organization may prefer hierarchical communication networks, like the star pattern, with themselves in position C because it helps them to maintain their power over the group. Patterns like that one serve the same purpose as one-way communication processes. They keep leaders off the psychological hook. Their weaknesses are hidden better in a position like C in the center of the star than in any position in the circle. They can screen information from others. They can blame errors on others, and maybe they can get away with it. The other people in such groups may have no way of checking on the real source of either an error or a bright idea. Often people argue for the star pattern over the circle on grounds of speed or businesslike efficiency, when an actual underlying reason for the preference is the protection of one's self-esteem. The same reasoning may hold for subordinates. It is easier for them, too, to hide in a hierarchical network.

But, of course, despite these issues, open nets are used more frequently in contemporary organizations. As we shall see later, their advantages in the modern world appear to outweigh their costs.

In summary

The simple structure of a communication network of a group or organization, independent of the people working in the network, sets limits on the group's performance.

Groups whose problems require the collation of information from all members work faster when one position is highly centralized and the others relatively peripheral. But the morale, self-correctiveness, and creativity of such groups may be better when the communication network is more egalitarian and when each member has more than one source of information.

Highly centralized groups may often be used for their consistency with larger organizational designs, their speed, and their controllability; but they are also often used as psychological defense mechanisms to protect key people's power and their control over other members.

20 Taking groups seriously: Designing organizations around small groups

In America, despite all the discussions and writings, managers have not taken groups very seriously—at least not until recently. Certainly, large Japanese companies, for example, focus much more on small groups than do most American organizations. And yet we know—"we" being both social scientists and managers—that groups play a crucial role in organizations. Moreover, we've known it for a long time.

But American culture is an individualistic culture, and American organizations (including educational organizations) reflect that emphasis on the individual as the central unit of analysis. When we draw organizational charts, we draw two things: the organization and the individual jobs within it. We seldom draw groups.

This chapter is both a fantasy and a bridge. It is a bit of a fantasy because it asks the reader to think—we hope creatively—about the role groups might play in modern organizations. It is a bridge because it tries to provide a transition from the chapters you have just read about small groups to the chapters that follow in part 4, chapters that focus on large numbers of people trying to work together in large organizations.

Let's start with a little context. Groups have been experimented with, observed, built, and taken apart in innumerable ways. Small groups have become the major tool of the applied behavioral scientist. Organizational development methods are group methods. Almost all of what is called participative management is essentially based on group techniques. So the idea of using groups as key organizational mechanisms is by no means new or extraordinary.

Yet right from the start, talk like that appears to violate a deep and important American value, individualism. But our fantasy may not turn out to be very anti-individualistic after all.

The rest of this chapter will briefly address the following questions: (1) Is it fair to say that groups have not been taken very seriously by American organizations? (2) Why are groups even worth thinking about as organizational building blocks? What are the characteristics of groups that might make them interesting enough to be worthy of serious attention? (3) What would it mean "to take groups seriously"? Just what kinds of things would have to be done differently? (4) If we wanted to have groups as the basic unit, what compensatory changes would be needed in other facets of the organization? (5) Is the idea of designing the organization around small face-to-face groups a very radical idea, or is it just an extension of a direction toward which we are already heading?

Haven't groups been taken seriously enough already?

The argument that groups have not been taken "seriously" doesn't seem a difficult one to make. Contemporary ideas about small groups in organizations didn't really come along until the 1930s and 1940s. By that time, a logical, rationalistic tradition for thinking about organizations was already solidly in place. Embedded in that tradition, it treated the individual as the organizational building block. The logic moved from the projected task backward. Determine the task, the goal; then find an appropriate structure and technology; then carve it all up into person-sized jobs; and last of all fit individual human beings into those predefined person-sized pieces of the action. That was, for instance, what industrial psychology was all about between the two world wars. Psychologists worried almost exclusively about differences among individuals in aptitudes and abilities, and worked in the service of structuralists to find the right square human pegs to fit into those predesigned, square organizational holes. The role of the psychologist was ancillary to the role of the designers of the whole organization. It was a backup, supportive role that followed more than it led organizational design.

It was not just the logic of that classical organizational theory that focused on the individual. The whole entrepreneurial tradition of American society supported it. Individuals, at least male individuals, were taught achievement motivation. They were taught to seek individual evaluation, to compete, to see the world, organizational or otherwise, as a place in which to strive for individual accomplishment and satisfaction.

In those respects, the classical design of organizations was quite consonant with its cultural landscape. Individualized organizational structures blended nicely into the larger environment of individualism. All the accessories fell into place: individual incentive schemes for hourly workers, performance evaluation and assessment schemes, batteries of tests to select individuals for jobs.

The unique characteristic of the organization was that it was not simply a racetrack within which individuals could compete but a system in which somehow the competitive behavior of individuals could be coordinated, harnessed, and controlled in the interest of common tasks. Of course, one residual effect of all that was a continuing tension between the individual and the organization. The organization tried to control and coordinate individuals' activities at the same time that it tried to motivate them; and at the same time, competitive individuals insisted on reaching well beyond those constraints imposed by the organization. One product of that tension was what came to be called the "informal organization"—typically an informal coalition designed to fight the system.

Then it was discovered that groups could be exploited for what management saw as positive purposes, *toward* productivity instead of away from it. The 1950s and 1960s were decades of active experimentation with small face-to-face groups. We learned to patch them on to existing organizations, as Band-Aids, to relieve tensions between the individual and the organization. We promoted coordination through group methods. We learned that groups were useful for disciplining and controlling recalcitrant individuals.

Thus, groups were retrofitted onto organizations. The group skills of individual managers gradually improved. They learned to coordinate their efforts better, to control deviants better, and to gain more commitment from subordinates. But groups were seen primarily as tools to be tacked on to the preexisting individualized organizational system. With a few notable exceptions, organizations were not designed around groups. On the contrary, as some of the ideas about small groups began to be added on to existing organizational models, they generated new tensions and conflicts of their own. Managers complained not only that groups were slow but that they diffused responsibility, and they vitiated the power of the hierarchy because they were too "democratic"; they created small in-group empires, which were hard for others to penetrate. There was a period, for example, of a great gap between sensitivity training (which had until then been conducted on isolated "cultural islands") and the organization back home. The sensitivity trainers in those days talked a lot about the "reentry problem," which meant the problem of moving back from the training culture, designed around groups, into the old organizational culture designed around individuals.

Of course, groups didn't die, despite their difficulties. How could they die? They had always been there, though not always in the service of the organization. They turned out to be useful—indeed, necessary. Organizations were not only growing; they were professionalizing. The need for better coordination was becoming obvious, and the personal expectations of individuals were also growing. "Acknowledged" groups (as distinct from "natural," informal groups) became attached even to conservative organizations. Mostly, though, they were seen as compensatory addenda, often reluctantly backed into by managers.

It was as though someone had insisted that automobiles be designed to fit the existing rough terrain, instead of building new kinds of roads to adapt to the automobile.

What makes groups worthy of serious attention?

Why would groups be more interesting than individuals as basic design units around which to build organizations? What are the prominent characteristics of small groups? And how are they useful?

First, small groups seem to be good for people. They can satisfy important membership needs. They can provide a moderately wide range of activities for individual members. They can provide support in times of stress and crisis. They are settings in which people can learn not only cognitively but empirically to be reasonably trusting and helpful to one another.

Second, groups seem to be good pathfinding tools. They are useful in promoting innovation and creativity.

Third, in a wide variety of decision situations, as we have seen, they actually make better decisions than individuals do.

Fourth, they are great tools for implementing. They gain commitment from their members; group decisions are more likely to be willingly carried out than individually made decisions.

Fifth, they can control and discipline individual members in ways that are often extremely difficult through more impersonal disciplinary systems.

Sixth, as organizations grow large, small groups appear to be useful mechanisms for fending off many of the negative effects of large size. They help to prevent communication lines from growing too long, the hierarchy from growing too steep, and the individual from getting lost in the crowd.

There is a seventh reason for taking groups seriously, although it is an altogether different kind of argument. It's the no-choice argument. Thus far the designers of organizations seemed to have had a choice. They could try to build either an individualized *or* a group-based organization. A group-based organization will, de facto, have to deal with individuals; but remember that individualized organizations must also, de facto, deal with groups. Groups are natural phenomena, facts of organizational life. They can be intentionally created, but their spontaneous development cannot be prevented. The problem is not whether we should have groups or not. The question is should we build planned groups or live with the groups that grow naturally? Individualized organizational gardens are likely to sprout weedlike groups all over the place, whether they are planted or not. By defining them as weeds instead of flowers, they continue, as in earlier days, to be treated as pests, forever fouling up our rationally designed individualized organizations, forever forming informally (and irrationally) to harass and outgame the planners.

It is likely that the reverse could also be true. If groups are defined as flowers, and carefully planted, they will not be a costless good. New problems will crop up. But that discussion can be delayed for at least a little while.

Who uses groups best?

So, groups look like interesting organizational building blocks. But before going on to consider the implications of designing organizations around them, it is useful to look at those places in the existing world where groups seem to have been treated more seriously.

One such place is in Japanese organizations. The Japanese seem to be very group-oriented and much less concerned than Americans about issues like individual accountability. As a result, Japanese organizations are, of course, consonant with the larger Japanese culture, where notions of individual aggressiveness and competitiveness are deemphasized in favor of self-effacement and group loyalty. Japanese organizations seem to get a lot done, despite the relative suppression of the individual in favor of the group. It also appears that the advantages of the group-oriented Japanese style have really come to the fore in technologically complex organizations.

Another place to look is at American conglomerates. They go to the opposite extreme, dealing with very large units. They buy large organizational units and sell units. They evaluate units. In effect, they promote units by offering them extra resources as rewards for good performance. In that sense, conglomerates, one might argue, are designed around groups, but the groups in question are often themselves large organizational chunks.

More recently still, we have had several interesting uses of small groups by well-managed large companies. The IBM PC, we are told, was developed by a fairly small group, consciously set outside the routine of the rest of the company. And Apple's Macintosh also came out of a small group, working by itself, in a separate location (and flying a flag consisting of a skull and crossbones with an apple in its eye). The Swedes, too, have been building their Volvos with small groups, each responsible for making a large part of the finished vehicle, successfully abandoning the traditional, individualized assembly line.

If we look carefully, we can find a number of places, even in the United States, where groups have taken on a new importance in recent years.

Groups in individualistic cultures

An architect can design a beautiful building that either blends smoothly with its environment, or contrasts starkly with it. But organizational designers may not have the same choice. If we design an organization that is structurally dissonant with its environment, it is *conceivable* that the environment will change to adjust to the organization. But it is much more likely that the environment will simply reject the organization. If designing organizations around groups represents too sharp a break from surrounding environmental trends, maybe we should abort the idea early on.

Our American environment, one can argue, is certainly highly individualized; groups do not seem consistent with it. But one can also make a less solid argument in the other direction: American society is becoming more group-oriented than individual these days; or at least it is becoming group-oriented as well as individual. The evidence is sloppy at best. We can reinterpret the student revolution of the 1960s and the growing distrust of the "establishment" as a reaction against the decline of the social institutions that most satisfied *social* group motives. Didn't American society used to be more group–oriented in the 1920s than in the 1960s? Weren't the village, the extended family, and the church more important then? And didn't they help to satisfy people's unsatisfied needs for membership and belonging? Certainly, popular critics of American society have laid a great deal of emphasis on the loneliness and anomie that seemed to result from our extraordinary emphasis on individualism. Isn't it fair to argue that recent changes in the work ethic in America has moved toward a belief that work should be *socially* as well as egoistically fulfilling, that it should satisfy human needs for affiliation and cooperation as well as needs for individual achievement?

The rising role of women also carries implications for the group orientation of organizations, doesn't it? In general, women have been socialized more strongly into affiliative and relational sorts of attitudes than men. Women probably do, other things equal, work more comfortably in group settings, where there are strong relational bonds among members than in much more competitive individualized settings. Moreover, as women occupy more important places in American organizations, some of their values and attitudes will spill over to the male side.

But groups are becoming more relevant for pragmatic organizational reasons as well as cultural reasons. Groups are particularly useful as coordinating and integrating mechanisms, for dealing with complex tasks that require many different kinds of specialized knowledge. In fact, the extensive use of project teams and task forces in high-technology industries can be viewed as one effort to modify individually designed organizations toward a group-oriented direction. This is not for humanistic reasons, but in order to cope with tremendous increases in the complexity of the organization's work.

What might a group-based organization look like?

At this point the reader may want to participate with us in a little intellectual voyage into space. Just what would it mean to design organizations around groups? Operationally, how would that be different from designing organizations around individuals? One approach is simply to take the things organizations do with individuals and try them out with groups. The idea is to raise the level from the atom to the molecule. Suppose, for example, that we were to *recruit* groups rather than individuals, *train* groups rather than individuals, *pay* groups rather than individuals, *promote* groups rather than individuals, *fire* groups rather than individuals, and so on down the list of activities that organizations have traditionally undertaken to use human beings.

Some of the items on that list seem easy to handle at the group level; others, much harder. For example, it doesn't seem terribly hard to design jobs for groups. In effect, that is what many senior managers already do. They give specific jobs to committees. Some set up a group and call it the "office of the president." The problem seems to be a manageable one: designing job sets that are both big enough to require a number of people, and also small enough to require only a *small* number of people. "Big enough" in this context means not only jobs that would occupy the hands of group members but would also provide opportunities for learning and growth.

Matters such as evaluating, promoting, and paying groups raise more difficult, yet still rather interesting problems. Maybe the best that can be said for such matters is that they provide opportunities for thinking creatively about pay and evaluation. Suppose, for example, that, as a reward for good work, the group gets a larger salary budget than it got last year. Suppose the allocation of increases within the group is left to the group members. One can think about all sorts of difficulties that might then arise. But are the potential problems necessarily any more difficult than those generated by individual merit raises? As we said earlier, few managers are satisfied with their existing individual performance-appraisal and salary-allocation schemes. At least the issues of distributive justice within small groups would presumably be open to group discussion and debate. One might even permit the group to allocate payments to individuals differentially at different times, in accordance with some criteria of current contribution that they might establish.

As far as performance evaluation is concerned, it is probably easier for people up the hierarchy to assess the performance of total groups than it is to assess the performance of individuals several levels down the hierarchy. Top managers of decentralized organizations do it all the time, except that they usually reward the formal leader of the decentralized unit rather than the whole unit.

The notion of promoting groups raises another set of difficulties. Think of the difficulties involved in physically transferring a whole group, for example, and the costs associated with training a whole group to do a new job. But there may be major advantages, too. If a group moves, its members already know how to work with one another. Families may be less disrupted by movement if several move at the same time.

Then there is the problem of recruitment and selection. Does it make sense to select whole groups? Initially, why not? Usually we select for knowledge and skill. Couldn't we also select for potential ability to work together? There is plenty of groundwork in the huge amount of research that has already been done.

Costs and danger points

If we play this game of designing organizations around groups, what might be the important dangers? In general, a group-based organization would be somewhat more like a free market than most present organizations. More decisions would have to be worked out ad hoc, in a continually changing way. One would need to schedule more negotiation time both within and between groups. One would encounter more issues of justice, for the individual vis-à-vis the group and for groups vis-à-vis one another. More and better arbitration mechanisms would probably be needed along with highly flexible and rapidly adaptive record-keeping systems. But modern information technology is both flexible and adaptive. Couldn't computers handle that job?

Another specific issue would be the provision of escape hatches for unhappy individuals. Groups have been known to be cruel and unjust to their deviant members. One currently available escape route for those individuals would, of course, continue to exist: departure from the organization. Another might be an easy means of transfer to another group.

Further danger accompanying a strong group emphasis might be a tendency to drive out highly individualistic, unusual, pathfinding people. But don't the tight organizational constraints now imposed do the same thing? Indeed, might not groups protect their unusual individuals better than the impersonal rules of present-day large organizations?

Another obvious problem: If groups are emphasized by being rewarded, paid, promoted, and so on, groups may begin to perceive themselves as power centers, in competitive conflict with other groups. Intergroup hostilities of the kind we described a couple of chapters ago might be exacerbated unless we could design some new coping mechanisms. One proposal for solving that sort of problem (and others) is the *linking-pin* concept. The notion is that individuals serve as members of more than one group, up and down the hierarchy as well as horizontally. But that scheme still assumes fundamentally individualized organizations. In a more group-based organization, the linking-pin concept would have to be modified so that an individual might be a part-time member of more than one group, but still a real member. That is, for example, a portion of an individual's pay might come from each group in accordance with that group's perception of that person's contribution.

Much more talk, both within and between groups, would be a necessary accompaniment of more group emphasis; however, we might argue about whether more talk should be classified as a cost or a benefit. In any case, careful design of escape hatches for individuals and connections among groups would be as important in this kind of organization as would stairways between floors in the design of a private home.

There is also a danger of overdesigning groups. All groups in the organization need not look alike. Quite the contrary; the shapes and sizes of different subgroups within the large organization would vary with task, technology, and other factors. Just as individuals end up adjusting the edges of their jobs to themselves, and themselves to their jobs, we should expect flexibility within groups, allowing them to adapt and modify themselves to their special current situations and purposes.

Another initially scary problem: What happens in a group-based organization to clear, formal, individual leadership? Without individual leaders, how will we motivate people? Without leaders, how will we control and discipline people? Without leaders, how will we pinpoint responsibility? But aren't such questions really relics of old-fashioned beliefs about organizations? They are questions that are themselves a product of the old individual-building-block design. Surely, groups will have leaders, but they will probably emerge from the bottom up rather than the top down. Given a fairly clear job description, some groups, in some settings, will set up more or less permanent leadership roles. Others may let leadership vary as the situation demands, or as a function of the power that individuals within any group may possess relative to the group's needs at that time. A reasonable amount of process time can be built in to enable groups to work on the leadership problem, but the problem will have to be resolved within each group. On the advantage side of the ledger, that may even get rid of a few hierarchical levels. There should be far less need for having individuals who are chiefly supervisors of other individuals' work.

There is another intergroup problem that may also become extremely troublesome in group-based organization. There is a real danger that relatively autonomous and cohesive groups may close themselves off, not only from other groups but, more important, from expert advice of staff members or from new suggestions and ideas.

Such problems already exist, of course, but they may be exacerbated by more emphasis on group units. There is no perfect way to handle them. One possibility would be to make individual members of staff groups also part-time members of operating groups. Another is to work harder to educate operating groups to the potential value of staff contributions. Of course, the reward system, the old market system, will probably be the strongest force for keeping groups from isolating themselves from a world of new technologies and new ideas.

Would group-based organizations pay off?

Finally, from an organizational perspective, what are the potential advantages to be gained from a group-based organization? The first might be a sharp reduction in the number of units that need to be controlled, because one would not have to control all the way down to the individual level. A group-based design would probably also cut the number of operational levels in the organization. Levels that are now primarily supervisory could be incorporated into the groups that they supervise.

By this means many of the advantages of the small individualized organization might be brought back. Those advantages would recur within groups simply because there would be a small number of blocks, albeit larger blocks, with which to build and rebuild the organization.

But most of all, and this is still uncertain, might not great human advantages follow?—increases in cohesiveness and motivation, more family feeling among group members, and more commitment, too? And from there, might not increased productivity follow?

But should individualism be killed off?

By this point, many readers, especially Americans, may be feeling a bit uncomfortable. All this group stuff seems to relegate individuals to a subordinate position, dependent almost entirely on the groups to which they belong. Where, in these hypothetical group-based organizations, does the individual come in? What happens to the creativity that individuals generate? What about the individualistic entrepreneur? the pathfinder? the risk taker? Aren't all those attributes of individuals rather than of groups? And don't groups tend to kill off those qualities?

Perhaps the greatest danger inherent in many group-based organizations lies right there. Groups drive toward conformity. They tend, as we said earlier, to punish deviants. And yet deviation is a major wellspring of innovation and change. It is the oddballs, the stubborn nonconformists, the independent spirits who make most of the breakthroughs and who take those risks that move organizations forward. But remember, it isn't *only* individuals. Small teams are often highly creative and entrepreneurial, too.

So we have a dilemma: Although there are good reasons in today's world for many organizations to take groups much more seriously, there are also very good reasons, particularly in the West, for modern organizations to develop and encourage individualists. Is a healthy marriage possible? Can groups live with and even encourage individuality and nonconformity? And can nonconforming individualists live with and even encourage collaborative, team-oriented groups?

The answer is yes. A marriage is possible, but it ain't easy. Some organizations have already done it. It's a challenge that takes imagination, hard work, and a willingness to tolerate some disorder.

In summary

The most powerful and beloved tool of modern participative management is the small face-to-face group. Behavioral scientists and managers have been learning to understand, exploit, and nurture groups. Groups attracted interest initially as devices for improving implementation and increasing human commitment. Today they are appreciated because they can also be creative and innovative. They often make better-quality decisions than individuals, and they make organizational life more livable for people.

But groups in organizations are not an invention of behaviorists. They are a natural phenomenon. It is both possible and sensible to describe most large organizations as collections of groups in interaction with one another, bargaining with one another, forming coalitions with one another, cooperating and competing with one another.

Small face-to-face groups are also great tools for disciplining and controlling their individual members, potentially much better than the elaborate, bureaucratic, quasi-legal sets of rules used in most organizations. Performance evaluation schemes and incentive systems are all individually based and all generate problems of trust and distributive justice. Any kind of organizational design that can eliminate much of that legalistic superstructure begins to look highly desirable.

But moving too far and too blindly toward groups could easily cost us the great benefits that derive from our traditional individualistic values. Individuals, at least in Western societies, are still the major wellsprings of entrepreneurial innovation and risk taking. Somehow—and it is quite possible—group-based organizations have to include mechanisms for supporting and encouraging those individuals who want to march to different drummers.

4

People in hundreds and thousands: Managing the whole organization

Introductory note

This fourth part of the book is about managing large numbers of people in modern organizations. Because the focus is on people *in organizations,* this section looks at the nature of organizations—their purposes and strategies, their cultures and structures. But the organization itself is not our core concern. *Managing* the organization and its people is the heart of the matter in this fourth part—the art and science of working out problems, through people, in complex organizations.

In earlier sections, we considered how issues such as reinforcement and motivation affect people in organizations. We also looked at several ways that we can influence the behavior of individuals and small groups and examined the tremendous extent to which situations, especially work situations, can shape, control, and limit people's behavior. In this part we try to put all those pieces together, focusing on the process of *managing* the whole complex show.

We start in chapter 21 by describing what managers really do, day by day, hour by hour. Then we go on to treat managing as a special case of working out problems. All of us work our way through problems all the time. But managers do it in those complex social and economic settings called organizations. Often they have to deal with problems that extend well beyond the boundaries of those organizations. So we try to lay out a simplifying model to help clarify the key aspects of "problem working" in organizations.

Chapter 22 is about the setting within which managers work and the organizational handles that managers can hold onto to steer, influence, and change their organization's behavior. Chapter 23 takes a historical look at how our ideas about managing people have evolved over the last 100 years and how that past has influenced present-day managerial beliefs and practices. Chapter 24 considers organizational missions and strategies, as well as how managers find and set their goals. Then, in chapter 25, we look once again at the people part of the organization, at how we have approached the complicated task of managing people in traditional organizations and how organizational *culture* can be used as a managing mechanism in contemporary organizations. We follow that, in chapter 26, with a look at people and organizational structure, how structure controls and often imprisons people, and how managers can modify the structures of their organizations.

Although part 4 contains quite a bit about organizational theory, it is mostly about the process of managing. Managing, after all, is an active, ongoing process. It doesn't stop after the organization chart has been drawn up. Managing means trying to spot the important things to do, figuring out how to tackle them, and getting them done, mostly through the help of many other people. That's what this fourth part is all about.

21

The managing process: Pathfinding, problem solving, implementing

This chapter is about the process of managing in the frenetic, changing milieu of the modern organization. What do managers actually do in organizations? And what should they do?

What do managers do?

Over the years, organizational researchers have tried to answer that question by simply (and sensibly) following managers around, observing and recording their behavior, hour by hour, day by day. The various studies have looked at managers at different organizational levels, in different parts of the world, and at different times (since about 1950). Yet their answers generally come out rather alike. The commonalities include these:

1. Managers do an enormous amount of work. They move at a fast pace for long hours. They usually take very little time for breaks and often work well beyond regular working hours.

2. Managers work on many different issues in the course of a day, often skipping quickly from one problem to the next.

3. Managers do most of their managing with little time to spare and often with limited and incomplete information. They usually work against deadlines and many other pressures, so they make many of their decisions on the fly. It is not that managers won't or can't think but that they don't usually have much time to think. They don't have much control over what, when, and to whom they must pay attention. They are frequently interrupted and generally work with limited, often impressionistic data and high levels of uncertainty.

4. Managers not only do a great deal of work on the fly; they do it from formally delineated roles, in elaborate organizational structures. They are not free and independent agents. They have to depend on others and coordinate their activities with those of many other people. They have to influence people in all parts of the organization—upward, downward, and sideways. They are always driving in heavy human traffic.

On the whole, then, the observable parts of managers' jobs are characterized by brevity, variety, discontinuity, and a lot of verbal communication. Managers spend a lot of time with their subordinates and superiors in scheduled and unscheduled meetings and on the phone, dealing with problems and requests, receiving or giving information, and providing direction and guidance. There may also be a certain amount of personal preference for this hectic, reactive style. Some managers seem to find their busy, frenetic world a sort of security blanket, reassuring them that they are really needed. Besides, managers tend to be impatient, action-oriented people, preferring to get things done today, rather than to sit back and reflect on next year's plans.

But is that busy activity all there is to what managers do? Probably not. That's only the part that is directly observable from outside. Things go on inside the manager as well as outside; and the fact that those inside thoughts, dreams, and feelings are not easy to see should not fool us into believing they aren't there. Managing is about much more than what managers actually *do*.

Managing as a three-stage process

One way to characterize the whole process of managing is to divide it into three phases. We shall call phase 1 the *pathfinding* phase. Pathfinding is the beginning of the process, the phase in which managers try to identify, create, or imagine where they want their organization to go. Phase 2 is *problem solving,* the often difficult process of figuring out good solutions to complicated and messy problems. That's where analysis, planning, and organizing come in. Phase 3 is the *implementing* phase; it is the action phase, when the process is carried out—getting the bricks laid, the product built, the service rendered.

Those three phases probably characterize large segments of everybody's lives, whether managers or not. But for managers the whole process takes place in a pressurized, deadlined, interdependent, organizational setting, and managers have to do it all while running fast. Managing is not a process that allows much time for contemplation or careful study of all possible alternatives.

We shall elaborate on this three-phase model in the next few pages. We won't talk much yet about the pathfinding part. We'll begin instead by considering what part the problem-solving phase plays in the managing process, and then go on to talk about the implementing phase of managing. Then we'll back up and take a look at the pathfinding phase to see how it fits into the larger managing scheme.

Phase 2
Problem solving

In the day-to-day world of managing, problem solving is a messy business, much messier than the neat problem solving we did in math classes at school. Yet the basic rules of the game are still the same. Remember those classroom rules? They were rules like these: "First gather the relevant information." Then how about something like "Consider the possible alternatives," or "Figure out the possibilities"? Then "Select the best solution." The emphases were on accurate observation, logical and orderly thinking, searching for causal connections, and assessing alternative courses and outcomes—in short, on mental discipline.

Probably, too, in most college courses that required you to solve problems, you were *given* the problems to be solved, as homework or in exams. Your job was to solve them, to produce the correct answers. Aptitude and intelligence tests also usually gave you the problem and then asked you to solve it. Sometimes, in such tests, getting the right answer was not enough. You also had to show that you understood the *proper method* for solving the problem. If you solved the problem intuitively or by using some private little tricks of your own, you lost points. Problem solving, that is to say, was (and is) often taught as a discipline that begins *after* the problem has been identified; existing best-known methods are what the student is expected to learn.

In much formal education, problem-solving practice drives toward convergent thinking, toward finding *the* best answer, by *the* best method. Often, formal education stops right there, at the point where we have applied the right method and found the right answer.

But managing out in the field is different from solving problems in a geometry class. Probably the first important difference is that, in the managerial world, problems are seldom given to us. We have to find, create, or select our own.

Second, getting the right solution is usually not enough; we have to do something with it after we get it, or even while we are getting it. Managerial problems, even when they are "given," are almost never as pure as those at school. We almost never have all the information we need; and we often have to solve the problem in irrational real time—that is, against deadlines that weren't set by teachers who knew that twenty minutes was "about right" for working that problem.

Third, the right answer often doesn't make obvious sense when we find it. It doesn't possess that helpful attribute of coming out even, like those math problems usually did.

Nevertheless, there are good reasons for school-type education in problem solving. We have been taught the power and value of analytic methods developed over centuries of philosophy, mathematics, and the natural and social sciences. Most of what the Western world calls progress has emanated from our mastery of such analytic methods. And much of what we do successfully in managing organizations, we do because we can apply some of those analytic skills, even in the complex and ill-structured managerial context.

It's worth reiterating that much of our formal education has been aimed at the problem-solving phase of the total managing process. It has taught us how to decompose problems, how to order chaos, how to try to get to the heart of the issue and come up with *the* solution. Most education, after all, is analytically oriented. We were taught reading, writing, and arithmetic, which are all essentially analytic skills using symbolic languages. But what most formal education has not taught us about problem solving is how to solve problems on the fly, how to choose among risky and uncertain solutions, how to use our intuition and judgment, how to find good heuristics. Managing requires a lot of all of those. We do not typically assign responsibility for teaching those skills to classroom teachers; we leave it instead to that vague nonhuman teacher called "experience."

Consider, for example, the issue of assessing people. Just about all managers have to do it. They talk to people for half an hour and decide which one to hire, or whether to trust a sales pitch. Or they go to a meeting and must assess very quickly what they will be up against in trying to sell their new plan to their colleagues. As we've seen in chapter 7, a great deal is known about the formal assessment of human capacities. We have developed tests and measuring instruments to help managers in the selection or promotion or evaluation of their people. But those kinds of analytic instruments are essentially useless when managers are confronted with thirty-minute first meeting with new clients or with a tough union negotiating session. They can't put their clients through a test battery. They can't—much of the time—have staff completely check out all the people they will encounter. So they must use the subtle, uncertain cues that are available at that moment. However, our education, at least our formal education, does very little to help us deal with that kind of on-the-spot problem solving.

The best advice this book can offer to its readers on those matters is the same advice offered in earlier chapters:

1. Get all the facts you can; collect and analyze the data.

2. While collecting data, pay attention as well to your own empathetic feelings, intuitions, and judgments.

3. Go plural; take counsel. Check your assessment with others who are observers of the same people or the same issues; and do it without making logical reasoning the sole criterion for your decision.

Phase 3
Implementing
Type A and Type B implementing

Phase 3 of the managing process is the *implementing* phase. This is the action part of the managerial world—the part involving building, selling, making it happen, and getting it done. The implementing phase gets things out of the laboratory to the marketplace, from the consultant's recommendations to really changing the company. Implementing is turning out the finshed product, opening up the new market, getting the new plant into production.

Managerial implementing, however, is not just doing it yourself. It is getting other people to do it—the customer to buy it, your subordinates to behave differently, the other guy to accept your new idea. Implementing in management, that is to say, is a *social* process that requires the manager to influence, persuade, bully, sell, and communicate to other people.

Theoretically, the implementing phase can stand independently of problem solving. Somebody else can solve the problem, and then you can implement the solution. Somebody else can make the policy, and then you can carry it out. In practice, however, problem solving and implementing are usually very closely tied together. Any fairly large-scale implementation program, for example, usually includes a series of problem-solving acts that serve as "subroutines" inside the larger implementing program. If our job is to implement the acceptance of product X in a new market, we will encounter many problems nested inside that larger one, and they will have to be solved along the way. We shall have to decide in which medium to advertise or whether to advertise at all, what outlets to use, and how to price the product. The implementing process generates problems that need to be solved in order to go on implementing.

Implementing is tied to problem solving in another more important way. If we are implementing a decision, that must mean, of course, that the decision has already been made. Or so it would at first appear, for the obvious logical connections between problem solving and implementing—between decision and action—are sequential. Implementing *follows* problem solving. First decide, then act. That sequential, decision-first view is a reasonable approach. But there are other reasonable approaches, too. For the moment, let's call that kind of implementing, which *follows* problem solving, *type A implementing.*

In the organizational world, type A implementing not only serially follows decision making; it also typically has another important characteristic: the implementers are usually different people than the problem solvers. The engineering group designs a pump, and then the manufacturing people build it. If that pump happens to be a salable product, a third group, the salespeople, sell it. So, two major characteristics of type A managerial implementing are (1) deciding precedes implementing, and (2) the problem-solving people are a different group than the implementing people.

But in the managerial world, there is another way to implement. Let's call the second way *Type B implementing*. It's a view that has mostly grown out of a mix of applied social science and the commonsense experience of managers. It is based more on ideas about the nature of people than on the nature of reason. Type B implementing emphasizes the *interaction* between problem solving and implementing. By this type B view, successful implementing requires the involvement of the implementing people in the problem-solving part of the act. So the B view argues for mixing rather than separating problem solving from implementing, blending the people and the process together.

The rationale is simple: People support what they help to create. If *you* must implement what *I* have decided, you will probably not implement it with as much love and commitment as I would. But if you are implementing what you yourself have helped to decide, then the decision is your baby; you are more likely to love it and to work hard at it.

The type B view appears to fly in the face of the more rational type A model. In effect, it seems to argue against simple logic, like aim first then fire. Instead, it wants aiming and firing to be one process. But the conflict is more apparent than real. The type B model focuses mostly on many-person organizational situations, where several sets of bodies may be involved. There, the notion of interaction between deciders and doers finds its logical support from psychological reasoning, which treats human beings as *emotional* as well as rational creatures.

But gaining the commitment of the implementers is not the only reason for using the type B model in organizations. Decisions are often better (and more implementable), even by type A standards, when the people who have to implement it can get their input into the decision-making process.

The differences between the type A and type B views go even deeper than they may look. The classic argument between the two views has been going on for a long time, and some creative outcomes have emerged.

If you are a proponent of type A methods, your thinking may run something like this: "The important thing is to get the right answer. There's no use implementing the wrong solution. Therefore, concentrate on solving the problem before you concentrate on implementing the solution."

Type B proponents tend to think this way: "There's no use making a good decision if you can't implement it, because that's not really a *good* decision. The bottom line is getting things done, not making elegant decisions."

In some fields, such as the natural sciences, the type A view does and should dominate. But in the managerial world, the type B view plays a very important role indeed.

Curiously, for most of us, the A-B issue seldom reaches the debate stage. We go about our problem solving and implementing quite implicitly, using the standards and beliefs with which we have grown up. Those of us raised in science and engineering learn mostly the type A approach, because our education usually rewards us more for high-quality solutions than for high-quality implementation. Also, orderliness is valued next to godliness.

However, if our education emphasized more humanistic issues, or if the problems we have had to confront were mostly small, face-to-face people problems, then we may have developed a type B approach. For salesmen, teachers, counselors, politicians, and many senior executives, emotional and often irrational issues play a large part in life. Such people tend to adopt more of a type B approach, to be more concerned wth issues of change, commitment, and persuasion, than with formal plans, decisions, or structures.

It seems moderately clear, too, if one looks over a whole variety of implementing problems, that type A styles have generally dominated large companies, governments, and military organizations. Those kinds of organizations have almost always separated problem solvers from implementers. Staff experts plan and analyze, top managers decide, and the "line" personnel out there in the field do the implementing.

Tools for type A and type B implementing

What kinds of tools do type A implementers use? Primarily, they use the tools of structure, authority, and, to some extent, socialization. If we have already decided what needs to be done, we then need the power of authority and structure to get other people to do it. We need to control rewards and punishments. We need to specify expected duties and to be able to monitor behavior so we can know that what we want done is in fact being done. We also need to socialize our people to be loyal to us and to perceive our authority as proper and legitimate.

Type B implementers tend to use social and psychological tools. They prefer smaller units, one-on-one relationships, and small groups. Whereas the type A manager has been reasonably successful in managing large armies, it is in counseling, selling, and managing small teams and project groups that the type B manager has generally worked best (and type A has often fallen flat). It makes sense that things should work out that way. In small units, even within large organizations, personal commitment is critical; individuals with their own individual motives and attitudes are critical.

The tools that have evolved around type B are, then, understandably mostly socioemotional tools, which take human personality and emotionality into account. They are tools such as small-group discussions, team-building sessions, nondirective interviewing methods, and participative management. It is when type A implementing moves downward, into the smaller units nested within larger organizations, that it begins to run into trouble. Though the general may find it easy and comfortable to use type A tools in running his corps, the second lieutenant may find that they will not quite do when it comes to leading a platoon. And certainly foremen will run into trouble in getting good work from their crews if their methods are exclusively type A.

Conversely, of course, type B tools often run into difficulty as they move up and try to deal with the whole large organization. We have been less successful in running armies participatively than in running individual departments that way. In the larger units, type A requirements for sequencing, coordinating, and regulating loom very large.

It's managers of moderate-sized units—plants or small companies—who find themselves right in the middle of the A-B battleground. That's where type A traditions are challenged by type B experiments. It is during the period of growth from small to large that managers suffer from the traditional conflict between the informal but disorganized humanism of the small company and the pressing demands for structure and formalization that growth seems to require. As companies grow larger, they really do have to tell themselves, "We have to get ourselves organized," which means, in our parlance, we need to work out the appropriate A-B mix.

Back to phase 1
Pathfinding

Debates between true believers in type A and type B styles have gone on for a long time. Yet neither camp has paid much attention to phase 1, the pathfinding phase, of the managing process. Pathfinding focuses on processes by which one creates and selects problems, the front-end questions of where we want to go and what we want to achieve. Pathfinding is not about getting answers, nor about getting results. It is about getting questions and setting agendas. It is about figuring out where it is that we want to go, deciding on the problems worth pursuing. Pathfinding is, necessarily, about some very soft stuff—about missions, dreams, and offbeat ideas.

Consider, for example, the question of building a new house. For building contractors, the first order of business is mostly implementational—getting houses built cheaply, quickly, and efficiently. They worry about finding and scheduling competent subcontractors, buying materials, and making it all happen according to plan.

For heating engineers, problem solving is the central issue. They have to plan an efficient and safe system, given the design for a house of size X, shape Y, in climate Z.

Now consider architects. One part of their role is probably just like the engineer's—solving the problems of size and location of closets, stairways, and bathrooms. But another part of their job, the part for which most of us hire them, is neither engineering problem solver nor implementer-builder.

It is the architect as designer, as artist, as creator of unique houses. This design part of their work is the pathfinding part. It is divergent, not convergent. There is no single best answer to design questions. An infinite number of house designs is possible, even given constraints on budget, site, and size. What architects add to the problem-working process is imagination and creativity. They must create houses that will not only be functional but interesting and beautiful as well.

Notice the soft, subjective quality of words like *interesting* and *beautiful*. This is the stuff of imagination, of dreams. Pathfinding is partially about the ways one generates (inside oneself) visions and beliefs about what is beautiful, important, and right. That inside-to-outside component, that active input from within the person, characterizes not only innovative architecture but also innovative management. That pathfinding aspect has, until recently, been sadly neglected in the literature of management.

The pathfinding phase of managing may be soft, but it is also active. It is through creating the right problems that managing becomes a way of moving and shaking the world. It is at the front end that managers create their organizations' futures.

Where does one find outstanding pathfinders? They exist in almost any field of endeavor: among religious leaders, like Jesus Christ and Mohammed; among dedicated leaders of peoples and nations, like Mahatma Gandhi and Charles de Gaulle; among founders and leaders of corporations, like Watson of IBM, Wilson of Xerox, and Land of Polaroid; and among pioneers in the professions, like Sigmund Freud and Florence Nightingale.

Like implementing or problem solving, however, managerial pathfinding can't stand alone. To be an effective pathfinder, one also needs to be an effective implementer. Note that, at the same time that all of those people just named have been dreamers of dreams, they were also effective persuaders and influencers of others.

What kinds of managers tend to be good pathfinders? Probably not the kinds we have typically tried to develop in modern schools of management. There, we have (at least until recently) tried to train mostly demon problem solvers with a bit of effective implementing skill thrown in. But we haven't tried very hard to develop visionary entrepreneurial pathfinders.

The pathfinding phase of managing has to do with vision, values, and determination—with beliefs about what is right and dreams about what could be. Although we don't have very good analytic rulebooks with which to map and define such fuzzy concepts, we can still get a reasonable fix on what they mean. Vision means exercising imagination to generate some shadowy picture of a desirable (and desired) future. Values can be thought of as internal control mechanisms, usually developed early in our lives. They help us define the boundaries separating right from wrong, the boundaries within which we are willing to act, and outside of which we will try not to act. To translate visions into realities, we also need determination. We need to be true believers who are stubbornly determined to push on with our visions, even against long odds.

Those pathfinding qualities depend much more on internal than on external search. They require search into oneself for answers to very difficult questions: "What do we really want?" "What do we believe is right?" "What would we really love to create?" "What would I really like to be when I grow up?"

Perhaps because we don't have good, known methods for approaching such pathfinding questions, we often try to deal with them by using methods that we do understand; that is, we use phase 2, problem-solving methods, which are analytic. A student may try to choose a career by figuring out which professions may be in high demand a decade hence. Or organization planners may try to decide what posture their company should take by analyzing five-year forecasts of economic and demographic trends. Often, that is to say, we finesse, even for ourselves, the proactive question of "What do I want?" by playing a passive-reactive game of trying to go where we think the route will be smoothest.

There are at least two things wrong with an exclusively analytical approach to "What do I want?" sorts of pathfinding questions. First, forecasting the future is quite a difficult task. We don't do it very well. But more important, such approaches assume that the future exists, like history in reverse, just lying out there waiting to be dug up. That view of the future as something to be discovered leaves no room for the future to be chosen, to be created by our own imagination and energy. If we spend our time trying to adapt to projected futures, we become servant rather than master. It is part of our Western heritage to believe that the future can be created.

The interaction among the three phases

It's worth looking at the transfer points among those three phases of the managing process, because it's at the points where the ball has to be passed from one part to another that it is most often fumbled.

Consider first the connection between phase 2, problem solving, and phase 3, implementing. If we do our problem solving first, we said earlier, we can expect trouble when we try to pass the ball on to others for implementing. We will lose commitment and perhaps even encounter sabotage. On the other hand, if we bring implementers in on the problem-solving phase, things will get messy, disorderly, and slow. Too many people with too many special interests will get into the act.

A comparison between Japanese and American managing styles may offer some help with that dilemma. The traditional American hierarchical model is to do the problem solving first and then to push through its implementation. Understandably, Americans often run into many problems in getting the implementing done effectively. Some implementers don't like the decision they have to implement. Some sabotage it; some don't understand it; some claim it can never work. We waste a lot of time trying to force the decision into the implementing stage, usually by tightening controls and exercising authority.

Large Japanese companies, in contrast, spend a much larger portion of their time getting many levels of the organization into the problem-solving phase from the beginning. By American standards, the Japanese discuss things endlessly in small groups before they finally make a decision. But the Japanese seem to make up that "lost" time at the other end, in implementation. By the time the Japanese decision is finally made, everybody seems to understand and support it. That is, of course, not exclusively true of the Japanese. The Scandinavians have been doing it for years, as have many progressive companies in the United States and throughout the world.

The interactions between problem solving and implementation are more complicated than we have made them sound. Indeed, the battle between those two phases has gone on for decades in Western organizations. The type A, decision-first approach clearly prevailed in the first half of this century, but it has gradually given way to more type B, interactive styles, especially since the 1950s. The reasons for the gradual shift to an implementation-oriented perspective are many: a better-educated work force, union pressures (in Europe more than the United States), and generally higher expectations by organizational members about their rights to speak up and to question authority. Sometimes the outcome has been a bit schizoid, with strange mixtures of participative, implementing-oriented styles in otherwise problem-solving–oriented organizations.

But the problem solving versus implementing issue is less complicated than the interfaces between these two areas and pathfinding. Architecture as a profession, again, provides an example. Someone once called architecture "the impossible profession." Perhaps the reason is that effective architects must combine some very different cognitive styles. They must be, at the same time, both divergent pathfinders and convergent problem solvers. They must design beautiful houses, but the plumbing has to work. Many clients of architects complain that their architect is "unreasonable" or "impractical." What those complaints often point to is the difficult transition from dreams to budgets, for the architect's dream may not match the client's budget or the builder's requirements. But do we want architects to work only from the constraints backward? They must also work from their imagination forward, doing so much more, one would guess, than the heating engineer or the electrician. And that forward movement often collides with practical concerns.

The same kinds of stresses are apt to arise for pathfinders in the organizational world. Nothing about the pathfinding process guarantees reason, compromise, or economic realism. Pathfinders—people with strong visions who are determined to fulfill them—can also be inflexible and stubborn. They may not be much influenced by hard evidence. Therefore, more pragmatic problem solvers can find them difficult and unrealistic; the pathfinders, in turn, may see problem-solving issues as unimaginative and dull.

Difficulties occur at the pathfinding–implementing interface, too. At the extreme, participative, type B implementers often substitute participation for purpose. They are apt to decide what ought to be done by taking attitude surveys. They tend to treat leadership as a set of administrative functions to be performed in the service of those who are led. Pathfinders, however, see leadership as an active process of influencing others to believe in what the leader believes. Participative implementers value consensus; pathfinders value their own beliefs. So the dilemma at the pathfinding-implementing interface typically takes this form: When do I try to influence others to do what I believe should be done, and when do I set my own beliefs aside to help the group members do what they want to do?

There are positive sides to these conflicts, too. Implementing, for example, can operate in the service of pathfinding. One way to find what we want to do is to look at what we do when we are free to do what we like. Playing, experimenting, and trying out a variety of actions is certainly one method many of us use to get a clearer understanding of our own preferences. Since we can't always see very far ahead, we encounter new ideas as we go along, and some of those may turn out to attract us more than others. That is, the process of implementing old decisions can also provide new pathfinding alternatives.

The pathfinding-implementing interface presents a number of important issues for contemporary managers. On the one hand, a world of more innovation is contributing to a resurgence of interest in individual creativity and a more intense search for unusual individuals. On the other hand, our managerial faith in teamwork and collaboration is also on the rise. The integration of individualism and groupism in the modern organization is one of the great challenges for managers of this generation.

At the societal level, conflicts betwen pathfinding and other phases of managing often provide stimulants for innovation. A society salted with many pathfinding people is likely to start many divergent fires. Some of those fires will turn out to be infeasible and die out. They don't make it when confronted with the hard realities of problem solving and implementing. But some survive and prosper. Although conflicts between pathfinding and problem solving or implementing may generate serious problems, the greater danger seems to lie in trying to eliminate those conflicts by suppressing pathfinding behavior. Indeed the greatest danger may be in letting any one of the three phases dominate the other two.

In summary

Managers perform a number of different roles. They receive, process, and give out information; they use information to make decisions; and they interact and deal with people. They often do their work against deadlines and are on the go at a fast pace. Therefore, they do not seem to be very thoughtful or contemplative; rather, they respond to the plethora of problems that come up day by day. But that active and reactive view of the manager is probably quite incomplete.

Managing can be viewed as a three-phase process of (1) pathfinding, (2) problem solving, and (3) implementing. Although the active implementing part is the most visible, the other phases must be there, too.

Pathfinding is about identifying purpose, about creating interesting problems. Though not always visible from outside, it is the active, leadership phase of managing; it is a phase that often calls for creative and divergent thinking. Pathfinding concerns personal vision, personal values, and personal determination. Much of pathfinding goes on within the person, in ways not easily seen by outside observers.

Problem solving is what most of us have learned about in school. Analytic methods are our most powerful tools here. But even in this realm, managing often requires intuitive as well as analytic thinking.

Implementing focuses on the action part of the process—on getting things done. Type A implementing—emphasizing authority and control—derives from the rational view that implementing should follow problem solving and decision making; it often needs to do so in large human organizations and in technical, nonhuman systems. Type B implementing emphasizes interactions between problem solving and implementing. It tends to use emotional, participative group-oriented tools and is based more on beliefs about the nature of human beings than on beliefs about the nature of reason.

Many productive conflicts arise at the points of juncture among the three phases. We encountered some of those in the preceding chapters, and we shall encounter more of them in the chapters that follow.

22 The volatile organization: Everything triggers everything else

In chapter 21 we treated the managing process as a kind of problem-working process, a continuous interrelating of pathfinding, problem solving, and implementing. But managers, whether they are pathfinders, problem solvers, or implementers, work in human organizations. So in this chapter we turn to the organizational setting within which the manager manages. We shall try to make three key points. First, organizations are, above all, dynamic human systems. They are not just the static structures depicted in organization charts, nor just random collections of people. Human organizations are constantly changing; they are both simple and complicated, both orderly and disorderly, both placid and volatile. Second, organizations are networks, usually quite loose ones, of tasks, structures, and information systems, which are managed and operated by fallible people. Third, organizations do not operate in a vacuum but within environments that are themselves in constant flux.

A diamond model of the organization

Consider the following imaginary case. Indeed let's call it a fable, because it couldn't happen in real life. Or could it?

You are a senior manager, but new to your lofty position. You think you have just identified a serious problem. One of your large units, division X, has turned in much poorer results than their forecasts had predicted. It doesn't seem to be performing its assigned tasks up to standard.

So you decide to hire one of the reputable older consulting firms, company S, the largest in town. They contract to take on the problem and send some of their consultants out to the unit to collect information.

When they finally come in with a report, you scan it and then turn to the consultants' recommendations. Their recommendations are fundamentally *structural:* (1) job descriptions at division X should be

246

rewritten with greater precision (to get rid of squabbles about overlapping responsibilities); (2) the functional form of organization now in
place at division X is obsolete and ineffective; it ought to be converted
to a divisional form; (3) in fact, division X has grown so large that it
ought to be partially decentralized, with more authority given to the
proposed new product managers; (4) You may have to move a few
people out, too; there is too much fat in the organization. And so on.

Since in this fable, you are a manager with an experimental turn of
mind and a pocket full of money, you decide not to act on consultant
S's report, at least not yet. You decide, instead, to knock on the door of
another consulting firm, company I, to get a second independent
opinion.

By now you are more familiar with the first firm, company S. You
have found that the people in it were highly regarded and experienced
in business organizations. You now note, with some discomfort, that
company I looks different. Although it has some impressive creden-
tials, its business experience is not as extensive as that of firm S.
Instead, company I is active in the Operations Research Society and
the Institute of Management Sciences, and its senior people all have
Ph.D. degrees. It looks like a group of whiz kids. But they have cut
their hair and they sound reasonable; and they seem very savvy about
modern stuff you don't fully understand, like computers, software, and
information systems. So you hire them to look at those same problems
at division X.

They, too, send a couple of people out to the unit, and after a few
weeks they come up with a report. But their conclusions turn out to be
very different from those reached by firm S. Instead of recommending
modifications in the structure of the organization, they recommend
major modifications in the *information* and *control* methods being
used—modifications, that is, in the technology of managing.

They tell you that division X is still living in the nineteenth century.
They want the unit to use more computers for processing and analyzing information. It should automate its inventory control procedures
as well as many of its purchasing and production operations. They
want to modify the information flows, so that decisions can be made
faster and at different points in the organization. Instead of discussing
decentralization and job descriptions, they talk a lot about modern
analytical techniques and the newest available software. You will have
to hire some hotshot MBAs if you want to carry out their recommendations, because neither you nor any of your top people can fully
understand what they are talking about.

Because (in this fable) you continue to hold to your experimental
style and because you are still not satisfied, you decide you want a

third opinion. So you call in another consulting firm, company P. Its members have Ph.D. degrees, too, but their affiliations are different. They are members of the American Psychological Association. They are mostly clinical and social psychologists who view the world from the human side. They don't carry computers or draw organization charts. Their favorite tools seem to be group discussions, face-to-face meetings, and the open-ended interview.

You ask them to take a look at division X, and they, too, come back with a report. Their report is, of course, different from the other two. It argues that the solution to division X's problems lies in changing the *culture* of that unit, in "unlocking the human potential of division X." Morale is low, they report; apathy is high. People are constricted and anxious, afraid to speak up and take risks. What division X needs is a more open culture, more participation, more involvement, and more creativity.

Firm P's recommendation is that you approach the problem from a *people* perspective. They want you to set up an organizational development program in which you take groups of your people out to the country for long weekends to talk things over, open up valid communication among them, express what they really feel, and develop much more mutual trust and confidence. Then, they suggest, you follow up with an ongoing team-building program within the organization.

But you go on experimenting. Your marketing manager tells you about a new consulting group, company T. They have built their reputation by focusing on market research studies and by advising companies about market prospects and competitive position. You still have some money left, so you decide to ask them to take a look at your problem as well.

This group doesn't talk much to people inside division X; they don't even look at its computers, information systems, and communication patterns. Instead, they talk to people outside the division who know something about the division's business—to its customers and competitors, to the trade press and security analysts, to members of its industry association, and so on.

Firm T's recommendations are, as expected, quite different from the other three. They don't say much about the organizational structure, information and control systems, or even people's morale and attitude. Instead, they focus on division X's assigned *tasks*—its products, market prospects, and competitive position. They suggest that the division needs to redefine its tasks, take a fresh look at its markets, and change its perception of its environment. They argue that division X's structure, the attitudes of its people and its information systems are symptoms, but not necessarily the cause, of its problems. The division is

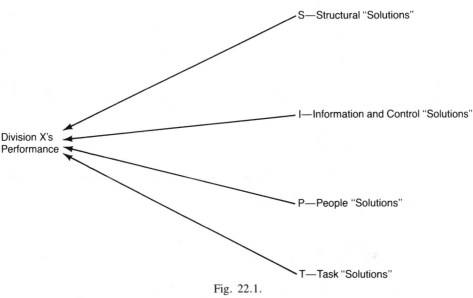

Fig. 22.1.

doing badly because it is working on the wrong tasks; it is working on tasks that are out of date, and out of tune with its current environment. Division X is in a mature industry with limited opportunities. To remain viable in the long run, it should look for new markets and more attractive business opportunities.

Probably you could go on experimenting, but the board members are giving you strange looks by now, and the people in division X have really had it with all those consultants.

So you stop there and look at what you've got. Which of the four recommendations should you follow? Which should you reject? Why? Since you are the manager in this story, we'll leave it to you to answer those questions!

As of right now, we face the following situation. All four groups have looked at the same division, but what they have seen seems to be determined more by what they are than by what's "really" there (fig. 22.1).

Group S sees the road to improvement through changing its organizational structure, changing the loci of authority and responsibility. Firm I looks at the same problem and sees it informationally. They want to improve the analytic quality of decisions by using sophisticated information technology and by applying new techniques for controlling and processing information. Firm P looks at the same problem and sees people issues. They want to work on the organization's "culture," on people's attitudes and interpersonal relationships to generate a spirit of teamwork. And firm T suggests that the problem isn't inside the organization at all; it is in its

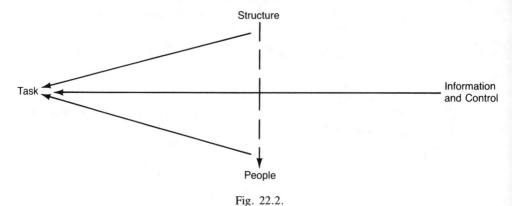

Fig. 22.2.

tasks, its relations with the environment, its mature markets and declining industry position. Therefore, the first priority is to redefine the division's tasks and its perceptions of opportunities.

But there is one more important point that needs to be made before you, the manager, can decide which of those alternatives to choose. The four are not mutually exclusive. Figure 22.1 is far from complete. No single one of those sets of recommendations, if implemented, will affect the performance of division X without also affecting each of the other variables in that model. *Structure, information and control, people,* and *task* are all interconnected in organizations. If we go with firm S and we decentralize the division, or if we give more authority to the newly proposed product managers, those changes will also cause changes (perhaps adverse ones) in people's attitudes and interpersonal relations. We will have to draw new arrows into that diagram, as in figure 22.2.

And if we continue to work on organizational structure, we will also affect information and control requirements. The kinds of techniques that are appropriate in a highly decentralized structure—accounting systems, for example—will be very different from those appropriate for highly centralized organizations. So add another arrow (fig. 22.3)

And the beat goes on. Suppose we hire the information technology–oriented consulting firm I and introduce new computers and new information systems. Then we should expect impacts not only on the way the job gets done but also on structure and on people. If we centralize information in locations where we couldn't centralize before, we will find decisions being made and responsibilities being taken in places different from where they were made and taken before. And although we may be claiming structural decentralization, our new information system may be pushing us toward greater informational centralization. We will probably also find that the kinds of people we need in our new, technically sophisticated organization may be quite different from those we needed before. Attitudes and

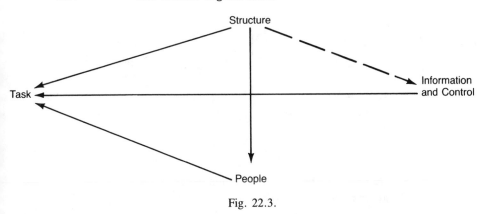

Fig. 22.3.

feelings will also change as technology moves in to supplement or even replace some human skills, judgment, and experience.

Suppose we go the people route, hiring people-oriented firm P. We start a major program to encourage more openness, more honesty in people's communication, more autonomy at lower levels, and more interaction across departments. Can we do such things effectively without also exerting great pressure on the preexisting organizational structure? The authority system will have to change, and old ideas about formal channels of communication will disappear. We will exert pressure on the information and control systems, too. Once people have developed new expectations, they may want new tools or the abolition of old ones that may have been managerially useful but psychologically frustrating.

Finally, suppose we follow firm T's recommendations and change division X's assigned tasks. We will have to come up with a new organizational structure to help carry out those tasks. We will also affect the people, because many of the existing folk may feel insecure and uncertain about their futures and their jobs. In fact, we may need to bring in new people with new capabilities to implement the new tasks.

And so we must keep adding more arrows until our diagram looks as it does in figure 22.4. In this version of our model, everything affects everything else! Although we started out worrying only about the relationship between structure and performance, or information system and performance, or people and performance, or task and performance, we end up worrying about what happens to all the others when we change any one. Some of those second-order changes may turn out to be very helpful, but some may be quite problematic. The wise manager has to somehow estimate those second- and even third-order effects before deciding which valve to turn.

All of this is to say that organizations are dynamic, changing entities. If we inject something into one part of the system, bells begin to ring and

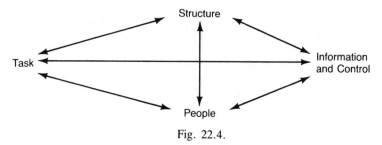

Fig. 22.4.

lights begin to flash all over the system, often in places we hadn't counted on and at times we hadn't expected.

No organization is an island, complete unto itself

The model we have just drawn is still incomplete. It portrays the organization in a world empty of everything but customers, competitors, and suppliers. Yet if American organizations have learned one thing in the last couple of decades, it is that the worlds they inhabit are anything but empty. The organization is influenced by its position in the broader environment, by government pressures, and by hosts of other organizations. The modern organization is a city dweller. The traffic jams are continuous. The organization lives in a pressing, crowded world. And it presses back.

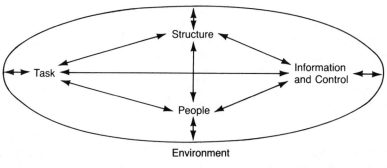

Fig. 22.5.

We will talk about the environment and its impact on organizations in part 5. For now, let's enclose our model in a world, so that managers can remember that changes in the organization are likely to affect that environment and that changes in the environment are likely to affect the organization (fig. 22.5).

Managing the whole organization

All this is not to say that the complexity of the organization is so great that managers can never predict what will happen when they try to change one variable. That is, the organization is complex enough to make any simple task, structural, informational, or people model inadequate. Over the last few decades we have made a lot of progress in understanding organizations. We now know a good deal more about effective methods for changing structure, culture, or information technology; and we know somewhat more about how those elements are related to one another. The four different solutions to the same problem proffered by our four imaginary consulting firms should not be taken as a sign that consultants don't know what they are doing. On the contrary, the different approaches are indications of how much we have learned about the complexity of organizations and how much we know about changing them.

Each of the four imaginary consulting firms in our fable may be sold on its own product. Each may be overly enthusiastic about all that can be done by changing structure, information systems, people, or tasks. Each may be partially and understandably blind to the perspectives of the others. But managers need not be blind. They have much more to work from than in the old days, when we so naively believed that a simple line drawing on an organization chart could capture the essence of a vital, volatile organization.

But we still haven't answered the question in our fable. Are there any sensible rules of thumb about where to *start* making changes in a given organization's performance? When should I start working on structure? When on information? When on people? When on tasks?

Here is a weak, but perhaps sensible, rule of thumb: To decide where one should devote attention, one should look first at the "programmability" of the "problem" that one is trying to solve. Where is the problem along the continuum from clear, well-defined, and familiar, on the one hand, to unclear, open-ended, and new, on the other. To what degree can that problem be defined operationally? Is the problem of a type the manager has solved before? Is there some known satisfactory method for solving it? If so, then the best entry point is probably structural. If, however, the "problem" is novel and ill-defined, if its shape isn't exactly obvious, the manager may do better starting from the people side first.

Why? The reasoning runs like this: If the problem is programmable, if we know what steps to take to solve it, then we can usually set out a sensible structure to carry out those steps. But if the problem is unfamiliar, if it has no clear precedents, then the best tool is the human head. In those unprogrammable problems, it doesn't make much sense to try to set up an orderly structure first, because no rational basis exists for choosing a structure.

Suppose, for example, the problem is to set up a new shoe factory in a new market in Texas. That's a fairly programmable problem. People who have worked in shoe manufacturing know a lot about how to go about solving that problem. They have enough experience and training in shoe manufacturing to specify the steps involved in setting up a factory to produce a certain number of thousands of pairs of shoes per month. They can make pretty good judgments about the equipment they will need, how that equipment ought to be aligned, how much space is required, what the steps from raw hides to finished shoes ought to be, and even how many people will be needed. That shoe factory problem is a moderately programmable problem. It is not programmable down to the fifth decimal place, but an experienced person knows how to go about solving it. For that sort of problem structural starting points for specifying the steps, rules, job descriptions, and so on seem to make good sense.

But what's an "unprogrammable" problem? It's an unclear, ill-defined problem that's new to you, for which you know no rules or solutions. You've had no prior experience in dealing with it and aren't even sure of the boundaries to the problem. The president of the United States thinks (but isn't perfectly sure) that the Russians are secretly placing offensive missiles in Cuba. How should he solve the problem? Our company's sales have suddenly started to drop for no obvious reason. How should I attack the problem?

Those are "unprogrammable" problems—at least the first time they happen. For such problems, what's the best entry point? Is it structure? Is it information systems? Probably not. The best bet is thoughtful people putting their heads together to try to figure out what to do.

If structure is a good place to start for programmed tasks, and people are a good place to start for unprogrammed tasks, what's the role of that third variable, information and control? One answer might be that information and control technology is the handmaiden of structure. The primary function of better information and control systems, one can argue, is to program what has hitherto been unprogrammable. Improving such systems helps us specify things that had formerly been done judgmentally, by the seat of the pants. What was unprogrammable yesterday becomes programmable today, and what we had to solve judgmentally last week can be tackled in a more systematic way this week.

Our rule of thumb now reads: If the task is programmable, go with structure first; if the task is unprogrammable, go people first; but remember that what was unprogrammable this year may be programmable next, given improved information technology.

We keep approaching the horizon, forever developing better ways to program the hitherto unprogrammable and to do systematically today what we did judgmentally yesterday. Yet, of course, though we may approach the horizon, we never reach it. New, unprogrammable problems keep popping up, even as we program the old ones. And as long as new issues, ideas,and crises arise, there is likely to be good reason for entering the organization through its human gate.

But one other rule is certainly in order: Look at what's happening out there in the world. Is your market changing? Will your present products or services become obsolete soon? If your organization lives in a volatile world, then assess the relevance of your present tasks and plug that information into your thinking.

The reader will note, as we conclude this chapter, that once again we approach some of the same issues raised in the preceding chapter. An unprogrammable task, for example, is one in which people initially don't know exactly what they're doing. That's not far from the nature of the pathfinding phase of the managing process. A programmable task is one in which we do know pretty much what we're doing. That's closer to the problem-solving phase of managing.

It's worth pointing out, too, that in large organizations it's usually the people at the top who know the least about what they're doing! In contrast, workers on the shop floor typically know a lot about what they're doing. Of course, that is precisely because we have, over time, learned to program what we call "low-level" jobs. They're considered "low-level" in large part precisely because they are programmable; it's fairly easy to teach many people how to do them. But we know very little about programming the jobs of scientists or CEOs, which is why we worry so much more about finding "outstanding" people for those roles. When we don't know how to tell people what we want them to do, we must be sure we get good people and hope they figure out good ways to handle all those (as yet) unprogrammable problems they'll have to confront.

Here is a second, weaker rule of thumb: As organizations grow larger, structural change generally becomes more useful. Large human systems need formal structures for coordination and control because face-to-face communication becomes too costly and unreliable. In very small organizations, face-to-face communication can do most of the job that structure tries to do for the large organization. The old dictum about growing organizations is probably true: As they get bigger, they have to get themselves organized, whether they like it or not.

And there is a third idea, not quite a rule of thumb: Managers are people, too. Before deciding to go either structural, people, task, or information and control, let the manager look forward: What do I [the manager] want? What do I believe in? What kind of organization would I just love to build? Let's use that pathfinding posture as a starting point, even if it creates some problems along the way.

In summary

Organizations can be thought of as lively sets of interrelated systems designed to come up with and perform complicated tasks in complex and volatile environments. We can try to manipulate at least four variables in those systems in order to improve the organization's performance. We can manipulate the organization's *tasks*. We can manipulate the organizational *structure*—the formal communication, authority, and accountability workflow systems. We can manipulate the *information and control* technology. And we can manipulate the *people* system, by changing the organization's culture, its people, and their attitudes and relationships. There is also an ever-present fifth, less controllable variable, which is growing more relevant every day: the *environment,* made up of the other organizations and institutions in which our organization is embedded.

When we tamper with any one of those variables—tasks, structure, information and control, or people—we are likely to cause significant effects in the others. Organizations are dynamic and volatile.

Here are some rules of thumb for where to start. For "programmable" tasks, structural change is often an appropriate starting point. Working on the people variable is usually more appropriate when taking on "unprogrammable" tasks. Structural change is also often an appropriate first step when trying to change very large units. Those are just rules of thumb, and they assume that the organization's tasks are right for its environment.

But one more rule of thumb is in order: Consider your mission, your philosophy, your vision of the kind of organization you want to create. Start there, even though you may have to do a lot of balancing and modifying of other parts in order to move sensibly in your chosen direction.

23 Four influential ideas: From scientific management to organizational culture

In chapter 22 we discussed several entry points for changing the organizational system: task, structural, informational, and people entry points. Useful ideas and techniques have developed around each of those points, adding to managers' tool kits for managing the organization.

In this chapter, we look back over the twentieth century to spotlight those ideas that have been most influential. Such a historical look gives us a way of making sense out of what might otherwise seem a jungle of conflicting notions about how managers should manage. There really is some order out there in the managerial world, and a historical perspective can help us to discern the dominant patterns.

Three caveats are in order here before we get into our historical review:

1. Managers, like everyone, are prisoners of history. This historical sketch is not here just to generate nostalgia; nor is it history for history's sake. The brick and mortar of much of our contemporary managerial thinking was laid down in those early years, setting a framework of beliefs and assumptions that still influences our thinking. Those same beliefs and assumptions, often implicit, can still be found out on Detroit factory floors, in Pittsburgh boardrooms, and in the startup companies of Silicon Valley.

2. Techniques—cheap and transferable techniques—have been a major catalyst of managerial change. Many of the ideas we shall consider in this chapter have been around for a long, long time; some have existed for centuries. But those ideas didn't take off and change managerial practice until someone invented some cheap and easily transferable techniques for implementing them. Techniques turn dormant ideas into instruments of major change; although many of the ideas are old, most of the techniques are relatively new.

3. In the managerial world, new ideas and techniques do *not* usually drive out the old ones that preceded them. Instead, the new shunts the old over into a somewhat different niche. Then the new and the old, which are often contradictory, coexist. When a new managerial invention comes along, it is added on to the old, just as television was added on to radio, so that the whole house got noisier. In management, too, that "layering"

effect of new ideas and techniques on top of old ones tends to make things noisier and more complicated as the years pass.

The history of managing is rather like the history of medical practice. Some of the same diseases that were around in 1900 are still around. But the practice of medicine must have been much simpler back then, not because those diseases were simpler but just because the medical tool kit was much more limited. The old Doc did what he could, and if the patient died he could still feel he had done what could be done. Modern physicians have to know a lot more about many more methods and techniques than their grandfathers. When patients die now, physicians have to worry about whether they were up to date on all the myriad of possible available courses of treatment. Modern managing, too, is more complicated than it was in 1900, and one reason is the same simple one: we have many more ideas and techniques now than we had then, and the modern manager, to make good choices, has to be on top of a much larger set of alternatives.

Let's go on now to look at four powerful ideas that have influenced American managerial thinking, and the techniques and practices that have evolved from them.

Scientific management and the separation of planning from doing

One very important set of managerial techniques got started in the United States back around 1910. It was called, by its founder, F. W. Taylor, "scientific management." That is a name and a set of techniques most readers probably remember from their college textbooks.

Taylor was an engineer—an unusually curious, creative, and imaginative engineer. If ever a movie is made about Taylor and "Taylorism," the climactic scene will take place in the yards of the Bethlehem Steel Works shortly after the turn of the century. Only two characters will be needed: Taylor himself and an immigrant laborer named Schmidt. In the first scene in that movie, Schmidt is going about his work, carrying heavy pigs of iron from one part of the smoky yards to another. Taylor, ever curious, is sitting on a pile of rusty iron bars, watching Schmidt, thinking, "There must be a better way."

As Taylor observes Schmidt, he makes something like the following analysis. Schmidt is really doing two kinds of things: (1) He is using his arms and legs to move those pigs of iron, but (2) he is also using his brain to make decisions. The decisions are small ones but real, nevertheless. Schmidt is deciding how to pile the iron, whether to bend from the knee or the hip, and so on.

Taylor argues to himself that, although Schmidt may have the better muscles, Taylor has the better brain. Schmidt is better suited for the *doing* part of the job, but Taylor is better fitted for the *deciding* part.

So Taylor goes to work and invents the technique of *time study,* which lets him measure and analyze the doing part of Schmidt's job. (Taylor, in the best American tradition, was gung ho on measurement.) Then he experiments with alternative ways of handling pigs of iron. From these, he and his colleagues go on to design an "optimal" plan for the way Schmidt's job should be done. The plan specifies the timing and sequences of movements Schmidt should follow, step by step, moment by moment.

Now Taylor returns to the mill yard, carrying his good news to Schmidt. "If you do it the way I have now laid out for you," Taylor tells Schmidt, "all sorts of goodies will follow. Start with your right hand, instead of your left; bend from the knee instead of from the waist," and so on. He points out to Schmidt that this analysis is in Schmidt's and everyone else's best interest, for three reasons. First, more pig iron will be handled by these new methods, and the increased productivity is certainly good for our young and developing nation. (Taylor called himself a "third force," working not in the interests of management or labor but of society at large.) Second, Schmidt will end the day less fatigued than he was before, for Taylor will have taught him how to use his muscles "scientifically." And third, Taylor, as an outside consultant, will urge the company to pay Schmidt increased wages accruing from his greater productivity. For all those reasons, Taylor proclaimed, it behooved Schmidt to do it Taylor's way. And it behooved the company and the world to adopt this new kind of "scientific management."

It worked, but it also didn't work. Taylor's new method spread rapidly, for it was cheap to use and the positive effects on productivity were often enormous. This new scientific management, in its envisioned ideal form, would produce a perfect fit between worker and work, so that all workers could do their work in the way best adapted to them personally and most closely adjusted to the interests of the firm. The flow of work from position to position would be scientifically determined, the limits of activity of each worker would be scientifically measured, and so on.

From Taylor's rib was born the whole concept of industrial engineering and the "efficiency expert." Moreover, scientific management fitted nicely with what was happening in the world around it. The United States, a developing country with a poorly educated immigrant labor force, needed more productivity, and Taylor offered just that. No wonder it caught on. Within a few years hardly a manufacturing firm in America was without "efficiency men" and the other paraphernalia that accompanied scientific management—job descriptions, work standards, individual incentive schemes, organization charts, work-flow diagrams, and all of their entourage.

Scientific management did indeed seem to pay off. As a result of the work of Taylor and many others in Europe and the United States, management became more formalized, jobs more specified, and mass-production technology, America's pride, came increasingly into being. The ideas that surrounded Taylorism became part of the standard beliefs of almost every manager in the nation. The notions that work processes should be spelled out, that tasks should be measured and programmed, and that responsibilities should be "commensurate" with authority were all ideas that were generated either out of Taylorism or from parallel sources that were quite consonant with Taylorism.

The costs of scientific management

The modern reader reviewing those last few paragraphs has probably already made a mental note of one nagging difficulty. It was made a manifest challenge by Taylor himself, with comments that were guaranteed to generate trouble, even in 1911. He wrote, for example, "Now one of the very first requirements for a man who is fit to handle pig iron . . . is that he shall be so stupid and so phlegmatic that he more nearly resembles . . . the ox than any other type. . . . He must consequently be trained by a man more intelligent than himself" (F. W. Taylor, *Scientific Management* [New York: Harper, 1911], 59).

The difficulty, of course, was *people;* and the people problem was later labeled by Taylorists as "resistance." What Taylor had done was to separate the planning and thinking parts of Schmidt's work from the implementing and doing parts. He argued for the separation, partially on the grounds that the Schmidts of the world were a dull group—a rather dull argument. But he also made his case on stronger grounds, often used in later years, arguing that specialized and highly trained experts, equipped with modern tools, could do a better job of specifying how work ought to be done than the people doing it.

But the human problem was to haunt Taylor and Taylorists for a good many years to come. Even in 1911, social reformers took up the cudgel against Taylorism. First, they argued that Taylor was demeaning and dehumanizing the American worker. What distinguished humans from oxen if not the human capacity to think and make decisions? If Taylor amputated the thinking part of a worker's job, he was indeed dehumanizing that person. An economic injustice argument was made even more loudly; if Schmidt's productivity had increased 300 percent, how come Taylor only wanted to pay him something like 60 percent more than he had been receiving before?

Overall, however, the observable increases in productivity generated by the new Tayloristic methods overwhelmed the social critics. Taylorism and the assembly line swept through the blue-collar ranks of U.S. industry.

The unhappy industrial engineer

So Taylor's methods proliferated and expanded. And with that expansion came the second wave of counterattacks. This time it did not come from social do-gooders but from the Schmidts themselves. Those human Schmidts behaved humanly. The second wave took the form of slowdowns, sabotage, pegged production, and socially organized resistance to Taylor's techniques. And it led to the era of the unhappy industrial engineer, "the efficiency man," being distrusted, often hated by the people in the plant. When he showed up, work slowed down. When he set high standards, people professed they couldn't possibly meet them. When he asked for suggestions, people hid the jigs they had rigged up to do the work faster.

At lower levels such human resistance was the major cost of Taylorism; the costs at higher levels were costs associated with tight authoritarian structure. Along with Taylorism, other parallel notions had emerged— about span of control, authority equaling responsibility, and rigid, logical designs for organizations. The costs showed in the form of inextricably overlapping areas of authority and responsibility that resisted all efforts at separation, as well as in the form of "depersonalization" of human relationships that followed from formalization of roles and restriction of communication. Those costs became greater and more noticeable as the decades passed, both because expectations were rising and because the number of people in middle-management levels was growing so rapidly. White-collar workers became more numerous, the complexities of staff relationships increased, and the varieties of specialists grew. Also, the problem of coordinating their activities became much more difficult than any simple formal structure could resolve.

Participative management

Under the influence of Taylorism, organizations had indeed grown and prospered; but through the 1920s, 1930s and 1940s, the human costs were becoming increasingly apparent, and human "resistance" had become a major problem. To fill this great breach, up stepped the "people people."

Let's try a second movie to dramatize a second important idea in the evolution of American managerial thinking—the people-oriented participative management phase. To do so, we must turn to another setting and another time.

This time we set our time machine back to the 1920s and to the Hawthorne Works of the Western Electric Company in Cicero, Illinois. In this second simplified film, the major characters are a group of Western Electric managers, researchers from the young Harvard Business School, and a group of blue-collar workers from the Western Electric plant. The researchers are there to study, among other things, the effects of working conditions on the productivity of those hourly workers. The interest in productivity, the focus on hourly workers, and the concern for physical conditions such as lighting and rest periods are all reminiscent of Taylor. But this time the workers are performing fine eye-hand tasks, assembling telephone relays and the like.

The researchers start their lighting studies by selecting a group of workers, placing them in a special workroom, and maintaining productivity records under varying conditions of light, over an extended period. In our movie, there is shot after shot of production charts, showing a clear rise in productivity as the foot-candles of light over the workbenches are increased.

With dramatic license, we now sneak a hero into the scene—an unknown (and imaginary) junior assistant. In the interests of science, this youngster argues, one more control is needed before one can safely conclude that better light yields better productivity. Quietly, the researchers begin to reduce the lighting. Productivity, if the lighting is what causes it, should now decline, but it doesn't. As the lighting drops, productivity continues to rise. That, of course, becomes the moment of truth. Now, those increases in productivity that seemed to have been *caused* by the lighting turn out to be quite independent of the lighting. It doesn't seem to matter whether the lights are bright or dim; in either case, those workers continue to produce at higher and higher rates.

At this point a new search begins. If it's not the lighting that's causing greater productivity, what is it? The search leads inexorably to just those issues that had plagued Taylor and his colleagues two decades earlier. It leads to the human side of the enterprise.

What did cause those increases in productivity? Probably some soft stuff like "morale," "motivation," or "attitude." Those workers had been separated from their peers, placed in a small private room, away from the noisy shop floor. The environment was less formal. A whole host of intangible social and psychological factors had been inadvertently changed along with the lighting. But intangible or not, those factors seemed to be the causes of higher productivity.

Incidentally, it is worth pointing out that Taylor and his colleagues were aware of such intangible human issues. They caused Taylor no end of trouble. But Taylor simply did not have very good tools for dealing with them. In the Western Electric studies, those same factors were suddenly and almost accidentally turned around to cause *increases* in productivity, instead of resistance.

So a new search soon got under way for better ways of harnessing those powerful psychological variables. By the early '30s, the "human relations" movement was making some headway. The people view began to gain a small foothold in American managerial thinking. Since then, that people point of view has slowly, but not steadily, grown and prospered. The initial idea was such a simple one by today's standards that it seems almost trivial: people would work better in organizations if they were willingly and enthusiastically involved in their work. Back in Taylor's days, that idea did not look so obvious at all. Would oxen work better if they were more "involved" in their work?

The next step was a search for methods and techniques for creating such involvement. Gradually, through a series of steps and missteps, two key developments emerged. The first key was the idea of *participation;* essentially, "people support what they help to create." In other words, people love their own babies more than other people's. The second was a technique—the *small group,* the team, as a mechanism for generating involvement. The group could serve almost as a substitute for authority. By participating in groups, people would develop loyalty to one another; they would develop commitment to their groups and the group's tasks.

The small war between scientific management and the new participative management

Together, the technique of the small group and the concept of participation led quite naturally to the notion that managers ought to involve workers more in planning and decision making, thereby generating motivation and commitment. But, of course, that idea didn't blend very well with the prevailing Tayloristic ideas. In fact, it was 180 degrees away from typical Tayloristic ways of dealing with the same problem of productivity. Taylor had argued that planning and decision making should be taken away from the Schmidts of the world and turned over to specialized planners and decision makers. Now along comes this new people-oriented view, recommending that Schmidt's head be put back on his shoulders. Encourage him to do his own planning—in groups with other Schmidts. It is no wonder that clashes and small wars began to break out between those two polar proposals.

At first the new participative people proceeded with considerable caution. They were a minority. They had to confront existing Tayloristic organizational structures and beliefs and work within them. For example, to apply the findings of their years of research, Western Electric developed an elaborate program of worker counseling. But the program was added on *outside* the operational scheme of the company. The counselors were available to help people blow off their frustrations, but they were not to feed back information to top management. They were not, themselves, to try to induce any organizational changes. That was management's business. The counselors listened. And when employees, having thus spilled out their anger or fear, felt a little better, they returned to the same setting that had been there before. The relief was likely to be temporary, and the "treatments" had to recur as new frustrations built up once again.

That external arrangement did not disturb the existing organizational philosophy. It was "sanitary." It worked only on people, without reference to structure or other managerial issues. Radical and revolutionary as it was at the time, in retrospect it seems a weak and compromising solution. Much more daring experiments were to follow.

Those new experiments used some of the same ideas, as well as some different ones. They used group methods especially, since resistance to change was seen more and more as a function of (1) individual frustration and (2) strong informal social groups that supported and enforced resistance. Therefore, if one could provide opportunities for greater job satisfaction and if one could also corner the group forces and redirect them toward more productive work, then the best of all possible worlds would result.

Where has participative management found its home?

In the 1950s, participative "experiments" were set up in several American companies. Again and again, despite mistakes and problems, they showed that this more human, more participative approach could clearly increase productivity among hourly workers. Yet participative management did not sweep American industry nearly as much as Taylorism had swept it in the decades earlier. And it certainly didn't supplant Taylorism. Work standards and job specifications are still a very large factor in modern American organizations. Those small wars of the 1950s between scientific managers and participative managers were not clearly won by the participative managers—at least not at the hourly worker level of American manufacturing industry.

One reason for the slow adoption of participative schemes was that senior managers feared the apparent loss of control implied by those participative changes. Workers allowed to control the speed of the production line might not be willing to give up that privilege at some future date; and they might abuse it. There were fears, too, about the coordination problems that might be generated by many small groups operating more or less autonomously. Some environmental developments, such as the rise of national labor unions and legal controls over wages and hours, required uniformity throughout the firm; and uniformity would be harder to achieve (or at least it so appeared) under participative schemes.

Whatever the reasons, by the mid-1960s in America, participative management had begun an orderly withdrawal from the hourly ranks, moving instead up into higher levels of the organization. There, it produced its greatest short-term impact. Within the rapidly growing ranks of middle management, new problems had begun to show up. Taylorism didn't work very well among people who worked with their heads more than their hands. So participative ideas moved in. Such words as *communication, motivation, feedback,* and *team building* became buzzwords in middle management circles. Group discussions, conferences, and management development programs grew and prospered. By the mid-sixties, participative management, which had been turned away from the main plant gate, had entered American industry through the white-collar doorway.

One disturbing result of all this was the unintentional construction, in the 1960s, of a rather thick, high, and impenetrable wall between hourly workers and managers; hourly workers operated in a Tayloristic environment, and managers in a more participative one. The old American idea of career mobility from apprentice to company president was almost killed off at that point. One does not move easily from blue-collar to management jobs in the modern company. Movement to the top is much easier for those who start out *above* the hourly worker barrier, coming into the company as technologists or management trainees. Hourly workers tend to stay hourly workers, in part because in their Tayloristic world they are trained differently, organized differently, and controlled differently than managers and supervisors. Whether that, too, is changing in the 1980s is not yet clear. Perhaps the shrinkage of the blue-collar sector will finesse some of the difficulties generated by that mutual isolation of the blue-collar and managerial worlds.

By the 1970s, however, the whole hourly worker question was once more reopened, as a consequence largely of environmental pressures. Job enrichment programs were starting and there was even talk about alternatives to the assembly line, such as group-based factories. European companies (Volvo of Sweden is a good example) and whole societies (such as Yugoslavia) had begun to experiment with extensive worker participation in all phases of work, from assembly lines to boards of directors. It was as though the costs of Taylorism had grown very large—compared with the payoffs—because expectations and attitudes had changed over those 50 years, among workers, among managers, and in society at large.

The brave new world idea of information technology

Our film series on the human organization is not yet complete. For the third film, we must once again change dates and costumes, this time to the 1950s and the era of the grey flannel suit. And we change cast, too. Our heroes in this round are not blue-collar workers or social researchers but mathematicians and computer types. Whereas Taylor and his colleagues were armed with stop watches, and the participative people used team-building groups as their primary tool, this new population rides on stage astride the glamorous new computer. They carry technology that did not exist for Taylor and powerful techniques for measuring and analyzing—not what people do with their arms and legs but what people do with their heads (and some things people can't do with their heads).

Like many movies, this one can be an updated repeat of an old plot—

the Taylor-Schmidt theme—in modern dress. We'll call it "The Son of Schmidt." Instead of old Mr. Taylor, the hands-on engineer, the son of Taylor is a management scientist of the '60s. And the new, young Mr. Schmidt, with a B.A., is a middle manager. Old Schmidt presumably achieved some fulfillment by being able to make minor decisions about how to handle pig iron. Young Mr. Schmidt, however, finds his fulfillment in making complicated judgmental decisions about how to allocate company funds among a variety of alternatives.

In the opening scene of this movie, young Mr. Taylor, much like his father, is sitting in the shadows at the back end of young Schmidt's skyscraper office, observing young Schmidt as he goes about his mental work. Taylor asks questions, collects data, and, like his father, concludes that there must be a better way to do Schmidt's job. Armed with his computer, he sets out to find it. After all, young Schmidt seems to be making his budget decisions by the seat of his pants, using "know-how," "judgment," and "experience." Surely there must be better, more scientific, more systematic, more logical ways to make those decisions.

With the help of his new machine and his new discipline that had come to be called "management science," young Taylor attacks the problem. (Were its creators conscious of the proximity of that phrase, "management science," to Taylor's old scientific management?)

In any case, our young management scientist, Taylor, believes he can use his machine to solve complex multivariate problems in standardized ways, better than the soft, experiential, commonsense ways used by young Schmidt. He also finds that he can make those complex decisions faster, and that one will no longer need ten years of experience to be able to make them well.

So, in the 1950s this third wave, the management science wave, began to make its impact felt at several levels of the organization. One effect was on the hourly worker, by programming already Taylorized tasks even further. One way, after all, to eliminate very routine and monotonous tasks from the human realm is to turn them over to the automated machine and the robot. Another effect was on some participative middle management jobs, an effect tantamount to what old Taylor had done to old Schmidt—to program their previously unprogrammed work.

Looked at another way, management science simply meant that once again humans had invented new, cheaper, and faster ways of programming the hitherto unprogrammable. Management science shared with its earlier forebear, scientific management, that push to order the disorderly, to analyze the previously unanalyzed, to do in systematic ways what had previously been done by human judgment.

Pathfinding and organizational culture

Notice that all three of those ideas—scientific management, participative management, and management science—dealt primarily with relationships between problem solving and implementing. Scientific management and management science, in their own ways, both tried to separate problem solving from implementing. Participative management dealt with the same issues in an almost opposite way, by generating more interaction between the two. None of the three said much about the individualistic, creative, pathfinding phase of managing.

But that does not mean that the pathfinding idea was new or unknown. It had been in vogue, in a modified version, way back before the turn of the century, at a time when individualists and entrepreneurs were even more the heroes of American society than they are today. But that early version of every individual cutting a personal path had somewhat faded away before the onslaught of the factory system with its focus on mass production and efficiency. Risk taking and charismatic pathfinding notions were also out of tune with both the strongly analytic, orderly thinking of management scientists and the small-group, consensus-building views held by proponents of participative management. By the 1970s, organizations didn't seem to value individualism anymore.

That, too, began to change in the late 1970s and early 1980s. Beginning in those years, a fourth set of ideas has been put forward that are consonant with individualistic pathfinding but also centrally concerned, like participative management, with implementing. This fourth set of ideas is about managing organizational cultures.

Culture is an umbrella word that encompasses a whole set of implicit, widely shared beliefs, traditions, values, and expectations that characterize a particular group of people. Culture is to the organization what personality and character are to the individual. It identifies the uniqueness of the organization, its values and beliefs. But organizational culture is also a system that controls the behavior of its members. Thus, the effective management of a company's culture can become just as relevant to the manager as the effective management of information. We shall devote most of chapter 25 to issues of managing organizational culture; for now, let's just put it into our historical context by calling it a fourth set of ideas about management that has followed scientific management, participative management, and management science. Just as both scientific management and management science stem from an analytic intellectual tradition, participative management and culture management share a behavioral, people-oriented tradition. Participative management was focused on small groups; its cousin, culture management, is a way of thinking about large groups.

One more point: In conjunction with a rising interest in the management of culture has come a resurgence of interest in pathfinding issues—individual leadership, creativity, and risk taking. One reason—not the only reason—is that the effective management of culture, as we shall see, is largely a pathfinding matter, for reasons such as these:

Pathfinding leaders define clear missions, and clear, shared missions are the foundations of organizational cultures. Of course, those missions have to be communicated, and other organizational members have to be persuaded to join up. And although cultures are communicated through acts of persuasion and reiteration (part of phase 3), they are shaped by beliefs (part of phase 1). Managing a culture becomes a combination of pathfinding ideas with implementing processes. But the keystone is the pathfinding part. That's where managers can create the meanings of the organization for their people.

Putting it together

Since about 1900, a series of powerful ideas and techniques have influenced the practice of management in America. To an extent, each of those ideas was a product of its times; Taylor's ideas were born when the United States was a developing, manufacturing-oriented society, populated by large numbers of eager but diverse and poorly educated immigrant groups. Participative management reflected evolving concerns with rising expectations, growing resistance to old Tayloristic methods, and even the intrusion of Freudian theory into our otherwise rational models of humankind. Management science, in its turn, rode on the shoulders of the computer and other technologies that evolved out of World War II and was welcomed as an aid in the new high-speed world of exploding technology and even larger, more complex organizations. Culture management began to make sense first in loosely structured high-tech organizations and older companies that were losing ground to competitors in productivity and quality.

Those were not meaningless oscillations. They can all legitimately be called progress. Taylor offered analysis to areas that had never before been analyzable. Participative management offered innovative ways for implementing change and for improving human satisfaction in an increasingly white-collar world. The management scientist added new, far more powerful phase 2–oriented analytic methods, addressing higher realms of information and decision. And the emphasis on culture may yet (though the evidence is not yet in) help us address the tensions between issues of control and participation, and also put our traditional values of creativity and entrepreneurship to work at all levels of even very large organizations.

None of those ideas can be applied without costs. Taylorism generated resistance and sabotage. Participation generated new problems of control, power, and coordination. Management science promised more than it could initially deliver and regenerated both old problems of resistance and new social concerns about displacement of humans by machines. And perhaps our recent attention to culture will create new sets of problems—this time of the *1984*, Big Brother variety, problems of overconformity and organizational rigidity.

If this historical rundown of overlapping waves of ideas seems only to complicate life for the manager, it should. The manager of this and coming generations will have to cope with problems of interrelating and estimating the relative impacts of all those approaches and the new ones that will yet arise. That manager will have to decide where in the organization each can best be applied and, if applied, what kinds of bells and whistles can be expected to sound off elsewhere in the organization.

In summary

Taylor's "scientific management" of the early 1900s separated phase 2, planning, from phase 3, implementing; it created the "efficiency man" and the industrial engineer. In doing so, Taylor also generated unforeseen problems of human resistance. Taylorism found its more lasting applications largely at hourly, blue-collar levels of American industry.

Participative management got seriously started in the United States in the 1930s and 1940s, recombining planning and implementing, but in groups. Though demonstrably applicable to hourly workers, it had its greatest impact on managerial levels, inadvertently contributing to a bigger barrier against movement from hourly worker to managerial jobs.

Management science, a label for the analytic, computer-based thrust of the fifties and sixties, again separated planning from implementing, but this time in "thinking" jobs, mostly at middle management levels; and it came into partial conflict with participative ideas as an alternative method for managing both managers and hourly workers.

In more recent years, the idea of the conscious management of organizational culture has taken hold. Driven by new technologies, changing expectations, and the success of Japanese practices, it offers a subtle, more social approach to many problems of organizational control and productivity.

Each of those developments is a step forward in helping us deal with the challenges of managing different kinds of organizations at different times in history. Of course, those four approaches are not the end of it. There will be a fifth and sixth and many more human inventions that will show up in the years ahead.

24 Organizational missions and strategies: Toward proactive pathfinding

"What's the mission of your organization?" the consultant asks the CEO. "What are this organization's long-term objectives? What do you want it to look like five years from now?"

Those are pathfinding questions. They are questions that are challenging, but a bit irritating, too. They are questions most of us can't easily answer, even about our personal lives. They are questions that can generate high-flown and silly answers, like "Our mission is to make the world a better place to live in, through men's cologne."

This chapter, nevertheless, is about such questions. Irritating or not, they're important to the spirit and the effectiveness of modern organizations. Organizations that can come up with *real* answers to such questions become organizations that know where they want to go; and knowing where you want to go is your most powerful weapon for coping with the uncertainties of a volatile environment.

This chapter will take a closer look at some of those soft pathfinding parts of managing—at missions and strategies, what missions are and why they are important, how organizations choose their missions and come up with strategies to achieve them, and the roles of "proactive" approaches to leadership in the total managing process.

At first glance, these may seem not only soft but trivial issues. There's no great mystery about what any particular organization is trying to accomplish. One company's long-term goal is to make and sell as many computers as it can; another wants to sell as many insurance policies as it can. They both try to do it profitably while growing and prospering en route. So why make such a big deal out of such issues?

The big deal derives from facts like these: Some companies in the same industry make a lot more profit than others. Some grow faster and provide better goods and services than others. Some are much more interesting and pleasant places to work in than others. Some seem to add value to the world, while others exploit their environments. Some companies start out cutting timber, then go on to run hotels, whereas others just keep on cutting timber. Some move beyond their national borders, becoming multinational;

some stay domestic. Some create new products and others keep grinding out the old ones. Some survive and prosper; others decline and die. Why?

Some of those differences can be ascribed to differences in managerial problem-solving or implementing skills; some to outside, uncontrollable environmental forces like economic recessions, wars, or shortages of capital; and some to timing or just plain luck. But a big chunk of the important differences also result from differences in "mission," "imagination," "strategy," or "leadership." Those front-end, internally driven differences are what this chapter is about.

Let's start with a real-world example about some real-world people and their real company:

The time is 1968. There's a war in Vietnam. Student uprisings, social turmoil, and racial strife are widespread in the United States. Our major character, Ken Oshman, has just completed his Ph.D. in electronic engineering. He is working in a large defense electronics company located in the area that will later come to be known as "Silicon Valley" in California.

Ken's tenure in this large organization, although successful, has carried its share of frustrations. Although a good place for a young engineer to work, it's still imposing bureaucratic restrictions, so typical of large organizations. Ken grows more and more restless. He feels the need to get out of this massive system, to do something that will give him more control over his own destiny. Perhaps, he begins to think, it may be about time to act on an old dream—founding his own company.

During the summer of 1968, that nascent dream gets a big push from some completely unforeseen events. An old friend, Walter Loewenstern, leaves the same company to start his own firm. Walter wants to develop an electronic gadget for locating cars—a device that might be used by organizations such as AAA and police departments—to help them locate cars and other vehicles quickly in busy urban areas. Walter and Ken talk at length about the idea. It seems technically feasible. Now Ken finds himself facing a clear and specific opportunity for moving his dream toward implementation.

Although Walter's electronic device catalyzes Ken into action, the development of the gadget itself soon fades away. But once Ken finds himself close to action, the dream of his new company continues to preoccupy him.

Oshman then contacts two other old college buddies, Bob Maxfield and Gene Richeson. The four decide to go for it. They join up to build a new company. They put a lot of their time and energy into trying to figure out what kind of a company they want to create, what business they ought to get into, what products they might develop. At the same time, they try to be realistic; they begin to look around for the capital they will need to get started.

Remember, it's 1968. The minicomputer boom is just getting underway. Our team decides to get their company off the ground by building on that emerging opportunity. All four have backgrounds in electronics, and three have worked for defense contractors. So they further decide to try to marry their electronics backgrounds and defense company experience to the mini-computer opportunity. They make up their minds to build a new type of minicomputer for the military market.

The idea is brand-new. The military has, until this time, used only custom-designed computers, which typically cost between five to ten times the standard product that the new team hoped to develop.

Now comes the search for capital. It's long, arduous, and frustrating. Their plan is rejected by one established venture capitalist after another. But they hang in and finally put their own heads on the block by turning to personal loans to finance the new company. They call it ROLM Corporation, an acronym made up of the first initials of the four founders' surnames.

The military version of the minicomputer, however, is not directly in line with the team's vision of its long-term mission. The military minicomputer looks like a desirable opportunity; it's a fairly small niche, not overly attractive to bigger competitors. But ROLM's larger mission, as initially formulated by Oshman and his team, is to become a major "commercial" company, not a defense contractor. Also, their mission is to become a company that is interested in more than commercial profitability, that can provide a challenging environment for its people with a minimum of bureaucracy. It must be a place where people can grow.

ROLM finally succeeds in developing and selling the standard military minicomputers. The group then begins its search for other niches that might help them become the "people-oriented commercial company" they have envisioned. Oshman and his team talk to friends and business associates and go to trade shows, always searching for business ideas that can build on ROLM's technological capability in computers, but also the opportunities that can generate the growth ROLM needs to move closer toward its mission.

Proactive search, luck, and a lot of talking and listening finally generate the idea of computer-controlled electronic telephone switching. A PBX (private branch exchange) is an automated switchboard that serves as a bridge between internal office phones and external lines. AT&T had held a monopoly on the PBX market, using mainly old electromechanical technology. By 1968, however, the industry has been partially deregulated, allowing other companies like ROLM to move into that business.

ROLM's expertise in computer technology looks promising here. Perhaps the old PBX can be turned into something that would do much more than just connect phones. A computer-controlled PBX, for example, might make it possible to route, track, and account for calls; to permit automatic redialing; to provide call forwarding, holding, and transferring; and to select the cheapest long-distance route at any given moment. All those features, if they could be put together into an electronic computer-controlled

PBX, could appeal to a broad spectrum of potential customers.

The PBX opportunity looks as if it might satisfy ROLM's growth aspirations of helping it become a "commercial" company. The idea also builds on its computer expertise. ROLM could probably develop a product with clear advantages over existing products.

It worked. That "strategy" helped ROLM become one of the most successful telecommunications companies in the United States—with a "people-oriented" reputation and culture. Within ten years, ROLM grew to a $700 million company. Eventually (in 1984) it was bought by IBM, IBM's first acquisition in more than twenty years.

We took several pages to tell you the ROLM story because it illustrates the key ingredients in the pathfinding process as it typically occurs (when it occurs) in the real world. Pathfinding is not an isolated process. It is inextricably intertwined with the problem-solving and implementing phases of the managing process. A clear mission and set of values have to be there; but so does a strategy that can help, in a realistic way, to achieve that purpose; and so do leaders who can stick with it and persuade others to join up. Luck and timing also play a big role in this uncertain world of technological innovations and short-lived market opportunities. ROLM did not grow by following a clear, predesigned master blueprint. But the process wasn't just random and catch-as-catch-can either.

Organizational mission:
What it is and why it is important

A "mission" is a dream; an organization's (or society's or individual's) long-term vision of where it wants to go or what it wants to become. It is partly a hope, partly a target, partly a commitment. Did ROLM have one? Or did it just have a fuzzy hope that the company would grow and prosper? ROLM saw its mission as becoming a large, profitable, commercial, and people-oriented Fortune 500 company. That sounds rather unclear and nonoperational. Yet it was that vague sense of mission that prompted ROLM to diversify into telecommunications. Military computers were neither going to satisfy its growth aspirations nor help it become a commercial company.

"Mission" is not about next year's objectives or even about specific goals. It's about dreams and desires, close to the soul of the individual's or organization's nature. The dream of getting rich, doing good, or being the biggest and the best—if it is internalized and pervasive—is a mission.

Mission provides the cues that broadly guide the organization's actions over time, an incentive to act, and a broad standard for judging the results of its efforts. Although missions can help an organization define more specific goals, they differ from goals along several dimensions. Missions are directional pathways; goals are more specific, timed "end points." Missions are dreams; goals are tangible benchmarks. Missions are almost never achieved but are always "in process"; goals are more achievable. One of an organization's overriding missions may be to have the highest rate of growth in its industry, but one of its goals may be to increase its sales by 10 percent every year for the next five years.

If "mission" is such a broad, directional set of dreams and values, what tangible benefits can it have? Why not simply stick to tangible, operational goals? Here are some reasons for having missions:

■ An organization's mission provides a broad guide for action and for decision, as was the case with ROLM's decision to get into the telecommunications business.

■ Mission provides an overarching framework within which the rest of the organization can develop more detailed and specific goals.

■ Mission can provide the glue to hold the organization together. In the real world, different individuals, different groups, and different units within the same organizations often strive toward different, local ends. Organizations try to solve a part of that problem by setting up formal roles and duties, expecting people to operate within them. But in complex organizations, it is almost impossible to set up a system of roles in such a way that everyone's goals are consonant with everyone else's. Conflicts arise. Organizations are more like political systems than smoothly operating machines. Overarching missions provide a broad umbrella that can keep the different parts of the organization together, even as all sorts of squabbles and conflicts are occurring beneath its protective cover.

■ Clear missions help build strong cultures, and strong cultures are controllers of human behavior in organizations. A sense of mission builds organizational cohesion, defining its common values. Identification, belonging, and loyalty can derive from clearly communicated, widely shared commitment to a common mission.

From Mission to Strategy: From the Dream to the Hard Work of Fulfilling It

Assume a clear mission, a vision of the future we want to build. What next? What should we do to help make it come true in the real world? That's where the concept of strategy becomes useful.

Strategy, like mission, is an umbrella concept. It is a bridging concept aimed at matching organizational capabilities and resources to environmental opportunities, helping an organization move toward its mission. Strategy bridges the pathfinding and problem-solving phases of the managing process. Strategy considerations can bring the visionaries into confrontation with the hard realities of what's feasible in this world and what isn't.

How do organizations develop their strategies? Mostly through a combination of analytic, intuitive, and accidental acts. On the one hand, they often use elaborate analytic techniques to forecast and assess markets, competitors, and emerging technologies; on the other hand, they have to blend motives, beliefs and values of the "dominant coalition"—leaders of the organization. Their commitment to a suitable strategy is absolutely critical. And sometimes unexpected opportunities suddenly appear (or disappear), sending everyone back to the drawing board.

Usually, corporate strategies evolve incrementally, piece by piece. The organization's leaders may have a clear sense of its mission and a fairly clear picture of what they have to do to move toward it. But in practice the process usually involves taking small incremental steps in the general right direction—probing, experimenting, learning, and reassessing along the way.

The ROLM team, for example, looked first at themselves: the top team's capabilities, personalities, and experience; their backgrounds in electronic engineering and in defense electronics; and their own beliefs and values. They then searched, in every way they could, for opportunities; what possibilities were out there.

They had to use their strengths and experience not only to capitalize on the opportunity they found but also to ensure that they could get a unique niche for themselves—something they could do better than others, or something that no one else was doing. They knew that, unless they could differentiate themselves from others in the same business, they could not build a sustainable business in the long run. That is how they got into the military minicomputer business; they had a unique way of building on their experience and capitalizing on an opportunity. That became ROLM's initial "strategy" for moving toward its mission.

In the old days, when the world was a bit more stable, strategies were often based solely on forecasts of future conditions. Let's forecast what the world will be like in five years; then we can figure out how best to position ourselves to take advantage of it. In the contemporary world, strategy has come to mean more than that. It tries to marry those forecasts and analyses to front-end, pathfinding factors. Let's not ask, "What's out there and how do we get the most out of it?" The newer and more realistic questions are "First, where do we want to go?" And second, "How can we use what's out there to help us go that way?"

Reactive and Proactive Strategies

Are words like *missions* and *strategies* phony words? Are they words used in textbooks but not consciously thought about in real organizations? Do organizations really spend time and energy worrying about their missions and strategies "proactively?" Or do they just react to events? Or, in fact, do they just go on doing again today whatever it was they did yesterday?

The answer, of course, is all of the above. Many organizations, like many individuals, don't think much about where they want to go or how they can get there. They just work on whatever comes across the desk. The company has always made light bulbs, and it just goes on making them, as cheaply, efficiently, and profitably as it can. People in my family have always been farmers. When I grow up, I will be a farmer, too. It's just "natural." What will I do today? I'll milk the cows or feed the pigs. That's what I always do.

Some organizations behave just a little differently. They let problems find them. "We don't have to think about what we ought to work on. My desk is loaded with problems every morning. We put out the fires that the world out there keeps starting."

It's certainly true that much of our individual and organizational lives seem to work that way, with problems finding us rather than us finding the problems. And it is also probably true, as some researchers have pointed out, that a special version of Gresham's law prevails: people respond first to the problems that find them and put aside the problems they find for themselves. When I have a specific deadlined problem (finishing the paper for that course by Friday), it usually gets priority over the more ephemeral things, like trying to figure out what I should do with the rest of my life.

But this is precisely where major organizational difficulties arise. Because programmed, specified, deadlined problems seem to grow like weeds and because they demand immediate attention, most of us respond to those problems first. When that becomes habitual in an organization, the organization becomes more *reactive* than *proactive*. It lets itself be buffeted by the waves instead of making on-course headway through them. The role of strategy, as a handmaiden of mission, is to give an organization a course of action that will help it move toward its mission, even in very rough and stormy seas.

How can organizations become proactive pathfinders?

How and why do some organizations (or individuals, for that matter) manage to get beyond that reactive state of forever putting out immediate, pressing fires that their environments keep starting?

Prudent organizations use several methods to try to add proactivity into their life-styles. They usually do it by working both sides of the strategy mix—the environmental side and the pathfinding side.

On the environmental side, proactive organizations build better and better organizational sensors. If we can get earlier warning of problems or opportunities, we will have some time to plan, to avert what would have become crises. It is important for organizations to develop their eyes and ears (which do not come naturally to organizations as they do to people), to sense market, social, and economic changes that are relevant to their mission.

But sensors aren't much help unless we can also respond quickly and appropriately. So proactive organizations also work to become fast on their feet, flexible and adaptive.

On the pathfinding end, proactive organizations try to build imaginative, experimental pathfinding cultures, to re-create in larger and older organizations the urgent, informal, purposive climate so characteristic of young, small start-ups. Suppose we focus on all three of those issues—better sensing of what's out there, more flexibility and responsiveness, and a creative pathfinding climate. What are the steps that reasonable people might take to generate them?

One general way is to loosen up structure and give people more elbow room. Another is to keep units small and decision-making authority decentralized. The reader can surely add to this brief list:

- We can encourage our people to keep in contact with the relevant constituencies—professions, minorities, political activities.
- How about monetary and nonmonetary rewards and incentives to stimulate search and creativity? How about sabbaticals or fellowships, which we talked about in chapter 14, to give people a chance to keep up with what's going on out in their fields?
- How about increasing "time spans of discretion"—the time between behavior and its evaluation—giving people a bit more time to experiment and explore, without having someone look over their shoulders constantly?
- How about aiming our recruiting much more toward finding creative, pathfinding, flexible people?
- And let's teach pathfinding skills (to the extent possible) through in-house education and, more important, through the role models set by the behavior of top managers.
- We can also rotate people around the organization, giving them the opportunity to broaden their perspectives and develop new skills in different jobs.
- We can set up, wherever possible, small, autonomous teams and task forces, to encourage both teamwork and flexibility.
- We can give elbow room to maverick members of the organization—a few oddball people who, by training or education or personality, insist on breaking Gresham's law, so that they can work on the unprogrammed, the new, and the unstructured. Such people often get into trouble in large organizations, precisely because they raise those disturbing questions that challenge the organization to think consciously about its direction and its strategies.

Perhaps most important of all is the day-to-day behavior of the organization's leaders, the men and women who are the primary source of its mission. Their commitment to a pathfinding mission, if it is communicated day by day, iteratively and believably, can stimulate and excite the whole organization toward proactive, forward movement, toward greater sensitivity to what's happening out there, and toward faster and more imaginative responses.

It is this passionate, charismatic, missionary aspect of leadership that is especially critical here. Leadership, after all, is a complex set of behaviors. the problem-solving, analytic part of leadership is certainly relevant; and so are the consensus-building, power, and authority sides. But most important for building proactivity, sensitivity, and flexibility is the communication, through the leader's own behavior, of an organizational vision and a sense of urgency and commitment for making it happen.

But no CEO, or king, or president, nor any small elite group, however brilliant, can generate all the bright ideas or all the dreams that organizations need to maintain vitality and urgency over the long haul. To build pathfinding organizations, leaders need to encourage pathfinding attitudes all over the organization, at all levels and for all jobs.

That requires something special even among charismatic, pathfinding leaders. It requires those leaders to be passionately concerned about developing other pathfinding people. Pathfinding leaders have been known to hurt their organizations over the long run because their own confidence and commitment has generated overly dependent, nonpathfinding, "yes sir" organizations. Such organizations are likely to be proactive for a while, but only as long as those leaders remain in charge; then they lapse into directionless bureaucracies.

In summary

This chapter has looked at some pathfinding aspects of organizational behavior, at organizational missions and visions, at strategies as mechanisms for turning those missions into operational plans and actions, and at the role of organizational leaders in helping their organizations take a more proactive, pathfinding stance.

Missions, although hard to define, can nevertheless give an organization a feeling for its values, its fundamental principles, its dreams for the future. Missions are important because they provide a basis for proactive actions and for evaluating alternative choices. Clear missions help build morale and a broad, organization-wide sense of identity by defining a few values that members share and a sense of a common future toward which all can strive. To be effective, missions need to be broad enough to allow people plenty of elbow room to develop more specific goals; yet they must be specific enough to spell out both the basic rules and the broad direction toward which the organization has chosen to go.

Strategy building is a mediating process to help move from mission to operational reality. It is an effort to match an organization's intentions, capabilities, and resources with the environmental opportunities and problems that surround it. Strategy is about how we can plot the best route to move toward where we already know we want to go, given the rocky world out there.

Most organizations use a combination of analytical and behavioral approaches to come up with their strategies. The process is usually quite informal in small, entrepreneurial organizations, where strategy is formed by the entrepreneurial team. Larger and more complex organizations tend to use elaborate formal procedures and staff workers to gather and analyze information about the company and its environment.

Missions are, by their nature, proactive, emerging from inside human beings. However, most strategies have in the past been formed reactively, as responses to perceived or forecasted environmental demands. But recent trends in strategic thinking have moved toward a marriage of proactive dreams to current and projected environmental (and organizational) pressures and opportunities.

Organizations can use several ways to inculcate more proactive pathfinding behavior. They can improve their sensors, loosen their structures, and generate incentives for creative thinking and initiative. But ultimately most of the responsibility rests on the leaders of the organization, who are not only the sources of its mission and strategy but the prime shapers of its culture and values.

Imaginative, dedicated pathfinding has been, until recently, a much neglected part of our thinking about the whole leadership process. It is quite different from other parts of leadership, such as brilliant problem solving or careful, participative nurturing of consensus. In modern, complex organizations, pathfinding leadership can't be the business of the CEO alone. Managers at all levels need the freedom and stimulus to innovate, inspire, and experiment.

25

Managing people in large numbers: From organizational pyramids to organizational cultures

Almost all of this book so far has been about managing people, so why a special chapter now? Because managing large numbers of people raises some very special problems that are different from the problems of managing small face-to-face groups. Managers in large organizations must often manage the work of people they have never met, may never even see, and who may work hundreds or thousands of miles away. Yet those managers set policies and make decisions that affect the attitudes, motivations, productivity, and economic fate of those people. It is that aggregate, policy-level, distant kind of managing that this chapter is about.

Two sets of assumptions about managing large numbers of people

We start by going backward, back to some historical issues we discussed in chapter 23. What are some fundamental assumptions about human beings that underlie the way large Western organizations have been managed in the past? And where have those assumptions led? Although the organizations of years past reflected the conditions of their times, they also set the foundation for the organizations that were to follow. The new in organizations, we proposed earlier, almost never completely replaces the old. Usually we just keep remodeling the old house. We add modern plumbing and electricity, but it's still the old house sitting on the old foundation. So here are a few old and widely held assumptions about people, not because they're curious and quaint but because they still set limits, often unconsciously, on our present thinking about how organizations should deal with human beings.

Assumption 1: *Work is not play; work is unpleasant, but it is good for the human soul.* Our early ideas about managing people were built around those assumptions. Largely out of the Protestant tradition, work was treated as a sort of righteous and purifying sacrifice. Play and other leisure activities ought to be separated from work. The eight (or twelve) hours a day that people spent at work were not there to provide earthly fulfillment and reward in and of themselves. They were working hours, hours of sacrifice and duty, the rewards of which were bread on the table and acceptance into heaven.

The young reader may find it hard to comprehend how pervasive a role those beliefs played in American (and Western) organizations in the bustling, expansive, mass-production–oriented era of the first half of this century.

Since then, of course, a dramatic rise in expectations has occurred, especially among younger age groups. That rise has taken place among all social classes and in almost all societies. People everywhere have come more and more to *expect* that life in general and work in particular are *supposed* to be rewarding and fulfilling in and of themselves. But that change in expectations has yet to be fully incorporated into the management practices of organizations solidly built to fit the old assumption.

Assumption 2: *Organizations should operate in an orderly, regular, and predictable way.* They should be logically designed, from the task backward. The test of optimality is clockwork efficiency. This second set of assumptions led us to the pyramidal shape of organizations, into which human cogs were to be fitted as neatly as possible. Given those assumptions, the role of people was to conform to prescribed rules and to carry out predefined duties.

But that set of assumptions has had to be remodelled, too. Although large industrial organizations were traditionally shaped like pyramids (and continue to be so), they get less orderly and more loose every day. The pyramidal shape remains useful because it simplifies problems of communication and sub-assembly, and it helps with the coordination of complicated, multigroup decisions. But the growing complexity and variability of organizational tasks has moved them gradually away from the clockwork efficiency model and toward (but not all the way to) what one observer has called "organized anarchies."

Those two sets of assumptions fitted together rather neatly. Together they functioned well in a world of mass production and were appropriate for the rather simple technologies of the day. But over the years a number of cracks slowly opened up, cracks that grew bigger as competition, interdependence, technology, and human expectations gradually changed.

Problems of interpersonal competition

The idea that work should not be fun, coupled with the idea of the organizational pyramid, generated many second-order notions about managing people. One, for example, is the positive value placed on interpersonal competition. A characteristic of the traditional pyramid is that it becomes narrower at higher levels. A characteristic of human beings (at least of most Americans) is that they try to move upward in pyramids. When those two characteristics meet, their encounter generates competition for advancement. That idea of competition is reasonably consistent with the hard work and efficiency assumptions. In fact, such competition probably has net positive effects when the pyramid is growing rapidly. But it can become debilitating and destructive when growth levels off. Fortunately, however, the world is bigger than any single company; even when an organization has stopped growing, some of its members can continue to climb by moving to other organizations.

Competition for advancement carries other organizational costs along with its benefits. Since people at higher organizational levels are the umpires in those competitive games, the lower-level competitors become critically dependent on personal evaluations by those at higher levels. So, one common negative consequence is political jockeying for approval. This redirects energy from productive work toward looking good, and perhaps toward making others look bad.

Another organizationally dangerous consequence can be restricted communication. Withholding bad news is a prime example, because carriers of bad news often lose their heads. The result: internal secrecy may grow, so that "I'll be sure to get the credit."

Competition for promotion certainly isn't all bad. It can be a stimulus for greater effort, especially if the jobs of the competitors can be kept independent, not interdependent, if work-related objective standards for advancement can be established, and if success for one person can be kept independent of failure for others.

Unfortunately, it was probably easier to establish those conditions in simple organizations of the past than in the technologically complex and fast-moving organizations of the present. Many jobs could be kept quite independent of one another then, and it was probably easier to establish objective measures of performance in the stable, repetitive work settings of that mass production era. In modern organizations, jobs are likely to be much more interdependent, and objective measures of individual performance are harder to pin down.

Another complicating factor is that many people, especially professionals, perceive themselves as participants in more than one pyramid. Therefore, promotion up the administrative company ladder may not always motivate them. Researchers and scientists, for example, may be more eager to move up their professional ladders than up the organizational hierarchy. Glory may, for them, be symbolized by a Nobel Prize much more than by a senior vice-presidency.

Thus, emphasis on competition inside the organization can cause problems in its own right. But those problems can be compounded by simply adding on, as many organizations have done, a simultaneous emphasis on "cooperation." Is competition between individuals within the company the key to productivity, or is it cooperation and teamwork? The word *teamwork* has slipped more and more into a central place in our organizational vocabularies over the last few decades. This reflects the shift from the old "clockwork" concept of individually independent jobs toward the contemporary recognition that the whole must be much more than the sum of the individual pieces. But many Western organizations are still a little schizophrenic about that combination. They carefully evaluate everyone's individual comparative performance and at the same time call for teamwork and collaboration among the competing players. Here is a puzzle for the reader: Might you solve that dilemma by holding a competition to determine who is the best teamworker on the team?

Authority and dependency

Roughly, power and authority parallel the pyramid. Higher levels have more of both; lower levels have less. That means that people at higher levels can tell those at lower levels what to do and not do; people upstairs can reward or punish people downstairs for doing it or not doing it.

The other side of that coin is the psychological one we discussed in part 1, the problem of dependency. People at lower levels are (and feel) more dependent on those at higher levels than vice versa.

Those facts and feelings of authority and dependency can affect the behavior of organizations in many ways. They can cause tensions between people at different levels; they can generate high degrees of stress; and they can distort communication. The boss's moods become subject matter for gossip and speculation. Offhand comments from upstairs are scrutinized downstairs for their hidden but presumably significant implications. Bad news is covered up; criticism and debate are muted.

Life in the traditional pyramidal organization is life in a medium of dependency. Any assigned job becomes two jobs. One is to carry out the assignment; the other is to please superiors.

Perhaps the most dangerous side effect of such dependency is the partial loss of a most valuable organizational asset—the sensitive, intuitive judgments of experienced people. Pressure on the superior to evaluate and on the subordinate to obtain a positive evaluation can team up to destroy subtle, unverbalizable judgments in favor of rationalizable justification.

Notice that "vertical" dependency, the psychological feelings of dependency associated with rank and authority, is the biggest troublemaker. Interdependencies among peers generate difficult problems, too; but in general, those are much easier to work at and work out. Vertical authority dependency is the real psychological villain in organizational life, the source of much of the stress and anxiety in our work lives.

The jigsaw puzzle of individual responsibility

A third related problem is generated by those two traditional assumptions—work isn't play and organizations should run like clockwork. These assumptions drive toward (or perhaps are themselves driven by) a "principle" of individual responsibility, a belief that tasks can and should be subdivided into person-sized pieces, each piece independent of every other and just the right size for an individual.

That principle of individual responsibility implies that actions and decisions should be reduced ultimately to single-person size; the whole of an enterprise should equal the sum of those separable, individual-sized pieces. Responsibility for failure, then, can and should be ascribed to individuals.

However, in large modern organizations, the parts turn out to be inextricably intertwined, as do individual areas of responsibility. It's hardly ever possible these days to single out the *one* person responsible for a particular event. But because we hold that principle dear, organizations often have to identify fall guys to throw to the wolves.

As organizations become bigger, individual jobs become more and more dependent on other, previously unrelated jobs. Manufacturing managers can't fulfill their responsibilities without sales department forecasts. Sales managers can't move without manufacturing schedules. The finance department needs timely information from every unit. Salespeople need backup from engineers; both may need clearances from the legal department. In the modern organization, no man or woman is an island.

When the individual-responsibility rule persists, private fiefdoms grow like weeds. Individuals become more and more territorial. They seek more and more authority to permit them to fulfill their unfulfillable individual responsibilities. They become increasingly resistant about encroachment by others and spend more time and energy in documenting even trivial acts so that they can later, if necessary, prove their own innocence of wrongdoing.

But what are the alternatives? Should no one be held responsible? Should we stop evaluating the individual's performance? Those seem unrealistic, even nonsensical, alternatives.

One route partially through those problems (an increasingly popular route in modern organizations) is, as we pointed out in chapter 20, to allocate considerably more responsibility to groups and considerably less to individuals. By treating the group as the responsible unit, we can evaluate the performance of the group and leave more of the evaluation of individuals within it to group members themselves. Groups can be great evaluators of individuals. The group, whether we call it a team, task force, or committee, has in fact become a cornerstone in the managing styles of many high-technology companies because so much of their work depends on the effective performance of small teams whose members can act together effectively. Individual evaluation, of course, doesn't go away; it just recedes a little.

Another effort to deal with interdependencies, one that became popular in the mid-1960s, is the "matrix" organization. That idea abandons the notion of one person–one boss in favor of multiple, shared patterns of responsibility and authority. But matrix organizations often run into trouble because they, too, make it difficult to pinpoint exactly who is responsible for what. That deep-rooted Western notion of individual responsibility is not likely to disappear. Therefore, the search continues both for more effective ways of maintaining our emphasis on individual responsibility and for alternatives in our highly interdependent modern organizational world.

Problems of size

As numbers of people increase, so do coordination and communication problems. Managing a thousand people is different from managing ten. Simple informal communication, so characteristic of small organizations, must give way to more formal procedures in larger ones. The organization becomes more and more "institutionalized." Size, in fact, generates a number of human problems:

- Size increases vertical distance between top and bottom, separating each of us from those who influence our organizational fate. Direct communication from bottom to top, and vice versa, become more difficult. Feelings of powerlessness and uncertainty increase, and feelings of frustration and anger can soon follow.
- As organizations grow, communication networks become more complicated, also increasing the probability of misinformation and error. Remember that, whereas the number of possible connections among five people is ten, the number for a hundred people is almost five thousand.
- Larger populations also mean more physical separation of related people, making communication more difficult and more costly.

Such changes not only affect people's attitudes and morale but also the quality of their decisions. Frustration and anger are the emotional accompaniments of obstacles to communication. How do you feel when you get busy signals repeatedly on an important phone call? Or worse yet, when you get an immediate "please hold"? Managers may try to compensate by forcing more information through long, fragile channels, sometimes ending up with a flood of information that further exacerbates the difficulties.

Organizations usually try to deal with problems of size, by changing their organizational structures. (We shall see this in chapter 26.) Sometimes we decentralize large organizations to keep the size of individual units reasonably small. Sometimes we tighten controls and specify more standard procedures, in the belief that more uniformity will make things run more smoothly in the larger system. Sometimes we try to improve the technology of communication, to substitute telephones and computers for committee meetings.

Doing something about the human problems of large organizations
1. "Structure first/people last" solutions.

How can organizations deal with problems of interpersonal competition, overlapping responsibilities, power and authority, and larger size?

In earlier years, our thinking almost always started in an analytical way—at the task part of the process—and worked backward. First, the analytical reasoning went, analyze the task we have to do, then design a structure (including all the jobs to be done) that is logically appropriate for that particular task. Finally pick the people and plug them into the pre-designed jobs. Then, should human problems arise—problems of competition, communication, or morale—work on those problems on an ad hoc basis. Try to alleviate them, for example, with incentive schemes, threats of punishment, tighter controls, or more precise definitions of responsibilities. But keep the structural design intact. In such systems, understandably, personnel people and psychologists usually played secondary, supportive roles. Their major function was to select the right people with the right skills to fit into the predefined boxes, and then to measure their performance.

Retrospectively, many of those efforts to "solve" people problems now look quaint and weak—like emptying the ocean with a teaspoon. Older readers will remember how elaborately we used to draw organization charts and specify "proper" and "improper" channels of communication, as well as how worried we used to be about maintaining management's "prerogatives" and setting the right spans of control. Those early efforts to cope with people problems often kept things from reaching crisis levels long enough to build profitable and productive organizations. But rising expectations and a changing world have forced those human problems into much greater prominence. Most of those older ideas have pretty much faded away.

If the old structure-first model is inappropriate for contemporary organizations, how about trying it the other way round? Suppose we design organizations *people-first* instead of structure-first, leaving the structural problems that might follow to be dealt with later.

2. Some "people first" solutions.

During the past three decades a number of people-first approaches have been put forward. Some were invented by pathfinding managers. Some emerged out of psychological studies of small groups. The applications typically took the form of "participative" experiments in units of large organizations. Those views have by now been extended beyond small units to encompass entire organizations, from designing their overall structures to developing their unique cultures.

In the early years, the people-first approaches sought first to build warm and open relationships among members of the organization, expecting that more efficient work would follow from the better morale and communication engendered. Gradually those approaches shifted focus more and more to the task, treating morale as a by-product. As they focused on developing task teams, the whole applied effort came to be known as "Organizational Development," or O.D.

O.D. approaches have typically used small groups as their building blocks, treating large organizations as assemblies of small groups. Effective small groups, in turn, are seen as emerging mostly from high levels of mutual trust among group members, open and accurate communication, and psychological commitment to the group. Toward those ends, O.D. works at developing emotional as well as factual communication among members and emphasizes sensitivity to group processes as a sine qua non to effective, collaborative teamwork. The small team becomes the key functional unit, and team building becomes one central activity of O.D. practitioners.

A second major element of Organizational Development follows from the team-building emphasis. Given a collection of effective teams, how can the whole set be glued together to form an effective organization? So the next step is to work on the connections among small groups, on issues of intergroup conflict and cooperation. Strongly motivated, task-oriented team members, not surprisingly, tend to identify with their own teams and therefore treat outsiders as unwelcome strangers or even as enemies. Developing good relationships *among* teams becomes critical in building up toward an integrated organization. Hence, O.D. practitioners use methods such as intergroup confrontational meetings and intergroup discussions of mutual perceptions. O.D. approaches also tend to *de*emphasize formal evaluation of individuals, focusing instead on the performance of total teams.

In recent years, O.D. people have widened their thinking from an emphasis on the small work group toward the design of total organizations. Both the rise of O.D. and its own increasing concern with broader issues of organizational design can be taken as indications that the people-first approaches have indeed been taking hold in Western organizations.

This growing tendency toward people-first designs has received a considerable boost in recent years from the emergence of the concept of "organizational culture." The "cultural" idea, as was suggested in an earlier chapter, permits other, earlier people approaches to begin to think big and to encompass the whole organization instead of just the small groups within it. So people-first types have understandably taken the concept of culture to their hearts. Notice, then, that the idea of culture may turn out to be an integrating bridge between the people views and the structural views of organizations. The cultural idea also promises to address one of the key concerns of the structure-first approaches, the concern for *control*. Strong cultures are themselves control systems, causing people to behave more uniformly and predictably, but accomplishing that end by social rather than structural means.

Why, in this world of robots, have people become more rather than less important?

The people-first approaches began to gather momentum in the United States at roughly the same time that we started to question our earlier assumptions about work versus play and about the inviolability of some early "principles" of pyramidal organizations. Traditional organizations had treated people as resources—substitutable, trainable, and usable for many different purposes. But people don't perceive themselves as resources. They think of themselves as people—unique, aspiring, and expectant. That difference in perspective underlies many of the "human relations" problems of the past. How can humans be "factors of production" and still be human?

Language often provides cues about underlying beliefs and values. In industry, we used to call people "hands"; we needed to "hire a hand." But, of course, we can't hire a hand. The whole person comes along, whether we like it or not. We are finally coming to understand that we have to take the whole human package. But why now? Why not forty years ago? Some of the reasons are these:

■ In our new "informational" society, people have to use their brains more than their hands; so far we haven't been able to program many substitutes for human brains. "Innovation," "change," and "flexibility" are buzz-words in modern organizations. Old words such as "efficiency" have not gone away, but our vocabularies are bigger now.

■ The key strategic resource of the old industrial organization was capital. But for new informational organizations, people have become key—people's knowledge, expertise, and creativity; capital tends to follow people.

■ With people as a key asset, the old separation between work and play becomes almost meaningless. When one works with one's brain and one's education, that work doesn't turn itself off at 5 o'clock. Moreover, "fulfilling" work has come to be seen more and more as a human *right* throughout the world. Certainly the new, well-educated informational employee expects interesting work and challenging tasks as the norm, not the exception.

■ Information technology, the backbone of our information age, is rapidly replacing many routine, administrative jobs performed at middle levels of old organizations. The new work force has to do more of the important "thinking" jobs, which can't be automated or delegated to technology, at least not yet. Of course, technology is a double-edged sword as far as people are concerned. On the one hand, it can eliminate many "routine" tasks and simplify problems of communication. But it also permits superiors to monitor lower-level activities accurately, quickly, and "unobtrusively." Whether managers will choose to use that new capacity to centralize decision making is still unclear.

■ A new model of the excellent manager began to take shape in the early 1980s. It is not the grey flannel suited organization man of the 1950s, nor the analytical whiz of the 1960s, but the charismatic, hands-on, inspirational manager of the 1980s. That manager is much more a leader and mentor than a monitor and controller.

■ Recent literature describing the practices of successful and respected companies have publicized a number of novel approaches to old problems of size, responsibility, and dependency. Most of the newer emphases go in the direction of loosening the organization, creating small autonomous divisions, reducing the size of control-minded corporate staffs, developing strong organizational cultures, encouraging people to define their own responsibilities, generating more open and informal communication, using open-plan physical layouts, and encouraging managers to "wander around." The overall direction is people-first.

■ Still another contributor to the growth of people-first approaches is the economic rise of Japan. This caused us to pay much more attention to how Japanese organizations dealt with their people. At first, impressed by their success, we extolled the virtues of Japanese organizational style—their guarantees of lifelong employment, the apparent bottom-up implementation-oriented participation by all levels in planning and decision making, and their emphasis on quality. But most of all, Japanese workers' discipline and loyalty stimulated our interest in the power of strong "organizational cultures."

Managing the organization's culture—another people-first solution

By the early 1980s, the people types had begun to explore well beyond their earlier small-group focus, looking more and more into the total organizational culture—the climate, belief systems, rituals, values, and myths and legends of the organization.

For the manager, the idea of organizational culture can be a powerful tool. By successfully socializing people into a desired culture, managers can accomplish two important results: (1) they can establish a base of shared attitudes, beliefs, and values throughout the organization, thereby fostering a sense of unity, common purpose, and mutual commitment; and (2) they can also establish a sense of common fate, a feeling shared by worker and manager alike, that what's good for all is good for everyone. In a traditionally adversarial world of manager versus worker, an idea that promises greater unity and cooperation is worth considering.

Culture is not a brand-new concept. Everyone has one, everywhere and always. We have national cultures—American, Italian, Indian, Chinese; and we have ethnic subcultures within those broader national cultures. And we even have regional and neighborhood cultures—the culture of New England, or New Orleans, or Haight Ashbury in San Francisco. Or we can cut it by age groups—teenage culture, yuppie culture. Culture has been a pervasive idea for a long time, but it has always also been a little soft and fuzzy around the edges. We know it's there; we can feel it when we visit cultures that are new (to us); but it's hard to pin down just exactly what it is that we're noticing.

Clearly, most national and tribal cultures have evolved over a very long time. Is it sensible, then, even to talk about the culture of a ten-year-old company? The answer is yes. Walk into the ten-year-old company and hang around for a day or two. You'll feel its culture.

Of course, the stronger and more unusual the culture, the easier it is to notice its special characteristics. That's true in strong organizational as well as national cultures. Consider IBM, for example. How might one describe IBM's culture? How about something like this: "At IBM, sales and marketing groups reign supreme. They really decide where the company is heading. No one gets to the top at IBM unless they've had sales experience. No new product gets developed unless it passes the critical eye of the sales force. IBM's heroes are members of the 'Hundred Per Cent' Club—salespeople who have consistently met or exceeded their sales quotas."

Does this give you some flavor of at least one aspect of IBM's organizational culture? Now add something like this: "IBM uses a 'contention system.' Internal competition between different groups is encouraged. The losers go out of favor quickly."

And: "Loyalty to IBM is so important that no one is ever hired back into the company once they leave to join another company."

And: "When I think of IBM, I think of white shirts and blue suits and highly professional managers."

In contrast, consider another respected American company, Hewlett-Packard. Here are some descriptions of parts of its culture: "Engineers are kings at H-P. The company was built around engineers, R&D, and technical excellence."

And: "H-P people talk a lot about the 'H-P Way'; it's an informal, caring style. H-P has open-plan offices. It coined the phrase MBWA—'management by wandering around.' It offers generous benefits and has the feeling of a big, close family."

And: "When I think of H-P, the first thing that springs to my mind is consensus and teamwork; no one can get anything done alone. You have to persuade all the relevant people to buy into it."

Such statements about the two companies' cultures are not very precise. But they still carry considerable meaning. The cultures of organizations are real. But often, like the weather, we are not very conscious of them. An organization's culture includes the following:

- Its dominant values and philosophies, such as the importance of sales at IBM and engineering at H-P
- Rules of the game for getting things done and for getting along, such as beating internal competitors at IBM or getting the key people to buy into an idea at H-P
- The general "climate" and style of the company, such as H-P's open-plan offices and informal atmosphere or IBM's more formal "white shirt and blue suit" style.

Indeed, culture is much more than all those. It is a broad set of beliefs that have been developed and shared by a group of people over a period of time.

But why is culture important to the manager? One reason, as we have said before, is that culture is a powerful controller of human behavior. Although culture may work largely unconsciously, it works. It teaches new employees how to behave around the organization, what is *really* important, and what is *really* off limits. It teaches everything from informal dress codes to the right ways of dealing with other people. It defines how late is late and how much work is a good day's work. If an organization can design and manage its culture, the organizational advantages can be enormous. But, although most organizations have cultures, most of those cultures have just grown; they haven't been managed.

Diagnosing an organization's existing culture

How does one get a sense of the culture of any organization? How does one find the tangible (and intangible) manifestations of culture?

One way is to use what is directly observable and to treat what we observe as indexes—the physical appearance of a building, the layout of offices, the paintings on the walls and other decor, the way people dress, the kinds of cars in the parking lot, and the times of day when they are parked there. Suppose, for example, one observes open offices, employees in blue jeans, children's drawings thumbtacked on the walls, and pickup trucks in the parking lot. And suppose most of those vehicles are still there after seven in the evening. Would you be willing to make any guesses about the probable "culture" of that company?

Another way to get a fix on an organization's culture is to identify the "recipes" it uses regularly. At IBM, for instance, the sales function had been given a prominent status, because it had worked well for a long time; so it became the "normal" way to work. On the other hand, H-P's success was built on its technical expertise in scientific instruments. Because that solution had been used and had worked time after time, it became the norm and the "proper" way to operate.

Notice the danger here. Strong cultures use characteristic styles in their approaches to the world that are rooted in their histories. But when situations and times change, some of those approaches that are taken for granted may become quite inappropriate, yet very hard to change.

Are organizational cultures manageable, and should they be managed?

All organizations have cultures. But most just evolve, unintentionally, inadvertently, sometimes detrimentally to all concerned. Most start with the beliefs of the original founders. Some develop strong adversarial counter-cultures within the larger culture. Some become lethargic, sloppy, and resistant to new ideas. But conscious management of a company's culture is quite possible, and some organizations do it rather well, steadily building the kind of culture they want.

What does managing an organization's culture mean? First, it means some imagination and vision—a pathfinding sense. What sort of culture, atmosphere, and value system do we want to try to build here? After that, it's a matter of determination, simplification, and reiteration.

Managing cultures is largely a question of managing *meanings,* of managing beliefs and perceptions, of getting many diverse people to subscribe to a few common beliefs, values, and principles. Although those people are all different, they will also become, in a few ways, the same.

Once managers figure out the pathfinding part—what they want—managing the culture then becomes a long, slow, day-by-day process of implementing, of communicating, persuading, and demonstrating the small set of key values and principles that most characterize the desired culture. How?

- The manager can focus, repeatedly and unswervingly, during daily discussions and decision-making sessions, on those few themes that exemplify the culture. If managers highlight the importance of "keeping costs under control"—raising questions about it over and over, in meetings and discussions—"cost consciousness" is likely to become a cultural characteristic. To get ahead, "think costs"; to get ideas accepted, demonstrate their cost advantages. One meaning of good, effective work in that culture will come to be equated with managing costs effectively.

- Managers can communicate positive cultural values by the example of their own behavior. Powerful leaders are models that others will emulate. When leaders of an organization debate openly with one another and with subordinates, when their day-to-day style is confrontational, that style is likely to spread and become characteristic of that organization's culture. If top management's approach is more well-mannered, characterized by quiet persuasion and delicate, diplomatic moves, the rest of the organization will begin to use similar methods. It is not just because we like to copy the powerful that we tend to move toward the leaders' ways of behaving; over time, newcomers enter the organization as strangers in a strange land, and in such situations most of us want to learn to live with the ways of this new world.

- The manager can try to manage culture by managing rewards. Is promotion unswervingly based on merit? Or do we get rewarded for looking busy, for clever ingratiation? Or for being creative, or for championing unusual projects?

- The manager can select people who have already acquired the cultural values the organization wants. One way that H-P has kept its engineering orientation, for example, is through heavy recruitment of outstanding young engineers from the major engineering schools.

- The stories, myths, and legends that are passed on from generation to generation can help carry a company's culture along. These reinforce key values and principles by communicating them to new people.

- The manager can build cultural "sameness" by setting up a series of filters to screen out differences among employees, thus selecting and promoting "good" exponents of cultural beliefs and values. Notice once again that there's no free lunch. That filtering process will also eliminate some valuable divergent views.

- Outside "enemies," like strong competitors, are powerful shapers of culture. All strong leaders know this technique. Threatening enemies— real or imagined—can help promote a sense of urgency and unity among our people.

- Managers communicate a great deal by their handling of crises. If, for example, a company must sharply cut its costs, it can go about it in many ways, each of which will convey a quite different meaning. If, instead of laying people off, the company decides to cut all salaries by 10 percent or to cut back to a four-day working week, the cultural meaning will come through: "If there are going to be cuts in this company, we are all in it together. Everyone shares in the sacrifice."

While you can readily add to this list of ways that managers can try to manage their company's culture, you might also feel that the game looks too easy. Somehow, it seems, *everything* a manager does becomes part of the process of managing culture.

And you will be right. Culture is pervasive and encompassing. Every move a manager makes—casual words, simple memoranda, manner of dress, office decor—communicates and moves the culture along. They all tell people what *really* is valued here, who *really* is believed, what *really* is expected. If those things are internalized by the members of the organization, then the organization's culture has been built.

The negative aspects of strong cultures

We can't end this section without an important caveat: Culture building has a lot in common with brainwashing. Managers try to develop culture, we said earlier, to develop *sameness,* some uniformity of beliefs and attitudes among all members. But when that sameness is carried to an extreme, we may find ourselves in the grey and miserably conforming world of Orwell's *1984.*

Therefore, en garde! Strong organizational cultures can be positive, when the sameness that evolves is limited to a small set of values, beliefs, and principles, and when diversity is encouraged in other respects. But there are many kinds of strong cultures, some of which most of us would abhor! So, when we try to manage an organization's culture, we had better look to our morality as well as our skill.

In summary

Managing large numbers of people is different from managing small, face-to-face groups. Over the years, several broad approaches have evolved, each more or less a product of its time and place.

Early in our industrial history we tended to view employees as "resources," as "factors of production," to be standardized so as to be interchangeable at will. They were plugged into the organization to carry out predefined and usually routinized jobs. Since work was not expected to be challenging and fulfilling, issues of frustration and hostility were not then of much concern.

The advantage of that kind of approach was high productivity from a poorly educated work force, in a developing society in great need of mass-produced goods. The approach paid off, but not without costs. The costs, which showed up slowly but forcefully, were not only employee apathy, frustration, and hostility and adversarial worker-manager relationships but also debilitating interpersonal competition, high levels of dependency, and "evaluation fear."

Over time, educational levels rose and organizations focused less on mass production and more on marketing, technology, and innovation. A second, more dynamic view of managing evolved. This one focused much more on people, seeking ways to release the "full" potential of the whole human being. That view, modified over the years, has gradually found increasing favor in modern organizations, in part as an acknowledgment of the higher expectations of modern workers about rights to a high and challenging quality of working life.

The early versions of those people-oriented approaches (in the 1950s and 1960s) focused on individuals, small groups, and units within organizations. By the 1980s, the concept of *organizational culture* extended these "micro-people" approaches to large numbers—indeed, to the whole organization.

An organization's culture is the whole implicit and explicit set of beliefs and values shared by the members of an organization. The culture defines the company's character, how it is different from others, and what its members particularly believe in.

Although cultures often are not consciously managed, they can be. Founders and leaders of organizations can exert a powerful influence on organizational culture. They "manage" culture by emphasizing and selectively communicating a few, important, inviolable values and standards. They do it by a great variety of means, ranging from reiterated day-by-day pronouncements, to selecting particular types of new employees, to offering rewards for certain kinds of behavior while ignoring or punishing others.

Strong cultures are powerful mechanisms of control. They promote conformity and sameness. Therefore, managers must think seriously about the ethical sides of their culture management and about the costs—economic, social, and psychological—of developing cultures that can become excessively uniform, restrictive, and conformist. But they also must think about the costs of ignoring culture. These days, managing the culture should be treated as an important part of every manager's job.

26 Organizational structure: Managing the situation to manage the people

We humans are probably much more influenced, constrained, and even imprisoned by formal organizational structures than we like to think. Those formal structures are powerful mechanisms for controlling and shaping the behavior of people in large organizations.

In an earlier chapter, we tried to show how changing the structure can be an important tool for managing the organization's performance. In this chapter we try to show how structure is also—intentionally or not—an important tool for shaping human behavior. When managers change their organization's structure, they also change people.

Structure imprisons us all to some degree. Structure, after all, is a set of limits on our roles. The paraphernalia of formal structure—spelled-out sets of duties, defined areas of authority, specified reporting relationships— all sharply, though often unconsciously, constrain and modify our behavior.

There are many dimensions of structure that managers can manage. We can set up new jobs, and we can wipe out old ones. We can centralize our structures, or we can decentralize them. We can tighten job definitions, or we can loosen them. We can enlarge the duties and responsibilities of certain roles, and we can limit others. We can redraw communication networks. And by changing one or more of those structural handles, we can try to generate specific changes in human behavior; and often we can succeed.

This chapter, then, tries to relate structure to behavior. To do that, we'll first take a look at the general functions of formal organizational structure. Then we'll examine the pros and cons of loose and tight structures and of important structural dimensions such as differentiation and integration. We'll conclude by exploring the rapidly changing nature of formal organizational structures, as well as some recent ideas for designing more effective structures for the contemporary organizational world.

What is organizational structure?

Managers set up formal structures primarily as implementing mechanisms, to help the organization perform its tasks effectively. Specifically the concept of structure includes:

- Dividing large tasks into smaller person-sized *jobs or roles,* and grouping and clustering those tasks into larger sets, usually labeled departments or divisions. Structure also usually includes some specification of rules for coordinating all the separate subactivities, through task forces, committees, and other devices.
- Specifying the reporting relationships of all roles, their scope of authority, spans of control, and location in a hierarchy of roles.
- Specifying standard procedures—what is expected from the occupant (any occupant) of a role, which channels of communication are defined as "proper" and which are "improper," how job occupants should interact and communicate with one another, and how their performance is to be monitored and evaluated.
- Defining desired decision-making procedures—what sources of information are to be used, how and when specific routine decisions should be reviewed, and who should participate in making different kinds of decisions.

Setting up a formal structure is a way of dividing tasks and then pulling them back together. It trades off between specialization and integration and balances centralization and decentralization.

Such structural efforts, although often quite effective, seldom fully succeed. That is because what we have described here is a traditional approach to the *intended* functions of organizational structure. It is a kind of formal set of "laws" intended to regulate and constrain the use of authority and the directions and patterns of communication and information flows, to distribute roles and responsibilities, and to control and coordinate the actions of the occupants of defined roles.

But there is another way of looking at organizational structure—a more current, more subtle, and more dynamic way. This second approach (let's call it a "responsive" approach) views structure as intertwined with, not separate from, human behavior. According to this view, structure is not a formal control and coordination tool, imposed from above, to which all members must then conform. Rather it's a set of organizational rules and procedures derived from the actual patterns of individual and group behavior that have evolved in an organization over time. By the responsive approach, pathways are paved *after* seeing where people have walked not because someone has decided where they should walk.

In contrast to the traditional view, which aims to create a formal, permanent, and stable organizational structure, this responsive view stresses the informal, dynamic, and temporary qualities of organizations and the relevance of "natural" human behavior. In this sense, the second view treats structure as a handmaiden of organizational culture.

Tight structures versus loose structures

Traditional, formal, hierarchical approaches to structure seek organizational effectiveness and productivity through tightly planned, rational, impersonal designs. These designs reflect the analytic thinking styles of their designers. Such designs usually start from the task end and work backward, ending with people. First, tasks are specified and broken down into a series of hierarchically coordinated roles. Only then are people slotted into those roles and assigned to behave within the constraints specified by their job descriptions.

In extreme and ideal forms of such tight structures, authority is seen as the primary mechanism of discipline and control. Communication lines are strictly specified. The "open space" on any job is squeezed to a minimum. Responsibilities of each job occupant are spelled out independently of others. And duplication of effort is eliminated. The primary criterion, implicit and explicit, is *efficient performance of predetermined tasks*.

In contrast, the looser, network approaches to structural designs treat the formal structure as a second-order concern to follow *after* the people issues have been examined. Structure is treated more as a servant of natural human motivation than as its master. In loose designs, people come first and roles second, and roles tend to change from time to time. Organizational stability is sought through relationships among people, rather than through tight specification of roles, reporting relationships, and hierarchy. Whereas authority is the mainstay of tight designs, communication is the key discipline of the loose organization.

The proponents of loose, people-oriented structures are generally also advocates of decentralization into smaller, autonomous units, flatter hierarchies with as few levels as possible, more emphasis on group and team (rather than individual) responsibilities, and flexible, often temporary, ad hoc structures, designed, abandoned, and redesigned as tasks change. While productive and efficient work remain important criteria, they recede a bit into the background in favor of more immediate concerns: the organization's adaptability to changing environments and its flexibility and responsiveness in dealing with opportunities and crises.

Both approaches nevertheless share the faith that structure does indeed influence behavior. One wants to focus people on specific desired behaviors; the other wants people to use their heads in more wide-open ways. In fact, most organizations do some of both, often tightening more at lower levels and loosening more at higher levels of the hierarchy.

The tight model offers benefits of clarity, stability, uniformity, and orderliness, but at the cost of inflexibility, especially for people in middle and lower levels. Unique ideas and new problems don't bubble up readily in such structures. And, of course, such structures often generate frustration and apathy in many people, who may feel overly constrained by the narrow definitions of their roles and by the frequent evaluations that follow. Informal communication—a wellspring of ideas and quick problem solving—is discouraged in tight structures, because appropriate communication channels, predefined and specified, are designed to foster clear, predictable, and uniform messages.

However, if you like the loose structure better, think twice. You may get less regular feedback about how you're doing in such structures, and perhaps less credit for your individual contributions. There may be continual change, a lot of confusion, and "slop" in the system, with important things happening before anyone bothers to tell you about them. Also, many meetings are probable, and much more time will be spent in persuading others to do the things you need to have done. You won't be able to ask the boss to order those people to do them.

Which is easier to manage? The tight structure looks easy because it is orderly and disciplined. But when you give your commands, nothing may happen, and you may find yourself overwhelmed by decisions that lower-level people don't dare make by themselves. People may bow to you, but they may not level with you. But you'll certainly be the boss.

In the looser designs, your subordinates may not pay much attention to you, except to complain when they can't get their own way. Indeed, it will not always be clear who is the subordinate. You'll be trying to manage something more like an oriental bazaar. Everybody will be negotiating for their own pieces of the action. The danger, of course, is that, if the organization becomes too loose, it may even fall apart. You'll have to be a charismatic leader and a rather effective negotiator and coach to manage well in the looser organization.

Differentiation and integration

Few organizations approach the extremes we've just caricatured. Looser organizations have to compromise; they have to be tight at some places just to hold themselves together. And tight organizations still have to be loose enough not only to cope with crises and coordination problems but also to motivate and keep their people. Organizations that can't do those balancing acts are probably heading down the road to self-destruction.

As one might expect, tight structural styles seem to fit just right on some organizational figures, and loose ones fit on others. Armies, ad agencies, hospitals, railroads, and software companies don't all look their best in the same structural outfits.

Over the *long* run, organizations seem to structure themselves to match the demands of the worlds they live in. They *differentiate* enough in order to cope with the different pressures of their environments. "Differentiation" here means dividing up their structures to fit the needs of their particular markets and other segments of their environments.

But as they put out those separate tentacles to cope with those different parts of the world, they must also make sure that they themselves don't break up. So, they typically make *integrating* moves to counterbalance their increased differentiation. They try to tie their rather different pieces together by developing more uniform control systems, stronger cultural values, or through coordinating devices.

Those simultaneous and opposing pressures to differentiate and integrate do not cause much trouble in organizations that live in very stable and slowly changing environments. But when the environment is volatile and unstable, managers must constantly worry about getting that differentiation-integration balance just right. They don't usually use those words when they worry about it. They talk instead about "regionalizing the structure" or "revising the financial reporting system."

Structure and the world out there

It's not just managers' personal preferences that determine the structural form an organization will take. A whole host of contextual factors tend to set limits on the manager's discretion. Here are some of those constraining factors.

The environment. As we'll see in more detail in part 5, organizations don't operate in a vacuum. They are parts of their broader environment, affecting and being affected by it. Their environments include many "stakeholders," such as customers, competitors, governmental bodies, pressure groups, stockholders, and a whole host of other organizations. Those entities influence the tasks that the organization can undertake, the speed at which it can move, and the structure that it will adopt.

Organizations that live in rapidly changing environments, such as high technology companies, need flexible structures, which can readily adapt to environmental changes, in which roles can be continually redefined and the loci of authority changed to suit changing situations. In general, such organizations develop looser structures, with many temporary task forces and teams, plenty of on-the-spot autonomy, and a lot of cross-communication among units.

But the environments of some organizations change more slowly and less often than others. The peacetime military is an example. In their relatively more stable environments, such organizations don't have to redefine their tasks or change their structures as often as some others. Therefore, they can choose more formal and durable structures, with tighter definitions of roles, hierarchical patterns of authority, and rules and procedures for coordinating and controlling their activities.

But can you think of many contemporary organizations that live in stable, unchanging worlds? They're becoming very rare indeed.

Societal conditions. Social, political, and economic conditions at the time of an organization's birth affect its adult structure. Tight, hierarchical structures, once in place, are very hard to change. If an organization develops that kind of structure early on, it may have trouble adapting to changed conditions later. The railroads, for example—first formed during the nineteenth century—tend even today to stay with formal hierarchical structures, small professional staff groups, and strong, tradition-based cultures. In complete contrast, recently formed high-technology companies typically show very different types of structure: looser organizations, flatter hierarchies, and more informal communication and procedures. They reflect not only the pressures of their fast-moving environments but also the social values and expectations of the contemporary professional work force.

Size. The number of employees is a driving factor in changes in organizational structure. As companies grow bigger, managers must (often reluctantly) switch from now infeasible face-to-face communication and informal controls to more formal procedures, standard job definitions, and more specialized jobs. Even with the compensatory advantages of modern technology, large numbers and physical distances still generate obstacles to human communication and decision making, forcing human organizations to become more "organized."

Collective tasks. Since structure is a device for implementing organizational work, it is inevitable that an organization's collective tasks also influence its structure. Organizations such as old railroads, whose sole task was railroading, typically developed functional structures. Other single-task organizations of the nineteenth century and the early part of this century— such as steel producers, oil refiners, meat packers, and tobacco makers— did so, too. Given their single overarching tasks, they designed structures around the major contributing functions: sales, production, distribution, and finance.

By the 1920s, many of those firms were no longer in just one business. Some had begun to diversify into new products and services. That diversification put a lot of stress on the old functional structures. How, for example, could one sales organization effectively sell many different products, destined for many segments of many markets? So the single, centralized, functional organization gradually—often too gradually—had to give way.

What it gave way to was a newly invented *divisional* structure, pioneered by such companies as General Motors and Du Pont in the 1920s. The divisional structure made its first structural cut not by functions but by product or service divisions. Each was more or less autonomously responsible for all phases of one product line; each had its own sales, production, and finance departments. The divisional structure also separated the long-term strategists, the senior corporate executives, from the operational general managers who managed the divisions on a day-to-day basis.

Many years later, during the 1960s and 1970s, as some U.S. companies began to cross national borders in increasing numbers, and as the technological complexity of tasks increased, they were driven to deal not only with diversified businesses but with new international markets and new large multidisciplinary projects. The old divisional structure could not cope with all those new demands, so some companies developed *matrix* structures, acknowledging the multidimensional interconnections of their organizations' parts and abandoning the notion of one task, one person, one job. Instead, they moved toward multiple, shared patterns of responsibility and authority, encompassing both product divisions and geographic markets. Although the matrix has had its difficulties, it seems clear that there will be no returning to earlier concepts that tried to design organizations so that all jobs would operate independently of one another.

Managerial Choice. Let's not forget that human managers play a part in all this, too. Such factors as environment, size, technology, and task are perceived and interpreted by people. So, managers' personal values, preferences and biases play a role in shaping organizational structures; and so do organizational power games and political manoeuvers, because some structural forms may serve the interests of some groups much more than others.

Fashion. Fashion plays its part, too. Often, organizations follow the fads and fashions of their time. They choose structural forms more for their stylishness than for their comfort and utility.

Some recent changes in managerial thinking about structure

Our beliefs about ideal organizational structures have changed over the years, reflecting the needs and priorities of their times and their history. Tight, formal, authoritarian structures dominated our thinking during most of this century. They derived in part from the fairly stable nature of the environment and in part from the available models of effective, older organizations, such as the military, the British civil service, and the Catholic church.

Gradually, however, more informal, flexible people-based forms have emerged. They reflect the demands of a faster-moving, competitive, interdependent, technological world. Here are some of the major features of the emerging, newer organizational forms.

Decline of authority. In the last couple of decades, the emphasis on authority has declined noticeably in our structural designs. Trade unions, with their strong countervailing power, helped make the arbitrary use of managerial authority quite unworkable. And more recently, professionalization and the dramatic rise of the technologist have challenged the usefulness of authority as the manager's most important tool. The human relations movement, participative management, and, recently, the rise of the concept of organizational culture have all contributed to the relative decline of the idea of authority from its earlier preeminence to a lesser (but by no means trivial) place in the managerial tool kit.

Flatter hierarchies. Organizational hierarchies have become flatter, too. But let us not confuse the decline of authority with a decline of the importance of organizational hierarchy. Hierarchies are not just systems for implementing authority from the top. They perform useful organizational tasks that have nothing to do with authority. They are an efficient way of dividing complex tasks into manageable subassemblies, each of which can then be put together to make the whole. Also, hierarchies serve purposes of coordination and integration.

But the kinds of hierarchies now gaining in popularity are flatter ones, with fewer levels between top and bottom. They are becoming flatter for a number of reasons:

- Information technology is providing a substitute for some of the middle levels of the old hierarchies. Those levels used to be assigned to people whose major job was processing and communicating information up and down the hierarchy. The informational revolution has made many such human jobs quite obsolete.

- The pace of change has gathered momentum in the lives of most organizations, encouraging a search for ways to increase responsiveness. One way to do that is to shorten the distance between the top and lower hierarchical levels.

- In modern interdependent companies, smaller autonomous units seem to work better than large, tightly controlled ones. People seem to work better in small groups, especially when they have to use their heads. Hence, flatter organization forms made up of many small units are often seen as more effective.

- Given the faster pace of change, communication is much more important than it used to be. Tall, hierarchical structures mean long communication chains and constraints about who can communicate with whom about what. Therefore they tend to limit and even choke the fast flow of relevant information.

Information technology. Information technology is also opening up some new and some rather old structural questions. For example, over the years the subject of centralization-decentralization has been a major preoccupation of structural designers, and organizations have gone back and forth between centralized and decentralized structures. During the early part of this century, tall, centralized, authoritarian structures were the order of the day. But they were challenged both by adventurous executives and by the then new human relations movement, both pushing for flatter, more decentralized structures. Then, with the rise of staff specialists and management scientists during the 1960s, we moved back once again toward more centralized structures.

That entire debate has been restarted in recent years, largely as a result of the dramatic impact of information technology on organizations. Perhaps the most interesting aspect of all is that the whole concept of decentralization is beginning to seem simplistic and inappropriate. With contemporary technologies, for instance, it is possible to centralize control and decentralize decision making simultaneously. Both the factory manager and the company president can have almost immediate access to information on many different aspects of the business. But decision making can reside at either end or at both, making the organization—informationally speaking—both centralized and yet decentralized. The full impact of information technology on organizational structure has yet to be fully understood and evaluated.

Temporary structures. Coupled with the idea of flexible, loose structures is that of temporary structures. These are structures that can change and regroup depending on the situation in which the organization finds itself. Today those once-dreaded reorganizations are an accepted feature of organizational life. In the past, reorganizations were often seen as signs of uncertainty or vacillation. Now, they are often looked on with favor, even as an indication of an organization's flexibility. Despite these general trends, though, appropriate design for a given company remains contingent on task, environment, people, size, technology, and the imagination and values of the organization's leaders. Organizational design, like architectural design, is a human creation. So we should not search for a single best answer. Rather, we should expect new designs, appropriate to their settings, to surface periodically.

If there is a general current trend, it is a combination of elements of both structure-first and people-first approaches. Structure (in the old sense) remains a useful but a limited tool, especially limited in managing a professional and expectant work force. The ideas of organizational structure and organizational culture are joining forces in modern organizations. Organizational structure is used to assign tasks to individuals or groups and to establish general lines of accountability and communication. Organizational culture defines the climate, values, and norms of behavior in which the structure is embedded.

In summary

The organizational structures we live and work in influence our behavior, perhaps more than most of us realize. They divide tasks among people;

they help define people's responsibilities, their relationships to one another, and the procedures that they should follow.

But structures are relatively manageable. Managers can tighten or loosen them, centralize or decentralize them. Both tightening and loosening, and all the other available alternatives, have clear advantages in specific situations, but they also engender costs for both manager and managed.

Though managers can modify structures with effort and imagination, they also have to cope realistically with constraints of tasks, size, age, and the environments in which they live. The more differentiated the world, the more differentiated the organization tends to become. More differentiation, however, requires some balance through integration. And the more volatile the organization's environment, the greater the need for a looser structure that can adapt to the changing needs of the time.

Although there is no ideal organizational structure, our ideas about what makes sense and what doesn't seem to evolve with the needs of the times. In recent years, with the emergence of a volatile, interdependent, technological society and a more professional and expectant work force, we have moved away from formal, tight, hierarchical designs toward more informal, flexible structures that can be adapted to the demands of changing situations.

Authority has generally become less important in modern structural designs than it was in the past. Hierarchies, though still there, have become flatter. We have shown more interest in improving communication and coordination. The idea of permanent structures has given way to more temporary changing ones. Structure and culture have joined forces as a way of managing and controlling people's behavior in organizations.

5

Organizations and environments: Managing in a turbulent world

Introductory Note

The relationship between an organization and its environment is much like the relationship between an individual and the big wide world. We can understand a good deal about an individual even without knowing much about that person's job, family, or birthplace. But to extend our understanding, we need to reach out to the environment and the people surrounding that person. No man, said the poet, is an island. And no organization is an island either, though some have acted as though they were—until the bell tolled for them.

Nor is it just the here and now but also the past environment that is relevant to organizations. The neighborhoods in which organizations spent their childhoods shape their adult perspective. Just as the contemporary society differs from the society of the early 1900s, the brash, youthful styles of many of today's start-up companies differ sharply from the ponderous styles of the heavy industrial firms that began life during those earlier years. And both differ from the impersonal, analytic styles of the staff-dominated conglomerates that grew up during the expansive sixties.

The surrounding environment has always influenced the shape and culture of organizations within it; but its role seems to have become far more critical and more intrusive in recent years. The organizations of our world have indeed moved sharply toward greater interdependence and complexity. Governments now exert tight regulatory (and deregulatory) influence on the lives of business organizations. Political and social pressures have increased enormously. Our shrinking world has made us highly sensitive not only to local but also world issues. Most organizations are now city dwellers, living in the crowded, noisy milieu of litigation, international crises, and novel technologies. And what changes the organization, changes the manager, too. The manager is not insulated from that turbulent environment. More and more of his work is affected by outside forces—privacy legislation, equal opportunity issues, import quotas, exchange rates, and safety regulations, to name but a few.

In this last part of the book, we shall try, mostly from the manager's perspective, to look at ways that organizations work (and used to work) with

309

their intrusive and lively environments. First, we'll examine how the environments of organizations have evolved over the past century and how some of our managerial thinking has been influenced by, and in turn has influenced, those developments. We will then explore alternative ways of getting a conceptual handle on the organization-environment relationship. Finally, we will consider some alternatives that managers have to influence their environments. We will even speculate a little about some of the environmental challenges that managers may have to face in future years.

27 The changing organizational environment: You'd hardly recognize the old neighborhood

Like most others, organizational environments have changed over the years. Indeed, during the last sixty or seventy years, the environments surrounding most organizations have changed so much that they would seem almost unrecognizable to our forebears. And, as the environment has changed, both the design of organizations and our ideas for managing them have also changed. This chapter takes a closer look at some of those changes and at their important effects on the managing process.

The early years and organization for productivity

Consider the American social, political, and economic environment of the early 1900s. In retrospect, that was an environment ripe for just the sorts of organization it spawned, organizations designed for one great purpose: productivity. We lived in a relatively sparse world then, sparse of people and of other organizations. Government was supportive. Vigorous entrepreneurs were society's heroes. The market begged for material goods. We were, after all, a developing country, growing and hungry. Our immigrant labor force was large, diverse, mostly non–English-speaking, and poorly educated, but dedicated to improving the lives of its children. Those were also years of personal immobility. People did not move easily from one part of the country to another. The extended family and the small town were the modes, out of the European and Asian traditions. It was a colonialist period, too. Among the upper classes, notions of the white man's burden and of an ignorant and somewhat irrational laboring class prevailed. And along with those beliefs went the paternalistic notion that the important planning had to be done by "superior" people, even over the objections of those ignorant masses, for their own good.

Into this ripe setting, and no wonder, marched the classical organizational theorists and the engineering technocrats—men like Frederick Taylor and Henry Ford—touting the gods of order, efficiency, and control. Taylor and his contemporaries, we said earlier, provided the tech-

niques to support classical organization theory, via their type A implementing systems. By separating planning from doing, they were able to
organize large numbers of unskilled and uneducated people into a system
that could produce large quantities of highly refined products. Taylor devised a system that could build crafted products without craftsmen. Out of
it he got what he (and most of the society at the time) was after: massive
increases in production.

A few decades later, by the 1930s and 1940s, the relevant U.S. environment had changed considerably, partially as a reaction to the past. Trade
unions were making themselves seriously felt. Franklin Roosevelt's New
Deal focused on social and welfare issues, particularly during the Great
Depression of the 1930s. The early image of the glorious, heroic entrepreneur gave way to the caricature of the ruthless robber baron. Our society
became more sensitive to some of the negative personal and social effects
of unfettered profit seeking. The pace of technological innovation gathered
momentum in those years, to be given a tremendous impetus by the pressures of World War II. Mobility increased as cheap and reliable transportation became available; and the distribution of information improved sharply
with better communications and the emergence of TV.

Did American organizations respond to those societal changes even
though they were partly responsible for causing them? Or did they, like
turtles, develop hard shells to try to keep themselves impervious to the
changing world around them?

The answer lies somewhere in between. Most of the initial responses
were ameliorative Band-Aids, intended to patch things up without changing very much. As some companies, for example, became aware—often
for the first time—of growing human frustration and resistance to their
tight control systems, they began to search for add-on ways that might
make people feel a little better, but without sacrificing basic operating
practices. They devised new individual piece-rate schemes; they set up
suggestion systems; they tried this and that to boost morale. But most organizations were not about to abandon those profitable Tayloristic structures
in which they had already invested so much. The physical layout of plant
and equipment had, after all, been designed for the old environment. So
we, in the United States, generally continued our practice of carving out
the organizational holes first, and then forcing human pegs to fit them.

The participative management movement had started to take shape during the 1930s and 1940s, when it began its modest confrontation with Taylorism on Taylor's own playing field. Protagonists of this new faith tried to
convince managers that participation and industrial democracy offered
better routes to the same nirvana of productivity than hard-nosed Taylorism. But they did it, at first, by adding their new ideas to what was already
there. In so doing, they actually helped to patch up Taylorism, to make it
more endurable, more human. If we can make employees *think* it's their

idea, although it's really ours, that early argument ran, they will produce even more.

The adolescent years:
Organization for marketing and product innovation

The single-minded emphasis on productivity began to show signs of cracking in the 1940s and 1950s, partially because of its own past success. Once we had produced a large number of refrigerators, the issue began to shift from producing more to marketing them better or developing new ones. By now, everybody could produce. Who could market? Who could innovate? Higher volumes and lower costs could no longer serve as exclusive targets. A new managerial focus began to grow, a focus not on the management of production workers but on the management of managers themselves. In this newly emerging executive world of marketers and technologists, the old Tayloristic methods were just about useless. Time clocks in the research division just didn't make sense; nor did stopwatches in the market analyst's office.

Those emerging issues drove changes in the internal design of organizations. White-collar workers proliferated, along with staff types and middle-level managers. A different kind of managerial philosophy was needed to replace the obsolescent style of the past. Gradually we backed into it. We began to worry about improving communication, about coordination, about setting up climates for creativity. Mostly, however, we did all that within the ranks of management itself, leaving the production worker pretty much in the same old Tayloristic hands. And it wasn't just that managers left it that way; so did the American trade unions. By the 1950s, American trade unions were as much a part of the basic old system as was management.

The new organizational form that began to emerge inadvertently was a two-tiered form, with the new, more open one stacked on top of the old, tight one below. The old one—at the blue-collar, shop floor level—remained tightly structured and generally authoritarian, with occasional bits and pieces of participation. For the new, more professional, better-educated middle managers doing their ill-structured white-collar jobs, the new, more open, "participative" form became the mode.

The implicit theory behind the new, upper-layer participative model was like old theories about the husbandry of plants. Agronomists didn't understand much about what really made plants grow, but they did the next best thing. They asked the "conditions-under-which" questions: What are the conditions under which plants grow best? The answers were *enabling* answers: they grow best when they get the right amounts of moisture and sunlight and the right soil chemistry. But what is the real nature of plant growth? That's for God to answer.

Participative types took a comparable position about human performance. We did not really understand what makes people imaginative, creative, or motivated; but we knew a lot about the conditions under which those processes seemed to flower. We knew that, under autocratic conditions, initiative and excitement tended to wither away. So, in the 1950s, we developed human-relations training, brainstorming programs, Organizational Development, attitude surveys, and a whole variety of other techniques, all intended to improve the conditions for growing effective human organizations.

The broader environment for U.S. business organizations remained relatively unobtrusive and even supportive during that period, and managers focused mainly on internal organizational matters. While the United States and most Western governments were increasingly on guard against monopolistic practices, in the main they remained friendly partners in promoting economic progress. The environmental turbulence generated by internationalism, social unrest, the technological revolution, and government regulation were yet to reach their zenith.

Then the informational organization

Once again our world insisted on changing. The wartime investment in research and development had its peacetime payoffs, spawning new technologies like radar and the transistor. All sorts of technological leaps occurred, especially in the late 1950s and the 1960s. We entered the information age, the age of the computer. With those new tools, we could now, for the first time, seriously look inside some of those "conditions" questions. We could ask, "What is the inner nature of the thinking processes underlying human problem solving and creativity?" We began to conceive of the human brain as a sort of ultrasophisticated information processor. Since excellent theories of information processing were evolving, we could begin to build problem-solving devices that would substitute for, or at least supplement, human thinking. Machines that were adaptive, that could "learn," that could make decisions began to look less and less like silly futuristic dreams.

This new analytic-informational package, when adapted to management, came initially to be called "Management Science"—perhaps an indicator of our continuing love of the pragmatic and the measurable. It was, in its underlying structure, much like its predecessor, Taylor's "Scientific Management," but its major tool was much more powerful than Taylor's stopwatch. Management Science had the computer.

Conceptually, "Management Science" was rather like "Scientific Management" in that it separated parts of the decision-making process from other activities such as implementation. Taylor had separated the planning of physical work from its implementation, taking the planning part away from the blue-collar worker and giving it to the new industrial engineer. Management science went a large step further, taking some of the planning part away from the middle manager (who had previously planned on the basis of personal experience and know-how) and giving it to the newly emerging staff planner, operations researcher, or systems analyst. Management science could work out the best answer to an inventory control problem, leaving for managers the job of getting their people to implement it.

What kinds of organizational changes, then, were likely to follow from that brand-new capacity to program the hitherto unprogrammable and the new ability to replace at least some classes of human judgment with clean systematic procedures? One major change was an almost incredible speedup in information flows in organizations. A new dynamism entered the scene; a new high-speed feedback cycle permitting the organization to learn the effects of its own actions very quickly, and thereby to become a more effective self-modifying system. This new high-speed quality was evident in the changing new information technology itself. Even now it continues to change at an exponential rate. This year's new equipment is next year's antique.

Attitudes changed, too. The new population of professionals who used and managed this new technology were a mobile group, with the typical attitudes of professionals everywhere: high professional loyalty and low organizational loyalty.

The new, however, doesn't entirely replace the old. More often it just gets added on to what was there before. Radio didn't disappear when TV took over its old spot in the living room. It just moved into the kitchen, the car, the bedroom, and the beach—and the house became noisier. As information technology and management science moved into organizations, participative management did not roll over and die; nor was Taylorism abandoned on the shop floor.

What happened instead was that organizations became even more differentiated, with the different parts operating by different organizational rules. For the people riding on the new systems—the staff planners and top managers—the new technology generated a *less* programmed world, a more ambiguous, more challenging, more judgmental, and more open-ended world. But for production workers and many middle-level people, the same new technology often meant much tighter Taylor-like controls, and often, too, the threat of displacement by the new machines.

By the late 1960s, the typical large organization had become not one structure but many. It wasn't an undifferentiated mass but a highly differentiated set of subsystems, capable of undertaking a wide range of tasks, from routine to creative. The new challenge lay not just in the operation of any particular part but in making all the parts mesh. Not surprisingly, our emphasis then began to shift from managing the individual and the small group to managing the whole complex organization.

This problem of articulation of the whole system, of managing the balance of differentiation and integration, became a new central problem for students of organizations. It was not just technology (and university students) that characterized the expansionist 1960s. The sixties were, some readers will remember, also a decade of very rapid growth and diversification for many companies. Conglomerates flourished. Multidivisional structures became the norm for large companies. Putting it all together was not easy.

Organizations came increasingly to be viewed by scholars as "open systems," drawing resources (such as people and raw materials) from their environment, and exporting goods and services back into that environment. In this new high-tech world, the old connotations of the word *productivity* began to fade. Productivity no longer conjured a picture of ten more engines rolling off the assembly line. It took on a "systems" connotation. Productivity meant integrating R&D, marketing, and manufacturing; it meant making the whole system work. Business schools gradually replaced their old production courses with new ones carrying exotic names like systems analysis and operations research. If you'd gone to a business school in the 1950s, you might have found an old laboratory full of brass instruments for measuring "ergs" of work, and you would have learned how to do time and motion analysis. By the late sixties, that was all ancient history. You were now solving linear programming problems instead.

Throughout the 1960s, staff managers, consultants, and academics developed increasingly elaborate models, simulating linkages among the environment, technology, structure, and management processes. Businesses and governments, too, turned more and more to formal and elaborate forecasting and planning techniques. Staff planners and systems analysts proliferated at corporate headquarters. The new organization had become a kind of technical-social-political quasi-society. Almost imperceptibly, large organizations had developed into elaborate sets of interacting power groups, each a kind of "constituency," with its own objectives, motives, values, and beliefs. But while large organizations were becoming elaborate though loosely coupled systems, interdependencies among the pieces were also increasing.

The interdependent organization

What about the 1970s and 1980s? For the manager, the 1970s was the decade of the intrusive world. The external environment began to occupy more and more of senior managers' attention. Environmental issues, exchange rates, trade barriers, minority concerns, tax structures, the women's movement, government regulations, inflation, and worldwide competition all moved to center stage. The organization was now living in a teeming, crowded world. Every time it moved, it found itself stepping on somebody else's toes.

In this intrusive organizational world of the seventies, even the population of organizations was exploding. The *Yellow Pages* phone directory became thicker than the white pages. Any given organization found itself beset with more and more competitors, more governmental agencies, and many other kinds of "stakeholders." Decision making slowed down, awaiting approval from this council or that committee. Interdependencies between organizations and their environments grew exponentially, echoed by more interdependency among the organization's own loosely coupled parts. For now, if one unit did X, another unit might suffer; or the whole organization might be blamed and held accountable. Interdependencies among nations, between organizations and governments, and among a multitude of different organizations all proliferated in the seventies.

It's worthwhile here to document a bit more fully just a few sources of these growing interdependencies.

Global interdependence

The degree of interdependence among global political and economic forces became dramatically obvious, for example, during the oil crisis of 1973. A number of oil-producing Arab nations, partly as a response to the West's support of Israel during the Yom Kippur War of 1973, partly as a consequence of their own growing sophistication, increased the price of oil almost fourfold and cut back their production, thus precipitating a worldwide energy crisis.

Even small local companies in distant parts of the world were thrown into economic chaos by that event. A worldwide economic recession followed. Managers who had no idea of where or what Kuwait was nevertheless found themselves fighting for their shoe factory's survival because of decisions made in those strange and distant places.

And that little shoe factory's unsolicited dependence on the world was not restricted to raw materials like oil. New competitors were entering "our" markets. In just a few years, global competition for markets became intense. Our competitive advantages over many other countries declined sharply. Other people showed themselves capable of low-cost production, technological innovation, and shrewd leadership. In steel, autos, textiles, and consumer electronics, others were becoming as good or better than we were. From a managerial perspective, by the late 1970s the world had indeed become a "global village."

Interdependencies between government and business

Governments' influence on the affairs of business has increased enormously since the early 1970s. Rules and regulations—like environmental
controls, equal opportunity laws, privacy legislation, and export restrictions—have proliferated. Deregulation of major industries (airlines, banks,
and telecommunications) has speeded up in the United States and elsewhere in the Western world. Controls over the economic and financial in-
frastructure (like interest and exchange rates), have had a profound impact
on the operations and profitability of almost all organizations. Small farmers have found themselves pawns in foreign policy decisions. Even under
"free enterprise" administrations, dedicated to market competition and *de*-
regulation, government/business interdependency continued to grow. Why?
Because larger environmental forces were at work.

- High economic growth rates during the 1960s had generated important
  negative side effects, like environmental pollution. Western societies
  began to question the costs of unfettered free enterprise, to reassess their
  social and economic priorities, and to reexamine questions of organizational legitimacy.
- The social unrest of the 1960s and early 1970s, including the civil rights
  movement, the rise of feminism, and student activism during the Vietnam War, led to new equal opportunity and employment legislation.
- Geopolitical forces contributed. What technologies should our companies be allowed to export to "enemy" countries? Should U.S. farmers' grain crop be used as a diplomatic bargaining chip in a hungry
  world? Competition from abroad led to cries for import quotas, to protect American jobs or British jobs or Belgian jobs.
- Technology's impact on our lives also increased, generating new interdependencies. From the noise of jet engines, to control of access to
  computer-based information, to nuclear power, new, politically sensitive, and socially important issues sprang up to affect organizational
  freedom.
- The size and scale of our projects grew. No single company could put a
  man on the moon; but a system of interconnected organizations could.
  No single company could build a space shuttle. No single hospital could
  afford to buy all the new medical equipment that was becoming available. It was not always sensible to go head to head directly against foreign competitors. They might have one kind of leading-edge technology,
  and we might have others. Joint ventures might work better technically,
  as well as economically and politically. The world was becoming smaller
  as our aspirations grew larger.

Interdependencies among organizations

The world's population of organizations is exploding at least as fast as, maybe even faster than, its human population; and as organizational density increases, so does interdependence.

Not only do managers have to contend with many more organizations in their once empty and nomadic world; they also have to manage many well-organized stakeholders, with their different demands, interests, and points of view. Organizations of investors, employees, customers, legislators, and pressure groups are everywhere around us, pushing, crowding, and demanding priority attention.

For almost any given organization, this growth in the population of stakeholding organizations has already generated an environment very different from that of the 1960s. Since the late 1970s, organizations have been living in noisy, bustling, aggressive "urban" environments. They do not drive on clear, open highways. Instead, they are caught in large, permanent traffic jams.

We discussed some of the more recent managerial ideas, like the concept of organizational culture, in chapter 23. It would be fair to say, however, that in recognition of our growing interdependence, we've begun to pay much more attention to issues outside the boundaries of the organization, to the way that organizations interact with their environments, to those external forces that affect their behavior. New management theories consider the sources of organizational "dependence" on the environment, be they people, resources, markets, or information, and whether and how they can be controlled and influenced. This development should not surprise us. Even in our roles as private citizens, the growing interdependencies are fairly obvious. We are all citizens of an interdependent world of organizations.

In summary

This chapter has looked at the history and evolution of organizations and their environments. Our thesis has been interactional: organizations respond to their times, and the times respond to their organizations. Our quick journey took us from the productivity-driven organizational world of the turn of the century, to the marketing and innovation-driven period of the 1930s, 1940s, and 1950s, to the informational organizations of the 1960s and 1970s, and finally to today's interdependent organization, confronting a multifaceted, crowded, and complex environment.

Although those stages reflect the pressures of their times, they have generally been additive, building on one another. Gradually, over the past few decades, the external environment has come to occupy a more central position in managerial thinking. That's not just for the CEO, but for managers at all organizational levels in organizations all over the world.

How should managers cope with this ever-closer interdependency with their environments? Is the world out there both unpredictable and uncontrollable? Should we just react and adapt as best we can? To what extent can we help shape and control our environments? The last two chapters look at different ways that organizations try to manage their complex relationships with their environments.

28

Organizations in intrusive environments: Can managers be masters of their fates?

Some scholars view organizations as powerless pawns tossed about by the stormy forces of their turbulent environments. Others take a more assertive stance: If managers stand up and fight, or if they at least anticipate opportunities that have not yet materialized, they can turn the tide in their own favor. This chapter looks at the world from both perspectives—the manager as the powerless pawn, and the manager as the assertive master. Both have their supporters and their truths. Then, we'll wrap up by putting the two views into an overall perspective.

Do environments manage managers? Who's in charge here, anyway?

Imagine the following situation:

You are the owner/manager of a small construction company. You specialize in building private homes in a prosperous community. Your business has been doing quite well during the past few years. Local high-technology industry has been booming, and affluent young professionals have been moving into the area. You therefore decide to borrow heavily to finance rapid expansion to meet the new demand; and the bankers back you. By now you've built a lot of speculative homes in the reasonable expectation that the boom will continue and that you will reap the benefits.

But others have noticed the regional boom in your town, too. Bigger construction companies have targeted the region as a lucrative area for future expansion. On top of that, the major banks just announced a sharp rise in interest rates, increasing the cost of mortgages for your potential customers. Moreover, the hot local high-technology industry has begun to cool off in the face of low-cost Asian competition. To make matters worse, the local authorities have announced a major tightening up of the building codes and more restrictions on new construction.

You must now (*a*) cope with more intense competition, (*b*) pay more for the money you need, (*c*) deal with a declining housing market, and (*d*) find ways of keeping your costs from getting out of line.

How will you, young owner/manager, deal with such a depressing state of affairs? Do you have to just wait and hope for the best? Can you take any actions to cope with this increasingly threatening and frightening environment?

Let's take a break here. We'll come back to our local contractor's difficulties later. First, let's look in a broader way at two alternative ways of thinking about that problem of organizations versus their environments.

The first view, which we'll call the "environmental imperative," or the "pawn" view, treats the environment as the boss, as the immutable controller of its inhabitants. The second, the "master" view ascribes more power to the little guy. Organizations and individuals, too, can, with effort and ingenuity, modify, manage, and even construct their own environments. We can make our environment serve us. That optimistic, perhaps arrogant, and typically American view urges us to be masters of our fates, shapers of our futures.

The environmental imperative view:
We are small boats in turbulent environmental seas

The environmental imperative argument takes an ecological, evolutionary position. Nature permits certain organisms to survive and flourish in certain ecological conditions, but not in others. Those organisms have no voice in selecting their environments. If they are lucky enough to be in the right place at the right time, they live; if not, they die. Even if polar bears preferred life in the gentle tropics, they couldn't survive there. Nor could tropical plants ever make it in the arctic cold.

Extend such thinking to organizations. In a given population of organizations, those that have particular resources and features appropriate to their environment will survive and prosper. Those that lack such features will, over time, decline and die.

This environmental imperative view is probably reasonably correct, over the *long* run, for the following reasons, among others

First, organizations can't be infinitely flexible. Their reaction time is slow. The time between decision and implementation is often long. Fixed investments that every business organization makes in facilities and machinery slow down the organization's capacity to modify itself, to be light on its feet, to change course, switch priorities, or re-allocate resources, even when it may be obvious that environmental changes call for such quick turnarounds.

An example? Try the U.S. auto industry during the 1970s. The dramatic (and presumably unforeseeable) increase in oil prices led to an immediate drop in the popularity of bigger cars. But billions of dollars had already been committed to physical plant and equipment for making the big cars.

There was no way that large auto companies could switch very quickly to smaller and more fuel-efficient cars. So Japanese and European auto manufacturers, already tooled up to build small cars, were able to capture a large share of the small-car market in the United States, pushing the U.S. manufacturers from their dominant position.

Second, organizations do not always have accurate and timely information about those external events that might affect them. Our local builder did not know in advance that larger competitors were about to move into the community, nor that interest rates were about to rise. Clearly, some organizations do better than others in keeping informed about their environments. Their eyes see more and their ears hear more. But even with good eyes and ears, many organizations have trouble passing the messages from their eyes to their brains, especially if the distance between the two is very great.

Even in well-managed organizations, messages must pass through many layers before getting to the key decision makers; and by then distortions and omissions can be colossal. Besides, as we indicated in chapter 21, the typical managers' day-to-day role demands focusing on short-term issues, putting out the most pressing fires. In such settings, weak early warning signals of distant disasters can easily be overlooked.

Third, to complicate matters further, internal political pressures inside organizations often block responsiveness to environmental changes. Even if a manager should decide to make quick adjustments, it might be difficult to make that decision politically palatable to the rest of the organization— especially to those groups whose interests might be adversely affected.

Fourth, history, tradition, and ideology affect organizational readiness to adapt to a changing world, as do structure, culture, and standard rules and operating procedures. Our local contractor may simply be unwilling to violate a personal sense of integrity by cutting quality or firing long-time employees. Or the contractor may just not be flexible enough to switch to new, more efficient building methods.

Fifth, there are other, larger external factors over which an organization may have almost no control. A new product, the hand calculator, makes the slide rule obsolete. A new technological breakthrough, the transistor, replaces the vacuum tube. A new government regulation kills off your chemical company's best-selling insecticide. Successes and failures can be driven by larger forces beyond the organization's control.

In the face of such overwhelming constraints, how can any organization hope to control its own fortunes? Looked at from this environmental imperative perspective, organizations don't control their own fortunes. It's simply a question of the survival of the fittest. And being fit is more a question of luck than of brains or exercise.

But is it really that hopeless? Even if fitness is mostly just a question of the right place and the right time, can't we still come to understand better how the surviving organizations acquire their special "genes," their fitness to survive?

The "genetic makeup" of an organization largely depends on the circumstances of the time, the nature of its business, and the background, experience, and values of its founders. If the organization begins its life with the right genetic makeup—right for its time, location, and industry—then, according to the environmental imperative perspective, it is likely to survive. If not, its inflexible genetic makeup can become a noose around its neck, making it too unresponsive to the pressures that will be imposed on it.

The environmental imperative point of view further argues that the environment selects the fittest organizations through the process of competition. Competition ensures that those organizations that fit their environment best will be "selected" to survive and prosper. If they produce the right products or services for their time and place, they will prosper.

But are some genetic makeups more flexible and adaptable than others, so they might make it in changing environments by changing themselves? Is there room, even in the environmental imperative view, for responsive and self-modifying organizations, better able to make choices, select goals, and change directions? Animals are a diverse lot. Some species (and some individuals within the species) are more likely to cope than others. Can't different organizations also respond in different ways? The answer is yes. More creative managers *can* devise unusual and often functional solutions to problems that would decimate others. It is rather like several architects who are given the same set of specifications for a new building. They don't all come up with the same designs. The solutions (or designs) depend largely on the managers' (or the architects') experiences, backgrounds, imaginations, values, and personal goals, not just the problem that needs to be dealt with. Given a flexible organization, perhaps some managers can carry it off despite the malevolence of their environments.

Moreover, although competition might cause the fittest organizations to survive in a *"pure"* environment, environments aren't always pure. Remember the U.S. government's rescue of Chrysler Corporation, and the British government's rescue of British Leyland, the auto and truck manufacturer, both during the 1970s? Failures of such large organizations can often bring totally unpalatable economic and political consequences to a whole society. So governments, investors, or other organizations often "interfere" with nature, to ensure the survival of "unfit" firms. In many European countries, such events occur frequently because employment considerations are significant determinants of policies, and critical industries, like railroads and electric utilities are often owned, managed, or otherwise kept alive through government subsidies.

Even without outside help, many "genetically unfit" organizations do not just die. They may be absorbed into other organizations through mergers and acquisitions, or restructured into different units and businesses; many more reincarnation possibilities are available to organizations than to us individual mortals.

Organizations are active. They don't just sit back passively in their environments. Those with mutual interests can take collective action either to change their environments or to insulate themselves against environmental pressures. Even small organizations can and do try to influence their environments. They form trade and industry associations, speak out collectively to protect their mutual interests, and seek changes in relevant laws or public attitudes.

In the long run, of course, even the smartest and most creative organizations can become victims of overwhelming environmental forces. If the bomb drops, the best of organizations is likely to die with the rest of us. So, in the long run, the environmental imperative view makes sense. In a given population of organizations, a long-run selection process must take place that selects the fittest organizations for survival. Viewed from that long-range perspective, individual managers are like individual soldiers in a large army. They don't usually have much influence over the outcome of the war.

We will return shortly to the options that face our local contractor, using that case to clarify some of the points in this chapter. First, however, let's go on to explore that second, more optimistic way of thinking about the organization—environment connection, the "master" view.

The proactive, enactive "master" view:
Get out there and change the world!

Managers can control their fates. They don't have to accept their environment as a given; nor do they have only to *react* to whatever happens out there. Some managers manage their environments better than others. They try to influence and even reshape their environments. They try to "sense" both opportunities and threats that may be lurking out there or that can be planted out there. They develop networks of contacts at points of influence. They take risks with bold strategies, explore new worlds, and plant new flags. Is that all nonsense? No, it's not.

Organizations can sometimes move from one environment to another, and even *create* aspects of their environments, such as new styles, new beliefs, and new wants. They can control their environments by choosing (and changing) the business they want to be in, the markets they go after, the products they launch, their target customers, the people they recruit, their structures, policies, and procedures, and the ways they allocate and use their resources. A sales manager can choose between spending more money on advertising or recruiting more salespeople; the CEO can, within certain limits, choose one type of organizational structure over another; the manufacturing manager can decide on the levels of inventory to hold and the rate at which to modernize the plant. Sometimes of course, they can also make unrealistic or just wrong choices, thus adding to their own environmental problems.

The environment is not just a source of pressure and threat for the organization. It is also a source of opportunity. Deregulation of the telecommunications industry, a major environmental change, provided tremendous opportunities for emerging long-distance carriers like US Sprint and MCI. Similarly, deregulation of airlines in the late 1970s made it temporarily possible for small companies like People Express to carve out initially profitable market niches. The same deregulation, however, later allowed the bigger airlines to close many of those niches.

So in the last analysis it is the quality of managers' decisions, their sensitivity to opportunities, their reservoir of entrepreneurial flair, and their capacity to reinterpret, reinvent, and redefine their worlds that will determine a large part of their organizations' fitness to survive, at least in the "middle run."

A few caveats are in order here. All organizations don't have the same degrees of control over their environments. It's easier to manage your environment if you're already a successful company with a good track record in a growing market than if you're a new kid on an old block. Suppliers will be eager to deal with you, customers eager to buy from you, and banks may even be eager to lend you money. Your major challenge is to come up with a winning strategy that can be sustained over time and to make the most of your opportunities. For you, the environment out there is warm, rich, and benevolent. But if you're a newcomer in a mature market and you have very limited resources, that environment is likely to look and act cold, cruel, and unforgiving.

One more issue: We "enact" much of our worlds. What kind of market, for instance, is a "mature" market? Is this market really mature, or do some of us just think of it as mature because we've been too close to it for too long? Given creativity and determination, maybe our panty hose market isn't mature. Maybe we can sell panty hose in a new way—not just in department stores but in supermarkets, at low prices. Or maybe we can make a niche for ourselves with superquality exotic ice cream in a "mature" ice cream market. Some organizations manage to turn their dry, infertile, threatening environments into lush, lively gardens.

What are some examples of companies making their environments work for them? A few years ago, a few mass merchandisers in the United States viewed those newly developing suburban and highway shopping centers as a golden opportunity for retailing. They joined up. Others, particularly those who had prospered in choice downtown locations, saw the new malls as either irrelevant or dangerous. By the time the second group realized that suburban shopping centers were there to stay, many of them were moribund. Did their changing environment kill them, or did they let themselves die? That they were unfit was true. But was it just a matter of luck?

Even as large, successful, and powerful a company as IBM can fail to see (or at least to exploit) potentially lucrative opportunities. In the late 1960s, IBM passed over the potentially huge impact of minicomputers, deciding to stay out of that market. That decision enabled Digital Equipment Corporation, then a small and insignificant company, to develop and capture most of that emerging and booming sector.

Once again, are managers masters or pawns?

Remember the local contractor we have cast you as? If you adopt a passive posture, you will most probably let your environment bury you. Local history will remember you as a loser and your organization as unfit for its time. But if you are proactive, if you start making or sensing opportunities that you can use to your advantage, maybe you can pull your company out of that seemingly hopeless situation.

How? What advice would the champions of the pawn and the master views give to you, the local builder? Perhaps the environmental imperative advice would be to accept your environment as a given. They might propose that you ought to have adopted a problem-solving posture. You should have analyzed the situation, forecasted changes in your environment, and developed contingency plans—all in the past tense. Right now, they might suggest, you better get out of the business.

The master types, on the other hand, would probably counsel you to take a pathfinding approach. Rethink the situation; try to redefine the problem. Look for bold, proactive moves you might make to turn your environment in your favor. Be creative! Come up with a totally different design concept, something unique and appealing to some growing segments of the population—yuppies or old people or single-parent families. Move faster than the big boys. Take risks. That's less practical advice, but is it foolish?

Much, albeit not all, of our destiny is in our own hands, at least in the "middle run." There is no guarantee that we can fully master our fates, but we can put up a good fight, and often we can win.

In summary

This chapter has looked at two opposite ways of thinking about relationships between organizations and their environments. At one extreme is the "pawn" or environmental imperative view. It holds that we have almost no influence over our environments; they control us. Our long-term survival depends on luck, on how well our "genes" match the environments we encounter. If we are lucky enough to be born with the right products for the right markets, at the right time, we go on to survive and prosper; if not, we'll decline and die over time.

The other view is more optimistic. The "master the world" view tells managers that they can (and should) become masters of their environments. They can get out of the slum or even stay there and turn it into a lovely resort. They can influence and change their environments through their own creativity and their proactive stance. Their survival depends on what they choose to do, not on their inheritance.

Both views are partially valid. The environment can be a source of great pressure; sometimes it can become so overwhelming that it destroys the organization. Political forces, new technologies, and unexpected catastrophes can all kill organizations. But managers can change the world, too. Those with imagination and determination can make the desert bloom. And if they fail, they would at least have given it a fair shot.

29 Managing our environments: Can managers create new worlds?

Can managers really "manage" their environments? The right answer, of course, is the standard academic answer: yes and no. More accurately, "It depends." The organizational world is crowded and frenetic. It is a world of large organizations and small ones, public and private, domestic and international, single business and diversified, manufacturing and service, and much more. Managing relevant environments in such a world is fairly easy for some organizations, and quite impossible for others.

Consider first the *why* question. Why should organizations bother with what's out there in the environment? Clearly, the manager of the local grocery store has to stay in touch with customers and suppliers, but why bother with anyone else? The answer is fairly obvious: The manager has to stay in touch with bankers and other creditors, keep one eye on competitors to make sure that they aren't offering better service or lower prices, and possibly have to worry about the city council's debate on rezoning or the cutback in local police patrols.

A large multinational company, of course, has to work with and through a much larger and more diverse set of environmental forces. In an oil company, the CEO's office may interact with governments of oil-producing countries, financial institutions, security analysts, regulatory and government agencies, and the media, among others. Division managers within the same company would have to work with trade unions, intermediate suppliers, community groups, local governments, and many more.

Though their environments are different in nature and complexity, both the grocery store and the oil giant have to "manage" their relationships with those crucial outside entities. In today's world it's not just customers or competitors who can make or break a company.

Here are a few of the reasons for the steadily increasing relevance of "outsiders" in the modern managing process:

- Crises, like the Tylenol tampering scare or the chemical explosion in Bhopal or the hijacking of the company aircraft just seem to have a way of turning up, especially for organizations with interests spread all over the world.

329

■ Unforeseen moves by competitors are nothing new, but they have now become almost a daily event for many organizations. Product life cycles are growing ever shorter, and competition now comes from many, often unexpected quarters. In the computer industry, for example, many companies were taken by surprise in 1981 by IBM's sudden decision to bring out its personal computer. Almost overnight, the IBM PC changed the market environments of many young computer companies, forcing some of them into bankruptcy.

■ Not surprisingly, the speed of technological change has accelerated considerably, making many old products obsolete and driving their producers into crises. Remember the impact of small, cheap electronic calculators on the makers of those big mechanical calculators back in the 1970s?

■ Governments now play a direct role in the lives of many organizations. Regulation, deregulation, tax reforms, minority employment, equal opportunity laws, interest rates, and foreign policy considerations all have an impact on managers and their organizations.

■ Worldwide markets and competitors are another source of change and uncertainty, from autos, chemicals, and computers to shoes, textiles, and videos.

■ Minority groups have helped transform the once-monolithic business world. Students lobbying for sanctions against South Africa, blacks and women fighting for fair treatment, and the aged asserting their rights in large numbers are all crowding the manager's world, demanding attention and swift action. By the time you read this chapter, many other groups will surely have made themselves felt.

All those forces and many others have pushed their way into the once pastoral and benevolent managerial world. They are all part of the manager's relevant environment because anything out there that can help or hinder an organization *is* the relevant environment.

Using organizational sense and senses: Seeing, smelling, processing, communicating, and acting

In order to manage our environment, it is first necessary to comprehend it. Clearly, some organizations do a better job than others at comprehending, knowing, and sensing their environments. Some may be more savvy and creative in their methods. Some use their eyes and ears to see and hear more. Some use their brains better to interpret what they see and hear.

And some organizations *respond* to those signals better and faster than others. Johnson & Johnson, Tylenol's parent company, for example, moved quickly—when some poisoned bottles of Tylenol were discovered in 1985—to dispel consumer fears by mounting a major advertising and public relations campaign. A few personal computer manufacturers reacted to

IBM's entry into their markets by refocusing on smaller but higher value-added niches; others just died. Sometimes crises, even if sensed as early as possible, may extend beyond any organization's control. But often it is within managers' ability both to get earlier warning of impending problems (or opportunities) and to do something about them.

An organization is a little like an individual. To manage its environment, it needs good sensors—eyes and ears—to gather information from the outside and effective internal communication channels to get the message to the right parts of its brain. It needs an effective processing capability to evaluate the information it receives and good muscles to take appropriate action. It needs something else, too—some means of knowing whether its actions went right or went wrong, and some way of modifying them when necessary. But the difference between individuals and organizations is that individuals have all those parts built into them to begin with; and they work almost automatically. Organizations have to design and build their own sensors, communication channels, processors, and muscles. Then they must make them work.

Suppose you manage a small sales office in a large widget manufacturing company. One day, one of your salespeople tells you that a customer said that your biggest competitor is about to announce a 15 percent price cut. You are assured that the information comes from a very reliable source. Your "sensor," the salesperson, has now given you the input.

What's next? You figure you ought to pass the information along to the marketing manager up at the head office, where pricing decisions are made. But you're due to be promoted and transferred to another division at the end of the month, at about the same time your competitor is supposed to announce the price cuts. You don't want to take a chance on jeopardizing your promotion by sending along rather flimsily supported bad news. You decide to ignore the salesperson's input. So, although the sensor has worked well, the transmitter—the manager—has failed to function. The input never gets to that part of the organizational system where it can be processed further. Nothing happens.

Consider an alternative scenario: You, the sales manager, are neither self-interested nor afraid to pass on the bad news. You phone the marketing manager to tell what you've heard, stressing the need for quick action. The marketing manager, also a responsible sort, calls a meeting of the marketing staff that same afternoon. They decide to preempt the competitor's move by announcing a 15 percent price cut immediately. They do so, and they get the word out. They hope the competitor will come in too late to reap any of the benefits. Your proactive, decisive, and swift action has made the difference. In this scenario, all the major elements, sensors, processors, transmitters, and action muscles have worked in harmony.

But the information was still flimsy. Suppose it was false. Shouldn't the processor have insisted on more search for confirmation? Maybe what you've done is to start a price war, forcing your competitor to cut his prices, too, though it had never planned to do it in the first place.

Now move on to an "in-between" situation. You communicate the information to the head office, but the marketing manager back there doesn't think it deserves immediate attention: "I have other pressing matters to deal with right now. Why don't we put this one on the back burner and just wait and see." In that case, it is the action muscle, the marketing manager in charge, who decides neither to collect more information nor to act. In due course, the market will judge whether the marketing manager was right or wrong.

So far, we have painted the picture as if each actor were a free agent, as if one could do as one pleased. But as we explained in part 4, real situations aren't like that. Organizational members occupy constrained roles. They are not free agents. They have to work in a given structure and a given culture, and they must follow rules, policies, and procedures. The salesperson may be required to write a report before anything can be done. The manager may have to get the approval of an immediate supervisor before passing that report on to the head office. Every important pricing decision may, according to procedures, have to be approved by the entire top management team. The manager may have to go through many different steps before taking any action. So the speed and flexibility of managerial sensors, transmitters, processors, and action muscles are constrained by the organization's structure, culture, rules, and procedures.

For the individual, eyes and ears are sensors; but what are the organizational equivalents of eyes and ears? A lot depends on the organization and its environment. Those in rapidly changing environments, like high-technology companies, use a whole host of sensors that can give them the information quickly—the people at the boundaries of their organizations, like salespeople, carefully developed networks of contacts, representatives at trade shows, and so on. Organizations in more stable environments, such as food and auto companies, may use more traditional sensors—staff groups, market research studies, and consumer surveys. But in the final analysis, watchful and sensitive people are the most important sensors in any organization. They gather and sense information by interacting with customers, suppliers, competitors, government agencies, universities, industry groups, and many others, as well as by reading and listening.

But as we've seen in our widget company, it's not enough just to have good sensors. Organizations, like individuals, can only act on information if that information is picked up by their "brains" and acted on by their muscles; that is, they also require ways of transmitting the right information to the right people, and effective muscles for acting on that information. The quality of transmission, processing, and action capabilities depend not only on people but also on the structure, culture, and internal working arrangements of the organization. Open channels of communication help by allowing information to be transmitted quickly and directly, up or down or sideways, along the shortest possible distance between sensors and action muscles. Also, the organization needs to be decentralized enough so that action can be taken quickly at lower levels, yet centralized enough so that subgroups don't run off in all sorts of conflicting directions.

But there are big differences between the organization and the individual. Although we individuals are great rationalizers and perceptual distorters, organizations do it even better. An organization's sensors are not just one pair of eyes and one pair of ears. There are many individuals in the organization, each watching the same environment from a different angle, each perceiving that environment differently. Some may see small shifts and read them as large; others may see large shifts but shut their eyes to them. The realities we each perceive are constructed in large part out of our particular motives and interests. A salesperson who feels angry, afraid, or just selfish may report a particular situation, but what the salesperson sees may be very different from what another observer sees. So, although managers need all the sources of relevant information they can get, they need to evaluate those diverse sources to try to extract a reasonably objective picture of what's really out there.

One important, though correctible cause of distortion is the tendency in many organizations to ostracize bearers of bad news and thereby to discourage future reporting of vital, but unfavorable information. Messengers carrying bad news, even in modern organizations, can lose their heads, so volunteers become scarce. Managers need to make sure that their organizational sensors can sense and transmit even what the organization doesn't like.

Problems also arise in transmitting and acting on information. Organizational hierarchies present many obstacles to the flow of information. By the time relevant information reaches the right action muscles in many organizations, it may have passed through a long, distorting human chain. Each link on that chain would usually, though mostly unconsciously, select, absorb, and discard, until the eventual message received bears only a slight resemblance to the message originally sent.

Developing effective sensors, processors, transmitters, and action mechanisms is the first necessary step toward managing the organization's environments. Without them, the organization floats deaf, blind, and paralyzed in a sea of sharks.

But even if you know what's out there, how do you manage it?

Over the centuries, human beings have created all sorts of mechanisms to help "manage" the environment. We developed mechanical tools to help us build shelters, discovered fire, and exploited natural resources to protect ourselves, to conquer our enemies, and to develop our communities. Gradually, over time, we have managed to reduce our dependence on our environments, if not to control some of them. Though we can't control rainfall, we invented umbrellas and raincoats. We have also created myths and rituals to help us in our quest for control over the uncontrollable parts of the environment.

Organizations use some of the same methods and some different methods to try to manage their dependence and to control, or to help them believe that they control, the critical aspects of their environments. Here are a few of those methods:

Choosing the right friends and neighbors. One simple way to finesse the problem of control over the environment is to select an environment in which we think our organization can prosper. Much as a family may look for a house in a neighborhood that's right for them, an organization looks for an environment they like and in which they feel at ease. They can, within certain limits, choose the kinds of businesses they go into or get out of. They can decrease their dependency on any one business or enter new businesses by selling off units, acquiring other firms, investing in other companies, or initiating new ventures. They can also convert enemies into friends by forging alliances with competitors, as, for example, GM and Toyota did, along with many others in the auto industry.

Managing relationships with critical constituents. If we can gain control over resources critical to our survival, we'll be less dependent on our environment. If we have our own water supply, can grow our own food, and can maintain a large stock of firewood, then those long winters in the wilderness may be more livable. Organizations think along similar lines. Some firms can, for instance, follow a strategy of vertical integration, by moving both forward to control their channels of distribution and backward to control their sources of supply.

Suppose a company makes athletic shoes. It might try to integrate forward by buying out some of its distributors and retail outlets, so as to control its marketing strategy more effectively. It can integrate backward by trying, for example, to acquire a few producers of its critical components and supplies.

It's not always easy or even possible for organizations to use such methods. Laws set limits on the activities of public and some nonprofit organizations. An organization needs money as well as broad managerial skills to pursue some of those options; they need resources that are not uniformly available to all organizations. Moreover, organizations require different degrees of control over their environments. How much does company X have to rely on outsiders for its critical resources? Are there hundreds of independent suppliers out there? Is the cost of switching from one source to another very low?

Building legitimacy. Organizations, like individuals, also influence their worlds by building relationships with the right people and the right organizations. In today's world of societal and public scrutiny, most business organizations are much more aware of the importance of building their legitimacy, gaining acceptance by society at large as "good citizens." So they spend resources on public relations to create the "right" image. They recruit people from other critical organizations and then use their influence and contacts to promote good relations. They appoint influential individuals to their boards of directors. They make contributions to popular causes and campaigns. They join together with other organizations, often in trade and industry associations, to promote their common interests. And they hire lobbyists to influence legislators in critical areas of concern.

Maintaining flexibility. When the world out there is changing rapidly and often unpredictably, flexibility is an essential weapon. Organizations may need to shift course quickly, re-allocate resources, and modify priorities. The rationale for maintaining flexibility is simple enough, but the implementing part isn't easy. The rationale for staying flexible is simply that the unexpected is bound to happen. Competitors will surprise you. Technological breakthroughs will make your products obsolete. Political upheavals in distant places will disrupt your activities and plans. Hurricanes will knock down your power lines. And new rules and regulations will make what you do today illegal tomorrow. But on the plus side, those same kinds of unforeseen changes often provide opportunities for alert and flexible organizations.

"Be flexible" may be good advice, but how does an organization follow that advice? One method that has become increasingly popular in recent years is to form tentative "strategic alliances." These are typically agreements between two or more firms interested in each other's financial resources, technological capabilities, marketing expertise, or geographic spheres of operations. Such relationships typically, although not exclusively, develop between small and large companies. By teaming up with the big boys, smaller companies can find money for research and development, enter markets they could not get into on their own, and, in some cases, obtain equity capital. The small company pays its part of the bill by supplying proprietary technology or new products and skills to its larger partner.

There are a number of reasons for the increasing popularity of such partnerships. Perhaps the most important one is those ever-shortening product (and service) life cycles, which foster the need for large capital injections to make investments in new products and new services. But that means more risk and more expense. Joint arrangements allow companies to get a better handle on the changing conditions of their environments, sharing the risks and costs as well as the potential rewards of their combined efforts.

Alliances between small, new biotechnology companies and large oil and chemical companies provide a current example. The startups need a lot of money to undertake risky projects, and big companies need those break-through products to build their long-term competitive positions.

Although the big firms may have enough resources to undertake developments of such products themselves, the costs and risks would be high, and it might take them a long time because of their bulky and relatively rigid structures. Smaller companies often have the knowledge, the technical expertise, and the entrepreneurial flair to move quickly and effectively. The big companies, on the other hand, are the ones that usually have the resources and access to large markets. They also provide the little guy with a security blanket should things go wrong.

These days even old competitors form strategic alliances when the situation looks right. GM gets together with Toyota to develop a world car; AT&T buys into Olivetti to develop products jointly and to have a better access to overseas markets. The psychology of interorganizational relationships has a lot in common with the psychology of interpersonal relationships.

Are there other ways to improve an organization's flexibility? How about subcontracting some operations (such as manufacturing) to specialized outside firms? That avoids the high costs of fixed assets such as plant and equipment. Or how about using part-time and temporary employees? At this writing, supplying temporary employees is one of the fastest-growing industries in America. But once again, there is no free lunch. Although using part-time help can provide some flexibility, the costs are reduced loyalty from those more casual guest employees and less understanding of the whole picture.

Organizations also try to develop more flexible structures, cultures, and internal working arrangements to encourage versatility and swift response from their employees and to inculcate the expectation of rapid change. Structurally the general direction, as we indicated in chapter 26, has been toward smaller, more autonomous units and more open and informal communication. The traditional steep and formal hierarchy has been steadily fading away. Other developments include leaner corporate staffs, easier access to senior management, effective use of new technology to speed up communication flows, and an emphasis on autonomy for people at all levels, rather than on job definitions, bureaucratic procedures, or paperwork. On the other hand, the trend toward complex, interconnected networks of products and markets is also pressing many companies in the opposite direction—toward integration into larger, more centralized units.

What does the future hold?

Since we are approaching the end of this book, it seems appropriate to use these last few pages to reflect on the past and speculate about (not forecast) the future.

Way back at the beginning, in the virgin world, companies were nomadic. They were wandering bands of entrepreneurial people. They were "companies" in the original sense of that word—companies of human beings, like traveling theatrical companies are today.

With the coming of Frederick Taylor and Henry Ford, among others, that nomadic form gave way to a more static organizational lifestyle. Companies became more like tough independent farmers, staking their claims, carving out their plots of land, routinely but also autonomously.

Then the knowledge explosion of the 1960s provided a kind of temporary rebirth of nomadism. Organizations no longer had to be anchored to their traditional tasks and structures. The new flexible technology and the new high-powered technologists made all sorts of changes possible. The organization could become mobile again, searching for tasks unlike anything it had undertaken before. It could become nomadic again, out hunting for new applications for its novel and flexible resources.

Today, the forecast is for change. It looks like the name of the game in the years ahead may be vision, intent, and purpose, coupled with flexibility and creativity, perhaps even more than with efficiency. Managers will live with change, ambiguity, and crises. In such a world, we will need flexible strategies and responsive organizations. But even more, organizations will have to be clear in their own "heads" about what they want and where they want to go.

Rigid, old authoritarian mechanisms have already largely disappeared. They were designed for an orderly, predictable, slowly changing world. Ambiguity, uncertainty, and irregularity have instead become normal states in the organizational milieu. New CEOs, if they are to juggle the conflicting forces rising from within and from outside their organizations, need the qualities of a good politician. But also, they need a vision of where their organizations are to go, a sense of purpose; they need to point the organizational way. Among the key assets of the manager in the managerial world ahead should be, and probably will be, a clear sense of purpose, a distinctive set of values, and a recognition of the responsibility that accompanies that important managerial role. Managing is more than a job or a way to make a living. It's a *leadership* position. And people in positions of leadership need clear vision, explicit values, and strong determination.

In summary

Crises, smart competitors moving in from unexpected quarters, technological breakthroughs, political changes, and many other factors have made the external environment much more a part of the manager's world. This chapter has tried to suggest ways that managers can try to manage the relevant parts of their direct and indirect environments, especially the indirect environment that has become the intrusive new kid on the manager's block.

To help manage their environments, organizations need what individuals need: good sensors (like eyes and ears) to find out what's happening out there, effective information transmitters (like the nervous system) to pass on the information, processors (like the brain) to deal with the information they receive, and action mechanisms (like muscles) to do something about what the brain has processed. While such organs come as original equipment in individuals, organizations have to design, build, and operate their own.

Managers can use many different methods to help reduce their dependency on their environments. Sometimes they can simply move to a more benevolent environment. Or they can try to gain some control over crucial resources through forward or backward integration. They can try to build their legitimacy so that the relevant world will love and support them. They can try to develop more flexibility to increase their chances of responding effectively to whatever may happen in their volatile surroundings.

Our general thesis in this last part of the book has been interactional: Organizations respond to their times and the times to their organizations. We have moved over the years from mostly productivity-oriented business organizations, to more marketing-oriented organizations, to more informational organizations, and recently toward ever more sociopolitical organizations. Right now we seem to be moving toward new types of networks among interdependent organizations. Each of those stages has reflected the pressures of its times, and some of them are reactions to even earlier pressures that organizations themselves have put on their times.

A final thought: Our environments will probably continue to grow more volatile, less predictable, and more risky. We can and should try to anticipate the environmental weather and prepare ourselves even for unexpected changes. But in dealing with a changing, unpredictable world, the best tool for both individuals and organizations is still an internal one; it is knowing ourselves and knowing where we want to go.

Suggested readings

Part 1

For an introduction to social psychology with a focus on patterns of human behavior, see:

Aronson, E. *The Social Animal*. 3d ed. San Francisco: W. H. Freeman & Co., 1980.

Myers, D. G. *Social Psychology*. New York: McGraw-Hill Book Co., 1983.

On motivation, try:

McClelland, D. C. *Human Motivation*. Glenview, Ill.: Scott Foresman & Company, 1985.

Maslow, A. H. *The Farther Reaches of Human Nature*. New York: Viking Press, 1973.

Weiner, B. *Human Motivation*. New York: Holt, Rinehart, and Winston. 1980.

On cognition and attribution, see:

Festinger, L. *A Theory of Cognitive Dissonance*. Evanston, Ill.: Row Peterson, 1957.

Harvey, J. H., and J. Weary, eds. *Attribution: Basic Issues and Applications*. Orlando, Fla.: Academic Press, 1985.

Hastorf, A. H. and A. M. Isen, eds. *Cognitive Social Psychology*. New York: Elsevier-North Holland, 1982.

On the emotional side of human behavior, see:

Izard, C. E. *Human Emotions*. New York: Plenum Press, 1977.

Lipman-Blumen, J. *Individual and Organizational Achieving Styles: A Handbook for Researchers and Human Resource Professionals*. Claremont, CA: Achieving Styles Institute, 1987.

For different perspectives on human reasoning and problem solving, see:

Newell, A., and H. A. Simon. *Human Problem Solving*. Englewood Cliffs., N.J.: Prentice-Hall, Inc., 1972.

Simon, H. A. *Reason in Human Affairs*. Stanford, Calif.: Stanford University Press, 1983.

On thinking and creativity, try:

Adams, J. L. *The Care and Feeding of Ideas*. Reading, Mass.: Addison-Wesley, 1986.

Hayes, J. R. *The Complete Problem Solver*. Philadelphia: Franklin Institute Press, 1981.

Ray, M., and R. Myers. *Creativity in Business*. New York: Doubleday and Company, 1986.

For an international survey of managerial attitudes and assessment procedures, see:

Bass, B. M., & P. C. Burger. *Assessment of Managers: An International Comparison*. New York: Free Press, 1979.

A couple of relevant collections of papers on psychological aspects of human behavior as related to management are:

Leavitt, H. J., L. Pondy, and D. Boje. *Readings in Managerial Psychology*. 4th ed. Chicago: University of Chicago Press, 1988.

Staw, B. M., ed. *Psychological Foundations of Organizational Behavior*. 2d ed. Glenview, Ill.: Scott Foresman and Company, 1983.

Part 2

Some useful books on influencing behavior are:

Allen, R. W., and L. W. Porter. *Organizational Influence Processes*. Glenview, Ill.: Scott Foresman and Company, 1983.

Cialdini, R. B. *Influence: The New Psychology of Modern Persuasion*. New York: Quill, 1984.

Kotter, J. P. *Power and Influence: Beyond Formal Authority*. New York: Free Press, 1985.

Zimbardo, P. B., E. B. Ebbesen, and C. Maslach. *Influencing Attitudes and Changing Behavior*. 2d ed. Reading, Mass.: Addison-Wesley Publishing Co., 1977.

For a comprehensive review of organizational reward systems, see:

Lawler, E. E. *Pay and Organizational Development*. Reading, Mass.: Addison-Wesley Publishing Co., 1981.

For an overview of communication processes in organizations, see:

Klauss, R., and B. M. Bass. *Inter-personal Communication in Organizations*. New York: Academic Press, 1982.

Rogers, E. M., and R. A. Rogers. *Communication in Organizations*. New York: Free Press, 1976.

For an overview of interpersonal relationships, see:

Athos, A. G., and J. J. Gabarro. *Interpersonal Behavior: Communication and Understanding in Relationships*. Englewood Cliffs, N.J.: Prentice-Hall, Inc., 1978.

Bennis, W., J. Van Maanen, and E. H. Schein, eds. *Essays in Interpersonal Relations*. Homewood, Ill.: Dorsey Press, 1979.

For a classic book on coercion, see:

Schein, E. *Coercive Persuasion*. New York: W. W. Norton Co., 1961.

For the application of collaborative models in organizations, see:

Bennis, W. G., K. D. Benne, and R. Chin. *The Planning of Change*. New York: Holt, Rinehart, and Winston, 1976.

Part 3

For an introduction to how small groups behave, try:

Forsyth, D. E. *An Introduction to Group Dynamics*. Monterey, Calif.: Brooks/Cole Publishing Co., 1983.

Shaw, M. E. *Groups Dynamics: The Psychology of Small Group Behavior*. 3d ed. New York: McGraw-Hill Book Co., 1980.

Stock-Whitaker, D. *Using Groups to Help People*. London: Routledge & Kegan Paul, 1985.

For a fascinating small-group analysis of some major decisions in U.S. history, see:

Janis, I. L. *Victims of Groupthink*. Boston: Houghton Mifflin Co., 1972.

For a work on how group pressure drives the individual toward conformity, see:

Kiesler, C. A., and S. B. Kiesler. *Conformity*. Reading, Mass.: Addison-Wesley Publishing Co., 1969.

For a useful model of group leadership, see:

Vroom, V. H., and P. W. Yetton. *Leadership and Decision Making*. Pittsburgh: University of Pittsburgh Press, 1973.

For works on managing conflict situations in organizations, see:

Brown, L. D. *Managing Conflict at Organizational Interfaces*. Reading Mass.: Addison-Wesley Publishing Co., 1983.

Filley, A. F. *Interpersonal Conflict Resolution*. Glenview, Ill.: Scott Foresman and Company, 1975.

For managing negotiation in organizations and groups, see:

Brazerman, M. H., and R. J. Lewicki, eds. *Negotiation in Organizations*. Beverly Hills, Calif.: Sage Publications, 1983.

For a work on managing small groups in organizations, see:

Bradford, D. L., and A. R. Cohen *Managing for Excellence*. New York: John Wiley and Sons, 1984.

Part 4

Some classic books on organizations and the managing process are:

Barnard, C. *The Functions of the Executive*. Cambridge, Mass.: Harvard University Press, 1938.

Chandler, A. D. *Strategy and Structure*. Cambridge, Mass.: MIT Press, 1962.

Cyert, R. M., and J. G. March. *A Behavioral Theory of the Firm*. Englewood Cliffs, N.J.: Prentice-Hall, Inc., 1963.

Drucker, P. *The Practice of Management*. New York: Harper, 1954.

Lawrence, P. R., and J. W. Lorsch, *Organization and Environment*. Boston: Harvard University Graduate School of Business Administration, 1967.

McGregor, D. *The Human Side of Enterprise*. New York: McGraw-Hill Book Co., 1960.

March, J. G., and H. A. Simon. *Organizations*. New York: John Wiley and Sons, 1958.

Thompson, J. D. *Organizations in Action*. New York: McGraw-Hill Book Co., 1967.

Weick, K. *The Social Psychology of Organizing*. 2d ed. Reading, Mass.: Addison-Wesley Publishing Co., 1979.

For different views of what managers actually do, see:

Kotter, J. P. *The General Managers*. New York: Free Press, 1982.

Mintzberg, H. *The Nature of Managerial Work*. New York: Harper & Row, 1973.

For a collection of papers on the historical evolution of business enterprise in the United States and Europe, see:

Chandler, A. D., and H. Daems, eds. *Managerial Hierarchies: Comparative Perspectives on the Rise of the Modern Industrial Enterprise*. Cambridge, Mass.: Harvard University Press, 1980.

For more on pathfinding and innovation, see:

Burgelman, R. A., and L. R. Sayles. *Inside Corporate Innovation.* New York: Free Press, 1986.

Kanter, R. M. *The Change Masters.* New York: Simon and Schuster, 1983.

Leavitt, H. J. *Corporate Pathfinders.* Homewood, Ill.: Dow Jones–Irwin, 1986.

For the processes of organizational decision making, see:

Allison, G. T. *Essence of Decision.* Boston: Little, Brown and Company, 1971.

Bower, J. L. *Managing the Resource Allocation Process.* Boston, Mass.: Graduate School of Business Administration, Harvard University, 1970.

George, A. L. *Presidential Decision Making in Foreign Policy: The Effective use of Information and Advice.* Boulder, Colo.: Westview Press, 1980.

Lindblom, C. E. *The Policy-Making Process.* Englewood Cliffs, N.J.: Prentice-Hall, Inc., 1968.

March, J. G., and J. P. Olsen. *Ambiguity and Choice in Organizations.* 2d ed. Bergen, Norway: Universitetsforlaget, 1986.

Quinn, J. B. *Strategies for Change: Logical Incrementalism.* Homewood, Ill.: Richard D. Irwin, Inc., 1980.

On leadership, try:

Bennis, W., and B. Nanus. *Leaders: Strategies for Taking Charge.* New York: Harper & Row, 1985.

Hunt, J. G., D.-M. Hosking, C. A. Shriesheim, and R. Stewart. *Leaders and Managers: International Perspectives on Managerial Behavior and Leadership.* New York: Pergamon Press, 1984.

Levinson, H., and S. Rosenthal, *CEO: Corporate Leadership in Action.* New York: Basic Books, 1984.

On organizational culture, see:

Deal, T. E., and A. A. Kennedy *Corporate Cultures: The Rites and Rituals of Corporate Life.* Reading, Mass.: Addison-Wesley Publishing Co., 1982.

Frost, P. J., L. F. Moore, M. R. Louis, C. C. Lundberg, and J. Martin. *Organizational Culture.* Beverly Hills, Calif.: Sage Publications, 1985.

Ouchi, W. G. *Theory Z.* Reading, Mass.: Addison-Wesley Publishing Co., 1981.

Schein, E. H. *Organizational Culture and Leadership.* San Francisco: Jossey-Bass, Inc., 1985.

For an overview of organization design and structure, see:

Child, J. *Organization: A Guide to Problems and Practice*. 2d ed. London and New York: Harper & Row, 1984.

Galbraith, J. R. *Organizational Design*. Reading, Mass.: Addison-Wesley, 1977.

Lawrence, P. R., and S. M. Davis. *Matrix*. Reading, Mass.: Addison-Wesley Publishing Co., 1977.

Mintzberg, H. *Structure in Fives: Designing Effective Organizations*. Englewood Cliffs, N.J.: Prentice-Hall, Inc., 1983.

Part 5

On the relationship between organizations and environments, see:

Aldrich, H. E. *Organizations and Environments*. Englewood Cliffs, N.J.: Prentice-Hall, Inc., 1979.

Pfeffer, J., and G. R. Salancik. *The External Control of Organizations: A Resource Dependence Perspective*. New York: Harper & Row, 1978.

Scott, R. W. *Organizations: Rational, Natural and Open Systems*. Second Edition, Englewood Cliffs, N.J.: Prentice-Hall, Inc., 1987.

Index